AWAKENING OF THE HEART

AWAKENING OF THE HEART

Essential Buddhist Sutras and Commentaries

Thich Nhat Hanh

PARALLAX
PRESS

Berkeley, California

Parallax Press
P.O. Box 7355
Berkeley, California 94707
www.parallax.org

Parallax Press is the publishing division
of Unified Buddhist Church, Inc.

Edited by Rachel Neumann
Cover and text design by Gopa & Ted2, Inc.
Cover drawing © Nguyen Thi Hop and Nguyen Dong
Interior illustrations © Richard Wehrman
Author photo © Phap Due

Library of Congress Cataloging-in-Publication Data

Nhât Hanh, Thích.
  Awakening of the heart : essential Buddhist Sutras and
commentaries / Thich Nhat Hanh.
    p. cm.
  Includes bibliographical references.
  ISBN 978-1-937006-11-2
  1. Tripitaka. Sutrapitaka—Commentaries. I. Tripitaka.
Sutrapitaka. English. Selections. II. Title.
  BQ1147.N 2012
  294.3'823—dc23
                                2011040382

2 3 4 5 / 16 15 14 13

Contents

Introduction

The word for a Buddhist scripture, the teachings of the Buddha, is *sutta* in Pali and *sutra* in Sanskrit. The sutras collected here are the key teachings of the Buddha, delivered during his lifetime and preserved in a continuous oral stream for the last twenty-five hundred years. For more than five hundred years the texts were transmitted orally. They were first written down on palm leaves in Sri Lanka in the first century BCE. Siddhartha, the man who became Shakyamuni Buddha, was born approximately twenty-six hundred years ago in India. He grew up in luxury as a prince of the Shakya clan. But he left the palace to search for a way out of suffering. He studied meditation with various teachers and then practiced on his own. He attained enlightenment under the Bodhi tree and was able to teach for forty-five years until he passed away at the age of eighty.[1] During his lifetime, the Buddha delivered his teachings, called the Dharma, in the Ardhamagadhi language, which was spoken primarily in the alluvial plain of the Ganges River. But his teachings spread far beyond and people began to study them in their own local languages. This was the Buddha's intention, as he wanted people everywhere to study his teachings and make them their own.

When we study the Buddha's teachings, we have to be careful to understand them correctly. If we misunderstand the teachings of the Buddha, it is not only unfair to the Buddha, it can also be harmful to ourselves and others. We should not study the Dharma just to become a skilled debater or to show off the knowledge that we have accumulated. The only reason to study the Dharma is to put it into practice. The teachings are deep and wonderful, but they are very easy to misunderstand. Many of the Buddha's contemporaries, even some of his own disciples, misunderstood him. So, of course, we might also misunderstand. The teachings of the Buddha are not a philosophy. They are a path, a raft to help us get across the river of suffering.

Each sutra in this book is presented by itself and then is followed by commentary. This is so you don't rush into the commentaries or become unduly influenced by them. Please read the sutra first. You may see things that no commentator has seen. You can read as if you were chanting, using your clear body and mind to be in touch with the words. Try to understand the sutra from your own experiences and your own suffering. It is helpful to ask, "Do these teachings of the Buddha have anything to do with my daily life?" Abstract ideas can be beautiful, but if they have nothing to do with our lives, of what use are they? So please ask, "Do the words have anything to do with eating a meal, drinking tea, cutting wood, or carrying water?"

The first sutra in the book is the Sutra on the Full Awareness of Breathing. I was so happy the day I discovered this sutra. I thought I'd discovered the greatest treasure in the world. Before, I'd been content to simply gain knowledge. I didn't know how to enjoy the present moment, how to look deeply into my life, and how to enjoy the positive conditions that were all around me. This sutra is so basic and so wonderful. There are many great sutras in this book, but approaching them without starting with the Sutra on the Full Awareness of Breathing is like trying to reach the top of a mountain without taking a path.

These sutras were originally given as talks to monastics, but they are intended for everyone. Anyone can practice mindfulness. If monks and nuns can practice the mindfulness of walking, standing, lying down, and sitting, then laypeople also can. Is there anyone who does not walk, stand, lie down, and sit every day? What is most important is to understand the fundamental basis of the practice and then apply it during our everyday lives, even if our lives are different from the way the Buddha and his monks and nuns lived twenty-five centuries ago. We have to read with the eyes of a person of today and discover appropriate ways to practice based on the teachings of the sutra.

There are many Buddhist sutras, but those compiled here are your foundation. These are the sutras to keep under your pillow, always with you. These sutras will shine light on the essence of living in an awakened way as taught by the Buddha. In them you will discover the true nature of all that is taking place in the present moment.

I invite you to read this book at a time when your body and mind are completely relaxed, for example after taking a comfortable bath.

You can light a candle or a stick of incense to give the room a pleasant glow or fragrance. Then, read one of these sutras slowly to discover its deepest meaning. These sutras are thousands of years old, but it is only by relating them to your own real-life experience that they come alive.

The Sutra on the
Full Awareness of Breathing

Anapanasati Sutta

Contents

The Sutra on the Full Awareness of Breathing

SECTION ONE

I heard these words of the Buddha one time when he was staying in Savatthi in the Eastern Park, with many well-known and accomplished disciples, including Sariputta, Mahamoggallana, Mahakassapa, Mahakaccayana, Mahakotthita, Mahakappina, Mahacunda, Anuruddha, Revata, and Ananda.[2] The senior *bhikkhus* in the community were diligently instructing bhikkhus who were new to the practice—some instructing ten students, some twenty, some thirty, and some forty; and in this way the bhikkhus new to the practice gradually made great progress.[3]

That night the moon was full, and the Pavarana Ceremony was held to mark the end of the rainy season retreat.[4] Lord Buddha, the Awakened One, was sitting in the open air, and his disciples were gathered around him. After looking over the assembly, he began to speak:

"O bhikkhus, I am pleased to observe the fruit you have attained in your practice. Yet I know you can make even more progress. What you have not yet attained, you can attain. What you have not yet realized, you can realize perfectly. To encourage your efforts, I will stay here until the next full moon day."[5]

When they heard that the Lord Buddha was going to stay at Savatthi for another month, bhikkhus throughout the country began traveling there to study with him. The senior bhikkhus continued teaching the bhikkhus new to the practice even more ardently. Some were instructing ten bhikkhus, some twenty, some thirty, and some forty. With this help, the newer bhikkhus were able, little by little, to continue their progress in understanding.

When the next full moon day arrived, the Buddha, seated under the open sky, looked over the assembly of bhikkhus and began to speak:

"O bhikkhus, our community is pure and good. At its heart, it is without useless and boastful talk, and therefore it deserves to receive offerings and be considered a field of merit.[6] Such a community is rare, and any pilgrim who seeks it, no matter how far he must travel, will find it worthy.

"O bhikkhus, there are bhikkhus in this assembly who have realized the fruit of arahatship, destroyed every root of affliction, laid aside every burden, and attained right understanding and emancipation.[7] There are also bhikkhus who have cut off the first five internal formations and realized the fruit of never returning to the cycle of birth and death.[8]

"There are those who have thrown off the first three internal formations and realized the fruit of returning once more.[9] They have cut off the roots of greed, hatred, and ignorance and will only need to return to the cycle of birth and death one more time. There are those who have thrown off the three internal formations and attained the fruit of Stream-Enterer, coursing steadily to the Awakened State.[10] There are those who practice the Four Establishments of Mindfulness.[11] There are those who practice the Four Right Efforts and those who practice the Four Bases of Success.[12] There are those who practice the Five Faculties, those who practice the Five Powers, those who practice the Seven Factors of Awakening, and those who practice the Noble Eight-fold Path.[13] There are those who practice loving kindness, those who practice compassion, those who practice joy, and those who practice equanimity.[14] There are those who practice the Nine Contemplations and those who practice the Observation of Impermanence.[15] There are also bhikkhus who are already practicing Full Awareness of Breathing."

SECTION TWO

"O bhikkhus, the method of being fully aware of breathing, if developed and practiced continuously, will have great rewards and bring great advantages. It will lead to success in practicing the Four Establishments of Mindfulness. If the method of the Four Establishments of Mindfulness is developed and practiced continuously, it will lead to success in the practice of the Seven Factors of Awakening. The Seven Factors of Awakening, if developed and practiced continuously, will give rise to understanding and liberation of the mind.

"What is the way to develop and practice continuously the method of Full Awareness of Breathing so that the practice will be rewarding and offer great benefit?

"It is like this, bhikkhus: the practitioner goes into the forest or to the foot of a tree, or to any deserted place, sits stably in the lotus position, holding his or her body quite straight, and practices like this: 'Breathing in, I know I am breathing in. Breathing out, I know I am breathing out.'

1. 'Breathing in a long breath, I know I am breathing in a long breath. Breathing out a long breath, I know I am breathing out a long breath.'

2. 'Breathing in a short breath, I know I am breathing in a short breath. Breathing out a short breath, I know I am breathing out a short breath.'

3. 'Breathing in, I am aware of my whole body. Breathing out, I am aware of my whole body.' He or she practices like this.

4. 'Breathing in, I calm my whole body. Breathing out, I calm my whole body.' He or she practices like this.

5. 'Breathing in, I feel joyful. Breathing out, I feel joyful.'[16] He or she practices like this.

6. 'Breathing in, I feel happy. Breathing out, I feel happy.' He or she practices like this.

7. 'Breathing in, I am aware of my mental formations. Breathing out, I am aware of my mental formations.' He or she practices like this.

8. 'Breathing in, I calm my mental formations. Breathing out, I calm my mental formations.' He or she practices like this.

9. 'Breathing in, I am aware of my mind. Breathing out, I am aware of my mind.' He or she practices like this.

10. 'Breathing in, I make my mind happy. Breathing out, I make my mind happy.' He or she practices like this.

11. 'Breathing in, I concentrate my mind. Breathing out, I concentrate my mind.' He or she practices like this.

12. 'Breathing in, I liberate my mind. Breathing out, I liberate my mind.' He or she practices like this.

13. 'Breathing in, I observe the impermanent nature of all dharmas. Breathing out, I observe the impermanent nature of all dharmas.'[17] He or she practices like this.

14. 'Breathing in, I observe the disappearance of desire. Breathing

out, I observe the disappearance of desire.'[18] He or she practices like this.

15. 'Breathing in, I observe cessation. Breathing out, I observe
cessation.'[19] He or she practices like this.

16. 'Breathing in, I observe letting go. Breathing out, I observe
letting go.'[20] He or she practices like this.

"The Full Awareness of Breathing, if developed and practiced continuously according to these instructions, will be rewarding and of great
benefit."

SECTION THREE

"In what way does one develop and continuously practice the Full
Awareness of Breathing in order to succeed in the practice of the Four
Establishments of Mindfulness?

"When the practitioner breathes in or out, a long or a short breath,
aware of his breath or his whole body, or aware that he is making his
whole body calm and at peace, he abides peacefully in the observation
of the body in the body, persevering, fully awake, clearly understanding
his state, gone beyond all attachment and aversion to this life. These
exercises of breathing with Full Awareness belong to the first Establishment of Mindfulness, the body.

"When the practitioner breathes in or out, aware of joy or happiness, aware of the mental formations, or to make the mental formations peaceful, he abides peacefully in the observation of the feelings
in the feelings, persevering, fully awake, clearly understanding his state,
gone beyond all attachment and aversion to this life. These exercises
of breathing with Full Awareness belong to the second Establishment
of Mindfulness, the feelings.

"When the practitioner breathes in or out with the awareness of
the mind or to make the mind happy, to collect the mind in concentration, or to free and liberate the mind, he abides peacefully in the
observation of the mind in the mind, persevering, fully awake, clearly
understanding his state, gone beyond all attachment and aversion to
this life. These exercises of breathing with Full Awareness belong to the
third Establishment of Mindfulness, the mind. Without Full Awareness

of Breathing, there can be no development of meditative stability and understanding.

"When the practitioner breathes in or breathes out and contemplates the essential impermanence or the essential disappearance of desire or cessation or letting go, he abides peacefully in the observations of the objects of mind in the objects of mind, persevering, fully awake, clearly understanding his state, gone beyond all attachment and aversion to this life. These exercises of breathing with Full Awareness belong to the fourth Establishment of Mindfulness, the objects of mind.

"The practice of Full Awareness of Breathing, if developed and practiced continuously, will lead to perfect accomplishment of the Four Establishments of Mindfulness."

SECTION FOUR

"Moreover, if they are developed and continuously practiced, the Four Establishments of Mindfulness will lead to perfect abiding in the Seven Factors of Awakening. How is this so?

"When the practitioner can maintain, without distraction, the practice of observing the body in the body, the feelings in the feelings, the mind in the mind, and the objects of mind in the objects of mind, persevering, fully awake, clearly understanding his state, gone beyond all attachment and aversion to this life, with unwavering, steadfast, imperturbable meditative stability, he will attain the first Factor of Awakening, namely mindfulness. When this factor is developed, it will come to perfection.

"When the practitioner can abide in meditative stability without being distracted and can investigate every dharma, every object of mind that arises, then the second Factor of Awakening will be born and developed in him, the factor of investigating dharmas. When this factor is developed, it will come to perfection.

"When the practitioner can observe and investigate every dharma in a sustained, persevering, and steadfast way, without being distracted, the third Factor of Awakening will be born and developed in him, the factor of energy. When this factor is developed, it will come to perfection.

"When the practitioner has reached a stable, imperturbable abiding in the stream of practice, the fourth Factor of Awakening will be born and developed in him, the factor of joy.[21] When this factor is developed, it will come to perfection.

"When the practitioner can abide undistractedly in the state of joy, he will feel his body and mind light and at peace. At this point the fifth Factor of Awakening will be born and developed, the factor of ease. When this factor is developed, it will come to perfection.

"When both body and mind are at ease, the practitioner can easily enter into concentration. At this point the sixth Factor of Awakening will be born and developed in him, the factor of concentration. When this factor is developed, it will come to perfection.

"When the practitioner is abiding in concentration with deep calm, he will cease discriminating and comparing.[22] At this point the seventh factor of Awakening is released, born, and developed in him, the factor of letting go.[23] When this factor is developed, it will come to perfection.

"This is how the Four Establishments of Mindfulness, if developed and practiced continuously, will lead to perfect abiding in the Seven Factors of Awakening."

Section Five

"How will the Seven Factors of Awakening, if developed and practiced continuously, lead to the perfect accomplishment of true understanding and complete liberation?

"If the practitioner follows the path of the Seven Factors of Awakening, living in quiet seclusion, observing and contemplating the disappearance of desire, he will develop the capacity of letting go. This will be a result of following the path of the Seven Factors of Awakening and will lead to the perfect accomplishment of true understanding and complete liberation."

Section Six

This is what the Lord, the Awakened One, said; and everyone in the assembly felt gratitude and delight at having heard his teachings.
—Majjhima Nikaya, Sutta No. 118, translated from the Pali

1: The Foundation of All Practice

In the Sutra on the Full Awareness of Breathing, in Pali the Anapanasati Sutta, the Buddha shows us how to transform our fear, despair, anger, and craving. Breathing is a means of awakening and maintaining full attention in order to look carefully, long, and deeply, see the nature of all things, and arrive at liberation. The Sutra on the Full Awareness of Breathing is the Buddha's way to help us remember to breathe and to enjoy our breath. When you breathe in slowly, mindfully, you can enjoy your in-breath. Just breathing in can make you very happy. Allow yourself to be happy while breathing in. You know that many people have stuffy noses. They don't enjoy their in-breath very much. So if you're able to breathe freely, that's already something good. You know that breathing out freely helps release toxins and that is something wonderful and healthy. For those of us who enjoy breathing in and out, this is already the practice of peace and happiness. Peace and happiness are already there inside of you and around you.

We all have the tendency to run away from suffering. But the fact is that without suffering, there is no way to cultivate understanding and compassion. I don't want to send my friends and children to a place without suffering, because a place without suffering is a place without understanding and compassion. Without understanding and compassion, there can be no happiness.

In Plum Village, where I live, we have a lotus pond. A lotus can never grow without mud. We cannot plant a lotus in a bowl of marbles. So just as the mud plays a very vital role in bringing out the lotus, suffering plays a vital role in bringing out understanding and compassion. When we embrace our suffering and look deeply into it, we can learn a lot.

In Buddhism, we often speak of taking refuge in the Buddha. The Buddha is not a person outside of us, but the energy of mindfulness, concentration, and insight in us. We have the seeds of compassion in us. There are times when we are capable of understanding and capable of being compassionate. The energy of understanding and compassion can be generated from within us. That is the energy of the Buddha inside. The Buddha is always there within you, and you can touch the Buddha at any time you like. One of the ways to reach the Buddha, anytime and anywhere, is through your breath.

Several years ago I was in Seoul, South Korea. The police had blocked traffic so that we could have a walking meditation in the city. When the time came to lead the walking meditation, I didn't know what to do. I couldn't walk, because hundreds of journalists and people with cameras were closing in. There was no path to walk. So I told the Buddha, "Dear Buddha, I give up, you walk for me." The Buddha came right away. He walked, and people made a path for the Buddha to walk.

The Buddha is in you, and the Buddha knows how to breathe and how to walk very beautifully. When you forget, you can ask the Buddha to come, and he will come, right away. You don't need to wait. I wrote these five *gathas*, small practice poems, to remind us of this.

BREATHING GATHA 1

Let the Buddha breathe,
Let the Buddha walk.
I don't have to breathe,
I don't have to walk.

We're lazy from time to time. We're human. We can allow ourselves to be lazy. This first gatha responds to my laziness; the Buddha is doing everything.

In the beginning, we distinguish between ourselves and the Buddha within ourselves. But as we let the Buddha walk and breathe for us, we can begin to enjoy the walking and breathing.

BREATHING GATHA 2

The Buddha is breathing,
the Buddha is walking.
I enjoy the breathing,
I enjoy the walking.

BREATHING GATHA 3

Buddha is the breathing,
Buddha is the walking.
I am the breathing,
I am the walking.

In the beginning, we believe that there must be someone in order for the breathing to be possible. There must be someone in order for the walking to be possible. But in fact the walking and the breathing are enough. We don't need a walker; we don't need a breather. Think of the rain. We're used to saying, "the rain is falling," or "the wind is blowing." But if it's not falling, it's not the rain. And if it's not blowing, it's not the wind. It's the same with breathing and walking with the Buddha. We begin to touch the reality of no-self. There is only the breathing going on; there's only the walking going on.

BREATHING GATHA 4

There is only the breathing,
There is only the walking.
There is no breather,
There is no walker.

BREATHING GATHA 5

Peace while breathing,
Peace while walking.
Peace is the breathing,
Peace is the walking.

In traditional Chinese medicine, doctors often offer their patients something healing that is delicious to eat. Just by eating, they begin to heal in a pleasant and relaxed way. The same thing is true with the practice. While you practice sitting, you enjoy the sitting. While you practice breathing, you enjoy the breathing. If you're able to enjoy yourself, then healing and transformation will take place.

When you're able to stop and breathe and enjoy each moment, you're doing it for all of your ancestors. Make a peaceful step. Smiling and touching the earth happily is very important. Your practice is not for yourself alone, it benefits the whole world.

We practice stopping and observing to arrive at liberation. We live as if we're in a dream. We're dragged into the past and pulled into the future. We're bound by our sorrows, agitation, and fear. In addition, we hold on to our anger, which blocks communication. "Liberation" means transforming and transcending these conditions in order to be fully awake, at ease, and at peace, joyful and fresh. When we live in this way, our lives are worth living, and we become a source of joy to our families and to everyone around us.

2: Exploring the Sutra

The Sutra on the Full Awareness of Breathing can be divided into six sections. The first part of the sutra describes the circumstances under which the Buddha delivered this Dharma talk. We are told about the community of his disciples during the time he was staying at the Eastern Park, a large park with many trees located right outside the city of Savatthi. The number of monks staying with the Buddha at that time may have been more than four hundred. The senior monks each taught ten, twenty, thirty, or forty newer monks.

Every morning after sitting in meditation, the monks went into the city together, bowls in hand, to beg for food. Before midday, when the sun was directly overhead, they returned to their retreat center to eat. From time to time, they would all be invited to eat at the king's palace or at the home of a wealthy patron, someone whose home was large enough to accommodate so many monks. Poorer households would wait for the bhikkhus to walk by so they too could make offerings. There were also some people who would bring food to the park to offer to the community.

The Buddha and his disciples ate only one meal a day, before noon. There was no cooking or baking at the retreat center itself. The monks had no responsibility for performing funerals or praying for sick or deceased laypersons, as is the case today in many Buddhist countries. Instead they offered a brief lecture to their sponsors either before or after eating the meal offered by them. They were able to speak clearly and powerfully, because they were living an integrated life, putting their study into practice.

While the sun was still up, the Buddha would teach his disciples under a shady grove of trees. Sometimes, he would also give a Dharma talk in the evening if the moon was bright enough, as was the case with this sutra. The Buddha had previously explained aspects of the practice of the Full Awareness of Breathing a number of times (there were many disciples already practicing it), but the evening he delivered this sutra was probably the first time he taught the entire method completely. He probably chose this occasion because there were so many bhikkhus from all over the country present, including a number of new disciples.

That year the retreat of the Buddha and his disciples in the Eastern Park was extended an additional month, to four months, so there would be a chance for disciples from all over the country to be together in one place. Many monks were able to attend because they had completed their rainy season retreat one month earlier than the monks staying at the Eastern Park. There may have been as many as one thousand bhikkhus present the evening the Lord Buddha delivered the Sutra on the Full Awareness of Breathing.

THE SIXTEEN EXERCISES

The second section is the heart of the sutra. This section elaborates the sixteen methods of fully-aware breathing in connection with the Four Establishments of Mindfulness.

The Four Preliminary Exercises

"Breathing in, I know I am breathing in. Breathing out, I know I am breathing out."

1. "Breathing in a long breath, I know I am breathing in a long breath. Breathing out a long breath, I know I am breathing out a long breath."
2. "Breathing in a short breath, I know I am breathing in a short breath. Breathing out a short breath, I know I am breathing out a short breath."
3. "Breathing in, I am aware of my whole body. Breathing out, I am aware of my whole body."
4. "Breathing in, I calm my whole body. Breathing out, I calm my whole body."

The first four exercises of fully-aware breathing help us return to our bodies in order to look deeply at them and care for them. In our daily lives, it is important that we learn to create harmony and ease in our bodies and to reunite body and mind. The Buddha never taught us to mistreat or oppress our bodies.

In exercises one and two, the object of awareness is your breath itself. Your mind is the subject, and your breathing is the object. Your breath may be short, long, heavy, or light. Practicing awareness in this way, you see that your breathing affects your mind, and your mind affects your breathing. Your mind and your breath become one. You also see that breathing is an aspect of the body, and that awareness of breathing is also awareness of the body.

In the third exercise, the breath is connected with the whole body, not just a part of it. Awareness of the breathing is, at the same time, awareness of the entire body. Your mind, your breath, and your whole body are one.

In the fourth breathing exercise, your body's functions begin to calm down. Calming the breath is accompanied by calming the body and the mind. Your mind, your breathing, and your body are calmed down, equally.

In these four breathing exercises, we can realize the oneness of body and mind. Breathing is an excellent tool for establishing calmness and evenness.

The Second Four Exercises

5. "Breathing in, I feel joyful. Breathing out, I feel joyful."
6. "Breathing in, I feel happy. Breathing out, I feel happy."
7. "Breathing in, I am aware of my mental formations. Breathing out, I am aware of my mental formations."
8. "Breathing in, I calm my mental formations. Breathing out, I calm my mental formations."

The second four exercises of fully-aware breathing help us return to our feelings in order to develop joy and happiness and transform suffering. Your feelings are you. If you don't look after them, who will do it for you? Every day you have painful feelings, and you need to learn how to look after them. Your teachers and friends can help you to a certain extent, but you have to do the work. Your body and your feelings are your territory, and you are the king or queen responsible for that territory.

Practicing the fifth exercise, we touch pleasant, unpleasant, and neutral feelings. As a result of conscious breathing and calming the body (the fourth method), joy, a pleasant feeling, arises.

In the sixth exercise, joy is transformed into peace and happiness, and you are fully aware of it. The seventh and eighth exercises bring your attention to all feelings that arise, whether produced by the body (*kayasamskara*) or the mind (*cittasamskara*). The mind's functions include feelings and perceptions. When you are aware of every bodily function and every mental action, you are aware of every feeling.

The eighth exercise calms the body and mind and makes them peaceful. At this point, we can perfectly and completely unify body, mind, feelings, and breath.

The Third Four Exercises

9. "Breathing in, I am aware of my mind. Breathing out, I am aware of my mind."
10. "Breathing in, I make my mind happy. Breathing out, I make my mind happy."
11. "Breathing in, I concentrate my mind. Breathing out, I concentrate my mind."
12. "Breathing in, I liberate my mind. Breathing out, I liberate my mind."

The third group of four exercises of fully-aware breathing has to do with our minds, which means the activities of our minds. Buddhist psychology in the Vijñanavada tradition lists fifty-one mental functions (*cittasamskara*). These exercises help us deal with whatever mental formations are present, cultivating mental formations that are beneficial, and being in touch with and transforming mental formations that are not beneficial. Mental formations are part of your territory, also. There are seeds buried deep in your consciousness that you do not touch often enough, seeds of love, understanding, compassion, and joy. Knowing right from wrong; having the ability to listen to others; nonviolence; and the willingness to overcome ignorance, aversion, and attachment are also present. Through the practice of mindfulness, you can learn to identify these traits in yourself and nurture them, with the help of teachers and spiritual friends, until they grow into beautiful flowers. When you survey your territory, you will also find destructive traits, such as anger, despair, suspicion, pride, and other mental formations that cause you suffering.

Because we don't like to look at these negative traits, we don't want to come back to ourselves. But with the aid of the practice of mindful breathing, we learn to take full responsibility for restoring our territory and taking good care of it.

The tenth exercise makes our minds happy, because it is easier for the mind to become concentrated when it's in a peaceful, happy state than when it's filled with sorrow or anxiety. We're aware that we have the opportunity to practice meditation and that there is no moment as important as the present one. Calmly abiding in the present moment, immense joy arises each time we touch in ourselves the seeds of faith, compassion, goodness, equanimity, liberty, and so on. These seeds are buried deep in our consciousness, and we need only to touch them and water them with conscious breathing for them to manifest.

Using the mind to observe the mind, the eleventh exercise, brings us to deep concentration. Mind is the breath. Mind is the oneness of the subject that illumines and the object that is illuminated. Mind is peace and happiness. Mind is the field of illumination and the strength of concentration. All mental formations that manifest in the present moment can become objects of our concentration.

The twelfth exercise can release the mind to freedom, if it is still bound. The mind is bound either because of the past or the future, or because of other latent desires, or anger. With clear observation, we can locate the knots that are binding us, making it impossible for our minds to be free and at peace. We loosen these knots and untie the ropes that bind our minds. Full Awareness of Breathing shines into the mind the light of the observation that can illumine and set the mind free. Looking deeply at the nature of mental formations such as fear, anger, anxiety, and so on, brings about the understanding that will liberate us.

The Four Final Exercises

13. "Breathing in, I observe the impermanent nature of all dharmas. Breathing out, I observe the impermanent nature of
all dharmas."
14. "Breathing in, I observe the disappearance of desire. Breathing out, I observe the disappearance of desire."

15. "Breathing in, I observe cessation. Breathing out, I observe cessation."

16. "Breathing in, I observe letting go. Breathing out, I observe letting go."

The mind cannot be separated from its object. The mind is consciousness, feeling, attachment, aversion, and so on. Consciousness must always be conscious of something. Feeling is always feeling something. Loving and hating are always loving and hating something. This "something" is the object of the mind. The mind cannot arise if there is no object. The mind cannot exist if the object of mind does not exist. The mind is, at one and the same time, the subject of consciousness and the object of consciousness. All physiological phenomena, such as the breath, the nervous system, and the sense organs; all psychological phenomena, such as feelings, thoughts, and consciousness; and all physical phenomena, such as the earth, water, grass, trees, mountains, and rivers, are objects of the mind, and therefore all are the mind. All of them can be called "dharmas."

The thirteenth breathing exercise sheds light on the ever-changing, impermanent nature of all that exists—the physiological, the psychological, and the physical. Breathing itself is also impermanent. The insight into impermanence is very important because it opens the way for us to see the interrelated, interconditioned nature, as well as the selfless nature, of all that exists. Nothing has a separate, independent self.

The fourteenth exercise allows us to recognize the true nature of our desires. It allows us to see that every dharma is already in the process of disintegrating, so that we are no longer possessed by the idea of holding on to any dharma as an object of desire, and as a separate entity, even the physiological and psychological elements in ourselves.

The fifteenth exercise allows us to arrive at the awareness of a great joy, the joy of emancipation and the cessation of illusion, by freeing us from the intention to grasp any notion.

The sixteenth exercise illuminates for us what it is to let go of ourselves, to give up all the burdens of our ignorance and our grasping. To be able to let go is already to have arrived at liberation.

These sixteen exercises can be studied and practiced intelligently. Although the first four exercises help our concentration very much, and every time we practice it is helpful to do these, it is not always necessary to practice the sixteen exercises in sequence. For example, you might prefer to practice only the fourteenth exercise for several days or months.

Although these exercises are presented very simply, their effectiveness is immeasurable. Depending on our experience, we can enter them deeply or superficially. The Lord Buddha did not intend to generate new theories or to confuse the minds of those new to the practice, so he used simple terms, like impermanence, disappearance of desire, cessation, and letting go. In fact, the deeper meaning of the term impermanence also includes the concepts of nonself, emptiness, (*shunyata*) interbeing, signlessness (*alakshana*), and aimlessness (*apranihita*). That is why it is so important to observe deeply that which lights your path and leads to emancipation.

SECTION THREE: THE FOUR ESTABLISHMENTS OF MINDFULNESS

After explaining the sixteen methods of conscious breathing, the Buddha speaks about the Four Establishments of Mindfulness and the Seven Factors of Awakening. Everything that exists can be placed into one of the Four Establishments of Mindfulness—the body, the feelings, the mind, and the objects of the mind. Another way of saying "objects of mind" is "all dharmas," which means "everything that is." Therefore, all of the Four Establishments of Mindfulness are objects of the mind. In this sutra, we practice full awareness of the Four Establishments through conscious breathing. For a full understanding of the Four Establishments of Mindfulness, read the Satipatthana Sutta.[24]

The phrases "observing the body in the body," "observing the feelings in the feelings," "observing the mind in the mind," and "observing the objects of mind in the objects of mind," appear in the third section of the sutra. The key to "observation meditation" is that the subject of observation and the object of observation not be regarded as separate. A scientist might try to separate herself from the object she is observing and measuring, but students of meditation have to remove the boundary between subject and object. When we observe something, we are that thing. "Nonduality" is the key word. "Observing the body in the body" means that in the process of observing, you don't stand outside your own body as if you were an independent observer, but you identify yourself one hundred percent with the object being observed. This is the only path that can lead to the penetration and direct experience of reality. In "observation meditation," the body and mind are one entity, and the subject and object of meditation are one entity also. There is no sword of discrimination that slices reality into many parts. The meditator is a fully engaged participant, not a separate observer.

Observation meditation is a lucid awareness of what is going on in the Four Establishments: body, feelings, mind, and all dharmas, "persevering, fully awake, clearly understanding his state, gone beyond all attachment and aversion to this life." "Life" means all that exists. Stubbornly clinging to all that exists, or resisting and rejecting it all, both lack the lucidity of an awakened mind. To succeed in the work of observation, we must go beyond both attachment and aversion.

The Four Establishments of Mindfulness are also called the Four Foundations of Mindfulness because they are at the base of our ability to be present in the moment. The first foundation of your being is your body. The practice of mindful breathing brings you back home to your body, to reconcile yourself with your body, to take care of your body, to look deeply into your body, to understand your body, and to allow transformation and healing to take place.

The second foundation of your being is your feelings. Very often, we leave our feelings unattended. Mindful breathing helps us go back to our feelings to recognize them, reconcile ourselves with them, and look deeply into their nature so that understanding is possible. By practicing mindful breathing, we take good care of our feelings; we can calm them, transform them, and heal them. Our feelings are very much interconnected with our bodies. You cannot take your feelings out of your body, and you cannot take your body out of your feelings. They inter-are.

The third foundation of our being is our mental formations. "Formation" means a thing that is conditioned by different kinds of elements. A flower is a physical formation. It is made of several elements. When these elements come together, a flower manifests itself. Among its elements we can see the sunshine. If we touch the being of a flower deeply, we touch the sunshine. We know that we cannot take the sunshine out of a flower. If we did, the flower would collapse. There would be no flower. The flower and the sunshine inter-are. When we touch a flower deeply, we also touch a cloud. There is a cloud in the heart of a flower, and we cannot take the cloud out of the flower. The cloud and the flower inter-are. If we continue to look deeply, we can see the earth, the minerals, the air, and everything in a flower. All these elements have come together to bring about the formation called "flower." All formations are impermanent. When one of the conditions is no longer sufficient, the formation dissolves. There is no flower.

There are other kinds of formations that are not physical, like fear. Fear is a mental formation; it is made of several elements, including the element of ignorance. Despair, anguish, attachment, love, and mindfulness are all mental formations. In the teaching of my tradition, there are fifty-one categories of mental formations. Mindful breathing brings us close to our mental formations as they manifest within us. Sometimes fear manifests, and our mindful breathing brings us back to our fear so that we can embrace it. We look deeply into the nature of our fear to reconcile ourselves with it. If we do well, we can calm our fear, look deeply into it, and discover its true nature. Insight into our fear helps us transform it.

This is true with all mental formations—such as anger, despair, agitation, and restlessness. Sometimes restlessness is present as a form of energy, and it prevents us from being peaceful. It prevents well-being. When restlessness manifests itself within us, we can practice mindful breathing in order to come back to it, to hold it mindfully, tenderly, and lovingly. The practice consists of two parts: the first part is calming, the second part is looking deeply. We calm down our mental formations, look deeply into them, and see their deep roots.

As soon as you use the energy of mindfulness to hold your mental formation, there is a tendency in that mental formation to calm down. As you continue holding your mental formation, you are capable of looking into it, and you begin to have the insight you need regarding what kinds of conditions have brought that mental formation to you. This is the practice of looking deeply, which we call *vipassana* in Pali, or *vipashyana* in Sanskrit.

The fourth foundation of our being is our perceptions. Most of our suffering comes from our wrong perceptions. We don't have correct insight about the nature of reality. Mindful breathing brings us back to ourselves to investigate the nature of our perceptions. Looking deeply into the nature of our perceptions, we discover the reasons why we suffer, or why our fear or despair is born. If we know how to practice looking deeply into the nature of our perceptions, the insight we get liberates us from our suffering, grief, and fear. We practice looking deeply into the true nature of reality, the true nature of a flower, the true nature of our bodies, of our feelings, or of our mental formations. Form, feelings, and mental formations are all the objects of our perceptions.

We cannot take form out of feelings nor take feelings out of form. The same is true of mental formations and perceptions. These four foundations of your being—form, feelings, mental formations, and perceptions—inter-are. We cannot take one out of the other three. If we know the art of looking deeply, we will discover reality as it truly is. By doing so, we remove all errors and wrong perceptions. This is liberation through understanding, and salvation by knowledge. If we speak in terms of grace, grace is understood here as wisdom, as knowledge, and as understanding. We know that sometimes we suffer because of our ignorance, jealousy, and anger. At the base of our jealousy and anger is ignorance, because we don't understand why we suffer. The moment we begin to understand our jealousy, our anger begins to dissolve. That is why understanding is the liberating factor, and the aim of the practice of meditation is to get this liberating insight. That is why our perceptions are so important. We have to go back to them and inquire about their nature.

SECTION FOUR: THE SEVEN FACTORS OF AWAKENING

In the fourth section of the sutra, the Buddha discusses the arising, growth, and attainment of the Seven Factors of Awakening, through abiding in them in conjunction with conscious breathing.

[1] Full attention is the main Factor of Awakening. Full attention is awareness, being fully awake. If full attention is developed and maintained, the practice of observation to shed light on and see clearly all that exists will meet with success. [2] The work of observation to shed light on the object of your attention and see clearly all that exists is investigation of dharmas. [3] Energy is perseverance and diligence. [4–5] Joy and ease are wonderful feelings nourished by energy. [6] Concentration gives rise to understanding. When we have understanding, we can go beyond all comparing, measuring, discriminating, and reacting with attachment and aversion. [7] Going beyond is letting go.

Those who arrive at letting go will have the bud of a half smile, which proves compassion as well as understanding.

Section Five: Emancipation

In this very short section, the Buddha reminds us that the Seven Factors of Awakening, if practiced diligently, lead to true understanding and emancipation.

Section Six: Conclusion

The sixth section is the concluding sentence of the sutra. This sentence is used at the end of every sutra.

3: The Sixteen Ways of Breathing

FORM

1. in/out
2. long/short
3. experiencing body
4. calming body

FEELINGS

5. experiencing joy
6. experiencing bliss
7. experiencing mental formations
8. calming mental formations

MENTAL FORMATIONS

9. experiencing mind
10. gladdening mind
11. concentrating mind
12. liberating mind

PERCEPTIONS

13. contemplating impermanence
14. contemplating non-craving
15. contemplating nirvana
16. contemplating letting go

4: Seven Ways to Practice

Here are seven different ways to focus on putting the Sutra on the Full Awareness of Breathing into practice. Please use whatever focus suits you in your present situation and practice those exercises first. Although the sixteen exercises of practicing full awareness breathing are intimately connected to one another, the order in which they're given in the sutra is not necessarily a progression from easy to difficult. Every exercise is as wonderful as every other, as easy and as difficult as every other one. We can, however, say that the preliminary instructions place greater importance on "stopping," and the later ones place more importance on "looking deeply," although, of course, stopping and looking deeply cannot exist separately from one another. If there is stopping, looking deeply is already present, more or less; and if there is looking deeply, there is a natural stopping.

The subjects for full awareness suggested below can be divided into seven categories: Following the Breath in Daily Life, Awareness of the Body, Realizing the Unity of Body and Mind, Nourishing Ourselves with Joy and Happiness, Observing Feelings, Caring for and Liberating the Mind, and Looking Deeply in Order to Shed Light on the True Nature of All Dharmas.

Laypeople as well as monks and nuns should learn how to practice both the first subject (following the breath in daily life) and the fourth (nourishing ourselves with the joy of meditation). Every time you practice sitting meditation, you should always begin with these two subjects. Only After that should we go into the other subjects. Every time you notice your state of mind becoming agitated, dispersed, or ill at ease, you should practice the fifth subject (observing in order to shine light on our feelings). The seventh subject (seeing things as they truly are) is the door that opens onto liberation from birth and death, and all those of great understanding have to pass through this door. This subject is the greatest gift the Buddha has given us. The first six subjects all involve stopping as well as looking deeply, but the seventh emphasizes looking deeply. Only after you have the capacity to concentrate your mind with great stability should you embark on this subject.

SUBJECT ONE:
FOLLOWING THE BREATH IN DAILY LIFE

"Breathing in, I know I am breathing in. Breathing out, I know I am breathing out."
1. "Breathing in a long breath, I know I am breathing in a long breath. Breathing out a long breath, I know I am breathing out a long breath."
2. "Breathing in a short breath, I know I am breathing in a short breath. Breathing out a short breath, I know I am breathing out a short breath."

Most of us don't live in forests or in monasteries. In our daily lives, we drive cars, wait for buses, work in offices and factories, talk on the telephone, clean our houses, cook meals, wash clothes, and so on. Therefore, it's important that we learn to practice full awareness of breathing in our daily lives. Usually, when we perform these tasks, our thoughts wander and our joy, sorrow, anger, and unease follow close behind. Although we're alive, we're not able to bring our minds into the present moment, and we live in forgetfulness.

We can begin to enter the present moment by becoming aware of our breath. Breathing in and breathing out, we know we are breathing in and out. As our awareness increases, we can smile to affirm that we are in control of ourselves. Through Full Awareness of Breathing, we can be awake in, and to, the present moment. Being attentive, we already establish stopping and concentrating the mind. Full Awareness of Breathing helps our minds stop wandering in confused, never ending thoughts.

Most of our daily activities can be accomplished while following our breath according to the exercises in the sutra. When our work demands special attentiveness to avoid confusion or an accident, we can unite Full Awareness of Breathing with the task itself. For example, when we are carrying a pot of boiling water or doing electrical repairs, we can be aware of every movement of our hands, and we can nourish this awareness by means of our breath: "Breathing in, I am aware of my hands carrying a pot of boiling water." "Breathing out, I am aware that my right hand is holding an electrical wire." "Breathing in, I am aware that I am passing another car." "Breathing out, I know that the situation is under control." We can practice like this.

It is not enough to combine Full Awareness of Breathing only with tasks that require so much attention. We must also combine Full Awareness of Breathing with every movement of our bodies: "Breathing in, I am sitting down." "Breathing out, I am wiping the table." "Breathing in, I smile to myself." "Breathing out, I light the stove." Stopping the random progression of thoughts and no longer living in forgetfulness are giant steps forward in our meditation practice. We can realize this by following our breath and combining it with full awareness of each daily activity.

There are people who have no peace or joy because they cannot stop their unnecessary thinking. They are forced to take sedatives to fall asleep, but even in their dreams, they continue to feel fears, anxieties, and unease. Thinking too much can give us headaches, and diminish our spiritual power. By following our breath and combining conscious breathing with our daily activities, we can cut across the stream of disturbing thoughts and light the lamp of awakening. Full awareness of an out-breath and an in-breath is something wonderful that anyone can practice. Combining Full Awareness of Breathing with full awareness of the movements of our bodies during daily activities—walking, standing, lying, sitting, and working—is a basic practice to cultivate concentration and live in an awakened state.

During the first few minutes of sitting meditation, you can use this method to harmonize your breathing and, if it seems necessary, you can continue following your breath with full awareness throughout the entire period. We simply recognize when we are breathing in and when we are breathing out. We can abbreviate "Breathing in, I know I am breathing in. Breathing out, I know I am breathing out," to "In, Out." We say these two words silently as we breathe in and out to help our concentration.

In this teaching, we consider our breath as part of our body. Our breathing is a physical formation. It is the door through which we go home to ourselves and reconcile with ourselves. The object of our mindfulness is our in-breath and out-breath, nothing else. We identify our in-breath as our in-breath and our out-breath as our out-breath. "In" is no longer a word; it is the reality of our in-breath, and all our thinking stops.

Don't suppress your thinking or make an effort to stop it. If you really enjoy your in-breath one hundred percent, then thinking suddenly stops. Sometimes we try to force ourselves to be mindful. This isn't good. Mindfulness is very enjoyable. The key is to make it interesting and pleasant. We breathe so that our in-breaths and out-breaths are pleasant, so that we are awake and mindful and our concentration is strong. If concentration is there, then insight will be born. Mindfulness, concentration, and insight give birth to one another. Mindfulness carries the energy of concentration within itself; and concentration carries the energy of insight within itself.

During sitting meditation, you can sit and enjoy your in-breath and out-breath and nothing else. Make your in-breath mindful and genuine. This is already resting and healing. Sometimes you may like to lie down and enjoy your in-breath and out-breath. When you sit, sit in such a way that your body can rest. You are erect with your head and spinal column forming a straight line, yet your muscles are completely relaxed. Sit in the lotus or halflotus position, or in a position that's comfortable for you, keeping your back straight. You can sit with or without a cushion. The cushion may be thick or thin; you need to find a cushion that suits your physical condition. If you sit in a chair, your back should be straight and your feet flat on the floor. Find a way of sitting that allows you to sit for at least twenty minutes without feeling tired or stiff. As soon as you sit down, begin to practice mindful breathing, paying attention to your breath. Then pay attention to your sitting position. Relax the muscles in your face—there are about three hundred muscles in your face. Every time you get angry, worried, or afraid, these muscles become tense. Other people can see the tension in your face. If you breathe in mindfully and become aware of your face, and breathe out mindfully and smile lightly, you relax the hundreds of muscles in your face. Then you move down to your shoulders and also let go. Don't try hard to practice. If you struggle or make an effort, you can't relax. Very soon you'll feel tension in your shoulder muscles, and you may get a headache.

When you sit and watch television, you don't make any effort. That's why you can sit there for a long time. When you sit in meditation, if you struggle, you won't be able to sit for very long. Please imitate the way you sit in your living room. Effortlessness is the key to success. Don't fight. Don't try hard. Just allow yourself to sit. This relaxing way of sitting is also resting. Allow your body to rest.

When you pour fresh juice into a glass and let it stand for fifteen minutes, all the pulp sinks down to the bottom of the glass. If you allow your body to sit in a relaxed, peaceful way, it calms your body and your mind. Sitting like this allows you to enjoy your in-breath and out-breath, to enjoy being alive, to enjoy sitting here. To enjoy your in-breath and out-breath is a miracle, the miracle of being alive. Just sit there and be yourself; don't try to become someone else. Your thinking will stop. You will touch the wonders of life that are available in the here and the now. The period of sitting is time worth living.

> "Breathing in a long breath, I know I am breathing in a long breath. Breathing out a long breath, I know I am breathing out a long breath."

> "Breathing in a short breath, I know I am breathing in a short breath. Breathing out a short breath, I know I am breathing out a short breath."

Our breath is usually short at first, but as we practice, our breath slows down and deepens. To practice these two exercises is to know whether our breath is short or long. We do not purposefully make our breath long. We don't say, "I will breathe in a long breath." Strictly speaking, we should say, "Breathing in, I know I'm breathing in a long (or a short) breath."

In the Anapananusmriti Sutra from the Chinese canon, the first of the sixteen breathing exercises is, "Breathing in, I know I am breathing in. Breathing out, I know I am breathing out." The second is, "Breathing in a long breath or a short breath, I know whether it is a long breath or a short breath. Breathing out a long breath or a short breath, I know whether it is a long breath or a short breath." This version is more in accord with the instructions given here, that we should just recognize the length of our breath.

As we continue to follow our breathing, we recognize its quality, "I know I am breathing in, and I know it is a short breath." If it's short, let it be short. It's not important to make it long. This is called "mere recognition." It's the same when we have a painful feeling. The first thing to do is to recognize it. If your breathing is fast, recognize that it's fast. If it's slow, recognize that it's slow. If it's uneven, recognize that it's uneven. If it's even, recognize that it's even. When we begin, our breathing may be uneven, but after a few minutes of practice, it will become even and it will bring us peace and joy. We don't force our breathing to be deep or slow. It's our continued practice that makes our breathing become deep or slow, quite naturally. When we recognize a deep, slow breath, we can say "Deep" as we breathe in, and "Slow" as we breathe out. With the first two exercises, the nourishment of the joy of meditation is already present, and once we have it, we can begin to share it with our family and friends. We don't have to wait until we're a Dharma teacher.

Sometimes we think and worry nonstop. It's like having a recording continually playing in our minds. When we leave a television set on for a long time, it becomes hot. Our head also becomes hot as a result of our thinking. Because we can't stop, we may not sleep well. Even if we take a sleeping pill, we continue to run, think, and worry in our dreams. The alternative medicine is mindful breathing. If we practice mindful breathing for five minutes, allowing our bodies to rest, then we can stop thinking for that time. The words "in" and "out" aren't thinking; they aren't concepts; they're a guide for mindfulness of breathing. When we think too much, the quality of our being is reduced. If we can stop thinking, we increase the quality of our being. There is more peace, relaxation, and rest.

When we look into the first two exercises, we see that when we practice the first exercise well, we're also practicing the second one well. "Breathing in, I know I'm breathing in." We're aware throughout our in-breath. Practicing with awareness, we're already doing the second exercise. And when we practice the second exercise well, we're also doing the first exercise. As we go along, we'll see the nature of interbeing of all sixteen exercises. We can train ourselves to see the nature of interbeing in everything, including one breathing exercise.

SUBJECT TWO: AWARENESS OF THE BODY

3. "Breathing in, I am aware of my whole body. Breathing out, I
   am aware of my whole body."

With this second subject, we embrace our bodies with mindfulness
rather than just embracing our breathing, as in the first two exercises.
We recognize the presence of the body and we "return home" to be
one with it. Breathing is the vehicle that brings us home to our body.
If we do not come back to our home and care for it, who will? When
we come home to it, our body breathes a sigh of relief and says, "She
has come back at last!" We do not blame our bodies, accusing them
of being a nuisance because we have a headache or an upset stomach.
We embrace our wounded bodies, care for them, and heal them with
right mindfulness.

In the Anapanasati Sutta, the Buddha teaches four exercises in connection with the body:

1. Breathing
2. Recognizing the body, and calming the body
3. Recognizing the positions of the body: standing, sitting,
   walking, or lying down, and knowing you are standing, sitting, walking, or lying down
4. Recognizing the actions of the body: bending down, drinking tea, and lifting a cup of tea

If your actions are hurried and forgetful, you recognize that and, once
you do, your hurriedness and forgetfulness disappear.

During the practice of meditation, the body and mind become
unified. In the sitting, lying, standing, or walking position, practice
awareness of your body. We know that the Buddha taught walking
meditation. Today, when we practice walking meditation, we can use
ideas from the Anapanasati Sutta to help us succeed in our walking. If
we're walking slowly, as in the meditation hall, we can take one step
and say "In" silently. It means, "Breathing in, I know I am breathing
in." For as long as the in-breath lasts, continue stepping with your left
foot. As soon as the out-breath begins, begin stepping with your right
foot and say the word "Out" silently, which means, "Breathing out, I
know I am breathing out." Just take a step and know you are breathing
in, and take a step and know you are breathing out. That is all you need

to do. There is nothing else besides that. If we put our whole body and mind into one step, we are successful in walking meditation. After practicing "In, Out" four or five times, our breath will become deeper and slower quite naturally. We can recognize that and say "Deep" as we breathe in and "Slow" as we breathe out. When we practice walking meditation outdoors, rather than taking one step with each breath, we take two or three steps for every breath. For every step, we say "In." So if we take three steps with each in-breath, we say "In, in, in." And if we take three steps with each out-breath, we say "Out, out, out." And then we say, "Deep, deep, deep. Slow, slow, slow."

Sometimes we identify ourselves with our bodies. Sometimes we believe our bodies are strangers to us, and we may hate our bodies. These attitudes show that we are alienated from our own bodies. So, you have to go home to your body and reconcile with it. Your breathing is part of your body. Your breath is the door through which you can go back to your body, your perceptions, and so on. With the energy of mindfulness, we embrace our breathing, our in-breath and our out-breath. We become one with our in-breath and out-breath. As our practice continues, our inbreath and out-breath become deeper, more harmonious, and more peaceful.

Then, you go a bit deeper and embrace your body and reconcile yourself with your body. You might do this in a sitting position or lying down. It's very important to go back to your body and show your concern, attention, and love. Your body might be suffering. It might have been abandoned for a long time. This is the beginning of the practice of love: You become aware of your body; you are determined to take good care of your body; and your body will feel much better when you're able to do so.

Sabbakaya means the whole body. During your in-breath, become aware of your body as a whole. Embrace your body in its entirety. The object of your mindfulness is no longer your in-breath alone; it now includes your body. Embrace your body tenderly during your in-breath and out-breath with the intention to reconcile yourself with it, to take care of it, and to show your concern and loving kindness. You may want to modify the language a little, but the content of the practice is the same: "Breathing in, I am aware of my body. Breathing out, I smile to my body." This is a smile of awareness; a smile that shows your concern and loving kindness.

How much time do you spend going back to your body, holding it tenderly with the energy of mindfulness, and smiling to it? Each of us knows that we need to do this frequently, with compassion and tenderness. Smile to your body with the smile of recognition, "Oh, my body, I know you are there. I will take good care of you."

One useful way to practice is to observe different parts of your body, one by one, and then observe the whole body. You can start with your hair, "Aware of my hair, I breathe in. Smiling to my hair, I breathe out." Then survey all the different parts of your body, down to the tips of your toes. You're in contact with each of them by means of mindfulness. You can practice this meditation when you're sitting or when you're lying down. Hospitals examine patients with a scanner, an instrument that scans the body using a laser beam to help diagnose what is wrong. Mindfulness also scans the body, though not with laser beams. Right mindfulness is a ray of light that recognizes the different parts of our bodies, helps us become acquainted with them, and shows us how to take care of them.

You can lie down and guide yourself in this meditation: "Breathing in, I am aware of my eyes. Breathing out, I smile to my eyes," and then do the same for the other parts of your body. If your concentration is strong, you will see how much joy your eyes bring into your life, and that alone will make you feel happy. Seeing how precious your eyes are will help you take good care of them.

During this practice, difficult feelings sometimes arise. For example, you may be observing your heart when suddenly you notice anxiety arising. Perhaps your friend has a heart condition, and you are anxious about that. In any case, do not push the feeling away. Just look at it and say, "Breathing in, I am aware that I'm anxious," and then continue observing your body under the supervision of the Full Awareness of Breathing.

Here is another example. As you become aware of your digestive organs, you may see millions of minute living beings that are living inside your intestines. Do not push this perception away. Simply remain aware of it, "Breathing in, I am aware of the minute organisms living within me." Your awareness of your symbiotic relationship with these organisms can be a rich subject for meditation. Recognize it as such, and make an appointment with yourself to return to this subject later, and then continue on your journey observing the rest of your body.

We call this practice "scanning the body with our awareness."

We generally pay very little attention to the organs of our bodies unless they cause us pain. You may pass half your life so caught up in your goals and projects that you never even take time to notice your little toe. Your little toe is very important. It has been kind to you for many years. If, one day in the future, there is a sign of cancer in it, what will you do? You may think somehow that being aware of your body is not an important spiritual practice, but that is not correct. Any physiological, psychological, or physical phenomenon can be a door to full realization. If you meditate on your toe, holding your toe between your fingers, that can lead to your goal of realization. The secret of practicing this second subject of full awareness, "Awareness of the Body," is to concentrate your mind and observe each organ of the body in full awareness. If you practice this way, one day you will see things in a new way that will change your view and your way of life. The hairs on your head may seem ordinary, but each hair is an ambassador of truth. Please receive the credentials of your hair. Observe them well and discover every message that each hair sends to you. According to the principle of interpenetration, each hair contains all the information of the cosmos. Are your eyes unimportant? Of course not. They are the windows that open up on to the miracle of reality. Don't neglect anything. Look deeply, and you will see.

In the Discourse on the Four Establishments of Mindfulness, the Buddha mentions thirty-six parts of the body. Each part should be embraced by our mindfulness, and we should smile to it. First we enjoy relaxing, either sitting or lying down. After a few minutes of relaxation with the help of mindful breathing—total relaxation cannot be perfect without mindful breathing—then you direct your attention to each part of your body. You breathe in and embrace each part of your body with mindfulness, and smile to it, like a mother holding her baby tenderly in her arms. This is very healing, and very important.

When you practice "Breathing in, I am aware of my liver. Breathing out, I smile to my liver," your liver might react right away: "Oh, I have been waiting for this for a long time. I have been sending SOS messages for help, day and night. But he just neglected me. He continues to drink and smoke, and it gives me a hard time. I couldn't tell him how hard it was for me to bear all of that. I suffered so much day and night; and I worked so hard day and night; and my message has been neglected." If you practice mindful breathing, you will get a lot of relief. If you pay attention to your liver and smile to it, you will get some insight into the condition of your liver. Your liver has been trying its best to maintain your well-being, but you have been neglectful.

Forgetfulness is the opposite of mindfulness. You have been forgetful, and you didn't know it. It may be the first time you pay attention to your liver. Your liver is comforted at that moment. If you continue for three, four, or five breaths, then insight will come. There is the intention to be kind to your liver, to protect it, because you know that your liver is a condition for your well-being. When that awareness is born, you know what to do and what not to do. You don't need anyone to tell you to stop drinking alcohol. You just embrace your liver and stop drinking and ingesting the poisons that harm it. Each part of your body should be embraced and taken care of in exactly the same way.

SUBJECT THREE: REALIZING THE UNITY OF BODY AND MIND

4. "Breathing in, I calm my whole body. Breathing out, I calm my whole body."

Now that we have observed and accepted the whole body, we can bring peace and calm to it. Sometimes our bodies don't function peacefully. We may work hard and notice that our bodies are not at peace. When we lie down, we see that our bodies are shaking from exhaustion. Our breath can be strained as well. When we are angry or exhausted, we may feel our bodies and our breathing coming apart at the seams. We can use this exercise to remind us to take care of our bodies: "Breathing in, I calm the functions of my body. Breathing out, I calm the functions of my body." Just by concentrating this way, we help our blood circulate better and make the rhythm of our hearts more even.

During another period of meditation, you can observe your whole body without discriminating between the parts: "Breathing in, I am aware of my whole body." At this point, allow your breathing, your body, and your observing mind to all become one. Breathing and body are one. Breathing and mind are one. Mind and body are one. Mind is not an entity that exists independently, outside of your breathing and your body. The boundary between the subject and the object of observation does not actually exist. We observe "the body in the body."

The mind is one with the object it is observing. This principle has been developed extensively in Mahayana Buddhism: Subject and object are empty. Subject and object are not two.

If you practice this way for ten or twenty minutes, the flow of your breathing and of your bodily functions will become very calm, and your mind will feel quite released. When you begin to practice, it may seem as rough as coarsely milled wheat, but as you continue to practice, the flour will become finer and finer. The fourth breathing exercise accompanies you along this path: "Breathing in, I calm my whole body. Breathing out, I calm my whole body." It is like drinking a glass of cool lemonade on a hot day and feeling your body becoming cool inside. When you breathe in, the air enters your body and calms all the cells of your body. At the same time, each "cell" of your breathing becomes more peaceful and each "cell" of your mind also becomes more peaceful. Body, breathing, and mind are one, and each one is all three. This is the key to meditation. Breathing brings the sweet joy of meditation to you. It is food. If you are nourished by the sweet joy of meditation, you become joyful, fresh, and tolerant, and everyone around you will benefit from your joy.

Although the aim of the fourth breathing exercise is to bring calmness to your body, its effect is to bring calmness to your breathing and to your mind as well. The calmness of one brings calmness to all three. In the calmness of meditation, discrimination between body and mind no longer exists, and you dwell at rest in the state of "body and mind at one," no longer feeling that the subject of meditation exists outside of the object of meditation.

The Buddha said that if you have a wound within your body or within your mind, you can learn how to take care of it. There are many ways of taking care of your wound. You allow the wound in your body and soul to heal. You don't stand in the way of its healing. But very often we do just that. We forbid our bodies to heal themselves; we do not allow our minds to heal themselves because of our ignorance. We know that our bodies have the capacity to heal themselves. When you cut your finger, you don't have to do much. You just clean it and allow it to heal—maybe for one or two days. If you tamper with the wound, if you worry too much or panic, it may not heal. We know that when an animal is wounded, it looks for a quiet place to lie down. Wisdom is present in the animal's body. It knows that rest is the best way to heal. It doesn't do anything, not even eat or hunt; it just lies down. Some days later, it can get up. It is healed. Human beings have lost confidence in their bodies. We don't know how to rest. Mindful breathing helps us to relearn the art of resting. Mindful breathing is like a loving mother holding her sick baby in her arms saying, "Don't worry, I'll take good care of you, just rest."

We have to relearn the art of resting. Many of us do not know how to make use of our vacations. Very often we are more tired after a vacation than before it. We should learn the art of relaxation and resting, and practice deep relaxation on our own or with others.

We have to believe in the body's capacity to heal itself. The power of self-healing is a reality, but many of us don't believe in it. Instead, we take a lot of vitamins and medicines that may sometimes be more harmful to our bodies than not. We have to trust the power of understanding, healing, and loving within us by taking good care of our bodies, eating well but not too much, sleeping, and drinking water. It is our refuge. It is the Buddha. It is the Kingdom of God existing within us. If we lose our faith and confidence in it, we lose everything. This is not abstract, it is very real. We can touch it, hold it, and take refuge in it. Instead of panicking or giving ourselves up to despair, we practice mindful breathing and put our trust in the power of self-healing, self-understanding, and loving within us. We call this the island within ourselves in which we can take refuge. It is an island of peace, confidence, solidity, love, and freedom. Be an island within yourself. You don't have to look for it elsewhere. Mindful breathing helps you go back to that precious island within, so that you can experience the foundation of your being.

When you find yourself in a dangerous or difficult situation, or when you feel like you are losing yourself, mindful breathing helps you go back to the island of self. Our practice is based on the insight that mindfulness is the energy of the Buddha that is within us. To be mindful means to be here, fully present, with body and mind united, not in a state of dispersion. Mindfulness is the energy we generate in mindful walking, mindful breathing, sitting, and even washing dishes. It is a protecting agent, because within mindfulness is the energy of concentration and insight. Mindfulness makes it possible for us to understand, to accept, to love, and to relieve suffering. That is why the island of mindfulness is our best refuge. Before passing away, the Buddha recommended to his students that they take refuge in the island of mindfulness within themselves.

"Experiencing my body, I breathe in. Smiling to my body, I breathe out. Calming my body, I breathe in. Smiling to my body, I breathe out." This is a wonderful practice that everyone can enjoy. We have to learn the art of mindful breathing, mindful living, mindful smiling, and mindfully taking care of our bodies. Students can set up mindfulness practice groups in their schools, because students are under stress, their bodies are under stress. Teachers are also under stress. They suffer because of their students. They can also set up a group to take care of their bodies. Psychotherapists can do the same. They take care of many people who suffer. If they don't take good care of themselves, they might become exhausted and give up. They can practice with other therapists or with a group of their clients. The police also suffer. They are victims of fear and stress. There is so much violence and suffering. They, too, can practice in a group and take good care of themselves. People living in correctional houses can also start a group. Anyone can practice mindfulness. You don't need to be a Buddhist. You don't need to be a Dharma teacher. You don't need transmission from a teacher in order to start a practice group. You can start a mindfulness practice group anytime, anywhere.

SUBJECT FOUR: NOURISHING OURSELVES WITH JOY AND HAPPINESS

5. "Breathing in, I feel joyful. Breathing out, I feel joyful."
6. "Breathing in, I feel happy. Breathing out, I feel happy."

Those who practice meditation should know how to nourish themselves with the joy and happiness of meditative concentration in order to reach real maturity and help the world. Life in this world is both painful and miraculous. The violet bamboo, the yellow chrysanthemum, the white clouds, and the full moon are all wondrous expressions of the Dharmakaya, the body of the Dharma. Your body, even though it is impermanent, without an independent self, and subject to suffering, is also infinitely wondrous. The joy of beginning to meditate is like leaving the busy city and going off to the countryside to sit under a tree. We feel ourselves filled with peace and joy. What a relief!

At the end of each day, you can sit cross-legged on a cushion, or sit on a chair, and begin to practice conscious breathing. If you do this, you will feel great joy. This is the initial sensation of the peace and joy of meditation. The fifth breathing exercise helps us touch this sensation. If you can set aside the stresses and difficulties of your day and enter your meditation filled with joy, it is easy to arrive at the state of peace and happiness.

Joy is a positive psychological and physiological state. Joy helps our blood circulate throughout our bodies, which makes us feel more alive. When we feel joyful, concentration is easy. When we do not feel joyful, it can be difficult to concentrate. When we are concentrated, we see more clearly and have a deeper understanding of things. How can we encourage the feeling of joy? Please try the following exercises:

"Breathing in, I know I have two good eyes. Breathing out, I feel joy."

"Breathing in, I recognize that my liver is in good condition. Breathing out, I feel joy."

"Breathing in, I am aware of my Sangha protecting me. Breathing out, I feel joy."

The last exercise is for those of you who are part of a Sangha, a community of practitioners. Your community may not seem to be doing anything special, but just by its existence, it is protecting you. When you attend a retreat and practice with the Sangha—sitting, eating, walking, breathing together in mindfulness—you feel great security and encouragement. In each session of sitting meditation, you can treat yourself to this kind of practice. Touching joy for twenty or thirty minutes is truly nourishing for your body and mind.

The sixth exercise allows us to experience happiness as we breathe in and out. Happiness is easiest when our bodies and minds are at ease, free of excessive worries and preoccupations.

Happiness is more than joy. According to the teachings of the Buddha, joy is less pure because there can be excitement in it. When we anticipate some special occasion, we may say, "I feel very excited. I can't wait." But when we feel too excited, our minds are not at peace. In Chinese, the characters "Peace" and "Joy" often appear together. One student said to me, "I can't wait to hear you teach on Friday!" If we are too excited about something in the future, how can we enjoy what is happening in the present moment? In the West, joy is often equated with excitement. According to the Buddha, joy is not the same as happiness. In the beginning, we need joy. But as we develop our happiness, the excitement that is present in joy disappears.

The example given in the sutra is of a man in the desert, about to die of thirst, who all of a sudden sees an oasis, a pool of water, in the midst of a grove of trees. He feels joy and excitement. His mind and body race towards the pool, and he bends down, puts his hands in the water and brings the water to his mouth. Until the very last moment before he drinks the water, joy is there. His hands are shaking from excitement. But when he finally drinks the water, he tastes real happiness, and his excitement has completely disappeared. The Buddha was not criticizing joy. We need joy very much, but we also need to go further than joy.

In the river of our feelings are many unpleasant ones. We want more than anything for them to change. The Buddha understood this. That is why the first two exercises that he proposed on the subject of feelings are to nourish us with joy and happiness. They are the medicine we need to strengthen us before we try to cure the deepest, most fundamental causes of our sickness. If we endeavor to write down one condition for happiness that exists in our lives right now, I think that before long we will surprise ourselves by being able to fill a whole sheet of paper. Whatever we are doing—sitting meditation, walking meditation, washing, cooking, or cleaning—we can ask ourselves, "What are the conditions that we have for happiness?" When we see one such condition, we can write it down. According to the Lotus Sutra, we are the heirs to many priceless jewels, but we wander around as if we were destitute children.

To succeed in the practice, we must "experience" joy and happiness. It is not enough to repeat the words "joy" and "happiness" to ourselves. If we do not use our eyes of understanding and practice right mindfulness, we will not be able to touch the conditions that can bring us joy and happiness in the present moment.

The Buddha taught us to look deeply at pleasant, unpleasant, and neutral feelings. Neutral feelings are those which are neither pleasant nor unpleasant. When we have a toothache, for example, we have an unpleasant feeling. But when we do not have a toothache, we do not enjoy the non-toothache. We think having a non-toothache is a neutral feeling. Having the toothache helps us see that not having a toothache is a very pleasant feeling. Only after we become blind are we aware that having eyes to see the blue sky and the white clouds is a miracle. While we are able to see, we rarely notice. We think seeing is neutral. The fact that we have a Sangha and the opportunity to practice may be just a neutral feeling, but when we are aware how precious a jewel a Sangha is, the feeling is very pleasant. The fact that we are alive is truly a miracle. We could say there is nothing special about it, but when we are deeply aware of being alive in this moment, we see how wonderful and how pleasant it is!

Through the practice of meditation, we learn to transform so-called neutral feelings into pleasant ones that are healthy and long lasting. Meditation helps us see what is painful and what is miraculous. Happiness in itself is nourishing. It is not necessary to look for happiness outside of ourselves. We only need to be aware of the existence of happiness, and we have it right away. We can enjoy pleasant feelings—like the sensation of the breeze on our cheeks—as we need them. Nourished by the happiness of meditation, we become tolerant, at ease and compassionate with ourselves and others, and our happiness is felt by everyone. With peace in ourselves, we can share peace with others, and we have enough strength and equanimity to face the many hardships in life with patience and perseverance.

Some of us feel that our lives make no sense nor hold any meaning. When we don't see a meaningful path in our lives, we suffer greatly. We're unhappy because we do not know where to go. Our confusion makes us suffer, no matter how rich and powerful we are. If we see a direction in our lives, find meaning in our lives, and live with compassion, we will know how to help ourselves and others around us to suffer less. We know the Dharma, have practiced it, and know that in difficult moments the Dharma can rescue us and the people we love. We have been freed by the Dharma. Just by touching the Dharma within us and touching our confidence in it, joy and happiness are born in us, making us truly happy.

If we know how to manage all twenty-four hours in a day, we realize that a day is a long time. What makes it long is our concentration. Older people live in a more concentrated way than the young, establishing themselves more in the present moment. With mindfulness and concentration, older people can appreciate each moment that is offered to them. Each moment of daily life can become a story for their children and grandchildren. This is possible. The Buddha did it. He didn't leave behind a set of dogmas and theories; he left behind his life. Every step he took was peaceful and solid. His compassion penetrated not only the living beings of his time, but also of our time. Each step, each breath, each word of the Buddha conveys and transports the energy of mindfulness, understanding, and compassion. From this source, his students continue to inherit compassion and knowledge. If they practice well, they can transmit this source of compassion, healing, and happiness to future generations.

SUBJECT FIVE: OBSERVING OUR FEELINGS

7. "Breathing in, I am aware of my mental formations. Breathing out, I am aware of my mental formations."
8. "Breathing in, I calm my mental formations. Breathing out, I calm my mental formations."

Mental formations are psychological phenomena. There are fifty-one mental formations according to the Vijñanavada school of the Mahayana, and fifty-two according to the Theravada. Feelings are one of them. In the seventh and eighth breathing exercises, mental formations simply mean feelings. They do not refer to the other fifty mental formations. In the Vimutti Magga, we are told that mental formations in these exercises mean feelings and perceptions. It is more likely that mental formations here simply mean feelings, although feelings are caused in part by our perceptions.

Some feelings are more rooted in the body, such as a toothache or a headache. Feelings that are more rooted in our minds arise from our perceptions. In the early morning when you see the first light of day and hear the birds singing, you might have a very pleasant feeling. But if once at this time of day you received a long distance telephone call that your parent had suffered a heart attack, the feeling that comes from that perception may be painful for many years.

When you feel sad, do remember that it will not last forever. If someone comes and smiles at you, your sadness may vanish right away. In fact, it has not gone anywhere. It has just ceased to manifest. Two days later, if someone criticizes you, sadness may reappear. Whether the seed of sadness is manifesting or not depends on causes and conditions. Our practice is to be aware of the feeling that is present right now:

"Breathing in, I am aware of the feeling that is in me now. Breathing out, I am aware of the feeling that is in me now."

If it is a pleasant feeling, when we are aware that it is a pleasant feeling, it may become even more pleasant. If we are eating or drinking something that is healthy and nourishing for us, the feeling of happiness will grow as we become aware of it. If what you are consuming is harmful for your intestines, your lungs, your liver, or your environment, your awareness will reveal to you that your so-called pleasant feeling has within it many seeds of suffering.

The seventh and eighth breathing exercises help us observe all our feelings—pleasant and unpleasant, neutral, and mixed. Feelings arising from irritation, anger, anxiety, weariness, and boredom are disagreeable ones. Whatever feeling is present, we identify it, recognize that it is there, and shine the sun of our awareness on it.

If we have an unpleasant feeling, we take that feeling in our arms like a mother holding her crying baby. The "mother" is mindfulness and the "crying baby" is the unpleasant feeling. Mindfulness and conscious breathing are able to calm the feeling. If we do not hold the unpleasant feeling in our arms but allow it just to remain in us, it will continue to make us suffer. "Breathing in, I touch the unpleasant feeling in me. Breathing out, I touch the unpleasant feeling in me."

In Buddhist meditation, looking deeply is based on nonduality. Therefore, we do not view irritation as an enemy coming to invade us. We see that we are that irritation in the present moment. When we are irritated, we know, "This irritation is in me; I am this irritation," and we breathe in and out in this awareness. Thanks to this approach, we no longer need to oppose, expel, or destroy our irritation. When we practice looking deeply, we do not set up barriers between good and bad in ourselves and transform ourselves into a battlefield. We treat our irritation with compassion and nonviolence, facing it with our hearts filled with love, as if we were facing our own baby sisters. We bring the light of awareness to it by breathing in and out mindfully. Under the light of awareness, our irritation is gradually transformed. Every feeling is a field of energy. A pleasant feeling is an energy that can nourish. Irritation is a feeling that can destroy. Under the light of awareness, the energy of irritation can be transformed into a kind of energy that nourishes us.

Feelings originate either in the body or in our perceptions. When we suffer from insomnia, we feel fatigue or irritation. That feeling originates in our bodies. When we misperceive a person or an object, we may feel anger, disappointment, or irritation. This feeling originates in our perceptions. According to Buddhism, our perceptions are often inaccurate and cause us to suffer. The practice of full awareness is to look deeply in order to see the true nature of everything and to go beyond our inaccurate perceptions. Seeing a rope as a snake, we may cry out in fear. Fear is a feeling, and mistaking the rope for a snake is an inaccurate perception.

If we live our daily lives in moderation, keeping our bodies in good health, we can diminish painful feelings that originate in the body. By observing each thing clearly and opening the boundaries of our understanding, we can diminish painful feelings that originate from perceptions. When we observe a feeling deeply, we recognize the multitude of causes near and far that helped bring it about, and we discover the very nature of feeling.

When a feeling of irritation or fear is present, we can be aware of it, nourishing our awareness through breathing. With patience, we come to see more deeply into the true nature of this feeling, and in seeing, we come to understand, and understanding brings us freedom. The seventh exercise refers to the awareness of a mental formation, namely a feeling. When we have identified the feeling, we can see how it arises, exists for a while, and ceases to be in order to become something else.

With mindfulness, a so-called neutral feeling can become a pleasant or an unpleasant feeling. It depends on your way of handling it. Suppose you are sitting in the garden with your little boy. You feel wonderful. The sky is blue; the grass is green; there are many flowers; and you are able to touch the beauty of nature. You are very happy, but your little boy is not. First, he has only a neutral feeling but, since he doesn't know how to handle it, it turns into boredom. In his search for more exciting feelings, he wants to run into the living room and turn on the television. Sitting with the flowers, the grass, and the blue sky is not fun for him. The neutral feeling has become an unpleasant feeling.

Mindfulness helps us to identify a feeling as a feeling and an emotion as an emotion. It helps us hold our emotions tenderly within us, embrace them, and look deeply at them. By observing the true nature of any feeling, we can transform its energy into the energy of peace and joy. When we understand someone, we can accept and love him, and there is no longer any feeling of reproach or irritation against him. The energy of the feeling of irritation, in this case, has been transformed into the energy of love. The Buddha had much love and compassion as far as the body and the feelings of people are concerned. He wanted his disciples to return to, look after, care for, heal, and nourish their bodies and minds. How deeply the Buddha understood human beings!

SUBJECT SIX: CARING FOR AND LIBERATING THE MIND

9. "Breathing in, I am aware of my mind. Breathing out, I am aware of my mind."
10. "Breathing in, I make my mind happy. Breathing out, I make my mind happy."
11. "Breathing in, I concentrate my mind. Breathing out, I concentrate my mind."
12. "Breathing in, I liberate my mind. Breathing out, I liberate my mind."

These four exercises refer to how our breath can help free our minds. In the Sutra on the Four Establishments of Mindfulness, we are taught to observe "the mind in the mind." We can observe mental formations in the spirit of nonduality, with no barrier between the subject and object of observation. When we look at the blue sky, the boundary between the observer and the infinite blue of the sky disappears, and we feel a deep contact between ourselves and the blue sky. When a grain of salt standing next to the sea asks, "How salty is the sea?" he is told that the only way to know is to jump into the sea and become one with it.

Mind here is composed of psychological phenomena that exist as seeds in our store consciousness. We have the chance to become aware of them when they manifest as mental formations in our mind consciousness. As soon a mental formation arises, you should breathe in and out and identify it. As you continue to observe it, you can see its connection with the whole of your mind. The meaning of the ninth breathing exercise is: "I breathe in and out and identify the mental formation that is present at this moment in me."

To identify a mental formation with the help of conscious breathing means to recognize, embrace, and become one with that mental formation. It does not mean to drown in that mental formation, because the subject that is recognizing, embracing, and becoming one with the mental formation is the energy of mindfulness. When our mindfulness is one with the mental formation, the mental formation quite naturally changes for the better.

The first four breathing exercises help us become one with our breathing and drop all thinking, discriminating ideas, and imaginings. The ninth exercise helps us identify psychological phenomena, such as thoughts or imaginings, as they arise. The term *citta* includes all psychological phenomena, such as feelings, perceptions, thoughts, reasoning, and so forth, along with their objects. It does not refer to a single, unchangeable psychological subject. Mind is a river of psychological phenomena that is always flowing. In this river, the arising, duration, and cessation of any phenomenon is always linked with the arising, duration, and cessation of all other phenomena. To know how to identify psychological phenomena as they arise and develop is an important part of meditation practice. When we recognize the mental formation that is manifesting in us, we recognize whether it is wholesome or unwholesome. Attachment, aversion, ignorance, pride, suspicion, and being caught in views are unwholesome mental formations, and they cause us to suffer. When we suspect someone of committing a wrongdoing, whether it is our teacher or our friends on the path, we suffer. When we doubt the teachings and have no confidence in anyone around us, we suffer a lot. We can only practice when we have faith and confidence. Pride is a great hindrance to progress. We think that we are better than others, that only we can see the truth. That is not at all conducive to peace and joy.

The activities of our minds, often unstable and agitated, are like torrents of water washing over rocks. In traditional Buddhist literature, the mind is often compared to a monkey always swinging from branch to branch or to a horse galloping out of control. Once our minds are able to identify what is happening, we will be able to see clearly our mental formations and make them calm. Just that will bring us peace, joy, and stillness.

We have to go home and take care of ourselves, first our bodies, then our feelings, and now our mental formations. We can begin by simply recognizing the presence of a mental formation. We do not try to grasp it, possess it, or be attached to it. We do not try to push it away, either. This is called simple recognition of a mental formation. Recognize it, call it by its true name, and say, "I am here to take care of you because you are myself."

We already know that many of us do not want to go home to ourselves. We are afraid. There is a lot of internal suffering and conflict that we want to avoid. We complain that we do not have time to live, but we try to kill our free time by not going back to ourselves. We escape by turning on the television or picking up a novel or magazine; we go out for a drive. We run away from ourselves and don't attend to our bodies, feelings, or mental formations.

We have to go home. If we are at war with our parents, friends, society, or church, it may be because there is a war raging within us. An internal war facilitates other wars. The Five Skandhas—forms, feelings, perceptions, mental formations, and consciousness—comprise a large territory. Each of us is the king or queen of our territory which is comprised of these five elements. But we have not been responsible monarchs. We don't want to survey our territory or to govern over it, we just want to abandon it. There are many wars being fought in it. It has turned into a mess, because we just want to escape and are afraid of going back to our own kingdom. The Buddha advised us to go home and tidy up, restoring our peace and harmony.

We are afraid of going home because we lack the tools or the means of self-protection. Equipped with mindfulness, we can go home safely and not be overwhelmed by our pain, sorrow, and depression. Going home mindfully, you can talk to your wounded child within using the following mantra: "Darling, I have come home to you. I am here for you. I embrace you in my arms. I am sorry that I left you alone for a long time." With some training, with mindful walking and mindful breathing, we will be able to go home and embrace our pain and sorrow.

If mental formations manifest during sitting meditation and prevent you from meditating, you may have to practice recognizing them one by one. This is also meditation. When a thought, feeling, perception, pain, or sorrow manifests itself, practice breathing in and out and recognize it for what it is. Say, "I know you. I know you are there. I am here for you," and embrace it. The object of our practice in the ninth exercise is any kind of mental formation—jealousy, fear, hatred, despair, restlessness—positive or negative.

When you're meditating on an interesting subject, your power of concentration is sufficient to quiet your mental formations. This is called guided or directed meditation. You choose a special subject for meditation and look deeply into it to discover something. The more interesting the subject, the stronger your concentration. If it is not interesting, then, even if you try hard, you will still feel sleepy, and other things will continue to come up. One guided meditation is identifying and writing down the names of all our attachments. Another is to write down what we can do for ourselves every day to bring ourselves joy. At first, you may think that there aren't many things, but when you sit and look deeply, you will discover dozens.

Another way of working with your mind is to allow things to come up and handle them with mindfulness. You nourish your mindful breathing and recognize each mental formation that manifests. Every time you embrace a wholesome mental formation, your joy and happiness grow, and the wholesome mental formation grows. You realize your compassion and faith in the Dharma, and use the happiness you receive to nourish yourself. Every time negative, unwholesome, and painful mental formations manifest themselves, you recognize and embrace them to calm them and look deeply into them.

The tenth breathing exercise is intended to gladden your mind. Compare this with the fifth and sixth exercises. The fifth aims at the experience of joy, and the sixth aims at the experience of happiness. These three methods can bring us to the land of great bliss, to a state of relaxation in meditative concentration. To better succeed in the practice of the tenth exercise, we must know how to recognize and touch the positive mental formations that are already present in us, such as faith, goodwill, compassion, understanding, tolerance, and equanimity. Our minds become joyful every time we recognize these positive mental formations.

This state brings us ease and can nourish the power of our concentration. The Buddha wants us to be nourished by feelings of peace and joy. To gladden the mental formations (as the tenth breathing exercise is sometimes expressed) or to make the mind happy is to see the beneficial mental formations that are within us. For instance, to have faith and confidence in the path we are following is beneficial. To know what it is right to do and not to do is also beneficial. If I see others practicing sitting meditation and I recognize that it is a good thing to do, I will have the intelligence to join them. If I do not want to kill a slug or caterpillar that is eating the lettuce in my garden because

I have the wholesome mental formation of nonviolence, I will know to go out with a flashlight while it is still dark and gently remove the slugs and caterpillars from the lettuce plants and put them somewhere else. Or I may decide to be a vegetarian because I do not feel happy about factory farming, the slaughter of animals, or the death from starvation of thousands of children because there is not enough grain for human consumption. These decisions arise from the mental formation of nonviolence in me.

There are ways you can practice the tenth breathing exercise during sitting meditation: "Breathing in, I recognize the mental formation of nonviolence in me. Breathing out, I feel happy." "Breathing in, I have faith in the practice I am doing. Breathing out, I feel happy." "Breathing in, I know that at this moment I am not caught in any desire. Breathing out, I feel happy." "Breathing in, I know that I am not angry at anyone. Breathing out, I feel happy." But we should not stop at this. We can continue by "observing the mental formation to shed light on it," in order to arrive at an awakened understanding. Only awakened understanding can lead us to complete freedom.

We cultivate joy because it helps us get the nourishment we need in order to be stronger and go further in the practice. The Buddha encourages us to relax our bodies, to embrace our pleasant feelings, and to create joy and happiness for our nourishment. Cultivating joy means to strengthen our happiness and nourish ourselves.

Deep in our consciousness there are many wholesome, positive seeds. If we know how to touch them and water them, they will manifest themselves on the upper level of our consciousness—the mind consciousness. We have to practice looking deeply to recognize our wonderful seeds—the seeds of mindfulness, enlightenment, understanding, joy, and loving kindness. We might think that we cannot love because we have not been able to touch the seed of love within us. Through our practice, and with the support of a brother or a sister, we are able to touch our seeds of love, forgiveness, compassion, and joy. Some people say, "I don't know what joy is. I have absolutely no joy within me." That is because that person has not been able to touch the seed of joy within himself. The practice is to touch it and recognize it. This is the practice of cultivating joy.

We need to organize our daily lives so that the positive seeds are watered every day and the negative seeds are not watered. We all have seeds of suspicion, despair, and anger. In one person, they are stronger;

in another person, they are weaker. We do not want the people who live around us to water our negative seeds. Every time a negative seed is touched and watered, we suffer.

But we can do better than simply not watering our negative seeds; we can water our positive seeds of happiness, loving kindness, forgiveness, and joy. We call this the practice of selective watering. We water the flowers, not the weeds, so that the flowers will bloom in the other person. When we make the other person smile, we benefit as well. It does not take long to see the result of our practice.

The eleventh exercise of mindful breathing proposed by the Buddha is concentrating our minds. We bring all our power of concentration and place it on the mental formation that is present. Concentration means to direct the energy of the mind towards one object. It is called *ekagatta* in Pali, which means "one-pointedness." The mental formation that is manifesting in the mind at that moment is a unique object, such as faith. We are in touch with that mental formation. We recognize it and we call it by its name. Through this practice the energy of joy arises, and our faith develops. If the mental formation is negative, we also recognize it and call it by its name, directing all our mental energy upon it. We embrace it and look deeply at it, and doing this already begins the work of transforming that negative mental formation. It is like waking up on a cold morning and lighting a fire. The cold air is warmed by the warm air of the fire. We do not need to open the door and force the cold air to go outside to make the room warm. All we have to do is tend the fire. In the case of a negative mental formation, all we have to do is look after it with the warmth of the fire of our mindfulness. Only by concentrating steadily on an object can we observe it. The object of your mind is lit up by your observation, like a performer standing in a spotlight on a stage. The object might be moving in time and space, since it is alive. But, your mind is also alive, and in the state of concentration, subject and object become one.

Breathing is an object of your concentrated mind. When you put all of your attention on your breath, and your mind and your breath become one, that is concentration. After practicing with the breath, we can practice with other physiological, psychological, and physical phenomena. Only if there is concentration can the work of looking deeply take place.

The twelfth exercise aims at untying all the knots of the mind—the sorrows and memories of the past, the anxieties and predictions concerning the future, feelings of irritation, fear, and doubt in the present, or confusion created by inaccurate perceptions. Only by concentrating the mind do we have the capacity to observe, illumine, and be emancipated from obstacles. Looking deeply into our bodies and consciousness, we recognize our internal knots. True happiness is not possible unless we know how to untie these knots and become free. When the person you love says something unmindful or unkind, you might get an internal knot—it may be a small knot, but it is a knot. It can become harmful if you don't untie it, and the next time your beloved makes the same mistake, the knot will grow. Out of forgetfulness, we create internal knots in each other and don't realize it, until one day we can no longer look each other in the eye, and we watch television instead. To untie the knot, we have to begin anew with our beloved. Say, "Darling, why did you say such a thing to me? Why did you do such a thing to me?" If we are skilled practitioners, we do not allow the knot to become stronger. Mindful living helps us know when an internal knot is being formed. If you are a good practitioner, you don't let it go unnoticed. You are aware that you must untie the knot right away to ensure your long-lasting happiness.

When we say "liberate my mind," "mind" refers to any mental formation that makes us anxious, makes us suffer, or pushes us in the wrong direction. We open our minds so the light of concentration will reveal what is there and liberate what is there. It is the same as trying to untie knots in thread. We have to be calm, and we need to take time. By observing your mind in all its subtlety, in a calm and self-contained way, you can free your mind from all confusion. "Breathing in, I open my heart for all the knots to be untied. Breathing out, I open my heart for all the knots to be untied."

The practice of concentration helps us to understand the nature of affliction, and with that kind of insight, we can burn affliction away. Concentration as energy has the power of transformation. Concentration is something extremely important in the teaching of the Buddha.

To concentrate means to concentrate on something. In the teaching of the Buddha, many kinds of concentration are proposed. According to our needs, we can apply one or two of these concentrations to free us, like concentration on impermanence, concentration on nonself, concentration on compassion, concentration on interbeing, and so on. Each concentration, each *samadhi*, has its own name.

The contemplation on love and compassion can bring you a lot of relief and can bring the nectar of healing to you. *Maitri* and *karuna* are Sanskrit for loving kindness and compassion. Suppose someone has made you suffer. You think of that person as being very cruel. They've inflicted a lot of suffering on you, your family, your country. This has made you suffer so much that you want revenge. You want that person or group of people to suffer so you can get relief. You want to punish them. But your hatred and anger and the desire for revenge are a kind of fire that continues to burn your body and your mind, and you are in hell. Hell is here in the here and the now. We've said that the Kingdom of God can be in the here and the now. That is also true of hell. Hell can be in the here and the now. If you allow the flame of affliction to burn you, there may be times you can't sleep because your whole body, your whole being is being burned by the fire of hate, of anger, or of despair.

The concentration on loving kindness and compassion, will help you to suffer less. With your attention focused on the other person, you can see that they also suffer a lot. The fact is that when someone suffers a lot and is not capable of handling her own suffering, she will spill her suffering all over, and you will become a victim of her suffering. You may be like that too. If you're suffering a lot and you don't know how to manage your suffering, you will continue to suffer and make others around you suffer, including the people you love.

Looking deeply, we may see that when that person was a child, he had no chance to learn love and compassion from his parents. They caused him many wounds that no one has helped him to heal. When he went to school, the teacher didn't help, the students didn't help. The seeds of anger, suffering, and hatred continued to grow. Such a person needs help, not punishment. By looking deeply and recognizing the presence of suffering in the other person, you might see that truth—that he needs help. And now if we punish him, he will suffer more.

This insight may motivate you to do something to help that person. This insight brings the nectar of compassion. Hate and anger vanish. The nectar of compassion is wonderful; you stop suffering right away. The fire that has been burning, stops burning. That is the effect of metta meditation, the meditation on loving kindness and compassion.

In my experience, the concentration on compassion is a wonderful practice. You may need only fifteen minutes of breathing deeply and looking deeply to recognize that the other person is a victim of their suffering. That person needs your help, not your punishment. Suddenly the nectar of compassion is born, your heart is blessed with that nectar, and you don't suffer anymore. Instead, you want to do something, to say something. If you're not capable of using loving speech, you can write a letter. You can say something kind to help that person. But you can't help another until you've been able to help yourself. Peace and compassion always begin with yourself.

SUBJECT SEVEN: LOOKING DEEPLY IN ORDER TO SHED LIGHT ON THE TRUE NATURE OF ALL DHARMAS

13. "Breathing in, I observe the impermanent nature of all dharmas. Breathing out, I observe the impermanent nature of all dharmas."
14. "Breathing in, I observe the disappearance of desire. Breathing out, I observe the disappearance of desire."
15. "Breathing in, I observe cessation. Breathing out, I observe cessation."
16. "Breathing in, I observe letting go. Breathing out, I observe letting go."

The thirteenth breathing exercise proposed by the Buddha aims at looking deeply to shed light on the impermanent nature of all dharmas. All phenomena, whether physiological, psychological, or physical, without exception, are impermanent. The meditation to look deeply at the impermanent nature of all phenomena is one of the basic practices. If we hear someone talking about impermanence, we may think we understand. But understanding impermanence is not a matter of words or concepts, but a matter of practice. Only through our daily practice of stopping and looking deeply can we experience the truth of impermanence.

Impermanent does not only mean, "Here today, gone tomorrow." The meditation on impermanence is a deep, penetrating, and wonderful path of meditation. There is no phenomenon whatsoever with a separate, lasting individuality. All things are in endless transformation, and all things are without an independent self. To be impermanent is to be without self (*anatman*). This is a fundamental recognition in Buddhism regarding the nature of all that exists. "Breathing in, I am looking deeply at some object. Breathing out, I observe the impermanent nature of that object." The object I am observing might be a flower, a leaf, or a living being. Looking deeply this way, we can see that change is taking place in every instant. The Sanskrit word for instant is *kshana*, the shortest unit of time. One second contains many kshana. The first kind of impermanence is called *kshana-anitya*, "impermanence in every instant." When something reaches the end of a cycle of arising, duration, and cessation, there is a marked change. This second kind of impermanence is called "cyclic impermanence." When we heat water, the water is getting hotter all the time. That is kshana-anitya. Then, suddenly, we see steam. The appearance of steam is a cyclic impermanence of water.

We have to look deeply at cyclic change in order to accept it as a necessary part of life and not be surprised or suffer so greatly when it occurs. We look deeply at the impermanence of our own bodies, the impermanence of the things around us, the impermanent nature of the people we love, and the impermanent nature of those who cause us to suffer. If we do not look deeply at impermanence, we may think of it as a negative aspect of life, because it takes away from us the things we love. But looking deeply, we see that impermanence is neither negative nor positive. It is just impermanence. Without impermanence, life would not be possible. Without impermanence, how could we hope to transform our suffering and the suffering of our loved ones into happiness? Without impermanence, how can we hope that a tyrannical regime might become democratic?

Impermanence also means interdependence, that there is no independent individual because everything is changing all the time. A flower is always receiving non-flower elements like water, air, and sunshine, and it is always giving something to the universe. A flower is a stream of change, and a person is also a stream of change. At every instant, there is input and output. When we look deeply at the flower, we see that it is always being born and always dying, and that it is not independent of other things. The components of the universe depend on one another for their existence. In the Majjhima Nikaya, it says, "This is, because that is. This is not, because that is not." Impermanence also means "signlessness" (*alakshana*). The reality of all that exists is beyond every concept and linguistic expression. We cannot go directly to their essential and true nature, because we are accustomed to grasping phenomena through the intermediaries of perception and thought. The categories of perception and thought are "signs."

The example of wave and water is often given to help us understand the "signless" nature of all that exists. A wave can be high or low, can arise or disappear, but the essence of the wave—water—is neither high nor low, neither arising nor disappearing. All signs—high, low, arising, disappearing—cannot touch the essence of water. We cry and laugh according to the sign, because we have not yet seen the essence. The essence (*svabhava*) is the very nature of everything that is, and it is the reality of ourselves. If we only see the wave with its manifestations of being born and dying, we will suffer. But if we see the water, which is the basis of the wave, and see that all the waves are returning to the water, we have nothing to fear. When we begin the practice, we want things to be permanent and we think things have a separate self. Whenever things change, we suffer. To help us not suffer, the Buddha gave us the truths of impermanence and nonself as keys. When we look deeply at the impermanent and nonself nature of all things, we are using those keys to open the door to reality, or *nirvana*. Then our fears and our suffering disappear, and we do not mind whether we are young or old, or even alive or dead. We realize that we do not die in the usual sense of having existed and then ceasing to exist. We see that all of life is ongoing transformation.

"Breathing in, I see the nature of impermanence. Breathing out, I see the nature of impermanence." We have to practice this many times to have success in the practice. We have to practice on our own and with a community, not just during sitting meditation but in whatever we are doing—watering the garden, washing the dishes, walking up and down the stairs, and so on. The reality of everything that exists is its signlessness, since it is a reality that cannot be grasped by concepts and words. Because it cannot be grasped, it is called empty. Emptiness here does not mean nonexistent as opposed to existent. It means signless, free from all imprisonment by concepts—birth/death, existent/nonexistent, increasing/decreasing, pure/impure. This is developed in the fifteenth breathing exercise. It says in the Prajñaparamita Heart Sutra, "All dharmas are marked with emptiness; they are neither produced nor destroyed, neither defiled nor immaculate, neither increasing nor decreasing."

Impermanence also means aimlessness (*apranihita*). The presence of everything that exists is not to attain a final goal. We cannot add on to the true nature of all that exists, nor can we remove anything from it. It has no origin and no end. We do not need to seek realization outside of all that exists. In the very "stuff " of every dharma, the awakened nature is already fully present.

Many teachers, including those of ancient Greece and China, gave teachings on impermanence. In the Buddhist tradition, impermanence is not just a description of reality but also an instrument for understanding. You cannot understand impermanence without understanding the teaching of interbeing or emptiness. Impermanence is the first key to unlocking the door of reality. Impermanence is a samadhi, a form of concentration. Intellectually, you may agree that things are impermanent, but you might behave as if reality were permanent. We have to train ourselves to maintain the insight of impermanence in every minute of our lives. Then we will always have wisdom and happiness.

Because life and reality are impermanent, we feel insecure. I think the teaching on living deeply in the present moment is what we have to learn and practice to face this feeling of insecurity. We have to handle the present moment well. We live deeply in the present moment so that in the future we will have no regrets. We are aware that we and the person in front of us are both alive. We cherish the moment and do whatever we can to make life meaningful and to make him or her happy in this moment.

When I drink a glass of water, I invest one hundred percent of myself in drinking it. You should train yourself to live every moment of your daily life like that. Hugging is a deep practice. You need to be totally present to do it correctly. When you open your arms and hold the other person, you practice three mindful breaths. "Breathing in, I know that he is still alive in my arms. Breathing out, I feel so happy." Life becomes real at that moment.

Impermanence is a key that can unlock the door of reality. It is also a concentration, a practice. Intellectually we know that things are impermanent. We can agree with the truth of impermanence. Our scientists also agree that things are impermanent. But in reality we still behave as though things are permanent. We have to keep the insight of impermanence alive. When we come in touch with anything, we should be able to see the nature of impermanence in it.

We have to distinguish between the notion of impermanence and the insight of impermanence. We may have the notion of impermanence, we may have understood what impermanence is, but we do not have the insight of impermanence. The insight is something alive. When you are able to see the nature of impermanence, you'll begin to see the nature of nonself. Nonself is not different from impermanence. Since everything is changing in every second, nothing can remain itself in two consecutive moments. So impermanence means nonself. They're the same thing. Looking in terms of time, we say impermanence. Looking in terms of space, we say nonself. They are exactly the same thing.

The fourteenth breathing exercise aims at looking deeply to shed light on the true nature of all dharmas and the true nature of our desire.[25] We see that happiness does not lie in ideas about what we want to realize in the future. Therefore, we're no longer attached to the objects of our desire that we thought would bring us future happiness. When people go fishing, they sometimes use synthetic bait. The fish thinks the bait is real and bites. If the fish knew that the bait was synthetic, it would never bite, because it would know that would only lead to suffering. When you have the thought, "If I could only have that, I would be happy," it's a good time to practice the fourteenth breathing exercise.

Many people think that if they don't have a Ph.D., they can't possibly be happy. Why do they have to have a degree to be happy? Thinking you'll be happy if you have a degree is only an idea you have. It's quite possible that after you have the degree, you still won't be happy. The idea that marriage or a divorce is the only thing that can bring happiness is also just an idea. There's no guarantee that after we've married or divorced, we'll have happiness for the rest of our lives. In fact, it could be quite the opposite.

If we can see that the nature of the object of our desire is always changing and is on the way to dissolution, our desire for it to be always the same will disappear. A rose, a cloud, a human body, an ancient tree, all are on the way to dissolution. All dharmas, all phenomena, pass through the stages of birth, duration, transformation, and disappearance. A practitioner should observe clearly the impermanent and fading nature of all things, including the Five Aggregates, the Five Skandhas, that comprise his or her own self. The Nine Contemplations were a special practice used at the time of the Buddha. In them, we observe the decomposition of a corpse from the time it becomes bloated to the time when it disappears into dust and ashes. In Lessons in Emptiness, King Tran Thai Tong of thirteenth-century Vietnam contemplates as follows:

> Formerly glowing cheeks and pink lips,
> today cold ashes and white bones.

Position, renown though unsurpassed,
they are but part of a long dream.
However rich and noble you are,
you are no less impermanent.
Jealousy, pride, and self-clinging,
but self is always empty.
Great strength, ability, and success,
but in them is no final truth.
Since the four elements come apart,
why discriminate old from young?
Crevices erode even mountains,
more quickly the hero is dead.
Black hair has hardly grown on our head,
when suddenly it has turned white.
Our well-wisher has just departed,
a mourner arrives on our death.
This six-foot skeleton of dry bones—
with what effort it seeks riches.
This wrapping of skin containing blood
suffers year after year just because of attachment.

This is a way of looking at our bodies, and it is also a way of seeing how our minds, so subtle and quick today, can become slow and senile tomorrow. Rivers, mountains, houses, riches, and health—all should be meditated on like this. The objects of our desire are all deceptive in appearance. In the light of deep looking, they are no different from the plastic bait containing a dangerous hook inside. Once their true nature is revealed, our desires vanish.

Perhaps you will smile and say that this contemplation is intended principally to bring you to a pessimistic state of mind, frustrating your love of life. This is both true and not true. Medicine may be bitter, but it can heal your sickness. Reality may be cruel, but to see things as they are is the only way to heal yourself. Reality is the ground of effective liberation. Life passes so quickly, and there is no stopping it from being cut off. The lifeblood of joy flows in every living thing, from the mineral world through the plant world, to the world of living beings. Only because we imprison ourselves in the idea of a small self do we create a state of darkness, narrowness, anxiety, and sorrow. According to our narrow view of a truly existing self, life is just my body, my house, my spouse, my children, and my riches. But if we can extend beyond every limit we have created for ourselves, we will see that our lives exist in everything, and that the deterioration of phenomena cannot touch that life, just as the arising and disappearing of the waves cannot influence the existence of the water. By observing in this way to shed light on the deterioration of everything, we can smile in the face of birth and death and attain great peace and joy in this life.

The Buddha advised us to look into the nature of the object of our desire so that reality can reveal itself strongly, and then we will no longer be caught in a wrong perception. Each of us has objects of desire, of craving. We believe that if we cannot get what we want, we cannot be happy, and we chase after these objects. The Buddha advises us to look deeply into that object, using mindfulness and concentration, so that it reveals its true nature. This is the aim of the exercise, "Experiencing non-craving, I breathe in." We might desire wealth, believing that if we don't have a lot of money, we cannot be happy. Those of us who have a lot of money know that it can make us very unhappy. Money is not an element of our happiness. With money, we may feel that we have power. That power can bring us a lot of suffering because it is often linked with notions of self, discrimination, delusion, and ignorance. Looking deeply into the object of our desire, our craving, we see that it is not really an object to chase after.

If you're addicted to alcohol, you think that we can't feel good without it. You need to look deeply into its nature; how it is made; what it is going to do to you and the people around you; what the relationship is between liquor and your liver, heart, feelings, and consciousness. If you look deeply enough, you see that the object of your craving is not an element of your happiness. We can suffer tremendously because of alcohol, or die because of it, yet we may have chased after it for a long time.

The Buddha used the image of a man who is thirsty who sees a glass of water. The water looks very cold, fresh, and sweet, but there is poison in it. Someone warns the man not to drink the water, "If you drink it, you could die or be close to death. Don't drink it, I warn you. Look for something else to drink. Use anything to quench your thirst, but don't drink this." But the man is so thirsty and the water looks so appealing that he decides that dying is okay. He drinks it and thinks, "I'll die later." And he suffers. It is the same with wealth, fame, sex, and food.

We don't want to die; we don't want to suffer; but because of our desire, we're dragged into the realm of suffering. Looking deeply into the nature of the object of our desire with mindfulness and concentration, we discover the true nature of our desire, and we stop chasing after it.

We behave in much the same way as the fish who bites the plastic bait. We have a wrong perception about the object of our desire. We think that life will have no meaning, and we will not be happy if we don't have it. There are a million ways to be happy, but we don't know how to open the door so that happiness will come. We just chase after the objects of our craving. Many of us have experienced the reality that the more we chase after the object of our craving, the more we suffer.

The Buddha said that you only consider the object of your craving to be happiness when you are sick. The object of our desire can kill us. While breathing mindfully, we look directly at our object of desire and look deeply into it. If we succeed, we'll be free from it and we'll look for happiness in other places, in the here and the now.

Each one of us has to study and practice this. We have to help our young people study and practice it, too. What is true happiness? Is happiness possible? Are the elements and conditions for happiness available in the here and the now? Do we need to chase after happiness in the future? All these questions are helpful. Therapists, teachers, politicians, everyone should learn about this, because we all want happiness and we all want to reduce suffering. Let us come together, practice looking deeply, and offer our collective insight to our community and nation. There is a way out of suffering. There is a way to build well-being. It is to look deeply into the nature of our suffering. When we can identify the elements that have brought us suffering, we can see the way out.

The Diamond Sutra advises us to throw away four notions. The first notion is the notion of self, that I am this body. Everything is made of elements that are not itself. The flower is made of the seed, the sun, the soil, the rain, and other elements. This is, because that is. If you are not there, I cannot be here. So it's very important to throw away the notion "I am," the notion of self, because it does not reflect the truth. By looking deeply into the nature of reality, you are capable of throwing away the notion of "I am." When we say the words "I am," we say them because we have the notion "I am." When the father looks deeply at himself, when the son looks deeply at his father, they see that they inter-are. The father is at the same time the son, and the son is at the same time the father. So a better statement is, "I inter-am."

The second is the notion of "human being." This is not too difficult to let go of. When we look into a human being, we see human and animal ancestors. If we look deeply, we can also see plant and mineral ancestors. The human is made of non-human elements. We see that we are at the same time a rock, a river, a cloud, a squirrel, and a rose. If we take away all the non-human elements, there's no human being left.

This is the deepest teaching on deep ecology. In order to protect the human being, you have to protect elements that are not human, because these elements are our ancestors, and if you destroy them, there is no way we can be here. That is why discrimination between man and nature is a wrong view. You have to see yourself as nature, as being one with nature. With this understanding, harmony and respect for life are possible. So throw away the idea that the human being is the boss, that man can do anything to nature. The key is the contemplations on impermanence and nonself. With liberation from the notion of human being, we become less proud and less arrogant as a species. We have to respect and protect the other species in order for us to have a chance. This is why we say the Diamond Sutra is the oldest text on deep ecology.

The third notion is the notion of living beings. When we say the words "living beings," it's because we want to distinguish living beings from non-living beings. But by looking deeply into living beings, we see elements that could be called non-living beings. Looking deeply, we can see that plants and minerals are alive also. So there is no real boundary separating human beings and nonhuman beings.

We have the notion that there is inert matter, non-living matter. But if you look deeply into the notion that matter is something without soul, without life, we see that's not true. First of all, matter is the object of our perceptions. For a long time we believed that matter existed as a separate entity, and matter was something that did not move. But now as science advances, we see that matter is not static and immobile as we thought. In fact, the atoms, the electrons, move a lot. They're very alive. Looking more deeply, we see the role our minds play in how we perceive things. We're no longer sure that things are the way we'd imagined them to be. So the distinction between living beings and non-living beings disappears after meditation. There's no longer any discrimination.

The fourth notion to be thrown away is the notion of life span. We believe that time is linear, that we are born at a certain point in time and that we shall die at another point in time. We believe we'll only spend seventy, eighty, ninety, or one hundred years on this planet. After that, we'll be gone. This is what we believe. But as we look deeply, we see that this is a notion, a wrong perception. Birth is a notion, and death is also a notion. It's not reality.

We have spoken of the deathlessness of a cloud. The cloud can never die. It can only become rain or snow. In our minds, to die means that from something you become nothing; from someone you become no one. But if you look deeply you don't see anything like that. You see that a cloud can never die. When you burn a piece of paper, that piece of paper transforms into smoke, heat, and ash. The piece of paper cannot be reduced to nothingness. The idea of annihilation is just an idea. You cannot annihilate anything.

If we look deeply we see that the nature of the cloud is also the nature of no birth. The cloud does not come from nothing. It has come from the water in the river and the ocean. It has come from the heat of the sunshine. You know that the birth of a cloud is a poetic image. The cloud is simply a new manifestation. Before being a cloud, the cloud has been many other things.

Our true nature is the nature of no birth and no death. Birth and death are notions that cannot be applied to reality, because there is nothing that can be born from nothing, and there is nothing that can become nothing at all. The meditation practice of looking deeply will bring about insight. It will dissipate our fear and our despair.

The four notions spoken of in The Diamond Sutra are the four basic notions that are at the foundation of our fear, our desperation, our suffering. That's why the Diamond Sutra advises us to practice looking deeply, so that we can throw them away. The practice of throwing away your notions, your views, is so important. Emancipation and liberation would not be possible without this practice of throwing away. If we suffer a lot, it's because we still entertain a number of ideas. The practice of meditation helps us to get free from these ideas.

The final breathing exercises help us look deeply in order to shed light on giving up desire and attachment; fear and anxiety; and hatred and anger. Usually we think that if we let go, we will lose the things that make us happy. But the more we let go, the happier we become.

We should not think that letting go means letting go of everything.

We do not let go of reality. We let go of all our wrong perceptions about reality. If we cannot let go of our wrong ideas, we cannot enter the world of reality. According to Tang Hoi, letting go means first of all letting go of ideas concerning self and life span. We have an idea that we began to exist the day our mothers gave birth and that the day we are buried, we cease to exist. We say we are our bodies, and outside of our own bodies we do not exist. "Breathing in, I let go of my idea of my body as myself." " Breathing out I let go of my idea that this period of fifty to one hundred years is my life span."

Anathapindika was a lay disciple who had always given a lot of support to the Buddha and the community of monks. When he was about to pass away and was in great pain, he was given teachings by the Venerable Shariputra to help him let go of ideas of self and life span. These teachings can be found in the Sutra on Teachings to Be Given to the Sick. After Shariputra guided Anathapindika in a meditation on the Buddha, the Dharma, and the Sangha to nourish the seeds of joy in him, he began to offer the cream of the Buddha's teachings: "Friend Anathapindika, please meditate like this: 'These eyes are not me. I am not caught in these eyes.'" He went from eyes to ears, nose, tongue, body and mind; to form, sound, smell, taste, touch and objects of mind; then to eye consciousness, up to mind consciousness. "All these things are not me. I have no need to be caught by them."

Shariputra continued, "Friend Anathapindika, all things exist because of causes and conditions. When the causes and conditions for them cease to exist, they no longer exist. The true nature of things is not to be born and not to die, not to come and not to go." When Anathapindika heard these teachings, he understood them immediately. He knew he had only a short time left to live, and that was enough motivation for him to put the teachings into practice without delay. When he practiced in this way, tears of happiness started to run down his cheeks, and Anathapindika passed away in peace. We, too, are fortunate to have the cream of the teachings available to us. We have to practice letting go of our ideas in order to see life everywhere, beyond space and time. Dear reader, do not wait until your last moments to practice this sutra. Practice it now so you can see that you are not enclosed in your small shell of your body or the small shell of your life span.

When you see that there is already a precious jewel in your pocket, you give up every attitude of craving or coveting. Seeing that we are lions, we do not long to nurse from a mother deer. Seeing that we are the sun, we give up the candle's habit of fearing the wind. Seeing that life has no boundaries, we give up all imprisoning divisions. We see ourselves and our lives everywhere. That is why we vow to help all living phenomena, all living species, like a *bodhisattva* who has attained great awakening. Letting go does not mean abandoning one thing in order to seek something else. It means giving up every comparison, seeing that there is nothing to be removed and nothing to be added, and that the boundary between ourselves and others is not real. We need not give up our human condition in order to become a buddha. We seek buddhahood in our very human condition, giving up nothing and seeking nothing. That is the meaning of apranihita, "aimlessness," sometimes translated as "wishlessness." It is the same as not seeking, a concept fully developed in Mahayana Buddhism. Let go in order to be everything and to be completely free. Many people have already done so, and each of us can do so as well, if we have the intention.

The fifteenth exercise helps us free ourselves from individuality, so that we can become part of the whole universe. Cessation in Pali and Sanskrit is *nirodha*. It means cessation of all erroneous ideas, of all notions that keep us from directly experiencing the ultimate reality, and of all suffering born of our ignorance. That means the cessation of ideas like birth and death, permanence and annihilation, increasing and decreasing, being and nonbeing, coming and going. We have to go beyond these ideas because they form the basis of our suffering, which is expressed as desire and attachment; fear and anxiety; and hatred and anger. When we stop having ideas like that, we are in touch with the wonderful true nature of how things are. How can we get beyond our ideas of birth and death, and coming and going? First we have to see that things are impermanent; they manifest and pass away. Then we are free to look more deeply and see that reality is beyond all ideas. It is like a coin. At first we see that it has two sides, but when we look more deeply we see that both sides of the coin are made from the same metal. The essence of the coin is the metal. The two sides both arise from the metal. In the same way, birth and death; coming and going; being and nonbeing; and permanence and annihilation all arise from the same essence.

Many years ago, I could not imagine that there would one day be nonsmoking flights. I suffered when I sat amongst the smokers. Yet awakening was possible. So many of us demanded nonsmoking flights, that they now exist. Awakening is possible if we are determined to practice. We practice to awaken ourselves and others. This is the only way to address a difficult situation. Now, we are much more aware of the foods we eat. Cigarette packages contain health warnings. This is the fruit of awakening. We should wake up as individuals and as nations. Now we can go on to make laws protecting us from other harmful things like weapons and films full of sex and violence.

Every one of us has the seeds of awakening, insight, compassion, and loving kindness. Once in touch with these, we inspire confidence in the people around us. We have to help each other practice as a Sangha. When we see a group of people living mindfully, we have confidence in the future. We cannot let the younger generation lose hope. That would be the end. We have to live our daily lives in a way that makes the future possible.

As I have mentioned previously, some of our children spend many hours a day watching television and touching violence, fear, craving, anger, and despair. The job of educators is to create a situation that helps them touch the healthy, healing elements inside and around them. Those of us who are teachers should use our intelligence and creativity to do this work. We have to ask our representatives in Congress to practice with us and make the kinds of laws that we need for our protection and the protection of our children. Now is not the time for us to meditate as sole practitioners; we have to practice meditation as groups, cities, and nations. Our collective insight comes from individual insight, and vice versa. We practice on both levels so that we will know what to do and what not to do on the individual, familial, and national levels. Mindfulness is our instrument. Without mindfulness, negative things will continue to take place everywhere. Awareness helps us know which actions to stop and which to continue.

ENJOYING OUR BREATHING

The Sutra on the Full Awareness of Breathing is a reminder that we can use the sixteen exercises and the Four Foundations of Mindfulness to bring our breath, bodies, and minds into harmony. We are able to use our breath to bring ourselves into a state of meditation, of stopping and looking deeply. Meditation is not an escape. It is the courage to look at reality with mindfulness and concentration. Our world needs wisdom and insight.

The practice of resting, of stopping, is crucial. If we cannot rest, it is because we have not stopped. We have continued to run. We started running a long time ago. We even continue to run in our sleep. We think that happiness and well-being aren't possible in the here and the now. That belief is inherent in us. We have received the seed of that belief from our parents and our grandparents. They struggled all of their lives and believed that happiness was only possible in the future. That's why when we were children, we already had the habit of running. We believed that happiness was something to seek in the future. But the teaching of the Buddha is that you can be happy right here, right now. The conditions for your well-being and happiness are found in the present moment.

5: Breathing Practices

BREATHING GATHAS

> Let the Buddha breathe,
> Let the Buddha walk.
> I don't need to breathe,
> I don't need to walk.
>
> Buddha is breathing,
> Buddha is walking.
> I enjoy the breathing,
> I enjoy the walking.
>
> Buddha is the breathing,
> Buddha is the walking.
> I am the breathing,
> I am the walking.
>
> There is only the breathing,
> There is only the walking.
> There is no one breathing,
> There is no one walking.
>
> Peace while breathing,
> Peace while walking.
> Peace is the breathing,
> Peace is the walking.

GUIDED MEDITATIONS

Following are some ways for you to guide yourself or each other in sitting meditation, based on the exercises in the sutra. You can practice each exercise for as long as you need in order to realize its meaning. You might like to practice one exercise for as long as ten minutes. If the practice is enjoyable and you feel nourished by it, you know you are practicing correctly.

The words in parentheses after each exercise are abbreviations of the exercise for you to recall easily the subject of your meditation. You do not have to practice all the exercises here during one sitting.

1. "Breathing in, I know I am breathing in. Breathing out, I know I am breathing out." (In, Out)
2. "Breathing in, my breath goes deep. Breathing out, my breath goes slow." (Deep, Slow)
3. "Breathing in, I am aware of my whole body. Breathing out, I calm my whole body." (Aware of my body, Calming my body)
4. "Breathing in, I know I am alive. Breathing out, I feel the joy of being alive." (Alive, Joy of being alive)
5. "Breathing in, I know I have the opportunity to meditate. Breathing out, I feel happy to have that opportunity." (Opportunity to meditate, Happy)
6. "Breathing in, I am embracing my unpleasant feeling. Breathing out, I am calming my feeling." (Embracing my feeling, Calming my feeling)
7. "Breathing in, I am aware of right mindfulness in me. Breathing out, it makes me happy." (Wholesome mental formation, I am happy)
8. "Breathing in, I concentrate on a mental formation which is present. Breathing out, I look deeply at that mental formation." (Concentrate on mental formation, Look deeply at it)
9. "Breathing in, I open up my mind to look deeply at my fear. Breathing out, there is liberation from fear." (Opening up my mind, Liberation)
10. "Breathing in, I observe a flower. Breathing out, I contemplate the impermanence of the flower." (Observing a flower, Contemplating its impermanence)

11. "Breathing in, I look deeply at the object of my desire. Breathing out, I see the disappearance of desire with regard to that object." (Object of desire, Disappearance of desire)

12. "Breathing in, I observe the coming and going of the wave. Breathing out, I contemplate the no-coming, no-going of the water." (Coming and going of the wave, No-coming, no-going of the water)

13. "Breathing in, I let go of the idea that this body is me. Breathing out, I am not caught in this body." (This body not me, I am not caught in this body)

14. "Breathing in, I let go of the idea that I did not exist before I was born. Breathing out, I let go of the idea that I will not exist After I die." (I am not born, I do not die)

In the second exercise, do not force your breathing to become deeper or slower. This is an exercise of mere recognition. Your breath has actually become deeper and slower as the result of practicing the first exercise. In the third exercise, because of your awareness of your body, you will know how calm it is and you will know what bodily factors need calming. In the fourth and fifth exercises, you do not want to repeat the words "joy" and "happy" without giving them a reason to exist. Here we have chosen the fact that you are alive and the fact that you have the chance to meditate as being occasions for your happiness, but you can find other reasons for joy and happiness and substitute them in this exercise. The first five breathing exercises are intended to calm, stop, focus, concentrate, and nourish us. Without these elements in your sitting meditation practice, you will tire of sitting. Only when you feel happy can you have concentration. You cannot achieve concentration by forcing yourself to concentrate.

Methods seven and eight in the Anapanasati Sutta become one breathing exercise here, number six. You are aware of an unpleasant feeling or a pleasant feeling that has the capacity to poison or excite you, and you calm these feelings. In the seventh exercise, your mind feels happy because you know that in your consciousness is the capacity to realize wholesome mental formations. The capacity to be mindful, caring, and loving is within everyone. The first seven exercises here cover the first ten methods of the Anapanasati Sutta, and they are to nourish and to calm.

In exercise eight, you concentrate your mind on a mental formation.

It could be wholesome, unwholesome, or neutral. When you concentrate, you have to concentrate on something; and when you are liberated, you have to be liberated from something. It is not fruitful to repeat the words "concentration" and "liberation" without there being an object for your concentration. When you concentrate and look deeply at a mental formation, you can see why it is there, and that understanding will help you be liberated from it. To open up your mind and liberate your mind in exercise nine, you need to have developed concentration in exercise eight. Exercises eight and nine are an opportunity for us to look at the mental formations that make us suffer.

In exercise ten, you can observe any phenomenon: yourself, another person, or an object in order to contemplate impermanence. Here we have chosen to observe a flower. Buddhist monks and nuns meditate every day on the impermanence of their own person.

In exercise eleven, you should meditate on a specific object of desire. It can be a person or a thing. If a person has become the object of your desire, it can be unpleasant for them if they feel they are losing their freedom. This exercise can help you not to be caught in wanting to possess or dominate others. Desire disappears when you see that the true nature of the object you desire is impermanent, has no separate self, and cannot be grasped. If you are not satisfied with what is available in the present moment, you will never be satisfied by attaining what you think will bring you happiness in the future.

In exercise twelve, you contemplate the cessation of ideas concerning birth and death; coming and going; and high and low, using the images of water and wave to help you.

In exercise thirteen, you contemplate that this body is not you, and that these feelings, perceptions, mental formations, and consciousness are not you either. The vegetation, the air, and the water are constantly contributing to this body. Feelings and perceptions are dependent on your education, your ancestry, your friends, your teacher, and your upbringing. Consciousness is a vast field containing all the seeds, with constant output and constant input.

In exercise fourteen, you have to see very clearly the reason for not being born and for not dying. Your so-called birthday was not the day you began to exist. You were in your parents before that, and prior to that in a line of ancestors. After death, you will continue in the clouds and in the dust that is part of the Earth, and in the descendants of your blood family and in your spiritual heirs.

I HAVE ARRIVED

A number of years ago, I went to India to visit the Buddhist community of the untouchables. A friend organized this teaching tour for me. He belonged to that caste, which has been discriminated against for many thousands of years. He was sitting with me in the bus, next to me on my right. I was enjoying the Indian countryside very much. When I looked at him, I saw that he was very tense. He had done everything to make my visit pleasant, but he continued to worry. This habit energy had been transmitted to him from many generations of ancestors. They had struggled all their lives, for many generations, against discrimination. It is very hard to transform that kind of habit. I said, "Dear friend, why are you so tense? There is nothing to do now here on the bus. We can enjoy the countryside. When we arrive, our friends will come to the station to get us. Sit back and enjoy the countryside and smile." He said, "okay," but just two minutes later, he looked exactly as before, very tense, thinking about the future, and not being able to be at ease in the here and the now.

Our practice is to be aware that all the wonders of life are available in the here and the now, and that we should stop running. While practicing walking meditation, we should stop. While practicing sitting meditation, we should stop. While enjoying our breakfast, we should stop. There are some people who sit down to have a meal but continue to run inside. They are not capable of stopping, being in the here and the now, and just enjoying a slice of tomato or a carrot. Let us support each other in order to really stop. The Buddha said, "The past is already gone. The future is not yet here. There is only one moment for you to live. That is the present moment." We have an appointment with life in the present moment. If we miss the present moment, we miss our appointment with life. We can all understand this.

But our habit energy is so strong. That is why we need each other in order to stop and establish ourselves in the present moment. Eating together is an occasion for us to stop. Walking together is also an opportunity to stop. Sitting together, enjoying our in-breath and out-breath, is another opportunity to stop. Every time the runaway horse of habit energy shows its head, pushing us on, we breathe in and out and say, "My dear friend, I know you, the habit energy of running." We smile to it, and it is not able to push us any more. It will go away. Sometime later, if it manifests itself again as a mental formation, we breathe in and out and say, "My dear friend, I know you." We simply recognize a mental formation. Every time we practice like this, it loses some of its strength. We don't have to fight. All we have to do is recognize it and smile to it.

> I have arrived. I am home
> in the here, in the now.
> I am solid, I am free.
> In the ultimate I dwell.

"I have arrived. I am home." Our true home is in the here and the now. It is in the island of self within. We can only touch life in all its wonders in the here and the now. It's like when we hear the bell. We practice, "Listen, listen. This wonderful sound brings me back to my true home."

Later, you might want to use the second line of the gatha, "In the here and in the now." "In the here" is for your in-breath; "in the now" is for your out-breath. "The here and the now" is the address of your true home. "In the here and in the now" means the same as "I have arrived. I am home." They are just different words. It is up to you how long to enjoy each exercise.

Later on, you may use the third line, "I am solid. I am free." This is not auto-suggestion. If you have arrived, then you have cultivated more solidity and freedom. As you walk mindfully, you touch your true home, and you become more solid, because you are not running anymore. You have reclaimed the freedom to be yourself. Before that, you were a victim of the past and the future, both pulling you in different directions. Now you are more yourself; you have reclaimed some of your liberty. "I am solid. I am free." You are no longer a victim.

In the teachings of the Buddha, solidity and freedom are the two characteristics of nirvana. You begin to touch nirvana when you cultivate mindfulness of walking or breathing. At the same time, you cultivate the elements of solidity and freedom. Happiness is possible on the ground of solidity and freedom.

"In the ultimate I dwell." We can't understand the last line unless we learn how to touch the ground of our being. There are two dimensions of reality: the historical dimension and the ultimate dimension. We live in history. In this dimension, there are: birth and death; a beginning and an end; being and nonbeing; high and low; and success and failure. We are used to dwelling in this dimension. We have not had the chance to touch this dimension deeply in order to dwell in the ultimate dimension. But the two dimensions belong to each other. You cannot take the historical dimension out of the ultimate dimension, or the ultimate dimension out of the historical dimension. It is like the wave and the water. You cannot take the wave out of the water, nor the water out of the wave.

Don't throw away impermanence and nonself in order to touch nirvana. If you throw away impermanence and nonself, there will be no nirvana left. It is like if you throw the water away, there will be no waves left, and if you throw all the waves away, there will be no water left. That is why when we touch the historical dimension deeply, we also touch nirvana. This is a very deep Buddhist teaching. We find relief from our suffering by embracing our despair, fear, and sorrow, but the greatest relief comes through touching nirvana.

This solidity and freedom introduces us to the world of the ultimate. The last line of the gatha, "In the ultimate I dwell" is best understood when we practice the last four exercises on mindful breathing concerning our perceptions. So let us help each other enjoy our sitting. Sitting is an enjoyment, not hard labor for enlightenment. Mindful walking is an enjoyment, and eating breakfast is an enjoyment. If we enjoy the practice, then the practice becomes pleasant, nourishing, and healing for us.

BEING AN ISLAND UNTO MYSELF

Being an island unto myself.
As an island unto myself.
Buddha is my mindfulness.
Shining near, shining far.
Dharma is my breathing, guarding body and mind.
I am free.
Being an island unto myself.
As an island unto myself.
Sangha is my skandhas, working in harmony.
Taking refuge in myself.
Coming back to myself.
I am free.

This practice brings us home. The Buddha said that there is an island in each of us, and when we go home to ourselves, we are on that safe island. There, we touch the energy of the Buddha, which sheds its light on any situation, enabling us to see near and far and to know what to do. We touch the living Dharma on that island by practicing mindful breathing. Mindful breathing and mindfulness practice are the living Dharma. They generate energy and protect our bodies and minds.

You can touch the energy of the Sangha within yourself in your Five Skandhas: body, feelings, perceptions, mental formations, and consciousness. Through mindful breathing, these elements come together to work in harmony. Unhappiness, sorrow, fear, and conflict are transformed into harmony. When we touch the energy of the Buddha, the Dharma, and the Sangha, we are safe, and not overwhelmed by the negative energy of confusion, despair, and panic. Returning to our island and practicing mindful breathing helps tremendously.

I always practice this gatha at the most difficult times. If I were in an airplane and thought it was going to crash, I would practice breathing in and out. It is the best thing to do. Please cherish this practice. It has saved many lives. It is a Dharma treasure. You can memorize this gatha and practice it while driving, making breakfast, or having lunch. Dwelling in the island of self, you chew each morsel of food with this gatha in mind. You can practice arriving, being at home, and being in a pure land. You will feel as though you are surrounded by the Sangha and are absorbing its energy. You are also producing energy and offering it to the Sangha at the same time.

6: A Point of View on Practice

Neither the Sutra on the Full Awareness of Breathing nor the Sutra on the Four Establishments of Mindfulness mentions the technique of counting the breath. There is also no mention of the Six Wonderful Dharma Doors: counting, following, stopping, observing, returning, and calming. Nor is there any reference to the *kasina* (visualized image) meditation, the Four Jhanas, or the Four Formless Concentrations. These teachings were probably developed somewhat later to serve many levels of students. We need not criticize them for being later teachings, certainly not before we have practiced them and seen for ourselves if they work well. Counting is an excellent technique for beginners.[26] Breathing in, count "one." Breathing out, count "one." Breathing in, count "two." Breathing out, count "two." Continue up to ten and then start counting over again. If at any time you forget where you are, begin again with "one." The method of counting helps us refrain from dwelling on troublesome thoughts; instead we concentrate on our breathing and the number. When we have developed some control over our thinking, counting may become tedious and we can abandon it and just follow the breath itself. This is called "following."

Well-known commentaries, such as the Patisambhida Magga (Path of No Hesitation) and the Visuddhi Magga (Path of Purity), teach that while we breathe, we should be aware of our nostrils, the place where air enters and leaves the body. Just as when we cut a log we keep our eyes on the place where the saw touches the log (rather than looking at the teeth of the saw), we pay attention to the nostrils and not to the air as it enters the body. Many commentators point out that if you follow the breath entering the body, then the object of your attention is not a single object, and thus concentration will be difficult. For this reason, they say that "the whole body" in the third method means the whole body of breath and not the whole body of the practitioner. If we study the sutra, we can see that their explanation is not correct. In the third breathing exercise, the object of attention is not just the breath. It is the whole body of the practitioner, in the same way that the object of the seventh exercise is all feelings and the object of the ninth exercise is the whole mind.

In the fourth exercise ("Breathing in, I calm my whole body"), the expression "whole body" cannot mean just the whole body of breath either. All four preliminary exercises take the physical body as the object, since the body is the first of the Four Establishments of Mindfulness. Even if in the first two exercises the object is just the breathing, that includes the body, since the breath is a part of our physical organism. In the third and fourth exercises, the entire physical body is the object.

All the commentaries—the Patisambhida Magga (Path of No Hesitation) by Mahanama, the Vimutti Magga (Path of Liberation) by Upatissa, and the Visuddhi Magga (Path of Purity) by Buddhaghosa—recommend that practitioners focus on the tip of the nose rather than follow the breath as it enters the body. If the practitioner follows the breath into the body, they say, the practitioner will be dispersed and unable to enter into the Four Jhanas. The Vimutti Magga was written at the end of the fourth century CE, the Patisambhida Magga at the beginning of the fifth, and the Visuddhi Magga shortly after that. All of these emphasize the necessity of stopping (*shamatha*) as the prerequisite for observing (*vipashyana*). Here, stopping means the Four Jhanas and the Four Formless Concentrations. Focusing the mind at the tip of the nose and being aware of the first moment of contact of air at its place of entry into the body, just as the carpenter looks only at the place of contact of the saw's teeth as they enter and leave the wood, gradually the rough, uneven breathing becomes delicate and subtle, and finally all discrimination disappears. At this point, the sign (*kasina*) will appear, like a ball of cotton, giving the practitioner a feeling of lightness and ease like a fresh, cool breeze. If the practitioner follows this sign, he or she enters concentration, the first of the Four Jhanas. The first jhana is the first step, followed by the second, third, and fourth jhanas. In each state of meditative concentration, the five sense organs are inactive, while the mind of the practitioner is lucid and awake. After the Four Jhanas come the Four Formless Concentrations:

the realm of limitless space, the realm of limitless consciousness, the realm of no materiality, and the realm where the concepts "perceiving" and "not perceiving" no longer apply.

We must examine the extent to which Buddhist meditation practice was influenced by the Yoga-Upanishadic systems. Before realizing the Way, Shakyamuni Buddha studied with many Brahman yogis, from whom he learned the Four Jhanas and the Four Formless Concentrations. After experiencing these, he said that concentrations like "the realm of no materiality" and "the realm where perceiving and not perceiving do not apply," taught by the masters Arada Kalama and Udraka Ramaputra, cannot lead to ultimate emancipation. As we have seen, he did not mention the Four Jhanas or the Four Formless Concentrations in the Anapanasati or the Satipatt hana, the two fundamental sutras on meditation. Therefore, we must conclude that the practices of the Four Jhanas and the Four Formless Concentrations are not necessary for arriving at the fruit of practice, the awakened mind. The methods of mindfulness taught by the Buddha in the Sutra on the Four Establishments of Mindfulness can be seen as the incomparable path leading to emancipation. There are meditation students who have practiced for many years and who, having failed to attain the Four Jhanas, think they do not have the capacity to realize awakening. There are others who stray into unhealthy meditation practices and lose all peace of mind, just because they want so much to enter the Four Jhanas. Only by practicing correctly, according to the teachings of the Buddha in the Anapanasati and Satipatthana Suttas, can we be sure we will not stray into practices we may later regret.

In Vietnam at the beginning of the third century CE, the meditation master Tang Hoi, when writing the preface to the Anapanasati in Chinese, referred to the Four Jhanas, but the Four Jhanas of Tang Hoi were combined with observation—observing the body, sky and earth, prosperity and decline, coming and going, and so on. Tang Hoi also spoke of the Six Wonderful Dharma Doors (counting the breath, following the breath, concentrating the mind, observing to throw light on all that exists, returning to the source of mind, and going beyond the concepts of subject and object). Moreover, Tang Hoi referred to the technique of concentrating the mind at the tip of the nose. The Xiu Hang Dao Di Sutra, in the chapter called "Enumerating," also refers to the Four Jhanas, the technique of counting the breath, the Six Wonderful Dharma Doors, and the technique of concentrating the mind at the tip of the nose.[27] The Zeng Yi A Han (Ekottara Agama), in the chapter on breathing, also refers to the Four Jhanas and the technique of concentrating the mind at the tip of the nose, but it does not refer to counting the breath or the Six Wonderful Dharma Doors.[28]

We should remember that the sutras were memorized and transmitted orally for hundreds of years before they were written down. Therefore, many sutras must have been at least somewhat altered according to a variety of influences and circumstances during those centuries. The Anapanasati and Satipatthana Suttas can be seen as two precious accounts of early Buddhist meditation practice, since they were handed down by the monks in an especially careful way. It seems to be the case that mistakes and outside additions were very few in these two sutras.

In the history of Buddhism, some classical sutras were affected during their transmission by outside influences, both in the Southern schools and the Northern schools, but especially in the Northern schools. Studying Mahayana sutras, we must remember to look again and discover the depth of the fundamental "source" sutras. The seeds of all important ideas of the Mahayana are already contained in these source sutras. If we go back to the source, we develop a more clear and unshakable view of the Mahayana sutras. If we merely sit on the two giant wings of the Mahayana bird, we may fly far away and lose all contact with the original abode from which the bird arose.

Although the Anapanasati and Satipatthana Suttas do not refer to the Four Jhanas and the Four Formless Concentrations, we should not conclude that they do not emphasize the importance of concentration. Meditation has two aspects: stopping (shamatha), and observation or looking deeply (vipashyana). Stopping is concentration, and looking deeply is insight. The Full Awareness of the Breath, or of any other object such as the body, the feelings, the mind, the objects of mind, and so forth, all aim at the goal of concentrating the mind on an object so that it is possible to see the object in all its depth. Concentrating the mind is stopping it from running around from one object to another in order to stay with just one object. We stay with one object in order to observe it and look deeply into it. In this way, stopping and observing become one. Thanks to our ability to stop, we are able to observe. The more deeply we observe, the greater our mental concentration becomes. Stopping and collecting our mind, we naturally become able to see. In observing, the mind becomes increasingly still. We do not need to search for anything more. We only need to practice the simple exercises proposed by the Buddha in these two sutras.

7: Other Translations:
The Anapananusmriti Sutras

Translated from the Chinese by Thich Nhat Hanh from the Samyukta Agama (Tsa A Han, Chapter 29, Taisho Revised Tripitaka, number 99)

SECTION ONE

This is what I heard. At that time the Buddha was staying in the Jeta grove in Anathapindika's park in the town of Shravasti during the rainy season retreat. At that time, many elder disciples were spending the retreat with the Blessed One. There were bhikshus staying all around where the Blessed One was, at the roots of trees or in caves. The number of young bhikshus present during that retreat was also quite great. They came to where the Buddha was staying, prostrated at his feet, and then withdrew and sat down to one side. The Buddha gave teachings to the young bhikshus on many subjects, instructing them, teaching them, enlightening them, and delighting them. After giving these teachings, the Lord was silent. When the young bhikshus had heard these teachings from the Buddha, they felt great joy. They stood up, prostrated to the Lord, and withdrew. After that the young bhikshus approached the elders. When they had paid respects to the elder monks, they sat down to one side. At this time, the elder monks thought to themselves, we should take charge of these young monks and give them teachings. Some of us can instruct one monk, others can instruct two or three monks or even more. They put this idea into practice immediately. Some elders taught one young monk, others taught two or three young monks, and others again instructed more than three young monks. There were elders who guided and instructed up to sixty young bhikshus.

At that time when it was the end of the retreat and time for the Inviting Ceremony, the World-Honored One looked over the assembly of bhikshus and told them, "Well done, well done. I am very happy to see you doing the things that are right and fitting for bhikshus to do. Please continue to study and practice diligently like this, and please stay here in Shravasti for another month, until the full moon day of the month of Kattika."

When many bhikshus who had been spending the rainy season retreat scattered about in the countryside heard that the World-Honored One would stay at Shravasti until the full moon day of Komudi, they performed the Inviting Ceremony, finished sewing their robes, and without delay took their robes and bowls and left for the town of Shravasti. When they came to the Anathapindika Monastery, they put away their robes and bowls, washed their feet, and went to the place where the Buddha was sitting. They paid their respects to the Buddha and then withdrew a little and sat down to one side. Then the World-Honored One taught the Dharma to the monks who had just arrived from the surrounding areas. He instructed them on many topics, enlightening and delighting them. When he finished, he sat in silence. When the monks from the surrounding areas heard the teachings, they were delighted. They stood up and prostrated, and then went to the elders. After they paid their respects to these monks, they withdrew a little and sat down to one side. At this time the elder monks thought to themselves, we should also accept the monks who have just come from the surrounding areas, and each of us can instruct one monk, or two monks, or three monks, or more than three monks. They put this idea into practice immediately. There were elders who taught just one of the newly arrived bhikshus, and there were elders who taught more. There were even elders who instructed up to sixty newly arrived bhikshus. The elders did the work of instructing and encouraging the bhikshus who came from the surrounding regions, teaching them everything in order, putting first what should go first and adding later what should be taught later, in a very skillful fashion.

When the day of the full moon came after the Uposatha observances had been performed, the World-Honored One sat before the assembly of monks. After he had cast his gaze over the whole community of bhikshus, he said, "Well done. Well done, bhikshus! I am delighted to see that you have done and are doing the things that are right and fitting for a bhikshu to do. I am very happy when I see that you have done and are doing the things that are necessary for a bhikshu to do. Bhikshus, the Buddhas of the past also had communities of bhikshus who did the things that are right and fitting for a bhikshu to do. The Buddhas of the future will also have communities of bhikshus like this community of bhikshus, and they also will do the things that are right and fitting for a bhikshu to do as you today are doing and have done.

"In this community of bhikshus, there are, among the elders, those who have accomplished the first *dhyana*, the second dhyana, the third dhyana, and the fourth dhyana. There are those who have accomplished the *maitri samadhi* (concentration of loving kindness), the *karuna samadhi* (concentration of compassion), the *mudita samadhi* (concentration of joy), and the *upeksha samadhi* (concentration of equanimity). There are those who have realized the limitless-space concentration, the limitless consciousness concentration, the concentration of no thing exists, and the concentration of no perception and no non-perception. There are those who are always able to remain in one of these samadhis. There are those who have untied the three basic internal knots and have attained the fruit of Stream-Enterer. They have no fear of falling into the paths of great suffering and are firmly on the way to perfect enlightenment. They only need to return seven times more to be born in the worlds of gods and men before being liberated from the suffering of birth and death. There are monks who, after they have untied the three basic internal knots and have nearly transformed the three poisons of craving, hatred, and ignorance, have realized the fruit of Once-Returner. There are monks who have untied the first five internal knots and have realized the fruit of non-returning. They are able to reach nirvana in this life and do not need to be born again in the world, which is subject to birth and death. There are bhikshus who have realized the immeasurable miraculous intelligence and even in this world are able to use the divine eye, the divine ear, knowing others' minds, recollecting previous births, knowing others' previous births, and ending all the ashravas (roots of affliction). There are monks who, thanks to practicing the meditation on impurity, have transformed the energy of attachment; thanks to the meditation on loving kindness, have transformed the energy of hatred; thanks to looking deeply at impermanence, have transformed the energy of pride; and thanks to the practice of conscious breathing, have been able to put an end to the ignorance and suffering that arise in the fields of feelings and perceptions.

"Bhikshus, what is the Way to practice conscious breathing so that we eliminate the ignorance and the suffering in the fields of feelings and perceptions?"

—Samyukta Agama, Sutta No. 815
translated from the Chinese

SECTION TWO

"A bhikshu who practices the method of conscious breathing very diligently will realize a state of peace and calm in his body and in his mind. Conscious breathing will lead to right mindfulness, the ability to look deeply, and a clear and single-minded perception, so that he is in a position to realize all the Dharma doors that give rise to the fruit of nirvana.

"A bhikshu who lives near a small village or a town puts on his *sanghati* robe in the morning, picks up his bowl, and goes into the inhabited area to seek alms. All the time he skillfully guards his six senses and establishes himself in mindfulness. After he has received alms, he returns to his place of abode, takes off his sanghati robe, puts down his bowl, and washes his feet. Then he goes into the forest and sits at the foot of a tree or sits in an empty room or out in the open air. He sits very straight, maintaining mindfulness before him. He lets go of all his cravings. He calms and clarifies his body and mind. He eliminates the five hindrances—craving, anger, dullness, agitation, and suspicion—and all the other afflictions that can weaken his understanding and create obstacles for him in his progress towards nirvana. Then he practices as follows:

1. 'Breathing in, I know I am breathing in. Breathing out, I know I am breathing out.'
2. 'Breathing in a long breath or a short breath, I know whether it is a long breath or a short breath. Breathing out a long breath or a short breath, I know whether it is a long breath or a short breath.'
3. 'Breathing in, I am aware of my whole body. Breathing out, I am aware of my whole body.'
4. 'Breathing in, I calm my whole body. Breathing out, I calm my whole body.'
5. 'Breathing in, I experience joy. Breathing out, I experience joy.'
6. 'Breathing in, I experience happiness. Breathing out, I experience happiness.'

7. 'Breathing in, I am aware of the feeling that is present now. Breathing out, I am aware of the feeling that is present now.'

8. 'Breathing in, I calm the feeling that is present now. Breathing out, I calm the feeling that is present now.'

9. 'Breathing in, I am aware of the activity of mind that is present now. Breathing out, I am aware of the activity of mind that is present now.'

10. 'Breathing in, I make the activity of my mind happy. Breathing out, I make the activity of my mind happy.'

11. 'Breathing in, I bring right concentration to bear on the activity of my mind. Breathing out, I bring right concentration to bear on the activity of my mind.'

12. 'Breathing in, I liberate the activity of my mind. Breathing out, I liberate the activity of my mind.'

13. 'Breathing in, I observe the impermanent nature of all dharmas. Breathing out, I observe the impermanent nature of all dharmas.'

14. 'Breathing in, I observe the letting go of all dharmas. Breathing out, I observe the letting go of all dharmas.'

15. 'Breathing in, I observe no craving with regard to all dharmas. Breathing out, I observe no craving with regard to all dharmas.'

16. 'Breathing in, I observe the nature of cessation of all dharmas. Breathing out, I observe the nature of cessation of all dharmas.'

"Bhikshus, that is the practice of conscious breathing, whose function it is to calm the body and mind, to bring about right mindfulness, looking deeply, and clear and single-minded perception so that the practitioner is in a position to realize all the Dharma doors that lead to the fruit of nirvana."

—Samyukta Agama, Sutra No. 803
translated from the Chinese

SECTION THREE

At that time, the Venerable Ananda was practicing meditation in a deserted place. It occurred to him, can there be a way of practice if, when it is practiced to fruition, one will realize the ability to remain in the Four Establishments of Mindfulness, the Seven Factors of Awakening, and the two factors of wisdom and liberation? With this in mind, he left his sitting meditation and went to the place where the Buddha was staying, bowed his head, prostrated at the feet of the Buddha, withdrew a little, and sat down to one side. He said, "World-Honored One, I was practicing meditation on my own in a deserted place, when the question suddenly occurred to me, can there be a way of practice if, when it is practiced to fruition, one will realize the ability to remain in the Four Establishments of Mindfulness, the Seven Factors of Awakening, and the two factors of wisdom and liberation?"

The Buddha instructed Ananda, "There is a way of practice which, if brought to fruition, will enable one to realize remaining in the Four Establishments of Mindfulness and, by remaining in the Four Establishments, the Seven Factors of Awakening will be realized. By realizing the Seven Factors of Awakening, wisdom and liberation will be realized. This way of practice is conscious breathing.

"How is conscious breathing to be practiced? A noble disciple practices as follows: 'Breathing in, I know I am breathing in. Breathing out, I know I am breathing out. Breathing in and breathing out, I know whether my in-breath and out-breath are short or long. Breathing in and breathing out, I am aware of my whole body.' While practicing like this, he dwells in the practice of observing body in the body, whether it be his own body or another body. At this point, the object of the bhikshu's observation that he follows closely is the body.

"A noble disciple practices as follows: 'Breathing in and out, I am aware of joy. Breathing in and out, I am aware of happiness. Breathing in and out, I am aware of the feeling that is present. Breathing in and out, I calm the feeling that is present.' As he practices like this, he abides in the practice of observing feelings in the feelings, whether they be his own feelings or the feelings of another. At this point, the object of his observation that he follows is the feelings.

"A noble disciple practices looking deeply as follows: 'Breathing in and out, I am aware of the activity of mind that is present. Breathing in and out, I make the activity of mind happy. Breathing in and out, I bring concentration to bear on the activity of mind. Breathing in and out, I liberate the activity of mind.' As he does this, he abides in the practice of observing mental activities in mental activities, whether the mental activity is his own or that of someone else. At this point, the object of observation that he follows is mental activities.

"A noble disciple practices as follows: 'Breathing in and out, I observe the impermanent nature of things. Breathing in and out, I observe the nature of letting go. Breathing in and out, I observe the nature of no more craving. Breathing in and out, I observe the nature of cessation.' As he practices like this, he abides in the observation of phenomena in phenomena, whether they are phenomena in his own person or outside his own person. At this point, the object of his observation that he follows is phenomena.

"Ananda, the practice of conscious breathing to realize dwelling in the Four Establishments of Mindfulness is like that."

The Venerable Ananda asked, "World-Honored One, the practice of conscious breathing to realize dwelling in the Four Establishments of Mindfulness is as you have described. But how do we practice the Four Establishments of Mindfulness in order to realize the Seven Factors of Awakening?"

The Buddha said, "If a bhikshu is able to maintain mindfulness while he practices observation of the body in the body, if he is able to abide in right mindfulness and bind mindfulness to himself in such a way that it is not lost, then he is practicing the Factor of Awakening called right mindfulness. The factor of right mindfulness is the means that leads to success in the Factor of Awakening called investigation of dharmas. When the factor of investigation of dharmas is fully realized, it is the means that leads to success in the Factor of Awakening called energy. When the factor of energy is fully realized, it is the means that leads to success in the realization of the Factor of Awakening called joy, because it makes the mind joyful. When the factor of joy is fully realized, it is the means that leads to success in the realization of the Factor of Awakening called ease, because it makes the body and the mind light, peaceful, and happy. When the factor of ease is fully realized, the body and the mind are happy, and that helps us to be successful in the practice of the Factor of Awakening called concentration. When the factor of concentration is fully realized, craving is cut off, and that is the means that leads to success in the practice of the Factor of Awakening called equanimity. Thanks to the continued practice, the factor of equanimity will be realized fully just as have been the other Factors of Awakening.

"When the noble disciple practices observation of the feelings in the feelings or observation of the activities of mind in the activities of mind or observation of phenomena in phenomena, he is also making it possible for the Seven Factors of Awakening to be fully realized in the same way as he does when he practices observation of the body in the body.

"Ananda, that is called the practice of the Four Establishments of Mindfulness with a view to full realization of the Seven Factors of Awakening."

The Venerable Ananda addressed the Buddha, "The World-Honored One has just taught the practice of the Four Establishments of Mindfulness that brings about the full realization of the Seven Factors of Awakening. But how do we practice the Seven Factors of Awakening in order to bring about the full realization of understanding and liberation? Lord, please teach us."

The Buddha taught Ananda, "When a bhikshu practices the Awakening Factor of mindfulness relying on putting aside, relying on no more craving, relying on cessation, he goes in the direction of equanimity, and then the strength of the Awakening Factor called mindfulness will help him realize fully the practices of clear understanding and liberation. When a bhikshu practices the other Factors of Awakening: investigation of dharmas, energy, joy, ease, concentration, and equanimity, relying on putting aside, relying on no more craving, relying on cessation and going in the direction of equanimity, the strength of these other Factors of Awakening will also help him to realize fully the practices of clear understanding and liberation. Ananda, we can call it becoming one of the different methods or the mutual nourishment of the different methods. These thirteen methods all advance when one of them advances. One of these methods can be the door through which we enter, and if we continue our journey after that using each of the other methods, we will arrive at the full development of all thirteen methods."

When the Buddha had finished speaking, Ananda was delighted to put the teachings into practice.

—Samyukta Agama, Sutra No. 810
translated from the Chinese

8: History of the Sutra on the Full Awareness of Breathing

The Sutra on the Full Awareness of Breathing presented here is a translation from the Pali of the Anapanasati Sutta. In the Chinese Tripitaka, there is a Da An Ban Shou Yi Jing (Greater Anapanasati Sutta).[29]

This text cites An Shi Gao as translator into Chinese. Master Shi Gao was a Parthian by birth who went to China in the later Han period.[30] There is also a preface to this sutra written by Master Tang Hoi. The Da An Ban Shou Yi Jing seems to be different from the Pali Anapanasati and is probably a commentary on it, and not just an expansion or embellishment of it. At the end of the text, the engraver of the wood block says, "Judging from the style of the sutra, it seems the copyist is at fault: the original text and the commentary are so intertwined that it is no longer possible to distinguish between them."

The original translation by Shi Gao of the Sanskrit (or Prakrit) text into Chinese has probably been lost. The Da An Ban Shou Yi Jing is only the commentary that was originally printed below the text of the sutra. It does not begin with the words that usually begin a sutra, "Thus have I heard." According to Tang Hoi's preface, the person responsible for the annotation and commentary was Chen Hui, and Tang Hoi himself only assisted in the work by correcting, altering, and editing it.

Chen Hui was a disciple of Master An Shi Gao, who traveled from Loyang, China to Giao Chi (present-day Tonkin or North Vietnam) with two fellow disciples, Gan Lin and Pi Ye. They may have brought the original translation of the Anapanasati Sutta with them. The commentary and preface were written by Tang Hoi in Vietnam before the year 229 CE.

Tang Hoi's parents were traders from Sogdia in central Asia who had settled in Vietnam, and Tang Hoi was born in Vietnam, became a monk in Vietnam, and studied Sanskrit and Chinese there. Before traveling to the kingdom of Wu in southern China in the year 255 to spread the Dharma, he had already taught the Dharma in Vietnam and had composed and translated many works into Chinese. He died in the kingdom of Wu in the year 280.

In the Chinese Tripitaka, there are a number of other sutras on the Full Awareness of Breathing: Zeng Yi A Han, Ekottara Agama, chapters seven and eight on the theme "Awareness of Breathing"; the sutra Xiu Hang Dao Di, Book Five, chapter twenty-three, on "Breath Counting"; and in the Tsa A Han (Samyukta Agama sutra collection), the chapter on Full Awareness of Breathing.[31] If we combine the three sutras 815, 803, and 810 of this collection, we have the equivalent of the Pali Anapanasati.

The sutra already presented here in English is a translation from the original Anapanasati Sutra in the Pali Tipitaka (Sanskrit: Tripitaka). In many countries of the Mahayana tradition, the Anapanasati Sutra (Full Awareness of Breathing) and the Satipatthana Sutra (Four Establishments of Mindfulness) are not considered important and, in some cases, are not even available for study.[32] There are Buddhist centers where practitioners are considered to have learned all there is to know about the Four Establishments of Mindfulness when they can repeat that the body is impure, the feelings are painful, the mind is impermanent, and the objects of mind are without self. There is even one book on Buddhist meditation that says that the practice of meditation does not need Full Awareness of Breathing or the Four Establishments of Mindfulness. The Four Establishments of Mindfulness are a daily practice, described in great detail in the Anapanasati and Satipatthana Suttas. These two texts, along with the Bhaddekaratta Sutra (Sutra on Knowing the Better Way to Live Alone), are fundamental to the practice of meditation, and I feel that it's very important to reestablish the importance of these three texts in all places of study and meditation.[33]

In the Southern traditions of Buddhism, the Full Awareness of Breathing and the Four Establishments of Mindfulness are still regarded as the most important texts on meditation. Many monks learn these sutras by heart and give them their greatest attention. Even though the spirit of these sutras is very much present and observable in the Mahayana meditation sutras, we would do well to become familiar with the sutra literature fundamental to meditation that was studied and practiced at the time of the Buddha. I hope that these texts will again be put into wide circulation in the Northern traditions of Buddhism. If we understand the essence of these two sutras, we will have a deeper vision and more comprehensive grasp of the scriptures classified as Mahayana, just as after we see the roots and the trunk of a tree, we can appreciate its leaves and branches more deeply.

From these sutras, we observe that practitioners of meditation at the time of the Buddha did not consider the Four Jhanas, the Four Formless Concentrations, and the Nine Concentration Attainments to be essential to the practice.[34] The Four Jhanas are mental states in which the practitioner abandons the desire realm and enters the realm of form, and although his or her mind remains perfectly awake, the five sense perceptions no longer arise. These four successive states (also called Four Absorptions) are followed by the Four Formless Concentrations, which are states of meditation in which the practitioner, having already abandoned the realms of form, enters four successive formless realms:

1. The Realm of Limitless Space
2. The Realm of Limitless Consciousness
3. The Realm Where Nothing Exists
4. The Realm Where the Concepts "Perceiving" and "Not Perceiving" No Longer Apply

The Nine Concentration Attainments are composed of the Four Jhanas and the Four Formless Concentrations, plus the attainment of cessation (*nirodha samapatti*), a concentration in which there is the absence of feeling and perception. There are many references in other sutras of the Southern traditions as well as in those of the Northern traditions to the Four Jhanas, the Four Formless Concentrations, and the Nine Concentration Attainments, but in these two basic sutras (Full Awareness of Breathing and Four Establishments of Mindfulness), there are no such references. Thus, we can infer that the Four Jhanas, the Four Formless Concentrations, and the Nine Concentration Attainments became a part of Buddhist practice after the death of the Buddha, probably due to the influence of the Vedic and other Yogic meditation schools outside of Buddhism. The teachers who introduced them gave them a Buddhist flavor and adapted them so they would fit with a Buddhist way of practice.

In the oldest Buddhist scriptures—the Dhammapada, the Suttanipata, the Theragatha, the Therigatha, the Itivuttaka, and the Udana—as well as in some of the most important of the other sutras—The Turning of the Dharma Wheel, the Anapanasati, and the Satipatthana—there is no mention of the Four Jhanas. But because they are mentioned in so many other sutras, we generally think they were a method of practice taught by the Buddha. However, from my research, it seems to me that the Four Jhanas, the Four Formless Concentrations, and the Nine Concentration Attainments were not introduced into Buddhism as Buddhist practices until one hundred years after the Buddha's passing. When we read the life story of the Buddha in the sutras, in the Vinaya, and in the account by Ashvagosha, we learn that before the Buddha was enlightened, he practiced meditation under the guidance of two teachers, Arada Kalama and Udraka Ramaputra. He practiced the Four Formless Concentrations with great success, but he expressed clearly that this practice did not lead to final liberation from suffering, and therefore he abandoned it. One of the reasons the Nine Concentration Attainments were made a part of Buddhist practice might have been that people feel the need for a practice marked by stages of progress, and here there is a progression from the first jhana, through the Four Formless Concentrations, to the cessation attainment.

Therefore, we may conclude that according to the Anapanasati and Satipatthana Suttas, the realization of the Four Jhanas and the Four Formless Concentrations is dispensable. Future generations of scholars should distinguish as much as possible between the essential, fundamental meditation practices of Buddhism (whether Northern or Southern) and elements that were incorporated later from other traditions. Throughout the history of Buddhism, new elements have always been added. This is the only way Buddhism can grow and stay alive. In the eighth century and afterwards, kung an (koan) practice developed. Some new methods have been very successful, and some have failed. Before we study and practice methods of meditation practice that were developed after the time of the Buddha, we should first firmly grasp the ways of meditation that the Buddha taught and practiced with his disciples after his enlightenment.

Analyzing their content, we can see that the Anapanasati and Satipatthana Suttas are perfectly compatible with one another. Throughout twenty-six hundred years of Buddhist history, all generations of the Buddha's disciples have respected these works and have not embellished them (as they have so many other scriptures). Although the Anapanasati Sutta was in circulation in Vietnam as early as the beginning of the third century CE, from the time Vietnamese Buddhists devoted themselves primarily to the study of great and beautiful Mahayana sutras like the Avatamsaka, the Lotus, and the Vimalakirti Nirdesha, this sutra ceased to be regarded as essential. It is time for us to restore the Sutra on the Full Awareness of Breathing to its proper place in the tradition of meditation practice. We can begin to practice mindfulness of breathing as soon as we enter a Buddhist meditation center.

THE SUTRA ON THE FOUR
ESTABLISHMENTS OF MINDFULNESS

SATIPATTHANA SUTTA

Contents

The Sutra on the Four Establishments of Mindfulness

SATIPATTHANA SUTTA, MAJJHIMA NIKAYA 10

SECTION ONE

I heard these words of the Buddha one time when he was living at Kammassadhamma, a market town of the Kuru people. The Buddha addressed the bhikkhus, "O bhikkhus."

And the bhikkhus replied, "Venerable Lord."

The Buddha said, "Bhikkhus, there is a most wonderful way to help living beings realize purification, overcome directly grief and sorrow, end pain and anxiety, travel the right path, and realize nirvana. This way is the Four Establishments of Mindfulness.

"What are the Four Establishments?

1. "Bhikkhus, a practitioner remains established in the observation of the body in the body, diligent, with clear understanding, mindful, having abandoned every craving and every distaste for this life.

2. "He remains established in the observation of the feelings in the feelings, diligent, with clear understanding, mindful, having abandoned every craving and every distaste for this life.

3. "He remains established in the observation of the mind in the mind, diligent, with clear understanding, mindful, having abandoned every craving and every distaste for this life.

4. "He remains established in the observation of the objects of mind in the objects of mind, diligent, with clear understanding, mindful, having abandoned every craving and every distaste for this life."

SECTION TWO

"And how does a practitioner remain established in the observation of the body in the body?

"He goes to the forest, to the foot of a tree, or to an empty room, sits down cross-legged in the lotus position, holds his body straight, and establishes mindfulness in front of him. He breathes in, aware that he is breathing in. He breathes out, aware that he is breathing out. When he breathes in a long breath, he knows, 'I am breathing in a long breath.' When he breathes out a long breath, he knows, 'I am breathing out a long breath.' When he breathes in a short breath, he knows, 'I am breathing in a short breath.' When he breathes out a short breath, he knows, 'I am breathing out a short breath.'

"He uses the following practice: 'Breathing in, I am aware of my whole body. Breathing out, I am aware of my whole body.' And then, 'Breathing in, I calm my body. Breathing out, I calm my body.'

"Just as a skilled turner knows when he makes a long turn, 'I am making a long turn,' and knows when he makes a short turn, 'I am making a short turn,' so a practitioner, when he breathes in a long breath, knows, 'I am breathing in a long breath,' and when he breathes in a short breath knows, 'I am breathing in a short breath,' when he breathes out a long breath, knows, 'I am breathing out a long breath,' and when he breathes out a short breath knows, 'I am breathing out a short breath.'

"He uses the following practice: 'Breathing in, I am aware of my whole body. Breathing out, I am aware of my whole body. Breathing in, I calm my body. Breathing out, I calm my body.'

"This is how a practitioner observes the body in the body. He observes the body from within or from without, or from both within and without. He observes the process of coming-to-be in the body or the process of dissolution in the body or both the process of coming-to-be and the process of dissolution. Or he is mindful of the fact, 'There is a body here,' until understanding and full awareness come about. He maintains the observation, free, not caught up in any worldly consideration. That is how to practice observation of the body in the body, O bhikkhus.

"Moreover, when a practitioner walks, he is aware, 'I am walking.' When he is standing, he is aware, 'I am standing.' When he is sitting, he is aware, 'I am sitting.' When he is lying down, he is aware, 'I am lying down.' In whatever position his body happens to be, he is aware of the position of his body.

"This is how a practitioner observes the body in the body. He observes the body from within or from without, or from both within and without. He observes the process of coming-to-be in the body or the process of dissolution in the body or both the process of coming-to-be and the process of dissolution. Or he is mindful of the fact, 'There is a body here,' until understanding and full awareness come about. He maintains the observation, free, not caught up in any worldly consideration. That is how to practice observation of the body in the body, O bhikkhus.

"Moreover, when the practitioner is going forward or backward, he applies full awareness to his going forward or backward. When he looks in front or looks behind, bends down or stands up, he also applies full awareness to what he is doing. He applies full awareness to wearing the sanghati robe or carrying the alms bowl. When he eats or drinks, chews or savors the food, he applies full awareness to all this. When passing excrement or urinating, he applies full awareness to this. When he walks, stands, lies down, sits, sleeps or wakes up, and speaks or is silent, he shines his awareness on all this.

"Further, the practitioner meditates on his very own body from the soles of the feet upwards and then from the hair on top of the head downwards, a body contained inside the skin and full of all the impurities which belong to the body: 'Here is the hair of the head, the hairs on the body, the nails, teeth, skin, flesh, sinews, bones, bone marrow, kidneys, heart, liver, diaphragm, spleen, lungs, intestines, bowels, excrement, bile, phlegm, pus, blood, sweat, fat, tears, grease, saliva, mucus, synovic fluid, and urine.'

"Bhikkhus, imagine a sack which can be opened at both ends, containing a variety of grains: brown rice, wild rice, mung beans, kidney beans, sesame seeds, and white rice. When someone with good eyesight opens the bag, he will review it like this: 'This is brown rice, this is wild rice, these are mung beans, these are kidney beans, these are sesame seeds, and this is white rice.' Just so the practitioner passes in review the whole of his body from the soles of the feet to the hair on the top of the head, a body enclosed in a layer of skin and full of all the impurities which belong to the body: 'Here is the hair of the head, the hairs on the body, nails, teeth, skin, flesh, sinews, bones, bone marrow, kidneys, heart, liver, diaphragm, spleen, lungs, intestines, bowels, excrement, bile, phlegm, pus, blood, sweat, fat, tears, grease, saliva, mucus, synovic fluid, and urine.'

"This is how the practitioner remains established in the observation of the body in the body; observation of the body from within or from without, or from both within and without. He remains established in the observation of the process of coming-to-be in the body or the process of dissolution in the body or both the process of coming-to-be and the process of dissolution. Or he is mindful of the fact, 'There is a body here,' until understanding and full awareness come about. He remains established in the observation, free, not caught up in any worldly consideration. That is how to practice observation of the body in the body, O bhikkhus.

"Further, in whichever position his body happens to be, the practitioner passes in review the elements which constitute the body: 'In this body is the earth element, the water element, the fire element, and the air element.'

"As a skilled butcher or an apprentice butcher, having killed a cow, might sit at the crossroads to divide the cow into many parts, the practitioner passes in review the elements which comprise his very own body: 'Here in this body are the earth element, the water element, the fire element, and the air element.'

"This is how the practitioner remains established in the observation of the body in the body: observation of the body from within or from without, or from both within and without. He remains established in the observation of the process of coming-to-be in the body or the process of dissolution in the body or both the process of coming-to-be and the process of dissolution. Or he is mindful of the fact, 'There is a body here,' until understanding and full awareness come about. He remains established in the observation, free, not caught up in any worldly consideration. That is how to practice observation of the body in the body, O bhikkhus.

"Further, the practitioner compares his own body with a corpse which he imagines he sees thrown onto a charnel ground and lying there for one, two, or three days, bloated, blue in color, and festering, and he observes, 'This body of mine is of the same nature. It will end up in the same way; there is no way it can avoid that state.'

"This is how the practitioner remains established in the observation of the body in the body: observation of the body from within or from without, or from both within and without. He remains established in the observation of the process of coming-to-be in the body or the process of dissolution in the body or both the process of coming-to-be and the process of dissolution. Or he is mindful of the fact, 'There is a body here,' until understanding and full awareness come about. He remains established in the observation, free, not caught up in any worldly consideration. That is how to practice observation of the body in the body, O bhikkhus.

"Further, the practitioner compares his own body with a corpse which he imagines he sees thrown onto a charnel ground, pecked at by crows, eaten by hawks, vultures, and jackals, and infested with maggots and worms, and he observes, 'This body of mine is of the same nature, it will end up in the same way, there is no way it can avoid that state.'

"This is how the practitioner remains established in the observation of the body in the body; observation of the body from within or from without, or from both within and without. He remains established in the observation of the process of coming-to-be in the body or the process of dissolution in the body or both the process of coming-to-be and the process of dissolution. Or he is mindful of the fact, 'There is a body here,' until understanding and full awareness come about. He remains established in the observation, free, not caught up in any worldly consideration. That is how to practice observation of the body in the body, O bhikkhus.

"Further, the practitioner compares his own body with a corpse which he imagines he sees thrown onto a charnel ground; it is just a skeleton with a little flesh and blood sticking to it, and the bones are held together by the ligaments, and he observes, 'This body of mine is of the same nature. It will end up in the same way. There is no way it can avoid that state.'

"Further, the practitioner compares his own body with a corpse which he imagines he sees thrown onto a charnel ground; it is just a skeleton, no longer adhered to by any flesh, but still smeared by a little blood, the bones still held together by the ligaments . . .

"Further, the practitioner compares his own body with a corpse which he imagines he sees thrown onto a charnel ground; it is just a skeleton, no longer adhered to by any flesh nor smeared by any blood, but the bones are still held together by the ligaments . . .

"Further, the practitioner compares his own body with a corpse which he imagines he sees thrown onto a charnel ground; all that is left is a collection of bones scattered here and there; in one place a hand bone, in another a shin bone, a thigh bone, a pelvis, a spinal column, and a skull.

"Further, the practitioner compares his own body with a corpse which he imagines he sees thrown onto a charnel ground; all that is left is a collection of bleached bones, the color of shells . . .

"Further, the practitioner compares his own body with a corpse which he imagines he sees thrown onto a charnel ground; it has been lying there for more than one year and all that is left is a collection of dried bones . . .

"Further, the practitioner compares his own body with a corpse which he imagines he sees thrown onto a charnel ground; all that is left is the dust which comes from the rotted bones and he observes 'This body of mine is of the same nature, it will end up in the same way. There is no way it can avoid that state.'

"This is how the practitioner remains established in the observation of the body in the body, observation of the body from within or from without, or from both within and without. He remains established in the observation of the process of coming-to-be in the body or the process of dissolution in the body or both the process of coming-to-be and the process of dissolution. Or he is mindful of the fact, 'There is a body here,' until understanding and full awareness come about. He remains established in the observation, free, not caught up in any worldly consideration. That is how to practice observation of the body in the body, O bhikkhus."

SECTION THREE

"Bhikkhus, how does a practitioner remain established in the observation of the feelings in the feelings?

"Whenever the practitioner has a pleasant feeling, he is aware, 'I am experiencing a pleasant feeling.' Whenever he has a painful feeling, he is aware, 'I am experiencing a painful feeling.' Whenever he experiences a feeling that is neither pleasant nor painful, he is aware, 'I am experiencing a neutral feeling.' When he experiences a pleasant feeling based in the body, he is aware, 'I am experiencing a pleasant feeling based in the body.' When he experiences a pleasant feeling based in the mind, he is aware, 'I am experiencing a pleasant feeling based in the mind.' When he experiences a painful feeling based in the body, he is aware, 'I am experiencing a painful feeling based in the body.' When he experiences a painful feeling based in the mind, he is aware, 'I am experiencing a painful feeling based in the mind.' When he experiences a neutral feeling based in the body, he is aware, 'I am experiencing a neutral feeling based in the body.' When he experiences a neutral feeling based in the mind, he is aware, 'I am experiencing a neutral feeling based in the mind.'

"This is how the practitioner remains established in the observation of the feelings in the feelings, observation of the feelings from within or from without, or observation of the feelings from both within and without. He remains established in the observation of the process of coming-to-be in the feelings or the process of dissolution in the feelings or both the process of coming-to-be and the process of dissolution. Or he is mindful of the fact, 'There is feeling here,' until understanding and full awareness come about. He remains established in the observation, free, not caught up in any worldly consideration. That is how to practice observation of the feelings in the feelings, O bhikkhus."

SECTION FOUR

"Bhikkhus, how does a practitioner remain established in the observation of the mind in the mind?

"When his mind is desiring, the practitioner is aware, 'My mind is desiring.' When his mind is not desiring, he is aware, 'My mind is not desiring.' When his mind is hating something, he is aware, 'My mind is hating.' When his mind is not hating, he is aware, 'My mind is not hating.' When his mind is in a state of ignorance, he is aware, 'My mind is in a state of ignorance.' When his mind is not in a state of ignorance, he is aware, 'My mind is not in a state of ignorance.' When his mind is collected, he is aware, 'My mind is collected.' When his mind is not collected, he is aware, 'My mind is not collected.' When his mind is distracted, he is aware, 'My mind is distracted.' When his mind is not distracted, he is aware, 'My mind is not distracted.' When his mind has a wider scope, he is aware, 'My mind has widened in scope.' When his mind has a narrow scope, he is aware, 'My mind has become narrow in scope.' When his mind is capable of reaching a higher state, he is aware, 'My mind is capable of reaching a higher state.' When his mind is not capable of reaching a higher state, he is aware, 'My mind is not capable of reaching a higher state.' When his mind is composed, he is aware, 'My mind is composed.' When his mind is not composed, he is aware, 'My mind is not composed.' When his mind is free, he is aware, 'My mind is free.' When his mind is not free, he is aware, 'My mind is not free.'

"This is how the practitioner remains established in the observation of the mind in the mind, observation of the mind from within or from without, or observation of the mind from both within and without. He remains established in the observation of the process of coming-to-be in the mind or the process of dissolution in the mind or both the process of coming-to-be and the process of dissolution. Or he is mindful of the fact, 'There is mind here,' until understanding and full awareness come about. He remains established in the observation, free, not caught up in any worldly consideration. This is how to practice observation of the mind in the mind, O bhikkhus."

SECTION FIVE

"Bhikkhus, how does a practitioner remain established in the observation of the objects of mind in the objects of mind?

"First of all, he observes the objects of mind in the objects of mind with regard to the Five Hindrances. How does he observe this?

1. "When sensual desire is present in him, he is aware, 'Sensual desire is present in me.' Or when sensual desire is not present in him, he is aware, 'Sensual desire is not present in me.' When sensual desire begins to arise, he is aware of it. When already arisen sensual desire is abandoned, he is aware of it. When sensual desire already abandoned will not arise again in the future, he is aware of it.

2. "When anger is present in him, he is aware, 'Anger is present in me.' When anger is not present in him, he is aware, 'Anger is not present in me.' When anger begins to arise, he is aware of it. When already arisen anger is abandoned, he is aware of it. When anger already abandoned will not arise again in the future, he is aware of it.

3. "When dullness and drowsiness are present in him, he is aware, 'Dullness and drowsiness are present in me.' When dullness and drowsiness are not present in him, he is aware, 'Dullness and drowsiness are not present in me.' When dullness and drowsiness begin to arise, he is aware of it. When

already arisen dullness and drowsiness are abandoned, he is aware of it. When dullness and drowsiness already abandoned will not arise again in the future, he is aware of it.

4. "When agitation and remorse are present in him, he is aware, 'Agitation and remorse are present in me.' When agitation and remorse are not present in him, he is aware, 'Agitation and remorse are not present in me.' When agitation and remorse begin to arise, he is aware of it. When already arisen agitation and remorse are abandoned, he is aware of it. When agitation and remorse already abandoned will not arise again in the future, he is aware of it.

5. "When doubt is present in him, he is aware, 'Doubt is present in me.' When doubt is not present in him, he is aware, 'Doubt is not present in me.' When doubt begins to arise, he is aware of it. When already arisen doubt is abandoned, he is aware of it. When doubt already abandoned will not arise again in the future, he is aware of it.

"This is how the practitioner remains established in the observation of the objects of mind in the objects of mind: observation of the objects of mind from within or from without, or observation of the objects of mind from both within and without. He remains established in the observation of the process of coming-to-be in the objects of mind or the process of dissolution in the objects of mind or both the process of coming-to-be and the process of dissolution.

Or he is mindful of the fact, 'There is an object of the mind here,' until understanding and full awareness come about. He remains established in the observation, free, not caught up in any worldly consideration. That is how to practice observation of the objects of mind in the objects of mind with regard to the Five Hindrances, O bhikkhus.

"Further, the practitioner observes the objects of mind in the objects of mind with regard to the Five Aggregates of Clinging. How does he observe this?

"He observes like this: 'Such is form. Such is the arising of form. Such is the disappearance of form. Such is feeling. Such is the arising of feeling. Such is the disappearance of feeling. Such is perception. Such is the arising of perception. Such is the disappearance of perception. Such are mental formations. Such is the arising of mental formations. Such is the disappearance of mental formations. Such is consciousness. Such is the arising of consciousness. Such is the disappearance of consciousness.'

"This is how the practitioner remains established in the observation of the objects of mind in the objects of mind with regard to the Five Aggregates of Clinging: observation of the objects of mind from within or from without, or observation of the objects of mind from both within and without. He remains established in the observation of the process of coming-to-be in the object of mind or the process of dissolution in the object of mind or both the process of coming-to-be and the process of dissolution. Or he is mindful of the fact, 'There is an object of mind here,' until understanding and full awareness come about. He remains established in the observation, free, not caught up in any worldly consideration. That is how to practice observation of the objects of mind in the objects of mind with regard to the Five Aggregates, O bhikkhus.

"Further, bhikkhus, the practitioner observes the objects of mind in the objects of mind with regard to the six sense organs and the six sense objects. How does he observe this?

"He is aware of the eyes and aware of the form, and he is aware of the internal formations which are produced in dependence on these two things. He is aware of the birth of a new internal formation and is aware of abandoning an already produced internal formation, and he is aware when an already abandoned internal formation will not arise again.

"The practitioner is aware of the ears and aware of the sound, and he is aware of the internal formations which are produced in dependence on these two things. He is aware of the birth of a new internal formation and is aware of abandoning an already produced internal formation, and he is aware when an already abandoned internal formation will not arise again.

"The practitioner is aware of the nose and aware of the smell, and he is aware of the internal formations which are produced in dependence on these two things. He is aware of the birth of a new internal formation and is aware of abandoning an already produced internal formation, and he is aware when an already abandoned internal formation will not arise again.

"The practitioner is aware of the tongue and aware of the taste, and he is aware of the internal formations which are produced in dependence on these two things. He is aware of the birth of a new internal formation and is aware of abandoning an already produced internal formation, and he is aware when an already abandoned internal formation will not arise again.

"The practitioner is aware of the body and aware of the object touched, and he is aware of the internal formations which are produced in dependence on these two things. He is aware of the birth of a new internal formation and is aware of abandoning an already produced internal formation, and he is aware when an already abandoned internal formation will not arise again.

"The practitioner is aware of the mind and aware of the objects of mind (the world), and he is aware of the internal formations which are produced in dependence on these two things. He is aware of the birth of a new internal formation and is aware of abandoning an already produced internal formation, and he is aware when an already abandoned internal formation will not arise again.

"This is how the practitioner remains established in the observation of the objects of mind in the objects of mind with regard to the six sense organs and the six sense objects: observation of the objects of mind from within or from without, or observation of the objects of mind from both within and without. He remains established in the observation of the process of coming-to-be in the object of mind or the process of dissolution in the object of mind or both the process of coming-to-be and the process of dissolution. Or he is mindful of the fact, 'There is an object of mind here,' until understanding and full awareness come about. He remains established in the observation, free, not caught up in any worldly consideration. That is how to practice observation of the objects of mind in the objects of mind with regard to the six sense organs and the six sense objects, O bhikkhus.

"Further, bhikkhus, the practitioner remains established in the observation of the objects of mind in the objects of mind with regard to the Seven Factors of Awakening.

"How does he remain established in the practice of observation of the Seven Factors of Awakening?

1 "When the factor of awakening, mindfulness, is present in him, he is aware, 'Mindfulness is present in me.' When mindfulness is not present in him, he is aware, 'Mindfulness is not present in me.' He is aware when not-yet-born mindfulness is being born and when already-born mindfulness is perfectly developed.

2. "When the factor of awakening, investigation-of-phenomena, is present in him, he is aware, 'Investigation-of-phenomena is present in me.' When investigation-of-phenomena is not present in him, he is aware, 'Investigation-of-phenomena is not present in me.' He is aware when not-yet-born investigation-of-phenomena is being born and when already-born investigation-of-phenomena is perfectly developed.

3. "When the factor of awakening, energy, is present in him, he is aware, 'Energy is present in me.' When energy is not present in him, he is aware, 'Energy is not present in me.' He is aware when not-yet-born energy is being born and when already-born energy is perfectly developed.

4. "When the factor of awakening, joy, is present in him, he is aware, 'Joy is present in me.' When joy is not present in him, he is aware, 'Joy is not present in me.' He is aware when not-yet-born joy is being born and when already-born joy is perfectly developed.

5. "When the factor of awakening, ease, is present in him, he is aware, 'Ease is present in me.' When ease is not present in him, he is aware, 'Ease is not present in me.' He is aware when not-yet-born ease is being born and when already-born ease is perfectly developed.

6. "When the factor of awakening, concentration, is present in him, he is aware, 'Concentration is present in me.' When concentration is not present in him, he is aware, 'Concentration is not present in me.' He is aware when not-yet-born concentration is being born and when already-born concentration is perfectly developed.

7. "When the factor of awakening, letting go, is present in him, he is aware, 'Letting go is present in me.' When letting go is not present in him, he is aware, 'Letting go is not present in me.' He is aware when not-yet-born letting go is being born and when already-born letting-go is perfectly developed.

"This is how the practitioner remains established in the observation of the objects of mind in the objects of mind with regard to the Seven Factors of Awakening, observation of the objects of mind from within or from without, or observation of the objects of mind from both within and without. He remains established in the observation of the process of coming-to-be in the object of mind or the process of dissolution in the object of mind or both the process of coming-to-be and the process of dissolution. Or he is mindful of the fact, 'There is an object of mind here,' until understanding and full awareness come about. He remains established in the observation, free, not caught up in any worldly consideration. That is how to practice observation of the objects of mind in the objects of mind with regard to the Seven Factors of Awakening, O bhikkhus.

"Further, bhikkhus, a practitioner remains established in the observation of objects of mind in the objects of mind with regard to the Four Noble Truths.

"How, bhikkhus, does the practitioner remain established in the observation of the Four Noble Truths?

"A practitioner is aware 'This is suffering,' as it arises. He is aware, 'This is the cause of the suffering,' as it arises. He is aware, 'This is the end of suffering,' as it arises. He is aware, 'This is the path which leads to the end of suffering,' as it arises.

"This is how the practitioner remains established in the observation of the objects of mind in the objects of mind with regard to the Four Noble Truths, observation of the objects of mind from within or from without, or observation of the objects of mind from both within and without. He remains established in the observation of the process of coming-to-be in the objects of mind or the process of dissolution in the objects of mind or both the process of coming-to-be and the process of dissolution. Or he is mindful of the fact, 'There is an object of mind here,' until understanding and full awareness come about. He remains established in the observation, free, not caught up in any worldly consideration. That is how to practice observation of the objects of mind in the objects of mind with regard to the Four Noble Truths, O bhikkhus."

SECTION SIX

"Bhikkhus, he who practices in the Four Establishments of Mindfulness for seven years can expect one of two fruits—the highest understanding in this very life or, if there remains some residue of affliction, he can attain the fruit of no-return.

"Let alone seven years, bhikkhus, whoever practices in the Four Establishments of Mindfulness for six, five, four, three, two years or one year can also expect one of two fruits—either the highest under-standing in this very life or, if there remains some residue of affliction, he can attain the fruit of no-return.

"Let alone one year, bhikkhus, whoever practices in the Four Estab-lishments of Mindfulness for seven, six, five, four, three, or two months, one month or half a month can also expect one of two fruits—either the highest understanding in this very life or, if there remains some residue of affliction, he can attain the fruit of no-return.

"Let alone half a month, bhikkhus, whoever practices the Four Establishments of Mindfulness for one week can also expect one of two fruits—either the highest understanding in this very life or, if there remains some residue of affliction, he can attain the fruit of no-return.

"That is why we said that this path, the path of the four grounds for the establishment of mindfulness, is the most wonderful path, which helps beings realize purification, transcend grief and sorrow, destroy pain and anxiety, travel the right path, and realize nirvana."

The bhikkhus were delighted to hear the teaching of the Buddha. They took it to heart and began to put it into practice.

1: What is Mindfulness?

We practice mindfulness in order to realize liberation, peace, and joy in our everyday lives. Liberation and happiness are linked to each other; if there is liberation, there is happiness, and greater liberation brings greater happiness. If there is liberation, peace and joy exist in the present moment. We don't need to wait ten or fifteen years to realize them. They're available as soon as we begin the practice. However modest these elements may be, they form the basis for greater liberation, peace, and joy in the future.

To practice meditation is to look deeply in order to see into the essence of things. With insight and understanding we can realize liberation, peace, and joy. Our anger, anxiety, and fear are the ropes that bind us to suffering. If we want to be liberated from them, we need to observe their nature, which is ignorance, the lack of clear understanding. When we misunderstand a friend, we may become angry at him, and because of that, we may suffer. But when we look deeply into what has happened, we can end the misunderstanding. When we understand the other person and his situation, our suffering will disappear and peace and joy will arise. The first step is awareness of the object, and the second step is looking deeply at the object to shed light on it. Therefore, mindfulness means awareness and it also means looking deeply.

The Pali word *sati* (Sanskrit: *smrti*) means "to stop," and "to maintain awareness of the object." The Pali word *vipassana* (Sanskrit: *vipashyana*) means "to go deeply into that object to observe it." While we are fully aware of and observing deeply an object, the boundary between the subject who observes and the object being observed gradually dissolves, and the subject and object become one. This is the essence of meditation. Only when we penetrate an object and become one with it can we understand. It is not enough to stand outside and observe an object. That's why the Sutra on the Four Establishments of Mindfulness reminds us to be aware of the body in the body, the feelings in the feelings, the mind in the mind, and the objects of mind in the objects of mind.

Mindfulness is always mindfulness of something. There are four areas of mindfulness, four areas where mindfulness has to penetrate in order for us to be protected, for joy to be nourished, for pain to be transformed, and for insight to be obtained. These are called the Four Establishments of Mindfulness. These four establishments, or foundations, are body, feelings, mind, and objects of mind.

The First Establishment of Mindfulness is mindfulness of the body in the body. This means that when you bring mindfulness into your body, mindfulness becomes the body. Mindfulness is not an outside observer. Mindfulness becomes the body, and the body becomes mindfulness. When a mother embraces her child, the mother becomes her child, and the child becomes her mother. In true meditation, the subject and the object of meditation no longer exist as separate entities; that distinction is removed. When you generate the energy of mindfulness and embrace your breathing and your body, that is mindfulness of the body in the body. Mindfulness is not an outside observer, it *is* the body. The body becomes the object and the subject of mindfulness at the same time.

It's like when nuclear scientists say that to understand an elementary particle and really enter into the world of the infinitely small, you have to become a participant and not an observer anymore. In India they use the example of a grain of salt that would like to know how salty the ocean is. How can a grain of salt come to know this? The only way is for it to jump into the ocean, and the understanding will be perfect; the separation between the object of understanding and the subject of understanding is no longer there. In our time, nuclear scientists have begun to see that. That is why they say that in order to really understand the world of the elementary particle, you have to stop being an observer, you have to become a participant.

The Second Establishment of Mindfulness is our feelings. The Third Establishment of Mindfulness is the mind, namely the mental formations. In the Sutra on the Full Awareness of Breathing, the Buddha offered us four exercises of mindful breathing to take care of each of these fields of our mindfulness.

The Fourth Establishment of Mindfulness is the realm of perception.

In the sutra it is spoken of as "the objects of mind," and we can understand this as perception. The Buddha also proposed four exercises on mindful breathing for contemplation of the objects of the mind in the mind, so that we can penetrate, embrace, and look deeply into the objects of our perception. Doing so gives us the insight that will liberate us from our delusion and our suffering.

Mountains, rivers, birds, the blue sky, houses, streams, children, and animals—everything is the object of your perception. And we have four exercises of mindful breathing in order to help us inquire about the true nature of all these things, including ourselves. The body is also an object of the mind; feelings are also objects of our minds; and mental formations become objects of our minds. We can always inquire about the nature of our bodies, our feelings, or our minds, as well as our perceptions, and other things. If we look deeply at the body in the body, it becomes an object of the mind. When we are looking at feelings, then feelings are the objects of the mind. When we are observing the mind, the mind becomes the object of our minds. All the establishments of mindfulness are in fact objects of the mind.

A monk once asked me how the mind can be an object of the mind. I said if we take our two fingers and rub them together, then the body is in touch with the body. The mind is the same. When we look into our bodies, the body is the object of our minds. When we look into form, form is the object of our minds. When we look into mental formations, mental formations are the objects of our minds. So we see that the field of objects of the mind is very vast. But the division into four establishments is a convenient tool to help us learn how to practice mindfulness.

2: Summary of the Sutra

The Sutra on the Four Establishments of Mindfulness uses the term *ekayana*, which means "one path" in Pali, to signify "the one way to practice." Ekayana is translated in this version of the sutra as "a most wonderful way to help living beings." This term, used by the Buddha to describe the method of the Four Establishments of Mindfulness, gives us an idea of the great importance this practice held in the Buddha's teachings during his lifetime. These teachings have since spread throughout the world, and the foundation of these teachings remains the practice of mindful observation. The Sutra on the Four Establishments of Mindfulness has been studied, practiced, and handed down with special care from generation to generation for over twenty-five hundred years.

The four methods of mindfulness described in the sutra are:

1. mindfulness of the body
2. mindfulness of the feelings
3. mindfulness of the mind
4. mindfulness of the objects of mind

In the establishment known as the body, the practitioner is fully aware of the breath, the positions of the body, the actions of the body, the various parts of the body, the four elements that comprise the body, and the decomposition of the body as a corpse. In the establishment known as the feelings, the practitioner is fully aware of pleasant, painful, and neutral feelings as they arise, endure, and disappear. He is aware of feelings that have a psychological basis and feelings that have a physiological basis. In the establishment known as the mind, the practitioner is fully aware of states of mind such as desire, hatred, confusion, concentration, dispersion, internal formations, and liberation. In the establishment known as the objects of mind, the practitioner is fully aware of the Five Aggregates that comprise a person (form, feelings, perceptions, mental formations, and consciousness), the sense organs and their objects, the factors that can obstruct understanding and liberation, the factors that can lead to awakening, and the Four Noble Truths concerning suffering and the release from suffering.

As you see, the sutra is divided into six sections: Section One describes the circumstances under which the sutra was delivered and the importance of the teachings of the sutra, and it lists the Four Establishments of Mindfulness. Section Two describes the method of mindfulness of the body in the body. Section Three describes the method of mindfulness of the feelings in the feelings. Section Four describes the method of mindfulness of the mind in the mind. Section Five describes the method of mindfulness of the objects of mind in the objects of mind. Section Six describes the fruits of the practice and the length of time needed in order to realize those fruits.

3: Exercises for Observing the Body

The First Establishment of Mindfulness is the body, which includes the breath, the positions of the body, the actions of the body, the parts of the body, the four elements of which the body is composed, and the dissolution of the body.

Exercise 1 | Conscious Breathing

> "He goes to the forest, to the foot of a tree, or to an empty room, sits down cross-legged in the lotus position, holds his body straight, and establishes mindfulness in front of him. He breathes in, aware that he is breathing in. He breathes out, aware that he is breathing out."

The first practice is the Full Awareness of Breathing. When we breathe in, we know that we are breathing in. When we breathe out, we know that we are breathing out. Practicing in this way, our breathing becomes conscious breathing. This exercise is simple, yet its effects are profound. To succeed, we must put the whole mind into our breathing and nowhere else. As we follow our in-breath, for example, we need to be watchful of distracting thoughts. As soon as a thought such as, "I forgot to turn off the light in the kitchen," arises, our breathing is no longer conscious breathing as we are thinking about something else. To succeed, our minds need to stay focused on our breathing for the entire length of each breath. As we breathe, our minds are one with our breath, and we become one with our breath. That is the meaning of "mindfulness of the body in the body."

Anyone can succeed in the practice of a single conscious breath. If we continue to breathe consciously for ten breaths, without our minds going astray, then we have taken a valuable step on the path of practice. If we can practice conscious breathing for ten minutes, an important change will take place in us. How can a practice as simple as this bring about such important results and what are the results that it can bring about?

The first result of conscious breathing is returning to ourselves. In everyday life, we often get lost in forgetfulness. Our minds chases after thousands of things, and we rarely take the time to come back to ourselves. When we have been lost in forgetfulness like that for a long time, we lose touch with ourselves, and we feel alienated from ourselves. This phenomenon is very common in our times. Conscious breathing is a marvelous way to return to ourselves. When we are aware of our breath, we come back to ourselves as quick as a flash of lightning. Like a child who returns home after a long journey, we feel the warmth of our hearth, and we find ourselves again. Coming back to ourselves is already a remarkable success on the path of the practice.

The second result of conscious breathing is that we come in contact with life in the present moment, the only moment when we can touch life. The life in us and around us is wonderful and abundant. If we're not free, we can't be in contact with it, and we're not really living our lives. We shouldn't be imprisoned by regrets about the past, anxieties for the future, or attachment and aversion in the present.

To breathe with full awareness is a miraculous way to untie the knots of regret and anxiety and to be in touch with life in the present moment. When we follow our breathing, we are already at ease, no longer dominated by our anxieties and longings. As we breathe consciously, our breath becomes more regular, and peace and joy arise and become more stable with every moment. Relying on our breathing, we come back to ourselves and are able to restore the oneness of the body and mind. This integration allows us to be in real contact with what is happening in the present moment, which is the essence of life.

Exercise 2 | *Following the Breath*

"When he breathes in a long breath, he knows, 'I am breathing in a long breath.' When he breathes out a long breath, he knows, 'I am breathing out a long breath.' When he breathes in a short breath, he knows, 'I am breathing in a short breath.' When he breathes out a short breath, he knows, 'I am breathing out a short breath.'"

The practitioner follows his breathing very closely and becomes one with his breathing for the entire length of the breath, not allowing any stray thought or idea to enter. This method is called "following the breath." While the mind is following the breath, the mind is the breath and only the breath. In the process of the practice, our breathing naturally becomes more regular, harmonious, and calm, and our minds also become more regular, harmonious, and calm. This brings about feelings of joy, peace, and ease in the body. When the mind and the breathing become one, it is only a small step for the body and mind to become one also.

Exercise 3 | Oneness of Body and Mind

"Breathing in, I am aware of my whole body. Breathing out, I am aware of my whole body."

The third exercise is to bring body and mind into harmony. The element used to bring this about is the breath. In meditation practice, the distinction between body and mind dissolves, and we talk of the oneness of body and mind. In this exercise, the object of our mindfulness is no longer simply the breath, but the whole body itself, as it is unified with the breath.

Some practitioners and commentators, because they attach so much importance to the realization of the states of concentration (Pali: *jhana*; Sanskrit: *dhyana*) of the Four Form Jhanas and the Four Formless Jhanas, have explained the term "whole body" to mean the "whole breath body" and not the physical body of the practitioner. The Patisambhida Magga, Vimutti Magga, and Visuddhi Magga, all well-known commentaries, tell us to concentrate on the tip of the nose, the place where the air enters and goes out from the body, as we breathe. We are not told to follow our breath into our bodies, because the commentators fear that our bodies may be too large an object for us to concentrate on. This kind of reasoning has led the commentators to interpret the word "body" (*kaya*) in the sutra as "breath body." But as we read the sutra, we see that the practice of being mindful of the whole "breath body" was already dealt with in the second exercise: "Breathing in a long breath, he knows, 'I am breathing in a long breath.' Breathing out a short breath, he knows, 'I am breathing out a short breath.'" Why then do we need to repeat this exercise?

The first four exercises of the Sutra on the Full Awareness of Breathing (Anapanasati) teach us to focus our attention on the body, so it is natural for the third exercise in the Sutra on the Four Establishments of Mindfulness (Satipatthana) also to focus on the full awareness of the physical body. Nowhere in either sutra are we taught to concentrate on the breath at the tip of the nose. Nowhere are we taught that we shouldn't concentrate on the whole physical body.

In recent times, the Burmese meditation master Mahasi Sayadaw taught the method of being attentive to the inflation and contraction of the abdomen caused by the in-breath and the out-breath. Using this method, the practitioner can realize concentration easily, but it isn't described by the Mahasi as a method of awareness of breathing. The basic reason for doing this practice, according to the Mahasi, is that understanding (*prajña*) arises naturally when there is concentration. Perhaps the reason Mahasi Sayadaw doesn't describe this method as a practice of awareness of breathing is because of traditional prejudice that conscious breathing should not follow the breath into the body and down into the abdomen.

Here it may be useful to say something about the purpose of concentration. Right Concentration (*samyak samadhi*), one stage of the Noble Eightfold Path, leads to an awareness and deep observation of the object of concentration and eventually to awakened understanding. The Pali compound word *samatha-vipassana* (Sanskrit: *shamatha-vipashyana*) means "stopping-observing," "calming-illuminating," or "concentrating-understanding."

There are also states of concentration that encourage the practitioner to escape from the complexities of suffering and existence, rather than face them directly in order to transform them. These can be called "wrong concentration." The Four Form Jhanas and the Four Formless Jhanas are states of meditational concentration that the Buddha practiced with teachers such as Alara Kalama and Uddaka Ramaputra, and he rejected them as not leading to liberation from suffering. These states of concentration probably found their way back into the sutras around two hundred years after the Buddha passed into *mahaparinirvana*. The results of these concentrations are to hide reality from the practitioner, so we can assume that they shouldn't be considered Right Concentration. To dwell in these concentrations for a duration of time for the sake of healing may be one thing, but to escape in them for a long time isn't what the Buddha recommended.

In the third exercise, the practitioner uses her breathing to bring body and mind together as one, so the object of concentration is simultaneously body, mind, and breath. This condition, known as "oneness of body and mind," is one of total integration. In our daily lives, we often find our minds and our bodies separated. The body may be here, while the mind is somewhere else, perhaps lost in the distant past or floating in a distant future. Through mindfulness, we can realize the oneness of body and mind, and we're able to restore the wholeness of ourselves. In this condition, every practice will take us back to the source, which is the oneness of body and mind, and we open to a real encounter with life.

When body and mind are one, the wounds in our hearts, minds, and bodies begin to heal. As long as there is separation between body and mind, these wounds can't heal. During sitting meditation, the three elements of breath, body, and mind are calmed, and gradually they become one. When peace is established in one of the three elements, the other two will soon have peace also. For example, if the body is in a very stable position and all the muscles and the nervous system are relaxed, then the mind and breath are immediately influenced, and they too gradually become calmed. Similarly, if we practice conscious breathing in the right way, our breathing becomes more regular, calm, and harmonious with every moment, and this regularity, calmness, and harmony of the breathing will spread to our bodies and minds, and the body and mind will benefit from it. It's only by these kinds of processes that the oneness of body and mind will be achieved. When there's oneness of body and mind, the breathing serves as "harmonizer," and we realize peace, joy, and ease, the first fruits of meditation practice.

Exercise 4 | Calming

"Breathing in, I calm my body. Breathing out, I calm my body."

This exercise, a continuation of the third, uses the breath to realize peace and calm in the whole body. When our bodies are not at peace, it's hard for our minds to be at peace. Therefore, we should use our breathing to help the functions of our bodies be smooth and peaceful. If we're gasping for breath or if our breath is irregular, we can't calm the functions of our bodies. So the first thing is to harmonize our breathing. Our in-breaths and out-breaths should flow smoothly and lightly. When our breath is harmonious, our bodies are also. Our breath needs to be light and even and not audible. It should flow smoothly, like a small stream of water running down fine sand into the ocean. The more subtle our breath is, the more peaceful our bodies and minds will be. When we breathe in, we can feel the breath entering our bodies and calming all the cells of our bodies. When we breathe out, we feel the exhalation taking with it all our tiredness, irritation, and anxiety.

As we breathe, we can recite the following gatha to ourselves:

Breathing in, I calm my body.
Breathing out, I smile.
Dwelling in the present moment,
I know this is a wonderful moment.

We know that when we're meditating, body and mind are one, so we only need to calm the body in order to calm the mind. When we smile, we demonstrate the peace and joy of body and mind. Feelings of peace and joy are the nourishment of the practitioner and help the practitioner go far on the path of practice. To learn more about this, you are encouraged to practice the fifth and sixth exercises of the Sutra on the Full Awareness of Breathing. These two exercises are designed to help the practitioner nourish herself with the joy of meditational concentration. The essence of meditation practice is to come back to dwell in the present moment and to observe what is happening in the present moment. "A wonderful moment" means that the practitioner can see the wonders of life in her body, mind, and breathing and can make the feelings of peace and happiness stable and strong.

Although we are now discussing the part of the sutra that teaches full awareness of the body in the body, since there are very close links between the body and the feelings, we should not hesitate to cross freely the boundary between the establishment of the body and the establishment of the feelings. As we already know, the peace of the body is the peace of the mind.

In exercises three and four, the practitioner follows the breath while returning to be one with the body and calming the whole of the body. Obviously, while practicing these breathing exercises, all your organs of sense perception—eyes, ears, nose, and tongue—are closed off so that the images of the world around don't come in and agitate the peace within. To return to the body in this way is also to return to the mind.

From time to time, we feel tired, and everything we do or say seems to come out wrong and create misunderstanding. We may think, "Today is not my day." At times like this, it's best simply to return to the body, cut off all contact, and close the doors of the senses. Following our breathing, we can collect the mind, body, and breath, and they will become one. We will have a feeling of warmth, like someone sitting inside by a fireplace while the wind and rain are raging outside. This method can be practiced anywhere at any time, not just in the meditation hall. We come back in contact with ourselves and make ourselves whole again.

We shouldn't think that to close the doors of the sense perceptions is to close ourselves off from life and the world, to sever our contact with life. When we're not truly ourselves, when we're divided and dispersed, we're not really in contact with life. The contact is profound only when we are really ourselves. If we're not ourselves in the present moment, when we look at the blue sky, we don't really see the blue sky. When we hold the hand of a child, we aren't really holding the hand of a child. When we drink tea, we're not really drinking tea. Therefore, the wholeness of ourselves is the basis of any meaningful contact. We can realize the wholeness of ourselves by means of conscious breathing, which brings us back to the body and mind. Realizing the wholeness of ourselves is also to renew ourselves in every moment. We become fresh, and others enjoy being with us. When we renew ourselves, we see everything else as new. The Bamboo Forest Zen Master once said: "Everything I touch becomes new."

Exercise 5 | Positions of the Body

"Moreover, when a practitioner walks, he is aware, 'I am walking.' When he is standing, he is aware, 'I am standing.' When he is sitting, he is aware, 'I am sitting.' When he is lying down, he is aware, 'I am lying down.' In whatever position his body happens to be, he is aware of the position of his body."

This exercise is the observation in mindfulness of the positions of the body. This is not just an exercise to be practiced at the time of sitting meditation or in the meditation hall. The meditation practices taught in the Sutra on the Four Establishments of Mindfulness can be used all the day long to help the practitioner remain in mindfulness. When doing walking meditation in the meditation hall or outside, the practitioner can combine her breathing with her steps in order to remain steadily established in mindfulness. Before beginning any kind of walking meditation, we can recite the following gatha:

> The mind can go in a thousand directions,
> But on this beautiful path, I walk in peace.
> With each step, a gentle wind blows.
> With each step, a flower blooms.

Any time we sit down, we can follow our breath and use this gatha:

> Sitting here
> is like sitting under the Bodhi tree.
> My body is mindfulness itself,
> entirely free from distraction.

We can use our breathing in order to be aware of the positions of sitting and standing. When we're standing in a line waiting to buy a ticket, or when we're just sitting down and waiting for anything, we can recite the gatha, "Breathing in, I calm my body," in order to continue dwelling in mindfulness and to calm the body and mind.

Exercise 6 | Bodily Actions

Moreover, when the practitioner is going forward or backward, he applies full awareness to his going forward or backward. When he looks in front or looks behind, bends down or stands up, he also applies full awareness to what he is doing. He applies full awareness to wearing the sanghati robe or carrying the alms bowl. When he eats or drinks, chews or savors the food, he applies full awareness to all this. When passing excrement or urinating, he applies full awareness to

this. When he walks, stands, lies down, sits, sleeps or wakes
up, speaks or is silent, he shines his awareness on all this.

This exercise is the observation and awareness of the actions of the
body. This is the fundamental practice of the monk. When I was first
ordained as a novice over sixty years ago, the first book my master gave
me to learn by heart was a book of short verses (gathas) to be practiced
while washing your hands, brushing your teeth, washing your face,
putting on your clothes, sweeping the courtyard, relieving yourself,
having a bath, and so on. On hearing the sound of the bell, we would
breathe consciously and recite this gatha:

Hearing the sound of the bell,
the afflictions are lifted.
Understanding grows strong,
and the awakened mind is born.

Practicing breathing in combination with reciting a gatha helps us
dwell more easily in mindfulness. Mindfulness makes every action of
our bodies more serene, and we become master of our bodies and
minds. Mindfulness nurtures the power of concentration in us. Many
of the gathas in the book I was given, *Gathas for Everyday Use*, a text by
Chinese master Du Ti, were taken from the Avatamsaka Sutra. I have
written a book of gathas in the same spirit, *Present Moment, Wonderful
Moment.*[35] These gathas are very easy to use and can also be combined
with conscious breathing.

Without mindfulness, our actions are often hurried and abrupt. As
we practice the sixth exercise, we may find that our actions slow down.
If a novice applies himself to the practice of the sixth exercise, he'll
see that his everyday actions become harmonious, graceful, and measured. Mindfulness becomes visible in his actions and speech. When
any action is placed in the light of mindfulness, the body and mind
become relaxed, peaceful, and joyful. The sixth exercise is one to be
used day and night throughout our entire lives.

Exercise 7 | Parts of the Body

Further, the practitioner meditates on his very own body
from the soles of the feet upwards and then from the hair on

top of the head downwards, a body contained inside the skin and full of all the impurities which belong to the body: 'Here is the hair of the head, the hairs on the body, the nails, teeth, skin, flesh, sinews, bones, bone marrow, kidneys, heart, liver, diaphragm, spleen, lungs, intestines, bowels, excrement, bile, phlegm, pus, blood, sweat, fat, tears, grease, saliva, mucus, synovic fluid, urine.'

This exercise brings us into even deeper contact with our bodies. Here we observe the body in all its parts, from the hair on the head to the skin on the soles of the feet. In the process of our observation, we scan all the parts of the body, including the brain, heart, lungs, gall bladder, spleen, blood, urine, and so forth. The Buddha gives us the example of a farmer pouring the contents of a sack filled with a variety of seeds onto the floor and then observing and identifying each kind of seed: "This is rice; these are beans; and these are sesame seeds."

We use our conscious breathing in order to observe mindfully all the parts of the body. For example: "Breathing in, I am aware of the hair on my head. Breathing out, I know that this is the hair on my head." Breathing consciously helps us dwell in mindfulness more easily and helps us sustain the work of observing each part of the body. In addition to the conscious breathing, we can use the method of silently calling each part of the body by name to enable these parts to become increasingly clear in the light of mindfulness.

Why do we need to mindfully observe the different parts of the body? First of all, it is to be in contact with the body. We often have the impression that we're already totally in touch with the body, but often we're wrong. Between ourselves and our bodies, there can be a large separation, and our bodies can remain estranged from us. Sometimes we hate our bodies. There are even people who see the body as a prison and a place of punishment. To come back to the body is to become familiar with it and to establish harmony with it. We know that if our bodies aren't happy, we're not happy, and so we want our bodies to be calm and peaceful. To do so, we come back to the body and make peace with it.

We can try touching the different parts of our bodies to make their acquaintance. We should touch each part in an affectionate and caring way. For several decades, our eyes, feet, and hearts have done their work devotedly and faithfully with us and for us, but we never really give them much attention or express our gratitude to them. It's necessary to establish a close relationship with the different parts of our bodies.

The second reason for mindfully observing the different parts of the body is that each part can be the door to liberation and awakening. At first we'll only recognize the presence of the part of the body being observed, but later we'll come to see its true nature. Every hair on our heads, and every bodily cell contains the entire universe. Observing the interdependent nature of a single hair can help us to see into the nature of the universe.

The exercise of observing every part of the body begins with the hair on the head and goes down to the skin on the soles of the feet. Sometimes we observe just one part of the body deeply, such as the eyes, the heart, or the toe. In the process of scanning from head to foot, some observations may spring up in our minds. For example, as we pass the heart, we may think, "My friend John has a heart condition. I must visit him soon to see if he's all right." We can note these observations and then continue with the work of observing the remaining parts of the body. Later we can return to those observations.

Exercise 8 | Body and Universe

> Further, in whichever position his body happens to be, the practitioner passes in review the elements which constitute the body: 'In this body is the earth element, the water element, the fire element, and the air element.'

This exercise shows us the interrelationship of the body and all that is in the universe. It's one of the principal ways of witnessing for ourselves the nonself, unborn, and never-dying nature of all that is. Seeing things in this way can liberate and awaken us.

The sutra teaches us that we should be aware of the presence of earth, water, fire, and air elements in our bodies. These are the Four Great Elements (Sanskrit: *mahabhuta*), also referred to as the realms (Sanskrit: *dhatu*). The earth element represents the hard, solid nature of matter; the water element represents the liquid, permeating nature; the fire element represents heat; and the air element represents movement. The Dhatuvibhanga Sutra and the second version of the sutra on mindfulness in this book both refer to six elements—the two additional elements are space (Sanskrit: *akasa*) and consciousness (Sanskrit: *vijñana*).

Our bodies are more than three-fourths water. When the practitioner looks deeply in order to see the water in his body, not only does he see the liquid, permeating nature of the blood, sweat, saliva, tears, and urine; but he also sees the water element in every cell of his body. There are clouds in the body, because without clouds there can be no rain. Without rain, we wouldn't have any water to drink, or grains and vegetables to eat. We see earth in us, earth as the minerals in our bodies. We also see that earth is alive in us because, thanks to Mother Earth, we have food to eat. We see air in us, air representing movement. Without air we could not survive, since we, as every other species on Earth, need air to live.

The practitioner observes her body mindfully to see all that is in it and to see the interrelated nature of herself and the universe. She sees that this life is not just present in her own body, transcending the erroneous view that she's just her body. In the book *The Sun My Heart*, I refer to the sun as a second heart, a heart which lies outside the body but which is as essential for the body as the heart inside the body.[36] When the heart inside the body ceases to function, we know very well that we will die, but we often forget that if the heart outside the body, the sun, ceases to function, we will also die immediately. When we observe mindfully the interdependent nature of our bodies, we see our lives outside our bodies, and we transcend the boundary between self and nonself. This practice of mindful observation helps us go beyond such limiting concepts as birth and death.

Exercise 9 | Body as Impermanent

The Nine Contemplations (the nine stages of decomposition of a corpse):

1. The corpse is bloated, blue, and festering.
2. The corpse is crawling with insects and worms. Crows, hawks, vultures, and wolves are tearing it apart to eat.
3. All that is left is a skeleton with some flesh and blood still clinging to it.
4. All that is left is a skeleton with some blood stains, but no more flesh.

5. All that is left is a skeleton with no more blood stains.
6. All that is left is a collection of scattered bones—here an arm, here a shin, here a skull, and so forth.
7. All that is left is a collection of bleached bones.
8. All that is left is a collection of dried bones.
9. The bones have decomposed, and only a pile of dust is left.

This exercise helps us see the impermanent and decomposing nature of the body. The objects of our mindful observation are the nine stages of the decomposition of a corpse. When we first read this, we may feel that this is not a pleasant meditation. But the effect of this practice can be great. It can be liberating and can bring us much peace and joy. The practitioner observes mindfully in order to see the corpse at each of these stages and to see that it is inevitable that her own body will pass through the same stages.

In former times, practitioners would actually sit in cemeteries and observe corpses in these various stages of decomposition. Of course, today, decomposing bodies aren't exposed for us to view. But we can visualize them according to the description in the sutra. This exercise should be practiced by those who are in good mental and physical health. It shouldn't be practiced by those who have not yet mastered desire and aversion. Its intention is not to make us weary of life, but to help us see how precious life is; not to make us pessimistic, but to help us see the impermanent nature of life so that we don't waste our lives. If we have the courage to see things as they are, our meditation will have beneficial results. When we see the impermanent nature of things, we appreciate their true value.

Have you ever stayed up at night to see a Cereus cactus flower open? The flower opens and dies in a few hours, but because we're aware of that, we appreciate its wondrous fragrance and beauty. We can be in real contact with the flower and not be sad or depressed when it fades, because we knew before it opened how ephemeral its life was.

Our dear ones who live with us and the beautiful and precious beings around us are all wonderful cactus flowers. If we can see their true nature as well as their outward form, we will know how to value their presence in the present moment. If we know how to value them, we'll have the time to be in real contact with them, and we'll take care of them, make them happy, and therefore be happier ourselves.

These Nine Contemplations help us see the preciousness of life.

They teach us how to live lightly and freshly, without being caught by attachments and aversions.

REMARKS ON THE FIRST NINE EXERCISES

When we practice the above nine exercises offered by the Buddha for observing the body in the body, we concentrate either on the breath, the body, the positions of the body, the actions of the body, the different parts of the body, the elements that form the body, or the decomposition of the body. When we observe the body this way, we are in direct contact with it, and we are able to see the process of coming-to-be and ceasing-to-be in the constituents that comprise the body. In the first version of the sutra, at the end of each meditation exercise to observe the body in the body, we read:

> This is how the practitioner remains established in the obser-
> vation of the body in the body, observation of the body
> from within or from without, or observation of the body
> from both within and without. He remains established in
> the observation of the process of coming-to-be in the body
> or the process of dissolution in the body or both the pro-
> cess of coming-to-be and the process of dissolution. Or he
> is mindful of the fact, 'There is a body here,' until under-
> standing and full awareness come about. He remains estab-
> lished in the observation, free, not caught up in any worldly
> consideration.

We should remember that the breathing, the positions of the body, the movements of the body, and the parts of the body all belong to the body and are the body. To be in touch with these aspects and to be able to see the process of birth and death, and the nonself and inter-dependent nature of the body, is the meaning of mindful observation of the body.

Therefore, the teachings of impermanence, selflessness, and interde-pendent origination—the three basic observations of Buddhism—are realized directly through the practice of the nine exercises for mindfully observing the body. These nine exercises can liberate and awaken us to the way things are.

In the second version of the sutra, the description of each body meditation exercise is as follows:

> This is how the practitioner is aware of body as body, both within and without, and establishes mindfulness in the body with understanding, insight, clarity, and realization. This is called being aware of body as body.

The words *recognition, insight, clarity,* and *realization* here mean that the practitioner recognizes, sees, sheds light on, and realizes the impermanent and interdependent nature of the body and all that is, by means of the mindful observation of the body.

Observing the impermanent, selfless, and interdependent nature of all that is doesn't lead us to feel aversion for life. On the contrary, it helps us see the preciousness of all that lives. Liberation doesn't mean running away from or destroying life. Many people present Buddhism as a path that denies life, that transcends the world of the Five Aggregates (Sanskrit: *skandha*) of form, feelings, perceptions, mental formations, and consciousness. To present Buddhism in this way is no different from saying that the object of our practice is to arrive at the absence of life or nothingness.

In the Dhammacakka Sutta, the first Dharma talk given by the Buddha in the Deer Park, the Buddha taught that to be attached to existence (Sanskrit: *bhava*) is no worse than to be attached to nonexistence (Sanskrit: *abhava*). In the Kaccayanagotta Sutta, the Buddha also taught that reality is not to be found in terms of existence or nonexistence. His meaning is perfectly clear: suffering is not brought about by life, the Five Skandhas, or the selfless and interdependent nature of all that is. The cause of ill-being is our ignorance. Because we're not able to see that the true nature of life is impermanence, selflessness, and interdependence, we become attached to things, believing that they're permanent. From this thinking arise the roots of affliction and the internal formations or knots: craving, hatred, pride, doubt, and so forth. Impermanence, selflessness, and interdependence are the essential conditions for life. Without impermanence, how can the corn seed become a corn plant and how can the baby grow up and go to school?

In fact, it's because of impermanence, selflessness, and interdependence that things come into existence, mature, decay, and cease to be. Birth, decay, and ceasing to be are the necessary steps of the lives of all species. Presenting impermanence, selflessness, and interdependence as problematic, we senselessly make life unacceptable. We need to do the opposite; we need to praise them as essential elements of life. Only when we're not able to recognize these attributes as they are do we get caught in the knots of attachment and sorrow.

The Ratnakuta Sutra gives the example of someone who throws a clod of earth at a dog. When the clod hits the dog, he runs after it and barks furiously at it. The dog doesn't know that the thing responsible for his pain isn't the clod of earth but the man who threw it. The sutra teaches:

> In the same way, the ordinary man caught in dualistic
>   conceptions
> is accustomed to thinking that the Five Aggregates
> are the root of his suffering, but in fact the root of suffering
> is the lack of understanding about the impermanent,
> selfless, and interdependent nature of the Five Aggregates.

Because we don't understand correctly, we become attached to things, and then we're caught by them. In the sutra, the term "aggregate" (Pali: *khanda*; Sanskrit: *skandha*) and the term "aggregate of clinging" (Pali: *upadanakkhanda*; Sanskrit: *upadanaskandha*) are used. Skandhas are the five elements that give rise to life, and the upadana skandhas are the five elements as objects of attachment. The root of suffering isn't the skandhas but the attachment that binds us. There are people who, because of their incorrect understanding of what the root of suffering is, instead of dealing with their attitude of attachment, think they have to deal with their organs of sense and the aggregates, and so they fear form, sound, smell, taste, touch, and objects of mind and feel aversion for the body, feelings, perceptions, mental formations, and consciousness.

The Buddha was someone who, because he wasn't attached to things, lived in peace, joy, and freedom with a healthy and fresh vigor. He always had a smile on his lips, and his presence created a fresh atmosphere around him. There are many stories in the sutras that show how much the Buddha loved life and knew how to appreciate the beautiful things around him. On many occasions, he pointed out beautiful scenery to Ananda, such as the sun setting on Vulture Peak, the golden rice fields surrounded by green paths, the fresh green landscape of the

Bamboo Forest Monastery, and the lovely town of Vaishali. The Buddha was not afraid of beautiful things, because he was able to see the impermanent nature of everything, beautiful or ugly. He didn't chase after things, and he didn't run away from them either. The way of freedom isn't running away from the Five Aggregates, but coming face to face with them in order to understand their true nature.

If we cut flowers from our garden to place on the altar, that is because we acknowledge the beauty of those flowers. All we can say is, "Although these flowers are beautiful, their beauty is fragile. When, in a few days time, these flowers die, their beauty will die with them." We understand this, and when the flowers wilt in a few days, we won't suffer or feel sad. Because we can see the impermanent nature of the flowers, we can appreciate all the more the beauty of each flower. To observe the impermanence of things is not to reject them, but to be in contact with them with deep understanding, without being caught in desire and attachment.

Freedom in Buddhism is the freedom that comes about by being awake and understanding. A practitioner doesn't need to struggle with desire. The two basic meditation sutras, the Sutra on the Four Establishments of Mindfulness and the Sutra on the Full Awareness of Breathing, both shed light on this principle: "When his mind is desiring something, the practitioner is aware, 'My mind is desiring'" (Satipatthana Sutta), and "Breathing in, I am aware of the functions of my mind" (Anapanasati Sutta). In identifying the mind of desire, in observing the nature of that mind and the nature of the object of desire, we'll see the impermanence, selflessness, and interdependence of it, and we'll no longer be dominated by that state of mind.

For many generations, some Buddhists have presented Buddhism as a path that destroys desire, and they have described liberated persons as emaciated *arhat*s with wrinkled skin and no vitality. We should define what is meant by desire. If we've had nothing to eat for three days, we feel like eating. Is that desire? Is the natural desire for the indispensable elements of life a desire we need to destroy? To eat when hungry, to drink when thirsty, is that to go against the path that leads to emancipation? But if so, then Buddhism would be a path that flees from and destroys life.

We know very well that to eat and drink enough are necessary to nourish our bodies and keep us strong. We also know that eating and drinking excessively can destroy our bodies. So we can say that to eat and drink, so that the body is strong and healthy, is to walk on the path of emancipation, while to eat and drink in a way that causes our bodies and others to suffer is to go against the way of liberation. In the first case desire isn't present, in the second case desire is present.

Other Buddhists have opposed the image of the emaciated arhat destroying desire and have described liberated persons as fresh, healthy *bodhisattvas*, beautiful to look at and full of vigor. The image of the bodhisattva is very close to the image of the Buddha entering life with a heart of love and compassion and a smile on his lips. Although the Buddha enjoyed the solitary life, he never refused to go deeply into the world in order to help living beings.

To know how to appreciate a beautiful sunset is not desire, if we "remain established in the observation, free, and not caught up in any worldly consideration" (Satipatthana Sutta). If we are able to see impermanence, selflessness, and interdependence, we are awake. To swim in a cool stream, to drink a glass of clear water, to eat a sweet orange, and to know how to appreciate the coolness, the clarity, and the sweetness, is not desire if we are not attached to these things. In the Southern tradition of Buddhism, and to some extent in the Northern tradition, generations of Buddhists have expressed fear of peace and joy and have not dared to practice peace and joy.

The tenth exercise is taken from the second version of the sutra. It is a practice of peace and joy.

Exercise 10 | Healing with Joy

> Further, bhikkhus, a practitioner is aware of body as body, when, thanks to having put aside the Five Desires, a feeling of bliss arises during his concentration and saturates every part of his body.
>
> Further, bhikkhus, a practitioner who is aware of body as body feels the joy which arises during concentration saturate every part of his body. There is no part of his body this feeling of joy, born during concentration, does not reach.
>
> Further, bhikkhus, a practitioner who is aware of body as body experiences a feeling of happiness which arises with the disappearance of the feeling of joy and permeates his whole body. This feeling of happiness which arises with the disappearance of the feeling of joy reaches every part of his body.

Further, bhikkhus, a practitioner who is aware of body as body envelops the whole of his body with a clear, calm mind, filled with understanding.

The purpose of this exercise is to bring about ease, peace, and joy; to heal the wounds of the body as well as of the heart and mind; to nourish us as we grow in the practice of joy; and to enable us to go far on the path of practice.

When the practitioner is able to put an end to agitation, desire, and hatred, he sits down in the lotus position and concentrates on his breath, and he feels a sense of ease and freedom. As a result, a feeling of joy arises in his body. You can practice according to the following exercises:

1. I am breathing in and making my whole body calm and at peace. I am breathing out and making my whole body calm and at peace. (Exercise 4 again.)
2. I am breathing in and feeling joyful. I am breathing out and feeling joyful. (This is the fifth exercise of the Anapanasati.)
3. I am breathing in and feeling happy. I am breathing out and feeling happy. (This is the sixth exercise of the Anapanasati.)
4. I am breathing in and making my mind happy and at peace. I am breathing out and making my mind happy and at peace. (This is the tenth exercise of the Anapanasati.)

While practicing in this way, the practitioner feels the elements of joy and peace permeate every cell of his body. Please read the following excerpt from the second version:

Like the bath attendant, who, after putting powdered soap into a basin, mixes it with water until the soap paste has water in every part of it, so the practitioner feels the bliss that is born when the desires of the sense realms is put aside, saturate every part of his body.

The feeling of joy that's born when the practitioner lets go of his life of agitation, desire, and hatred will strengthen and penetrate more deeply when he has mastered the way of applying his mind:

Like a spring within a mountain whose clear, pure water flows out and down all sides of that mountain and bubbles up in places where water has not previously entered, saturating the entire mountain, in the same way joy, born during concentration, permeates the whole of the practitioner's body; it is present everywhere.

When the state of happiness is really present, the joy of the mind settles down to allow happiness to become steadier and deeper. For as long as the joy is still there, there goes with it, to a greater or lesser extent, conceptualization and excitement. "Joy" is a translation of the Sanskrit word *piti*, and "happiness" is a translation of *sukha*. The following example is often used to compare joy with happiness: Someone traveling in the desert who sees a stream of cool water experiences joy. When he drinks the water, he experiences happiness.

Just as the different species of blue, pink, red, and white lotus, which grow up from the bottom of a pond of clear water and appear on the surface of that pond, have their tap roots, subsidiary roots, leaves, and flowers all full of the water of that pond, and there is no part of the plant which does not contain the water, so the feeling of happiness which arises with the disappearance of joy permeates the whole of the practitioner's body, and there is no part which it does not penetrate.

At the time of the meditation, the practitioner feels happy and at peace. He lets his consciousness of this peace and happiness embrace his whole body, so that his body is saturated by it:

Just as someone who puts on a very long robe which reaches from his head to his feet, and there is no part of his body which is not covered by this robe, so the practitioner with a clear, calm mind envelops his whole body in understanding and leaves no part of the body uncovered. This is how the practitioner is aware of the body as the body, both within and without, and establishes mindfulness in the body with recognition, insight, clarity, and realization. This is called being aware of the body as the body.

As we've already seen, the function of this exercise is to nourish us with joy and happiness and to heal the wounds within us. But we have no doubts about letting go of this joy in order to embark on the work of observation. Joy and happiness come about because of physical and psychological conditions and are as impermanent as all other physical and psychological phenomena. Only when, thanks to mindful observation, we realize the impermanent, selfless, and interdependent nature of all that is, can we achieve freedom and liberation.

4: Exercises for Observing the Feelings

Exercise 11 | Identifying Feelings

Whenever the practitioner has a pleasant feeling, he is aware, 'I am experiencing a pleasant feeling.' Whenever he has a painful feeling, he is aware, 'I am experiencing a painful feeling.' Whenever he experiences a feeling which is neither pleasant nor painful, he is aware, 'I am experiencing a neutral feeling.'

There are three sorts of feelings: pleasant, unpleasant, and neutral. The teaching of this exercise is to identify and be in touch with these feelings as they arise, endure, and fade away.

When there is an unpleasant feeling, the practitioner is not in a hurry to chase it away. She comes back to her conscious breathing and observes, "Breathing in, I know that an unpleasant feeling has arisen within me. Breathing out, I know that this unpleasant feeling is present in me." Whenever there is a pleasant or a neutral feeling, she practices mindful observation in accordance with that feeling. She knows that her feeling is her, and that for the moment she is that feeling. She is neither drowned in nor terrorized by that feeling, nor does she reject it. This is the most effective way to be in contact with feelings. If we call a pleasant, unpleasant, or neutral feeling by its name, we identify it clearly and recognize it more deeply. Our attitude of not clinging to or rejecting our feelings is the attitude of letting go (Pali: *upekkha*, Sanskrit: *upeksha*) and is an important part of meditation practice. Letting go is one of the Four Unlimited Minds (Sanskrit: *brahmavihara*), which are love, compassion, joy, and letting go.

A person is comprised of the Five Aggregates: form (the body), feelings, perceptions, mental formations, and consciousness. Each aggregate is a river. The body is a river in which every cell is a drop of water, and all of them are in constant transformation and movement. There is also a river of feelings in us, in which every feeling is a drop of water. Each of these feelings—pleasant, unpleasant, neutral—relies on all other feelings to be born, mature, and disappear. To observe the feelings is to sit on the bank of the river of feelings and identify each feeling as it is arises, matures, and disappears.

Our feelings usually play an important part in directing our thoughts and our minds. Our thoughts arise and become linked to each other around the feelings that are present. When we are mindful of our feelings, the situation begins to change. The feeling is no longer the only thing present in us, and it is transformed under the light of our awareness. Therefore, it no longer sweeps us along the way it did before there was mindfulness of the feeling. If we continue to observe the feeling mindfully, we will be able to see its substance and its roots. This kind of seeing empowers the observer. When we are able to see the nature of something, we are able to transcend it and not be led astray or corrupted by it anymore.

Exercise 12 | *Seeing the Roots of Feelings and Identifying Neutral Feelings*

> When he experiences a pleasant feeling based in the body, he is aware, 'I am experiencing a pleasant feeling based in the body.' When he experiences a pleasant feeling based in the mind, he is aware, 'I am experiencing a pleasant feeling based in the mind.' When he experiences a painful feeling based in the body, he is aware, 'I am experiencing a painful feeling based in the body.' When he experiences a painful feeling based in the mind, he is aware, 'I am experiencing a painful feeling based in the mind.' When he experiences a neutral feeling based in the body, he is aware, 'I am experiencing a neutral feeling based in the body.' When he experiences a neutral feeling based in the mind, he is aware, 'I am experiencing a neutral feeling based in the mind.'

This exercise is a continuation of Exercise 11 and has the capacity to help us see the roots and the substance of the feelings we have. Our feelings—pleasant, unpleasant, and neutral—can have a physical, physiological, or psychological root. When we mindfully observe our feelings, we discover their roots. For example, if you have an unpleasant feeling because you stayed up late the night before, your unpleasant feeling has a physiological root. Nevertheless, to be able to identify the roots of your feelings is not enough. We have to look more deeply in order to see how these feelings manifest and to understand their true substance. To know a feeling is not just to see its roots but also to see its flowering and its fruits.

When one person takes a sip of whiskey or inhales from a cigarette, for example, he may have a pleasant feeling. If he observes this feeling mindfully, he can see its physiological and psychological roots. We know that not everyone shares the same pleasant feeling when they drink whiskey or smoke cigarettes. If another person were to do either of these two things, she may cough or choke, and the feeling would be unpleasant. Thus, the roots of that feeling are not as simple as they might appear at first. The elements of habit, time, and our own psychology and physiology are all present in the roots of any feeling. Looking into our feelings, we can see physiological, physical, and psychological habits; not only our own habits, but also those of the society whose products we are consuming.

Looking into our feelings, we see the nature of whiskey and the nature of tobacco. Looking into the glass of whiskey, we can see the grains that are needed for its production. We can see the effect that the alcohol will have on our bodies now and in the near future. We can see the connection between the consumption of alcohol and car accidents. We can see the link between the consumption of alcohol and the severe lack of food in the world. We have squandered large amounts of grain in producing alcohol and meat, while in many places in the world, children and adults are dying for want of grain to eat. An economist at the University of Paris (Charles Perrault) once said: "If the Western world were to consume fifty percent less alcohol and meat, the problem of starvation in the world could be solved." If we look into any one thing with the eyes of mindful observation, we can see the roots and the results of it. If we mindfully observe a feeling, we can see the roots of that feeling and the results it is likely to produce. The mindful observation of a feeling can lead to a deep insight into the nature of life.

When we hear someone praise us, we may have a pleasant feeling. That pleasant feeling also needs to be examined. Obviously, we have the right to accept a pleasant feeling, but we know that in our meditation practice we need to observe mindfully in order to have clear insight into the nature of our feeling. If in our mindful observation, we see that those words of praise were based in flattery rather than reality, then we discover that our pleasant feeling arose out of ignorance and self-love. Such a pleasant feeling can take us farther along the path of illusion. When we see that, the pleasant feeling disappears, and we come back to the ground of reality with both feet planted firmly. The danger of being deluded no longer exists, and we become healthy again. The pleasant feeling we have when we drink alcohol will also disappear when we see its roots and its effects. When pleasant feelings like this disappear, they can give rise to pleasant feelings of another kind, such as the awareness that we are now living in a way that leads to health and awakened understanding. Pleasant feelings of the second kind are healthy because they nourish us and others and cause no harm.

Even though we feel that the words of praise are in harmony with the truth, we should continue to observe the pleasant feeling brought about by those words of praise. The work of mindful observation helps us avoid pride or arrogance—the two things that above all obstruct our progress on the path. We see that if we keep on with what we have started, we will make additional progress, and the words of praise, instead of making us proud or arrogant, become elements of encouragement for us. If we observe mindfully like that, the pleasant feeling on hearing words of praise becomes a healthy feeling and has a nourishing effect.

When we observe our feelings, we can see their relative nature. It is our way of seeing the world that determines the nature of our feelings. One person while working might feel that work is nothing but agony, and he will only feel happy when he is not working. There are other people, however, who feel uneasy when they have nothing to do and would be happy with any work rather than doing nothing. In the latter case, work brings joy, a pleasant feeling, while in the former case, work gives rise to unpleasant feelings, such as boredom or drudgery. Often we do not see that we have all the conditions necessary for happiness, and we go looking for happiness in another place or in the future. To be able to breathe can be a great source of real happiness, but often, unless we have a congested nose or asthma, we are not able to realize that. To be able to see beautiful colors and forms is happiness, but often only after we have lost our sight do we become aware of this. Having sound and healthy limbs to be able to run and jump, living in an atmosphere of freedom, not being separated from our family—all these things and thousands more can be elements of happiness. But we rarely remember, and happiness slips from our grasp as we chase other things that we believe to be necessary for our happiness. Generally, only after we lose an element of happiness do we appreciate it. Awareness of these precious elements of happiness is itself the practice of Right Mindfulness. We can use conscious breathing to shine light on their presence:

> Breathing in, I know that I have two good eyes.
> Breathing out, I know that I have two able hands.
>
> Breathing in, I know that I am holding my child in my arms.
> Breathing out, I know that I am sitting with my family at
> the table.

Exercises such as these nourish Right Mindfulness and bring much happiness into our daily lives.

Peace, joy, and happiness are above all the awareness that we have the conditions for happiness. Thus, mindfulness is the basic and essential ingredient for happiness. If you do not know that you are happy, it means that you are not happy. Most of us only remember that not having a toothache is happiness at the time when we have a toothache. We are not aware of the joy of a non-toothache, because we do not practice mindfulness.

When a feeling is born in us, we know that it is born. As long as that feeling continues to be present, we know that it continues to be present. We look into it mindfully in order to be able to recognize its nature—pleasant, unpleasant, or neutral; its roots—physical, physiological, or psychological; and its fruits—physiological, psychological, or social. We can use conscious breathing to assist us in carrying out this work of mindful observation:

> Breathing in, I know that a pleasant feeling has just arisen in me.
> Breathing out, I know that this pleasant feeling is still there.
>
> Breathing in, I know that this feeling has a psychological basis.
> Breathing out, I can see the roots of this pleasant feeling.

Breathing in, I can see the influence of this feeling on my health. Breathing out, I can see the influence of this feeling on my mind. And so on.

When roots of affliction such as anger, confusion, jealousy, and anxiety manifest in us, they generally disturb our bodies and minds. These psychological feelings are unpleasant, and they agitate the functioning of our bodies and minds. We lose our peace, joy, and calm. In the Sutra on the Full Awareness of Breathing, the Buddha teaches us to take hold of our breathing in order to produce awareness of the unpleasant feeling and gradually to master it: "Breathing in, I know that I have an unpleasant feeling. Breathing out, I am clearly aware of this unpleasant feeling." If our breathing is light and calm (a natural result of practice), then our minds and bodies will slowly become light, calm, and clear again: "Breathing in, I calm the feelings in me. Breathing out, I calm the feelings in me." In this way, the practitioner continues to use conscious breathing to mindfully observe and calm his feelings. Every time she sees the substance, roots, and effects of her feelings, she is no longer under the control of those feelings. The whole character of our feelings can change just by the presence of mindful observation.

Fear and anger are fields of energy that arise from a physiological or psychological base. The unpleasant feelings that arise within us are also fields of energy. The Buddha teaches us not to repress fear or anger, or the unpleasant feelings brought about by them, but to use our breathing to be in contact with and accept these feelings, knowing that they are energies that originate in our psychological or physiological make-up. To repress our feelings is to repress ourselves. Mindful observation is based on the principle of nonduality. Our unpleasant feelings and ourselves are one. We have to be in contact with and accept the unpleasant feelings before we can transform them into the kinds of energy that are healthy and have the capacity to nourish us. We have to face our unpleasant feelings with care, affection, and nonviolence. Our unpleasant feelings can illuminate so much for us. By our work of mindful observation, we see that experiencing certain unpleasant feelings allows us insight and understanding.

Both in the sutras and the *shastras* (the commentaries on the sutras), the ancestral teachers say the painful, unpleasant feelings are easier to recognize than the neutral feelings. But in fact, neutral feelings are also easy to recognize. They are not suffering feelings and they are not happy feelings. In us there is a river of feelings, and every drop of water in that river is either a suffering feeling, a happy feeling, or a neutral feeling. Sometimes we have a neutral feeling and we think we don't have a feeling at all. But a neutral feeling is a feeling; it doesn't mean the nonexistence of feeling.

When we have a toothache, we have a feeling of pain, and when the toothache is no longer there, we think we don't have a feeling anymore. But in fact, we have a neutral feeling. It's not a painful feeling, so it must be either neutral or pleasant. Actually, it can be a pleasant feeling. When we have a very bad toothache, we just wish it would stop. We know if it were to stop, we would have a very pleasant feeling. Therefore, a non-toothache is a pleasant feeling. But once the toothache has been gone for some time, we no longer appreciate the non-toothache. We could call it a neutral feeling, but with awareness it can become a pleasant feeling. In Plum Village, we usually say someone who practices mindfulness can change all neutral feelings into pleasant feelings. In fact, neutral feelings are the majority of our feelings.

For example, a father and son are sitting on the lawn in springtime. The father is practicing mindful breathing and he sees how wonderful it is to sit on the grass, feeling fresh and happy, with the yellow flowers coming up and the birds singing; so he has pleasant feelings.

But the child is bored, he doesn't want to sit with his father. He's in exactly the same environment as his father. To begin with his feeling is neutral, and at some point the neutral feeling becomes an unpleasant feeling, because he doesn't know how to deal with this neutral feeling. So, wanting to run away from his unpleasant feeling, he stands up and goes into the house and turns on the television. But his father is feeling very content sitting in that same environment that was not able to bring happiness to the son.

We're the same. When we don't have a pleasant or unpleasant feeling, naturally we have a neutral feeling. If we don't know how to deal with or manage our neutral feeling, it will turn into an unpleasant feeling. However, if we know how to manage it, it will become a pleasant feeling, a feeling of well-being. Every neutral feeling, when held in mindfulness, will become a pleasant feeling.

5: Exercises for Observing the Mind

The Third Establishment of Mindfulness presented in the sutra is the establishment of the mind. The contents of the mind are the psychological phenomena called mental formations (*cittasamskara*). Feelings are also mental formations, but they were dealt with on their own in the Second Establishment of Mindfulness, because the sphere of feelings is so wide. What remains are all the other psychological phenomena, such as perceptions, mental formations, and consciousness. These are all mind functions and are the objects of our mindful observation of the mind in the mind. Formations can be either mental, physical, or physiological.

Different schools of Buddhism list different numbers of mental formations. The Abhidharmakosha school lists forty-six, the Satyasiddhi school lists forty-nine, and the Dharmalakshana school lists fifty-one. The Sutra on the Four Establishments of Mindfulness lists only twenty-eight mental formations, including desire, anger, ignorance, disturbance, narrowness, limitedness, lack of concentration, lack of freedom, dullness and drowsiness, agitation and remorse, doubt; their opposites: not-desiring, not-hating, non-ignorance, non-disturbance, tolerance, unlimitedness, concentration, freedom, absence of doubt, absence of dullness and drowsiness, absence of agitation; as well as mindfulness, distaste, peace, joy, ease, and letting go. The second version of the sutra lists one additional mental formation, impurity, which could include other mental formations that are considered to be defilements. The third version considers sensual craving as a formation separate from desire. Any of these mental formations can be the object of our mindful observation of the mind in the mind.

The exercise of observing the mind in the mind isn't different from observing the body in the body or observing the feelings in feelings. We mindfully observe the arising, presence, and disappearance of the mental phenomena which are called mental formations. We recognize them and look deeply into them in order to see their substance, their roots in the past, and their possible fruits in the future, using conscious breathing while we observe. We should remember that when the lamp of mindfulness is lit up, the mental formation under observation will naturally transform in a wholesome direction.

Exercise 13 | Observing the Desiring Mind

When his mind is desiring, the practitioner is aware, 'My mind is desiring.'

When his mind is not desiring, he is aware, 'My mind is not desiring.'

When his mind is hating something, he is aware, 'My mind is hating.'

When his mind is not hating, he is aware, 'My mind is not hating.'

When his mind is in a state of ignorance, he is aware, 'My mind is in a state of ignorance.'

When his mind is not in a state of ignorance, he is aware, 'My mind is not in a state of ignorance.'

When his mind is tense, he is aware, 'My mind is tense.'

When his mind is not tense, he is aware, 'My mind is not tense.'

When his mind is distracted, he is aware, 'My mind is distracted.'

When his mind is not distracted, he is aware, 'My mind is not distracted.'

When his mind has a wider scope, he is aware, 'My mind has widened in scope.'

When his mind has a narrow scope, he is aware, 'My mind has become narrow in scope.'

When his mind is capable of reaching a higher state, he is aware, 'My mind is capable of reaching a higher state.'

When his mind is not capable of reaching a higher state, he is aware, 'My mind is not capable of reaching a higher state.'

When his mind is composed, he is aware, 'My mind is composed.'

When his mind is not composed, he is aware, 'My mind is not composed.'

When his mind is free, he is aware, 'My mind is free.'

When his mind is not free, he is aware, 'My mind is not free.'"

Desire means to be caught in unwholesome longing. Form, sound, smell, taste, and touch are the objects of the five kinds of sense desire, which are desire for money, sex, fame, good food, and sleep. These five categories of desire produce obstacles on the path of practice as well as many kinds of physical and mental suffering.

Whenever the practitioner's mind and thoughts turn to desiring, she immediately gives rise to awareness of the presence of that mind. "This is a mind longing for wealth. This is a mind of sexual desire. This is a mind desiring reputation. This is the root of the arising of a mind longing for wealth. This is the feeling of pain caused by sexual desire."

The Satipatthana Sutta teaches that when desiring is not present, the practitioner also needs to observe that it is not present. We can practice like this: "At this time, the mind desiring wealth is not present; at this time, sexual desire is not present; at this time, the mind desiring reputation is not present, etc. This is the root of the absence of the desire for wealth. This is the root of the absence of the mind desiring reputation, etc. This is the sense of ease that accompanies the absence of the mind desiring riches. This is the sense of ease that accompanies the absence of a mind desiring reputation, etc."

The Buddha often said that many people confuse desire with happiness. In the Magandiya Sutra (Majjhima Nikaya no. 75), a man is forced to live in the forest because he has leprosy, suffering from severe itching and stinging. He dug a hole, filled it with dry branches and logs, and set them on fire. When the fire became red-hot charcoal, he stood at the edge of the hole and stretched his arms and legs out over it to catch the heat. When he did this, his suffering was relieved. On days when he could not make a charcoal fire to warm himself, his itching was unbearable. Miraculously, some years later, he was cured of the disease and went back to live in the village.

One day he went into the forest and saw a number of lepers dragging their bodies to warm themselves by a charcoal fire, and he felt tremendous pity for them. The charcoal was extremely hot, he couldn't go near it. If someone had dragged him to the hole to warm his body over the charcoal, his suffering would have been great. That which in former times had brought him happiness and relief was now a source of agony. The Buddha said, "Desire is also just a hole of burning charcoal in the forest. Only those who are sick look on desire as happiness." Before he became a monk, the Buddha had tasted a life of trying to satisfy the five desires, so his words came from experience. True happiness, he said, is a life with few desires, few possessions, and the time to enjoy the many wonders in us and around us.

The scriptures record how the monk Baddhiya tasted happiness and ease when he observed his life of no desire. One night while sitting in meditation at the foot of a tree in the Bamboo Forest Monastery, Baddhiya suddenly twice called out the words, "O happiness!" The next morning, another bhikkhu reported this to the Buddha, thinking that the monk Baddhiya regretted losing the high position he had had when he was a governor. That afternoon after the Dharma talk, the Buddha summoned Baddhiya and asked, "Is it true that yesterday during your meditation you called out twice, 'O happiness!'?" Baddhiya replied, "Venerable Sir, it is true that last night I called out twice, 'O happiness!'"

"Why?" the Buddha asked him. "Please tell the community."

Baddhiya replied, "Venerable Sir, when I was a governor, I lived in luxury and had great power and influence. Wherever I went, a regiment of soldiers assisted me. My residence was guarded day and night, inside and out, by soldiers. In spite of this, I was always anxious, afraid, and insecure. Now as a bhikkhu, I go into the forest on my own, sit alone at the foot of a tree, sleep alone without a curtain or a mat, and I never have any feelings of unease or fear. I feel a great sense of ease, joy, and peace that I never felt when I was a governor. I do not fear assassins or thieves, because I have nothing to be stolen or fought over. I live at ease like a deer in the forest. During last night's meditation, I felt clearly that feeling of ease, and that is why I raised my voice and called out twice, 'O happiness!' If I disturbed any of my fellow practitioners, I sincerely apologize, Venerable Sir."

The Buddha praised the monk Baddhiya and said to the community, "The monk Baddhiya is making steady and stable progress on the path of contentment and fearlessness. His are the feelings of joy even the gods long for."

In the Vijñanavada school of Buddhist psychology, "desirelessness," the absence of longing for something, is classified as one of the eleven wholesome mental formations. Desirelessness was the basic condition that made possible the feelings of joy, peace, and ease that the monk Baddhiya realized while living the simple life. Simplicity is to have few desires and to be content with just a few possessions. Desirelessness is the basis of true happiness, because in true happiness there must be the elements of peace, joy, and ease.

Exercise 14 | Observing Anger

> When anger is present in him, he is aware, 'Anger is present in me.' When anger is not present in him, he is aware, 'Anger is not present in me.' When anger begins to arise, he is aware of it. When already arisen anger is abandoned, he is aware of it. When anger already abandoned will not arise again in the future, he is aware of it.

This exercise is to observe our anger in mindfulness. In Buddhism, we learn that a person is comprised of the Five Aggregates of form, feelings, perceptions, mental formations, and consciousness. Anger belongs to the aggregate of mental formations, and the unpleasant feeling that goes along with the anger belongs to the aggregate of feelings. The mastery of our anger is an important step on the path of practice. Identifying the presence and the absence of anger in us brings many benefits. For our work of mindful observation to be wholehearted, we combine the work of observation with conscious breathing.

The first benefit of mindfully observing the presence and absence of anger is that we see that when anger is not present, we are much happier. Anger is like a flame blazing up and consuming our self-control, making us think, say, and do things that we will probably regret later. The actions of body, speech, and mind that we perform while we're angry take us a long way along the road to hell. We may never have seen the Avici hells, but we can see clearly that whenever someone is angry, he is abiding in one of the hot hells. Anger and hatred are the materials of which the Avici hells are made. A mind without anger—cool, fresh, and sane—is one of the eleven wholesome mental formations. The absence of anger is the basis of real happiness, the basis of love and compassion.

The second benefit of mindfully observing the presence and absence of anger is that by just identifying our anger, it loses some of its destructive nature. Only when we're angry and not observing our anger mindfully does our anger become destructive. When anger is born in us, we should follow our breathing closely while we identify and mindfully observe our anger. When we do that, mindfulness has already been born in us, and anger can no longer monopolize our consciousness. Awareness stands alongside the anger: "I know that I am angry." This awareness is a companion for the anger. Our mindful observation is not to suppress or drive out our anger, but just to look after it. This is a very important principle in meditation practice. Mindful observation is like a lamp that gives light. It's not a judge. It throws light on our anger, sponsors it, looks after it in an affectionate and caring way, like an older sister looking after and comforting her · younger sibling.

When we're angry, our anger is our very self. To suppress or chase away our anger is to suppress or chase away ourselves. When we're joyful, we are joy. When we're angry, we are anger. When we love, we are love. When we hate, we are hatred. When anger is born, we can be aware that anger is an energy in us, and we can change that energy into another kind of energy. If we want to transform it, first we have to know how to accept it. For example, a garbage can filled with decomposing and smelly organic material can be transformed into compost and later into beautiful roses. At first, we may see the garbage and the flowers as separate and opposite, but when we look deeply, we see that the flowers already exist in the garbage, and the garbage already exists in the flowers. The beautiful rose contains the garbage in it; if we look carefully, we can see that. It only takes one week for a flower to become garbage. The smelly garbage already contains beautiful flowers and fragrant herbs, such as coriander and basil. When a good organic gardener looks into the garbage can, she can see that, and so she does not feel sad or disgusted. Instead, she values the garbage and doesn't discriminate against it. It takes only a few months for garbage to transform into fragrant herbs and flowers. We also need the insight and nondual vision of the organic gardener with regard to anger and despair. We need not be afraid of them or reject them. We know that anger is a kind of garbage, but that it's within our power to transform it. We need it in the way the organic gardener needs compost. If we know how to accept our anger, we already have some peace and joy. Gradually we can transform anger completely.

When anger arises, other mental formations, which are lying latent in the depths of our consciousness, are not arising. This deep consciousness is called *alaya* by the Vijñanavada school. Joy, sadness, love, and hate, for example, are present in alaya when we are angry, but they are lying beneath the surface without manifesting, like seeds (Sanskrit: *bija*) in the ground. If we let the anger express itself without giving it a sponsor, it can do a lot of damage inside and outside of us. When the mental formation mindfulness arises from alaya, it can become the spiritual friend of the mental formation anger. As we follow our breathing and sponsor our anger with mindfulness, the situation becomes less and less dangerous. Although the anger is still there, it gradually loses its strength and begins to transform into another kind of energy, like love or understanding.

Mindfulness is like a lamp illuminating ourselves. As soon as the lamp is brought into the room, the room changes. When the sun rises, the light of the sun only has to shine onto the plants for them to change, grow, and develop. The light of the sun appears not to be doing anything at all, but in truth it is doing a lot. Under the influence of the sun, the plants produce chlorophyll and become green. It is thanks to the growth of plants that the animal species have what they need to survive. If the sun keeps shining on the bud, the flower will open. When the light of the sun penetrates the flower bud, the photons transform it, and the flower opens. Our mindfulness has the same function as the light of the sun. If we shine the light of full awareness steadily on our state of mind, that state of mind will transform into something better.

Thanks to the illuminating light of awareness, we can see the roots of our anger. The point of meditation is to look deeply into things in order to be able to see their nature. The nature of things is interdependent origination, the true source of everything that is. If we look into our anger, we can see its roots, such as misunderstanding (or ignorance), clumsiness (or lack of skill), the surrounding society, hidden resentment, and habit (or our conditioning). These roots can be present both in ourselves and in the person who played the principal role in allowing the anger to arise. We observe mindfully in order to be able to see and to understand. Seeing and understanding are the elements of liberation that allow us to be free of the suffering that always accompanies anger. Seeing and understanding bring about love and compassion. They are the balm of the bodhisattva's compassion that cools our hearts and minds. As we have already seen, our anger is a field of energy. Thanks to our mindful observation and insight into its roots, we can change this energy into the energy of love and compassion—a constructive and healing energy.

Usually when people are angry, they say and do things that cause damage to others and themselves. There are people who speak and act in ways that wound others. They believe that doing so will release the field of angry energy that is burning in their hearts. They shout and scream, beat things, and shoot poisoned arrows of speech at others. These methods of release are dangerous.

Sometimes people try to find ways to express their anger in a less dangerous way. They may go into their room, close the door behind them, and pound a pillow with all their might. Naturally if you beat a pillow until your energy is exhausted, your anger will subside, and you'll probably experience a temporary feeling of relief—exhaustion is easier to bear than anger—but the roots of the anger remain untouched, and when the conditions are right, the same anger will arise again. Therefore, the method of mindful observation in order to see and to understand the roots of our anger is the only method that has lasting effectiveness.

As we've seen already, when anger arises, we first need to come back to our conscious breathing and sponsor our anger with mindfulness. We concentrate on our breathing in order to maintain mindfulness. We avoid listening to or looking at the person whom we regard as the cause of our anger. Usually when we're angry, we don't return to ourselves and take care of healing our anger. We want to think about the hateful aspects of the person who has made us angry—rudeness, dishonesty, cruelty, maliciousness, and so on. The more we think of them, listen to them, or look at them, the more our anger flares up. Their hatefulness may be real, imaginary, or exaggerated, but whatever it is that's making us angry, we're inclined to give our full attention to that. In fact, the root of our problem is the anger inside of us, and we have to come back to it and take care of it first of all. Like a firefighter, we must put water on the blaze immediately and not waste time looking for the person who set the house on fire. "Breathing in, I know that I am angry. Breathing out, I know that I must take care of my anger." So it's best not to listen to, look at, or think about the other person, or to say or do anything as long as anger persists. If we put our minds into the work of observing and calming our anger, we'll avoid creating damage that we would probably regret later. We may like to go outside and practice walking meditation. The fresh air, green trees, and the plants will help us greatly. As we walk, we can recite this verse:

> Breathing in, I know that anger is still here.
> Breathing out, I know that anger is me.
> And I know that mindfulness is me also.

> Breathing in, I know that anger is an unpleasant feeling.
> Breathing out, I know that this feeling has been born
>   and will die.

> Breathing in, I know that I can take care of this feeling.
> Breathing out, I calm this feeling.

Mindfulness embraces the feeling, as a mother holds her crying child in her arms and transmits all her affection and care. If a mother puts all her heart and mind into caring for her baby, the baby will feel the mother's gentleness and will calm down. In the same way, we can calm the functioning of the mind.

In order to lessen the unpleasant feeling brought about by the anger, we wholly give our hearts and minds to the practice of walking meditation, combining our breath with our steps and giving full attention to the contact between the soles of our feet and the earth. After a while, our anger will calm down, and we will become stronger. Then we can begin to observe the anger and its true nature.

We know that we can't eat potatoes without cooking them first. We fill our pot with water, put the lid on, and light the fire. The lid of the pot, which keeps the heat inside, is the power of concentration—not to speak, not to listen, not to do anything at all, but just to concentrate our minds entirely on our breathing. As soon as the pot is on the fire, the water begins to get warm. When we practice conscious breathing, although our anger is still there, it's accompanied by mindfulness, the fire under the potatoes. The anger—the potatoes—has started to transform. Half an hour later, the potatoes are cooked, and our anger is transformed. We can smile, and we know that we understand the roots of our anger, and we can face the person who precipitated it.

Our anger is rooted in our lack of understanding of ourselves and of the causes, deep-seated as well as immediate, which have brought about this unpleasant state of affairs. Anger is also rooted in desire, pride, agitation, and suspiciousness. Our method of dealing with events as they arise reflects our state of understanding as well as our state of confusion. The chief roots of our anger are in ourselves. Our environment and other people are only secondary roots.

We can put up with the damage brought about by an earthquake or a flood, but if people had caused the same damage, we might not show much patience, and anger and hatred may arise in us. But if we know that earthquakes and floods have causes, we should also be able to see that there are causes (deep-seated or immediate) of the harm done to us by people. We need to see and understand these causes also. We have to see hardships brought about by others as a sort of natural disaster. These people make our lives difficult because they're ignorant, prisoners of their desires or their hatreds. If we speak angrily to them and treat them as the enemy, then we're just doing what they are doing, and we're no different from them. In order to realize the state of no anger in our conscious and subconscious minds, we have to practice the meditations on love and compassion.

Exercise 15 | Love Meditation

> When anger is not present in him, he is aware, 'Anger is not present in me.' When already arisen anger is abandoned, he is aware of it. When anger already abandoned will not arise again in the future, he is aware of it . . . When his mind is not attached, he is aware, 'My mind is not attached.' When his mind is not hating, he is aware, 'My mind is not hating.'

In the Anguttara Nikaya (V, 161), the Buddha teaches, "If a mind of anger arises, the bhikkhu can practice the meditation on love, on compassion, or on equanimity for the person who has brought about the feeling of anger." Love meditation is a method for developing the mind of love and compassion. Love (Pali: *metta*; Sanskrit: *maitri*) is a mind that is intent on bringing peace, joy, and happiness to others. Compassion (Sanskrit: *karuna*) is a mind that is intent on removing the suffering that is present in others. That is the meaning of the phrase, "Love is the capacity to give joy. Compassion is the power to relieve suffering." When love and compassion are sources of energy in us, they bring peace, joy, and happiness to those dear to us and to others also.

We all have the seeds of love and compassion in us, and we can develop these fine and wonderful sources of energy. Maitri and karuna aren't the kinds of love that try to possess and appropriate, to dictate and bring about suffering for ourselves and those we love. Maitri and karuna are the kinds of unconditional love that don't expect anything in return. Consequently, they don't result in anxiety, boredom, or sorrow.

The essence of love and compassion is understanding, the ability to recognize the suffering of others. We have to be in touch with the physical, material, and psychological suffering of others. To do so, we have to put ourselves "inside the skin" of the other. We must "go inside" their body, feelings, and mental formations and experience their suffering. A shallow observation as an outsider won't help us see their suffering. In the Satipatthana Sutta, we're taught to be one with the object of our observation. We observe the body in the body, the feelings in the feelings, the mental formations in the mental formations.

When we're in contact with the suffering of another, a feeling of compassion is born in us immediately. Compassion literally means "to suffer with" the other. Looking in order to see the suffering in another person is the work of meditation. If we sit cross-legged, follow our breathing, and observe someone mindfully, we can be in contact with his suffering, and the energy of compassion arises in us. We can also do this while walking, standing, lying down, sitting, speaking, and acting, not just when we are sitting in meditation. The physical and psychological suffering of that person will be clear to us in the light of our mindful observation.

When the mind of compassion arises, we have to find ways to nourish and express it. When we come into contact with the other person, our thoughts and actions should express our mind of compassion, even if that person says and does things that are not easy to accept. We practice in this way until we see clearly that our love is not contingent upon the other person apologizing or being lovable. Then we can be sure that our mind of compassion is firm and authentic. We'll recognize in ourselves some of the beautiful signs of the compassionate mind:

1. our sleep is more relaxed
2. we do not have nightmares

3. our waking-state is more at ease
4. we're not anxious or depressed
5. we're protected by everyone and everything around us.

The person who has been the object of our meditation on compassion will also, eventually, benefit from our meditation. His suffering will slowly diminish, and his life will gradually be brighter and more joyful.

We can begin our meditation on compassion with someone who is undergoing suffering of a physical or material kind—someone who is weak and easily ill, poor, or oppressed, or has no protection. This kind of suffering is easy to see. We observe it deeply, either during sitting meditation or when we're actually in contact with it. We must have enough time if we're going to be in deep contact with the suffering of that person. We have to observe until the mind of compassion arises, and the substance of the mind of compassion penetrates into our being. Then the mind of compassion will envelop the object of our observation. If we observe deeply in this way, the mind of compassion will naturally be transformed into action. We won't just say, "I love her very much," but instead, "I must do something so that she'll suffer less." The mind of compassion is truly present when it has the capacity of removing suffering.

After that, we can practice being in contact with more subtle forms of suffering. Sometimes the other person doesn't seem to be suffering at all, but we may notice that she has sorrows which have left their marks in hidden ways. Someone with more than enough material comforts can also be subject to suffering. There are very few people who are not suffering to some degree. The person who has made us suffer is undoubtedly suffering too. We only need to sit down, follow our breathing, and look deeply, and naturally we'll see her suffering.

We may be able to see how her misery has come about because of the lack of skill of the parents who raised her. But her parents may have been the victims of their parents. The suffering has been transmitted from generation to generation, and it has been reborn in her. If we can see that, we'll no longer blame her for making us suffer, because we understand the way in which she is also a victim. To look deeply is to understand. Once we understand, it's easy to embrace the other person in our mind of compassion.

To look deeply into the suffering of those who have caused us to suffer is a miraculous gift. Thanks to our observation, we now know that the person is suffering. He may think that his suffering will be lessened if he can cause us to suffer. Once we're in touch with his suffering, our enmity and bitterness towards him will vanish, and we'll long for him to suffer less. The spring water of the compassionate mind begins to flow, and we ourselves are the first to be cleansed by it. We feel cool and light, and we can smile. We don't need two people to bring about reconciliation. When we look deeply, we become reconciled with ourselves and, for us, the problem no longer exists. Sooner or later, the other will see our attitude and share in the freshness of the stream of love which is flowing naturally in our hearts.

After we experience the fruit of the meditation of compassion, the meditation on love becomes relatively easy. Just as with the mind of compassion, the mind of love brings peace, joy, and happiness to the practitioner first. We know that if we don't have peace and joy ourselves, we won't have peace and joy to share with others. That's why the meditation on compassion and the meditation on love bring benefits both to the practitioner and to others.

When we reduce the suffering in others, we also bring them happiness at the same time. Although life is suffering, it also has many wonderful things like the early morning sky, the harvest moon, the forsythia bush, the violet bamboo, the stream of clear water, and the beautiful child. When we pay attention only to our suffering, we're not able to make contact with these wonderful things, and anything we say or do will not untie the knot of suffering and bring about the conditions for living joyfully. Mindful observation is the element that nourishes the tree of understanding, and compassion and love are the most beautiful flowers. When we realize the mind of love, we have to go to the one who has been the object of our mindful observation, so that our mind of love is not just an object of our imagination but is a source of energy that has an effect in the real world.

The Buddha teaches that during our meditation we can send our mind of love and compassion into the four directions and embrace all species of living beings. But we must be careful not to think that the meditations of love and compassion consist in just sitting still and imagining that our mind of love and compassion will spread out into space like waves of sound or light. Sound and light have the ability to penetrate everywhere, and love and compassion can do the same. But if our love and compassion are only a kind of imagining—for example, if we imagine they are like a pure white cloud that slowly forms and gradually spreads out and out to envelop the whole world—then they'll have no effect; they're only a cloud of the imagination. A true cloud can produce rain. It's only in the midst of our daily lives and in our actual contact with people and other species, including the objects of our meditation, that we can know whether our mind of love and compassion is really present and whether it is stable. If love and compassion are real, they'll be evident in our daily lives, in the way we talk with people and the way we act in the world. The sitting meditation position is not the only position in which we can give rise to the spring water of love and compassion.

Many people think that if they don't have influence and money, they can't realize love and compassion. In fact, the source of love and compassion is in us, and we can help many people suffer less and realize a lot of happiness without being rich or influential. One word, one action, or one thought can reduce another person's suffering and bring him joy. One word can give comfort and confidence, destroy doubt, help someone avoid a mistake, reconcile a conflict, open the door to liberation, or show him the way to success and happiness. One action can save a person's life or help him take advantage of a rare opportunity. One thought can do the same, because thoughts lead to words and action. If love and compassion are in our hearts, every thought, word, and deed can bring about a miracle. Because understanding is the very foundation of love and compassion, the words and actions engendered by love and compassion will be ones that are helpful. When we want to help, we know how to avoid the kind of love that does more harm than good. We must always remember that love is none other than understanding.

6: Exercises for
Observing the Objects of Mind

Exercise 16 | Discriminative Investigation

> When the factor of awakening, investigation-of-phenomena, is present in him, he is aware, 'Investigation-of-phenomena is present in me.' He is aware when not-yet-born investigation-of-phenomena is being born and when already-born investigation-of-phenomena is perfectly developed.

Ignorance, or delusion, is the erroneous perception of things. In order to correct our erroneous perceptions, the Buddha teaches us a method of discriminative investigation, which relates to the establishment of the mind and the establishment of the objects of mind. The objects of mind are also called dharmas (all that can be conceived of as existing). They include the six sense organs, the six sense objects, and the six sense consciousnesses. The six sense organs are the eyes, ears, nose, tongue, body, and mind. The six sense objects are form and color, sound, smell, taste, tactile objects, and mind objects (every concept and every thing that belongs to the sphere of memory and mental experience). The sense six consciousnesses are: eye consciousness (or sight), ear consciousness (or hearing), nose consciousness (or smelling), taste consciousness (or tasting), body consciousness (or touching), and mind consciousness. All dharmas are contained within these Eighteen Realms (Sanskrit: *dhatu*), which include all psychological, physiological, and physical aspects. All Eighteen Realms are also called objects of mind, including mental formations. When mind is observing mind, the mind becomes an object of mind.

The basic characteristic of all dharmas is interdependent origination. All dharmas arise, endure, and fade away according to the law of interdependence. In the Majjhima Nikaya, it is taught: "This is, because that is; this is not, because that is not. This is produced, because that is produced. This is destroyed, because that is destroyed." The Buddhist principle of interdependence, put forward with the utmost simplicity, is immeasurably deep. According to this teaching, no single dharma can arise by itself, endure by itself, and fade away by itself. The coming-to-be of one dharma is dependent on the coming-to-be, endurance, and destruction of other dharmas, in fact, of all other dharmas. Dharmas do not have independent existence. They're empty of a separate, independent existence.

In our daily lives, we're inclined to perceive things as real and independent of each other. Take, for example, a leaf we see on the branch in front of us. We may think that this leaf exists independently of all the other leaves, independently of the branch, the trunk, and the roots of the tree; independently of the clouds, the water, the earth, and the sky. In truth, this leaf could not be here without the presence of all the other things that we see as different from it. This leaf is one with the other leaves, the branch, the trunk, and the roots of the tree; with the clouds, the river, the earth, the sky, and the sunlight. If any one of these things were not present, the leaf could not be. If we look deeply into the leaf, we can see the presence of all these things. The leaf and these things are present together. This is the principle of interbeing and interpenetration, the principle of one is all and all is one, which the Avatamsaka Sutra, the most complete and sufficient expression of the Buddhist principle of interdependent origination, teaches. Things do not exist outside of each other. Things exist within each other and with each other. That is why the Buddha said: "This is, because that is." With the power of concentration, we can observe all that is in the light of this principle. All phenomena in the universe, including the thoughts, words, and feelings of both ourselves and those around us, need to be observed in the light of interdependence.

This method of discriminative investigation begins by classifying the dharmas into categories like the six sense organs, the six sense objects, and the six sense consciousnesses, namely, the Eighteen Realms, which can also be classified according to the Five Aggregates of form, feeling, perceptions, mental formations, and consciousness. By "form," we mean all physiological and physical phenomena. "Feelings" means pleasant, unpleasant, and neutral feelings. "Perceptions" means basic conceptualizations and naming. "Mental formations" means psychological states that arise and manifest in us. "Consciousness" is the function of maintaining, cognizing, comparing, storing, and remembering all the seeds. The basic Abhidharma writings and the teachings of the Vijñānavada school of Buddhist psychology give very thorough explanations of the essential nature of these five categories and the ways in which they function.

The Heart of the Prajñaparamita Sutra tells us that the Bodhisattva Avalokita, thanks to his observation of the Five Aggregates, was able to see the interdependent nature of all dharmas and realize their essential birthlessness and deathlessness, and so transcend the fear of birth and death. The same sutra refers to the essential emptiness (Sanskrit: *shunyata*) of all dharmas. Emptiness, here, means interdependence. All dharmas depend on each other in order to arise and to endure. There is no dharma that can exist apart from other dharmas, which is why we say that the real nature of dharmas is emptiness. Nothing can exist on its own.

Through discriminative investigation, we realize the interdependent nature of all that is. This is to realize the empty nature of all things. With insight into emptiness, we'll go beyond concepts of "it is" and "it is not," birth and death, one and many, coming and going, and we'll transcend the fear of birth and death. Our concepts of it is/it is not, birth/death, one/many, coming/going, and so on, will dissolve when we're witness to the interdependent nature of all that is. To be able to end the concept of birth and death is the essential point of discriminative investigation.

Some days before the layman Anathapindika passed away, the Buddha sent the Venerable Shariputra and the Venerable Ananda to visit him and instruct him in his practice. Sitting at the layman's bedside, the Venerable Shariputra began his instruction: "Layman Anathapindika, you should meditate like this: 'These eyes are not me. I am not caught in these eyes.'" Anathapindika breathed and meditated according to the instructions. Shariputra continued his instructions: "These ears, nose, tongue, body, and mind are not me. I am not caught by forms, sounds, smells, tastes, contacts, or the thoughts that I have." Anathapindika observed in this way in order to see gradually the interdependent nature of all that is, to see that he himself was not restricted to the Eighteen Realms (the six sense organs, the six sense objects, and the six sense consciousnesses), and to see that there's no birth that brings us into existence and no death that takes us from existence to nonexistence.

When he had practiced this much, Anathapindika began to weep, the tears falling down his cheeks. The Venerable Ananda asked, "What is it? Do you regret anything? Did you not succeed in the meditation?" Anathapindika replied, "Venerable Ananda, I have nothing to regret, and my meditation has been very successful. I'm crying because I am so moved. I have been lucky enough to have served the Buddha and his community for many years, but I have never heard a teaching so deep, so wonderful, and so precious as the teaching transmitted by the Venerable Shariputra today."

"Layman Anathapindika, do you not know that the Buddha is always giving this teaching to monks and nuns?" Ananda said.

"Venerable Ananda, please tell the Buddha that laypersons such as myself could also listen to this wonderful teaching. There are laypeople who are too busy to hear, understand, and put into practice these wonderful and deep teachings, but there are also laypeople with the capacity to listen, understand, and put into practice these wonderful and deep teachings."

This excerpt about the layman Anathapindika (Majjhima Nikaya no. 143) shows us that anyone can practice the mindful observation of the interdependent and empty nature of things, not just monks or nuns. The life of a layperson is not so busy that he is not able to enjoy the taste of the highest teachings of Buddhism.

The Sutra on the Four Establishments of Mindfulness also describes the mind that is not in a state of ignorance and confusion, as when we are conscious of impermanence, interdependence, and selflessness; when our mind rests in Right View. Right View is one of the eight ways of practice called the Noble Eightfold Path.

In the section that teaches how to be mindful of the objects of mind, among the Seven Factors of Awakening (Sanskrit: *saptabodhyanga*), the investigation of dharmas is mentioned. Investigation of dharmas means the detailed examination of the source and the nature of phenomena whether physical or psychological. Investigation of dharmas has a meaning similar to discriminative investigation and is also intended to see the source and the nature of dharmas. If we can understand in depth the source and the nature of dharmas, then our minds are not in a state of ignorance or confusion.

Each of the above fifteen exercises from the Satipatthana Sutta has, to a greater or lesser degree, the function of mindfully observing the source of dharmas. The most obvious examples are the eighth exercise—observation of the interdependence of the body and all that is in the universe: earth, water, air, and fire—and the twelfth exercise—the observation of the source and the nature of our feelings.

When sitting in meditation, we concentrate our minds on the object of our observation—sometimes a physical phenomenon, sometimes psychological—and we look deeply into that object in order to discover its source and its nature. The role of our conscious breathing is to nourish and maintain our power of concentration on one object. If we look carefully and deeply, naturally we'll see that the arising, enduring, and ending of the object is dependent on other things. Eventually we'll see that the true nature of all dharmas is birthlessness and deathlessness, and that although dharmas are not everlasting, they're never totally destroyed. Thus, the mindful observation of interdependence is the road that leads us to transcend the limits of birth and death. A student of Buddhism who doesn't practice the mindful observation of interdependence hasn't yet arrived at the quintessence of the Buddhist path.

Exercise 17 | *Observing Internal Formations*

> He is aware of the eyes [ears, nose, tongue, body, mind] and aware of the form [sound, smell, taste, touch, objects of mind], and he is aware of the internal formations which are produced in dependence on these two things. He is aware of the birth of a new internal formation and is aware of abandoning an already produced internal formation, and he is aware when an already abandoned internal formation will not arise again.

In the section of the sutra that refers to the observation of the six sense organs and the six sense objects, we see the term "internal formations." The word in Sanskrit is *samyojana*, which can also be translated as "knots," "fetters," "agglomeration," or "binding together."

Internal formations can be classified as two kinds, the Five Dull Knots: confusion, desire, anger, pride, and doubt; and the Five Sharp Knots: view of the body as self, extreme views, wrong views, perverted views, and superstitious views (or unnecessary ritual prohibitions). The latter are easier to correct. When the eyes see form, the ears hear sound, the nose smells a scent, the tongue tastes something, the body touches something, or the mind cognizes an object, knots may or may not be tied, depending on the way in which our minds receive these impressions. When someone speaks unkindly to us, if we understand the reason and we do not take the words to heart, we won't feel at all irritated, and knots won't be formed in our minds. If we don't understand the reason and we feel irritated, a knot will form. The substance of this knot will be hatred. When we misunderstand someone's words or behavior, the knot that forms is confusion, which often gives rise to irritation, pride, attachment, and doubt. The knot of confusion, a lack of clear seeing, or ignorance (Sanskrit: *avidya*), is the basis for every other knot.

The feelings associated with internal formations are usually unpleasant, but sometimes internal formations are associated with pleasant feelings. When we are attached to a form, sound, scent, taste, touch, or mind object, an internal formation of the nature of desire is formed. To begin with, it can be associated with a pleasant feeling. But because we become attached to it, we are bound, and when the demands of the attachment are not met, the feelings become unpleasant. Anything from wine, tobacco, or opium to beautiful forms, good food, music, or words of praise can produce a knot in us, an internal formation that begins as a pleasant feeling. Once we have a such a knot, we are tied tightly by it, and we are forced to seek out the object of sense again and again in order to repeat the pleasant feeling.

Falling in love is also an internal formation, because in it there is the material of blind attachment. The term to "fall" in love in itself sounds disastrous. People often refer to love-sickness, as if falling in love were a disease. The French expression *coup de foudre* (struck by lightning) describes falling in love as a sharp blow. But being in love can be transformed, so that blind attachment, selfishness, and domination are replaced by the capacity to understand and bring happiness to the person we love, without demanding specific conditions and expecting something in return. To transform being in love in this way is to transform an internal formation.

Feelings of sorrow in us are also internal formations that arise from confusion, desire, hatred, pride, and doubt. If these roots of affliction are not transformed, the feelings of sorrow will remain intact in us. In everyday life, seeds of sorrow can be sown in our consciousness with or without the collaboration of others. Others may say or do things that produce knots in us, but if we give birth to the seeds of understanding, tolerance, love, and compassion, then what they say and do will not produce any internal formations in us. It depends on the way in which we receive what happens to us in our daily lives. If we are stable, relaxed, understanding, loving, compassionate, and not caught in egotism, then the things others do and say will not have the force to produce an internal formation in us.

If we live according to the teachings of the Four Establishments of Mindfulness, we practice mindful observation of the arising, duration, and transformation of internal formations. In our daily lives, we practice full awareness in order to be able to recognize the internal formation just born and find a way to transform it. If we allow internal formations to grow strong in us, the time will come when they will dominate us, and the work of transforming them will be extremely difficult. An internal formation of hatred, desire, or doubt needs our full attention as soon as it arises so that it may be transformed. When it arises for the first time, the knot is still very "loose" and the work of "untying it" is easy.

When we live with another person, we should help each other transform the internal formations that we have produced in each other. By practicing understanding and loving speech, we can help each other a great deal. Happiness is no longer an individual matter. If the other person is not happy, we will not be happy either. Therefore, to transform the internal formations in the other is to bring about our own happiness as well. A person can create internal formations in her partner, and her partner can do so for her, and if they continue to create knots in each other, one day they'll have no happiness left. A person needs to recognize quickly any newly formed knot inside herself. She should take the time to observe it and, with her partner's help, transform the internal formation. She might say, "Darling, I have an internal formation. Can you please help me?" This is easy when the states of mind of both partners are still light and not loaded with many internal formations.

As we have already seen, the material of any internal formation is ignorance or confusion. If we can see the ignorance that is present during the creation of a knot, we can easily untie it. In the twelfth exercise (mindfully observing the source and nature of feelings), the fourteenth exercise (mindfully observing anger), and the fifteenth exercise (observing with compassion), we have seen that if we're aware of interdependence and multiple causation, we can see the roots and the nature of our minds and transform and transcend unpleasant states.

Mindful observation is to look and be able to see the nature of dharmas. The transformation of an internal formation is the result of this insight.

Exercise 18 | *Transforming Internal Formations*

> He is aware of the eyes [ears, nose, tongue, body, mind] and aware of the form [sound, smell, taste, touch, objects of mind], and he is aware of the internal formations which are produced in dependence on these two things. He is aware of the birth of a new internal formation and is aware of abandoning an already produced internal formation, and he is aware when an already abandoned internal formation will not arise again.

This exercise uses the same quote from the sutra as Exercise 17. This exercise aims at putting us in touch with and transforming internal formations that are buried and repressed in ourselves. The internal formations of desire, anger, fear, feeling worthless, and regret have been suppressed in our subconscious for a long time. Although they are suppressed, they are always seeking ways to manifest in our feelings, thoughts, words, and actions. It is easy for us to observe our internal formations when they appear as feelings on the surface of consciousness, but internal formations that are repressed cannot appear in a direct and natural way in the conscious mind. They only disclose themselves indirectly. Thus, we're not aware of their presence, although they continue to tie us up and make us suffer in a latent way.

What is it that represses them and does not let them appear? It is our conscious, reasoning mind. We know that our desires and anger are not wholly acceptable to society and to our own reasoning mind, so we've found a way to repress them, to push them into remote areas of our consciousness in order to be able to forget them. This is the work of a mental formation called *mushita smrti*, forgetfulness. Contemporary psychology understands repression. Because we want to avoid suffering, there are defense mechanisms in us that push our psychological pains, conflicts, and unacceptable desires into our unconscious so that we can feel more at peace with ourselves. But our long-standing repressions are always looking for ways to manifest in words, images, and behavior unacceptable to society and can later become symptoms of physical and psychological illness. We may know that our words, thoughts, and behavior are destructive, but we can't do anything about them because our internal formations are so strong.

Take for example a daughter who, on the one hand, wants to be with a partner or do her own things in the world, and on the other hand does not want to leave her mother to live all alone. The daughter understands and loves her mother, but she also wants to be independent and/or live with the person she loves. However, her mother is sick and needs someone to support her, and the daughter can't bear the thought of leaving her alone. The opposing desires and feelings bring about an internal conflict in the daughter. And so her defense mechanism represses the pain of the conflict in her unconscious and tells her to devote her life to supporting her mother. Nevertheless, the desire to be with her own partner is still there, and the psychological conflict remains an internal formation looking for a way to manifest. She becomes irritable and says things that even she herself does not understand, and she has dreams that are incomprehensible to her. She is not happy, and so her mother can't be happy either. In fact, her mother has been haunted for years by the fear that her daughter will leave her, and it is this psychological factor that made her unexpectedly fall sick and grow weak, although she's not aware of it. When she heard her daughter say that she was going to stay, she was very pleased, but in the depths of her heart, she suffers because she knows that her daughter is prevented from doing something she wants to do. This conflict becomes an internal formation in the mother, that makes her suffer, and the mother also becomes irritable and says things that she herself does not understand. She also has dreams she doesn't understand, and she does things without knowing why she's doing them. Neither the mother nor the daughter is happy, and both continue to suffer.

The method of curing the sorrow that comes when internal formations are repressed is the deep observation of these internal formations. But to observe them, first of all we have to find ways to bring them into the realm of the conscious mind. The method of the Sutra on the Four Establishments of Mindfulness is to practice conscious breathing in order to recognize our feelings, thoughts, words, and actions, especially those that arise automatically, as reactions to what is happening. Our reactions may have their roots in the internal formations buried inside us.

When we're aware of what we are feeling, thinking, and doing, we can ask ourselves questions like: Why do I feel uncomfortable when I hear someone say that? Why do I always think of my mother when I see that woman? Why did I say that to him? Why didn't I like that character in the film? Whom did I hate in the past who this person resembles? Practices like this can help us discover the roots of our feelings, thoughts, words, and behavior and gradually bring the internal formations buried in us into the realm of the conscious mind.

During our sitting meditation, because we have closed the doors of our sensory input in order to stop listening, looking, and reasoning, the internal formations that are buried in us have the opportunity to reveal themselves in the form of feelings or images that manifest in our conscious mind. To begin with, there may be just a feeling of anxiety, fear, or unpleasantness, whose cause we can't see. We have to shine the light of mindfulness on it and be ready to see this feeling.

When this feeling begins to show its face and to gather strength and become more intense, we may feel it robs us of all our peace, joy, and ease. We may not want to be in contact with it anymore. We may want to move our attention to another object of meditation. We may not want to continue with the meditation, and we may say that we're sleepy and would prefer to meditate some other time. In modern psychology, this is called resistance. Deep down we are afraid to bring into our conscious mind the feelings of pain that are buried within us, because they'll make us suffer.

There are people who practice sitting meditation many hours a day, but they do not really dare to face and invite their feelings of pain into their conscious mind. They deceive themselves that these feelings aren't important and they give their attention to other subjects of meditation—impermanence, selflessness, the sound of one hand clapping, or the reason Bodhidharma came to the West. This isn't to suggest that these subjects are unimportant, but they should be considered in the light of our real problems in order to be authentic subjects for meditation practice.

We don't practice mindfulness in Buddhism in order to repress our feelings, but as a way of looking after our feelings, being their sponsor in an affectionate, nonviolent way. When we're able to maintain mindfulness, we're not carried away by or drowned in our feelings or in the conflicts within ourselves. We nourish and maintain mindfulness through conscious breathing and try to become aware of our internal formations and conflicts as they manifest. We receive them with love as a mother takes her child in her arms: "Mindfulness is present, and I know that I have enough strength to be in contact with the knots in me." In this kind of an environment, our internal formations will manifest as feelings and images in our minds that we can contact and identify fully and deeply.

Without judgment, blame, or criticism for having these feelings or images, we just observe, identify, and accept them in order to see their source and their true nature. If there's pain, we feel the pain. If there's sadness, we are sad. If there's anger, then we are angry, but our anger is accompanied by mindfulness. We don't lose ourselves in the pain, the sadness, or the anger, but we calm them down. Even if we haven't seen the roots of the internal formations, the fact that we can greet our pain, our sadness, and our anger in mindfulness already causes our internal knots to lose some of their strength. Thanks to our vigilant observation, eventually we'll see their roots and transform them. The teaching of the Sutra on the Four Establishments of Mindfulness on how to be in direct contact with our feelings and invite them up to manifest on the surface of our consciousness is wonderfully effective. The practitioner can work with difficult internal formations with the help of a teacher or of a co-practitioner. The teacher and the co-practitioners, because of their mindful observation, can help point out to him the manifestations of the internal formations that lie deep in his consciousness.

In his lifetime, the Buddha was praised as being a King of Doctors, and he helped thousands of people, including King Ajatashatru of Magadha, deal with mental problems. Those who practice mindful observation can learn the Buddhist way of dealing with internal formations in order to help themselves and others. Because many people live without practicing mindfulness and don't know how to transform internal formations, over time these internal formations become strong and lead to agitation, anxiety, and depression, which express themselves in speech and behavior that are not easily acceptable by society. Those with strong internal formations have difficulty relating to and working with others, and these difficulties make them feel more and more unsuccessful in society. As their internal formations increase, their behavior becomes more and more inappropriate, and eventually, the pressure may become so great that they'll have to quit their job or abandon their marriage.

If we know how to live every moment in an awakened way, we'll be aware of what's happening in our feelings and perceptions in the present moment and won't let internal formations become too tight in our consciousness. If we know how to observe our feelings, we can find the causes of long-standing internal formations and transform them.

Exercise 19 | Overcoming Guilt and Fear

> When agitation and remorse are present in him, he is aware, 'Agitation and remorse are present in me.' When agitation and remorse are not present in him, he is aware, 'Agitation and remorse are not present in me.' When agitation and remorse begin to arise, he is aware of it. When already arisen agitation and remorse are abandoned, he is aware of it. When agitation and remorse already abandoned will not arise again in the future, he is aware of it.

In Buddhist psychology, remorse or regret (Sanskrit: *kaukrtya*) is a mind function that can be either beneficial or damaging. When it's utilized to recognize errors we've made and to resolve not to commit the same mistakes in the future, then regret is a wholesome mental formation. If regret creates a guilt-complex that follows and haunts us, then it's an obstacle to our practice.

We have all made mistakes in the past. But these mistakes can be erased. We may think that because the past is gone, we can't return to the past to correct our mistakes. But the past has created the present, and if we practice mindfulness in the present, we naturally are in contact with the past. As we transform the present, we also transform the past. Our ancestors, parents, brothers, and sisters are all closely linked to us—our suffering and happiness is closely linked to theirs, just as their suffering and happiness is closely linked to ours. If we can transform ourselves, we also transform them. Our own emancipation, peace, and joy is the emancipation, peace, and joy of our ancestors and our parents. To take hold of the present in order to transform it is the unique way to bring peace, joy, and emancipation to those we love and to heal the damage done in the past.

Confession in Buddhism is based on the fact that we commit errors by means of our minds, and so by means of our minds those errors can be erased. If we take hold of life in the present moment in order to transform ourselves, we can create joy for ourselves and for everyone else as well. This transformation will bring about real joy and peace in the present and also in the future. It's not just a hollow promise to do better. If we can take hold of our breathing and live in a mindful way, thus bringing joy and happiness to ourselves and others in the present moment, we can overcome our complexes of guilt so that we're no longer paralyzed by them.

For example, the guilt complex that follows someone who has caused the death of a child out of mindlessness is a very strong complex. But if that person practices mindfulness and is able to be in real contact with the present moment, knowing what to do and what not to do in the present moment, she can save the lives of many children. Many small children die for want of medicine. Many children die through accidents or for want of proper care and attention. So she can work to save the children who are dying instead of imprisoning herself and dying slowly in the chains of regret.

Fear is also a dominant internal formation in many of us. The ground of fear is ignorance, the failure to understand our "not-self" nature. Insecurity and fear of what might happen to us and those dear to us are feelings we all have, but for some, these insecurities and fears dominate their consciousness. In Mahayana Buddhism, the bodhisattva Avalokitesvara is described as the one who has transcended all fear. He offers all beings the gift of non-fear (Sanskrit: *abhaya*), which comes from the mindful observation of the no-birth, no-death, no-increase, and no-decrease nature of all that is. The Prajñaparamita Heart Sutra is an exhortation on fearlessness. If we can observe deeply the interdependent and selfless nature of all things, we can see that there is no birth and no death and pass beyond all fear.[37]

Since everything is impermanent, disease and accidents can happen to us or to those we love at any time. We must accept this reality. If we live every moment of our lives mindfully and relate beautifully with those around us, we'll have nothing to fear and nothing to regret, even when there is a crisis in our lives. If we know that birth and death are both necessary aspects of life, we'll see that if our mother the Earth has brought us to life once, she will bring us to life one hundred thousand times more, and we will not be afraid or suffer when she reaches out her arms to welcome us back. An Awakened One remains unperturbed while riding the waves of birth and death.

Some people, because they received so many internal formations during childhood, are obsessed by feelings of insecurity. Their parents may have terrorized them, filled them with guilt, and exploited them.

For people like this, receiving and practicing the Five Mindfulness Trainings is a most effective means of protection. Practicing the mindfulness trainings, they will be able to reestablish the balance between themselves and their environment. Taking and observing the trainings is an effective means for healing the wounds of the past and influencing society for the better in the present and the future. Practicing mindfulness in order to guard the six senses, dwell in the present moment, and be in contact with life is a wonderful way of establishing a sense of security in everyday life. If in addition we have friends who also observe and practice mindfulness, our practice will have a firm and stable support.

Exercise 20 | Sowing Seeds of Peace

> When the factor of awakening, joy (ease, letting go), is present in him, he is aware, 'Joy is present in me.' When joy is not present in him, he is aware, 'Joy is not present in me.' He is aware when not-yet-born joy is being born and when already-born joy is perfectly developed.

The purpose of this exercise is to sow and water the seeds of peace, joy, and liberation in us. If internal formations are the seeds of suffering, then joy, peace, and liberation are the seeds of happiness.

Buddhist psychology talks of seeds as the basis of every state of mind and the content of our consciousness. Certain seeds were transmitted to us by our parents and our ancestors. These are seeds of Buddha, Bodhisattva, Pratyekabuddha (one who has reached liberation by one's own efforts but just for one's own sake), Sravaka (one who practices as a disciple by listening to the teachings), God, Human, Warrior-God, Animal, Hungry Ghost, and Hell-Being. This means that before we were born, there were already many kinds of wholesome and unwholesome seeds in us. In addition, there are many kinds of seeds that form in us from an early age, planted by our family, school, and society. Seeds that produce suffering we can call "unwholesome," and seeds that produce happiness we can call "wholesome."

According to the principle of interdependent origination, seeds do not have a fixed nature. Every seed is dependent on every other seed for its existence, and in any one seed, all the other seeds are present. Any unwholesome seed contains within it the germ of wholesome seeds, and a wholesome seed contains within it the germ of unwholesome seeds. Just as there has to be night for there to be day and death for there to be birth, an unwholesome seed can be transformed into a wholesome seed, and a wholesome seed can be transformed into an unwholesome seed. This fact tells us that in the darkest times of our lives, in the times of the greatest suffering, the seeds of peace, joy, and happiness are still present in us. If we know how to contact the seeds of joy, peace, and happiness that are already present in us, and if we know how to water and look after them, they will germinate and bring us the fruits of peace, joy, and liberation.

The sutra is always reminding us of the two contrasting aspects of the mind. The state of mind that has no desire is a wholesome state of mind called "desirelessness." The state of mind that has no anger is a wholesome state of mind called "no-anger." Desirelessness, no-anger, and freedom are wholesome seeds in the mind that need to be watered and cared for.

The sutras often refer to the mind as a plot of ground in which all sorts of seeds are sown. That is why we have the Sanskrit term *cittabhumi*, "the mind as the earth." When we practice mindfulness, we should not just observe the phenomena of birth, old age, sickness, death, desire, hatred, aversion, ignorance, doubt, and wrong views. We should also take the time to observe objects of the mind that lead to health, joy, and emancipation in order to enable wholesome seeds to germinate and flower in the field of the mind. Observing Buddha, Dharma, Sangha, love, compassion, joy, letting go, mindfulness, investigation of dharmas, ease, happiness, and equanimity, is always encouraged in Buddhism. Joy (Sanskrit: *mudita*), for example, is not just the joy that arises from the joy of others, but also the feeling of well-being that arises in ourselves. Mudita is one of the Four Unlimited Minds; love, compassion, and letting go or equanimity are the other three. The seeds of mudita are in all of us. Only when we have joy in our lives can we be happy and have the means to share our happiness with others. If we do not have joy, what can we share with others? If the seeds of our joy are buried under many layers of suffering, how can we smile and share joy with others? This exercise helps us stay in touch with the wholesome seeds in us so that they have a chance to develop.

Life is filled with suffering, but it is also filled with many wonderful things. There is spring as well as winter, light as well as darkness, health as well as sickness, gentle breezes and delightful rains as well as tempests and floods. Our eyes, ears, hearts, half-smiles, and breathing are wonderful phenomena. We only need to open our eyes and we can see the blue sky, the white clouds, the rose, the clear river, the golden fields of wheat, the shining eyes of a child. We only have to attune our ears to hear the whispering pines and the waves washing up on the shore. Everything is impermanent. Everything is in a temporary form. Nevertheless, there are many wonderful things. In us and around us, there are so many wondrous phenomena in nature that can refresh and heal us. If we can be in contact with them, we will receive their healing benefits. If peace and joy are in our hearts, we will gradually bring more peace and joy to the world.

The blue sky, the white clouds, the gentle breezes, the delightful rains, political stability, free speech, good schools for children, beautiful flowers, and good health—these are the positive ingredients of peace and happiness that exist alongside the negative ingredients such as war, sexism, social injustice, racial discrimination, economic inequality, and hunger and starvation. It is important that we be aware of these ugly, dangerous things in the world, so that we can begin to improve the situation. But if, day after day, we are only in contact with our anxieties and our anger about what is ugly and corrupt, we will lose our joy and our ability to serve others. That is why we have to be in contact with the peaceful and positive aspects in and around us and be able to enjoy them. We need to teach our children how to appreciate these wondrous and precious things. If we know how to appreciate them, we will know how to protect them. This basic practice will protect our happiness and our children's happiness as well.

There are many people who, although they know in theory that a flower is a wonderful thing, are unable to be in contact with it, because the sorrow in their hearts has closed them off. In the past, they may not have allowed themselves to be in contact with the refreshing, healthy seeds in their consciousness, and as a result, they are now cut off from them. The seventh precept of the Order of Interbeing reminds us to practice conscious breathing in order to stay in contact with the many healing and refreshing elements that are already around us. At times we may need the support of a friend to help us get back in touch with what is wonderful in life. "A meal needs soup as the practice needs friends" is a Vietnamese proverb about the importance of practicing with friends. Such a community of friends and fellow practitioners is called a Sangha. On the path of practice we need the support of this community, and so we say, "I take refuge in the Sangha."

Having one calm, joyful friend who is balanced and can understand and support us in times of difficulty is a great fortune. When we feel helpless, depressed, and discouraged, we can go to that friend, and, sitting with him, we can reestablish our equilibrium and once again be able to contact the flower and the other wonderful, refreshing things that exist within us and around us. If we receive the benefits of the joy that our friend brings us, we can refresh the seeds of healing in us that have become weak because they have not been cared for or watered for a long time.

The seeds of understanding, love, peace, joy, and liberation need to be sown and watered constantly by living our daily lives in mindfulness. The Sutra on the Four Establishments of Mindfulness offers many exercises for living in mindfulness. By the process of conscious breathing, smiling, walking meditation, sitting meditation, by our way of looking, listening and mindfully observing, we help the seeds of happiness flourish. The realms of love, compassion, joy, and letting go are the realms of true joy and happiness. If we have joy and can let go, we can share happiness with others and reduce their sorrows and anxieties.

7: Principles for the Practice of Mindfulness

All dharmas—physical, physiological, and psychological—are objects of mind, but that does not mean that they exist separately from the mind. All Four Establishments of Mindfulness—body, feelings, mind, and dharmas—are objects of mind. Since mind and objects of mind are one, in observing its objects, mind is essentially observing mind. The word "dharma" in Buddhism is understood to mean the object of the mind and the content of the mind. Dharmas are classified as one of the Twelve Realms (Sanskrit: *ayatana*). The first six of these realms are the sense organs: eyes, ears, nose, tongue, body, and mind. The remaining six are form, sound, smell, taste, touch, and dharmas. Dharmas are the object of the mind, as sounds are the object of the ears. The object of cognition and the subject of cognition do not exist independently of each other. Everything that exists has to arise in the mind. The culminating phase of the development of this principle is expressed in the phrase, "All is just mind. All phenomena are just consciousness," which means, "Because of mind, all can exist. Because of consciousness, all phenomena can exist." This is developed in the Vijñaptimatra school of Mahayana Buddhism.

In the Southern traditions of Buddhism, the idea of mind as the source of all dharmas is also very clear. The term *cittasamutthan* (mind-arising) and the term *cittaja* (mind-born) are often used in the Pali Abhidhamma writings. In the Patthana (equivalent to the Sanskrit Mahapakarana), the phrase *cittam samutthanam ca rupanam* ("and mind is the arising point of forms") is found.

The object of our mindful observation can be our breath or our toe (physiological), a feeling or a perception (psychological), or a form (physical). Whether the phenomenon we observe is physiological, psychological, or physical, we know that it is not separate from our minds and is of one substance with our minds. The mind can be understood as individual mind and as collective mind. The Vijñanavada teachings make this very clear. We need to avoid thinking that the object we are observing is independent of the mind. We have to remember that it is manifested from our individual and collective consciousnesses. We observe the object of our mind in the way the right hand takes hold of the left hand. Your right hand is you and your left hand is also you. So the hand is taking hold of itself to become one with itself.

BE ONE WITH THE OBJECT OF OBSERVATION

The subject of observation is our mindfulness, which also emanates from the mind. Mindfulness has the function of illuminating and transforming. When our breathing, for example, is the object of our mindfulness, it becomes conscious breathing. Mindfulness shines its light on our breathing, transforms the forgetfulness in it into mindfulness, and gives it a calming and healing quality. Our bodies and our feelings are also illuminated and transformed under the light of mindfulness.

Mindfulness is the observing mind, but it does not stand outside of the object of observation. It goes right into the object and becomes one with it. Because the nature of the observing mind is mindfulness, the observing mind does not lose itself in the object but transforms it by illuminating it, just as the penetrating light of the sun transforms trees and plants.

If we want to see and understand, we have to penetrate and become one with the object. If we stand outside of it in order to observe it, we cannot really see and understand it. The work of observation is the work of penetrating and transforming. That is why the sutra says, "observing the body in the body, observing the feelings in the feelings, observing the mind in the mind, observing dharmas in dharmas." The description is very clear. The deeply observing mind is not merely an observer but a participant. Only when the observer is a participant can there be transformation.

In the practice called bare observation, mindfulness has already begun to influence the object of consciousness. When we call an in-breath an in-breath, the existence of our breath becomes very clear. Mindfulness has already penetrated our breathing. If we continue in our mindful observation, there will no longer be a duality between observer and observed. Mindfulness and breath are one. We and our breath are one. If our breath is calm, we are calm. Our breathing calms our bodies and our feelings. This is the method taught in the Sutra on the Four Establishments of Mindfulness and the Sutra on the Full Awareness of Breathing.

If our minds are consumed by a sense desire or by what we are observing, mindfulness is not present. Conscious breathing nourishes mindfulness, and mindfulness gives rise to conscious breathing. When mindfulness is present, we have nothing to fear. The object of our observation becomes vivid, and its source, origin, and true nature become evident. That is how it will be transformed. It no longer has the effect of binding us.

When the object of our mindful observation is totally clear, the mind that is observing is also fully revealed in great clarity. To see dharmas clearly is to see the mind clearly. When dharmas reveal themselves in their true nature, then the mind has the nature of the highest under-standing. The subject and the object of cognition are not separate.

TRUE MIND AND DELUDED MIND ARE ONE

"True mind" and "deluded mind" are two aspects of the mind. Both arise from the mind. Deluded mind is the forgetful and dispersed mind, which arises from forgetfulness. The basis of true mind is awakened understanding, arising from mindfulness. Mindful observation brings out the light that exists in true mind, so that life can be revealed in its reality. In that light, confusion becomes understanding, wrong views become right views, mirages become reality, and deluded mind becomes true mind. Once mindful observation is born, it will penetrate the object of observation, illuminate it, and gradually reveal its true nature. The true mind arises from deluded mind. Things in their true nature and illusions are of the same basic substance. That is why practice is a matter of transforming deluded mind and not a matter of seeking for a true mind elsewhere. Just as the surface of a rough sea and that of the sea when it is calm are both manifestations of the same sea, true mind could not exist if there were no deluded mind. In the teaching on the Three Doors to Liberation (Pali: *vimokkha-mukha*), aimlessness

(Sanskrit: *apranihita*) is the foundation for realization. What is meant by aimlessness is that we do not seek after an object outside of ourselves. In Mahayana Buddhism, the teaching of nonattainment is the highest expression of the oneness of true mind and deluded mind.

If the rose is on its way to becoming garbage, then the garbage is also on its way to becoming a rose. She who observes discerningly will see the nondual character of the rose and the garbage. She will be able to see that there is garbage in the rose and that there are roses in the garbage. She will know that the rose needs the garbage for its existence, and the garbage needs the rose, because it is the rose that becomes garbage. Therefore, she will know how to accept the garbage in order to transform it into roses and will not be afraid when she sees the rose wither and turn into garbage. This is the principle of nonduality. If true mind (the rose) can be discovered in the raw material of deluded mind (the garbage), then we can also recognize true mind in the very substance of illusion, in the substance of birth and death.

To be liberated is not to run away from or abandon the Five Skandhas of form, feelings, perceptions, mental formations, and consciousness. Even if our bodies are full of impurities and even if the world is of the nature of illusion, it does not mean that to be liberated we need to run away from our bodies or from the world. The world of liberation and awakened understanding comes directly from this body and this world. Once Right Understanding is realized, we transcend the discriminations between pure and impure and illusory and real objects of perception. If the gardener is able to see that the rose comes directly from the garbage, then the practitioner on the path of meditation can see that nirvana comes directly from birth and death, and she no longer runs away from birth and death or seeks after nirvana. "The roots of affliction (Sanskrit: *klesa*) are the same as the awakened state. Nirvana and birth and death are illusory images in space." These quotations express deep insight into nonduality. The substance of this insight is equanimity or letting go (Sanskrit: *upeksha*), one of the Four Unlimited Minds.

The Buddha taught very clearly that we should not be attached to being or nonbeing. Being means the desire realm. Nonbeing means the realm of nihilism. To be liberated is to be free from both.

THE WAY OF NO-CONFLICT

The realization of nonduality naturally leads to the practice of offering joy, peace, and nonviolence. If the gardener knows how to deal with the organic garbage without conflict and discrimination, then the practitioner of meditation should also know how to deal with the Five Aggregates without conflict or discrimination. The Five Aggregates are the basis of suffering and confusion, but they are also the basis of peace, joy, and liberation. We should not have an attitude of attachment or aversion to the Five Aggregates. It is clearly stated in the sutra that the practitioner observes, having put aside every craving and every distaste for this life (Pali: *vineyya loke abhijjha domanassam*).

Before realizing the awakened state, Siddhartha practiced austerities, repressing his body and his feelings. Methods such as these are violent in nature, and the results are only negative. After that period of practice, he changed and practiced nonviolence and no-conflict in relation to his body and his feelings.

The method taught by the Buddha in the Sutra on the Four Establishments of Mindfulness clearly expresses the spirit of nonviolence and no-conflict. Mindfulness recognizes what is happening in the body and the mind and then continues to illuminate and observe the object deeply. During this practice, there is no craving for, running after, or repressing the object. This is the true meaning of the term bare observation. There is no coveting and no distaste. We know that our bodies and our feelings are ourselves and therefore we do not repress them, because to do so would be to repress ourselves. On the contrary, we accept our bodies and our feelings. Accepting does not mean craving. By accepting, we naturally reach a degree of peace and understanding. Peace and joy arise when we drop the discrimination between right and wrong; between the mind that observes and the body that is being observed (which we say is impure); between the mind that observes and the feelings that are being observed (which we say are painful).

When we accept our bodies and our feelings, we treat them in an affectionate, nonviolent way. The Buddha taught us to practice mindfulness of physiological and psychological phenomena in order to observe them, not in order to suppress them. When we accept our bodies, make peace with them, and calm their functioning, not feeling aversion to them, we are following the teachings of the Buddha: "Breathing in, I am aware of my whole body. Breathing out, I am calming the functions of my body" (Sutra on the Full Awareness of Breathing). In observation meditation, we do not turn ourselves into a battlefield with the good side fighting the bad. When we can see the nonduality of the rose and the garbage, the roots of affliction and the awakened mind, we are no longer afraid. We accept our afflictions, look after them as a mother looks after her child, and transform them.

When we recognize the roots of affliction in us and become one with them, whether we are entrapped in them or not depends on our state of mind. When we are forgetful, we may be caught by our roots of affliction, and so we become our roots of affliction. When we are mindful, we can see our roots of affliction clearly and transform them. Therefore, it is essential to see our roots of affliction in mindfulness. As long as the lamp of mindfulness shines its light, the darkness is transformed. We need to nourish mindfulness in ourselves by the practices of conscious breathing, hearing the sound of a bell, reciting gathas, and many other skillful means.

We need an attitude of kindness and nonviolence toward our bodies. We should not look on our bodies as only instruments or mistreat them. When we are tired or in pain, our bodies are trying to tell us that they are not happy and at ease. The body has its own language. As practitioners of mindfulness, we should know what our bodies are saying to us. When we feel a lot of pain in our legs during sitting meditation, we should smile and change our position slowly and gently in mindfulness. There is nothing wrong with changing our position. It does not waste our time. As long as mindfulness is maintained, the work of meditation continues. We should not bully ourselves. When we push ourselves around like that, not only do we lose our peace of mind and our joy, but we also lose our mindfulness and concentration. We practice sitting meditation to have liberation, peace, and joy, not to become a hero who is capable of enduring a lot of pain.

We also need a nonviolent attitude with regard to our feelings. Because we know that our feelings are ourselves, we do not neglect or overrule them. We embrace them affectionately in the arms of mindfulness, as a mother embraces her newborn child when it cries. A mother embraces the child with all her love for the child to feel comforted and stop crying. Mindfulness nourished by conscious breathing takes the feelings in its arms, becomes one with them, calms and transforms them.

Before the Buddha attained full realization of the path, he tried various methods of using the mind to suppress the mind, and he failed. That is why he chose to practice in a nonviolent way. The Buddha recounted in the Mahasaccaka Sutra (Madhyama Agama 36):

> I thought, why do I not grit my teeth, press my tongue against my palate, use my mind to overrule my mind, use my mind to repress my mind? Then, as a wrestler might take hold of the head or the shoulders of someone weaker than him, and, in order to restrain and coerce that person, he has to hold him down constantly without letting go for a moment, so I gritted my teeth, pressed my tongue against my palate, and used my mind to overrule and suppress my mind. As I did this, I was bathed in sweat. Although I was not lacking in strength, although I maintained mindfulness and did not fall from mindfulness, my body and my mind were not at peace, and I was worn out by these exhausting efforts. This practice caused other feelings of pain to arise in me besides the pain associated with the austerities, and I was not able to tame my mind.

It is clear from this passage that the Buddha regarded this kind of practice as not useful. Yet this passage was inserted into the Vitakkasanthana Sutra (Majjhima Nikaya no. 20), with the opposite meaning to what the Buddha intended:

> Just as a wrestler takes hold of the head or the shoulders of someone weaker than himself, restrains and coerces that person, and holds him down constantly, not letting go one moment, so a monk who meditates in order to stop all unwholesome thoughts of desire and aversion, when these thoughts continue to arise, should grit his teeth, press his tongue against his palate, and do his best to use his mind to beat down and defeat his mind.

This same passage was inserted into the second translation of the Sutra on the Four Grounds of Mindfulness: "The practitioner who observes body as body closes his lips tightly or grits his teeth, presses his tongue against his palate, and uses his mind to restrain and to oppose his mind." This extract does not appear in most versions of the sutra, but is also found in the Kayasmrti Sutra (Madhyama Agama 81) whose content is very similar to that of our second version. The corresponding sutra in Pali is the Kayagatasati Sutta (Majjhima Nikaya 119).

OBSERVATION IS NOT INDOCTRINATION

In Buddhist practice centers throughout the world, students are taught to recite such phrases as "body is impure, feelings are suffering, mind is impermanent, dharmas are without self," as they observe the Four Establishments. I was taught in this way as a novice, and I always felt that it was a kind of brainwashing.

The method of the Four Establishments of Mindfulness is observing deeply in the spirit of "not craving and not feeling distaste." Mindfulness does not cling, push away, reprimand, or repress, so that the true nature of all dharmas can reveal itself in the light of mindful observation. That the impermanent, selfless, and impure nature of all dharmas has the effect of causing suffering can be seen while we observe dharmas, but that is not because we repeat some formulas like the above, in an automatic way. When we look deeply and see the true nature of all dharmas, they will reveal themselves.

When we mechanically repeat, "Body is impure," we are reciting a dogma. If we observe all physiological phenomena and see their impure nature, this is not dogma. It is our experience. If, during our mindful observation, we see that phenomena are sometimes pure and sometimes impure, then that is our experience. If we look even more deeply and see that phenomena are neither pure nor impure, that they transcend the concepts of pure and impure, we discover what is taught in the Heart of the Prajñaparamita Sutra. This sutra also teaches us to resist all dogmatic attitudes. We should not force ourselves to see the body as impure or the feelings as suffering. Although there may be some truth in the sentences, just repeating them dogmatically has the effect of cramming us with knowledge. While we observe in mindfulness, we may see that we have many painful feelings, but we will also see that we have many joyful and peaceful feelings and many neutral feelings. And if we look more deeply, we will see that neutral feelings can become joyful feelings, and that suffering and happiness are interdependent. Suffering is, because happiness is; and happiness is, because suffering is.

When we repeat, "Mind is impermanent," our attitude is still dogmatic. If the mind is impermanent, then the body must be impermanent and the feelings too. The same is true of "dharmas are selfless." If dharmas are selfless, so are body, mind, and feelings.

Therefore, the special teaching of the Sutra on the Four Establishments of Mindfulness is to observe all dharmas but not to have any fixed ideas, just to keep on observing mindfully without comment, without assuming any attitude towards the object you are observing. In this way, the true nature of the object will be able to reveal itself in the light of mindful observation, and you will have insight into wonderful discoveries such as no-birth no-death, neither pure nor impure, neither increasing nor decreasing, interpenetration, and interbeing.

8: Finding the Highest Understanding

The last part of the Sutra on the Four Establishments of Mindfulness reads: "He who practices the Four Establishments of Mindfulness for seven years can expect one of two fruits: the highest understanding in this very life or, if there remains some residue of affliction, he can attain the fruit of no-return. Let alone seven years, bhikkhus, whoever practices the Four Establishments of Mindfulness for six, five, four, three, two years, or one year, or even six, five, four, three, two months, one month or half a month can also expect one of two fruits: either the highest understanding or the fruit of no-return. It may take seven years to attain the fruits of the practice, but people who have great willingness to practice don't need seven years; it is enough to have half a month. That is why we say that this path of the Establishments of Mindfulness is the most wonderful path, which helps beings realize purification, transcend grief and sorrow, and destroy pain and anxiety. The bhikkhus were delighted to hear the teaching of the Buddha. They took it to heart and began to put it into practice."

Mindfulness is the core of Buddhist practice. This practice can be done not only in sitting meditation but also in every minute of our daily lives. When we are able to take hold of our bodies in mindfulness, we begin to master our minds, and our bodies and minds become one. If our practice of mindfulness is still weak, our bodies are like wild buffalo. Mindfulness is the herdsman and the mind is the wild buffalo.

The Ten Oxherding Paintings of the Zen tradition represent stages on the path of awakening, stages on the path of mastering the body and mind. In the beginning the trainer approaches the wild buffalo; trainer and buffalo are two separate entities. With the practice of mindfulness, the trainer comes to know the buffalo. Gradually, the trainer and the buffalo become one, and eventually the trainer is able to ride on the back of the buffalo, singing or playing the flute, and the buffalo can go wherever he likes.

When we stand, walk, sit, lie down, or work in mindfulness, we are practicing what the Buddha taught us in the sutra. But in order for the practice to be easy and successful, it is very helpful to practice with a community, called a Sangha. The presence of those who practice mindful living is a great support and encouragement to us. Seeing people walking, sitting, being, and doing things in mindfulness, we are reminded to maintain mindfulness ourselves. In Buddhist communities, people use bells of mindfulness to remind one another to practice. The bell sounds from time to time and calls us back to being mindful. The presence of the people who practice around us is equivalent to the presence of several bells of mindfulness.

With a Sangha, we get support whenever we need it, and we profit from the experience and insight of its members and also from their advice and guidance. A teacher is a treasure, but without a Sangha, the practice can still be difficult.

Therefore, getting in touch with an existing Sangha or setting up a small Sangha around us is a very important step. We should be able to participate from time to time in a retreat of five days or a week to practice mindfulness in a concentrated atmosphere. With friends we can organize from time to time a Day of Mindfulness to practice together. A Day of Mindfulness can also be organized in the family for all the adults and children to practice together. It is good if we can invite a number of friends to join us.

Practicing Buddhist meditation is not a way of avoiding society or family life. The correct practice of mindfulness can help us bring peace, joy, and release both to ourselves and to our family and friends as well. Those who practice mindful living will inevitably transform themselves and their way of life. They will live a more simple life and will have more time to enjoy themselves, their friends, and their natural environment. They will have more time to offer joy to others and to alleviate their suffering. And when the time comes, they will die in peace. They will know that to die is to begin anew or just to continue with another form of life. When we live our lives this way, every day is a Happy Birthday, a Happy Continuation Day.

9: History of the Sutra on the Four Establishments of Mindfulness

Three versions of the Sutra on the Four Establishments of Mindfulness have come down to us. The main version presented in this book is a translation from the Pali Satipatthana Sutta (number 10 in the Majjhima Nikaya), a first century BCE scripture of the Theravada school. This version is exactly the same as the Pali Mahasatipatthana Sutta (number 20 in the Digha Nikaya), except that the latter has a little more text at the end. For purposes of this commentary, the Mahasatipatthana Sutta is regarded as version one.

The second and third versions are from the Chinese Canon. The second version, the Sutra on the Four Grounds of Mindfulness, is a translation of the Nian Chu Jing (number 98 in the Madhyama Agama and number 26 in the Taisho Revised Tripitaka) of the Sarvastivada school, translated into Chinese from the Sanskrit Smrtyupasthana Sutra. The third version, The One Way In Sutra, is a translation of the Yi Ru Dao Jing (Ekottara Agama, sutra number 125 in the Taisho Revised Tripitaka). It comes from the Mahasanghika school, not in its original but in its later form.

In the Chinese Canon, the name of the translator of the Sutra on the Four Grounds of Mindfulness is given as Gautama Sanghadeva. Master Sanghadeva came from what is now Afghanistan and traveled to China in the fourth century, living from the year 383 in the capital Chang An, and after that in Jian Kang, the capital of Dong Chin. He began the work of translation between 391 and 398. He probably had learned Chinese when he lived in Chang An.

The Chinese Canon also ascribes the translation of The One Way In Sutra to Gautama Sanghadeva. However, there are many reasons for thinking that the sutra was translated by the monk Dharmanandi. Master Dharmanandi was Khotanese. He traveled to China in the fourth century and took up residence in Chang An, where he translated sutras from 384 to 391. The book *Marking the Era of Buddhism* (K'ai Yuan Shi Pi Chiao Lu) says that the Ekottara Agama was translated by Sanghadeva. Master Tao An, in his introduction to The One Way In Sutra, says that it was Master Dharmanandi who read the original Sanskrit version for Zhu Fo Nian to translate into Chinese and for Gautama Sanghadeva to write down. After that, they brought the translated version to be examined by the translation school of Master Sanghadeva in Jian Kang, the capital of Dong Chin.

The Li Tai San Pao Chi, Volume 7 (Sui dynasty), the Ta T'ang Nei Tien Lu, and the Ta T'ang Ch'an Ting Chung Ching Mu Lu, all say that there were two translations of the Ekottara Agama, one by Master Dharmanandi and one by Master Sanghadeva. The books Ch'u San Tsang Chi Chi and the Chung Ching Mu Lu of the Sui dynasty, and the Sutra Index of the T'ang dynasty, all say that the Ekottara Agama was translated by Master Dharmanandi. Judging from all of this information and from the literary style of the text, we conclude that there was only one translation of the Ekottara Agama, the translation of Master Dharmanandi.

The Mahasanghika school, which came into existence after the council at Vaishali, later divided into two branches, one going to the northwest and one to the south. There were five branches of Mahasanghika in the northwest, including the Lokottaravada, which was Mahayana in outlook. It was the Ekottara Agama of this branch, including the third version of the sutra on mindfulness presented in this book, that Dharmanandi translated. Therefore, our third version is more influenced by the Mahayana and can be said to be less close to the original teaching of the Buddha than the first two versions, because many later elements have infiltrated into it. Still, it contains the essence of the original teachings.

10: Related Sutras

THE SUTRA ON THE FOUR GROUNDS OF MINDFULNESS

Nian Chu Jing (Sarvastivada) from Madhyama Agama (number 26 in Taisho Revised Tripitaka). Translated by Gautama Sanghadeva from Sanskrit into Chinese, and by Thich Nhat Hanh and Annabel Laity into English.

SECTION ONE

I heard these words of the Buddha one time when the Lord was staying in the town of Kammassadharma in the land of the Kuru people.

The Lord addressed the bhikshus:

"There is a path which can help beings realize purification, overcome anxiety and fear, end pain, distress, and grief, and attain the right practice. This is the path of dwelling in the Four Grounds of Mindfulness. All the Tathagatas of the past have attained the fruit of true awakening, the state of no further obstacles, by establishing their minds in the Four Grounds of Mindfulness. Relying on these Four Grounds, they have abandoned the Five Hindrances, purged the poisons of the mind, been able to transcend the circumstances which obstruct awakened understanding, and, practicing according to the Seven Factors of Awakening, have attained the true, right, and highest awakening. All Tathagatas of the future will also attain the fruit of true awakening, the state of no more obstacles, thanks to establishing their minds in the Four Grounds of Mindfulness. Relying on the Four Grounds of Mindfulness, they will be able to put an end to the Five Hindrances, purge the poisons of the mind, and overcome whatever weakens the ability to understand, practice the Seven Factors of Awakening, and attain the true, right, and highest awakening. All Tathagatas of the present (including myself) have attained the fruit of true awakening, the state without obstacles, thanks to establishing their minds in the Four Grounds of Mindfulness. Relying on the Four Grounds of Mindfulness, we have been able to put an end to the Five Hindrances and overcome whatever weakens the ability to understand, practice the Seven Factors of Awakening and attain to the true, right, and highest awakening.

"What are the Four Grounds of Mindfulness? They are the four methods of observing body as body, feelings as feelings, mind as mind, and objects of mind as objects of mind."

SECTION TWO

"What is the way to remain established in the awareness of body as body?

"When the practitioner walks, he knows he is walking. When he stands, he knows he is standing. When he sits, he knows he is sitting. When he lies down, he knows he is lying down. When he wakes up, he knows he is waking up. Awake or asleep, he knows he is awake or asleep. This is how the practitioner is aware of body as body, both inside the body and outside the body, and establishes mindfulness in the body with understanding, insight, clarity, and realization. This is called being aware of body as body.

"Further, bhikshus, when practicing awareness of the body, the practitioner is clearly aware of the positions and movements of the body, such as going out and coming in, bending down and standing up, extending limbs, or drawing them in. When wearing the sanghati robe, carrying the alms bowl, walking, standing, lying, sitting, speaking, or being silent, he knows the skillful way of being aware. This is how the practitioner is aware of body as body, from both within and from without, and establishes mindfulness in the body with understanding, insight, clarity, and realization. This is called being aware of body as body.

"Further, bhikshus, a practitioner is aware of body as body so that whenever an unwholesome state of mind arises, he can immediately apply a wholesome state to counterbalance and transform the unwholesome state of mind. Just as a carpenter or carpenter's apprentice stretches out a piece of string along the edge of a plank of wood and with a plane trims off the edge of the plank, so the practitioner, when he feels an unwholesome state of mind arising, immediately uses a wholesome state of mind to counterbalance and transform the existing state. This is how the practitioner is aware of body as body, from both within and from without, and establishes mindfulness in the body with understanding, insight, clarity, and realization. This is called being aware of body as body.

"Further, bhikshus, a practitioner is aware of body as body when, closing his lips tight, clenching his teeth, pressing his tongue against his palate, taking one part of his mind to restrain another part of his mind, he counterbalances a thought and transforms it. Just as two strong men might hold onto a weak man and easily restrain him, so the practitioner presses his lips together and clenches his teeth, presses his tongue against his palate, takes one part of his mind to restrain another part of his mind, to counterbalance and transform a thought. This is how the practitioner is aware of body as body, from both within and from without, and establishes mindfulness in the body with understanding, insight, clarity, and realization. This is called being aware of body as body.

"Further, bhikshus, a practitioner is aware of body as body, when, breathing in, he knows that he is breathing in, and breathing out, he knows that he is breathing out. When breathing in a long breath, he knows that he is breathing in a long breath. When breathing out a long breath, he knows that he is breathing out a long breath. When breathing in, he is aware of his whole body. Breathing out, he is aware of his whole body. Breathing in and out, he is aware of what he is doing and he practices stopping while acting. Breathing in and out, he is aware of what he is saying and he practices stopping while speaking. This is how the practitioner is aware of body as body, from both within and from without, and establishes mindfulness in the body, with recognition, insight, clarity, and realization. This is called being aware of body as body.

"Further, bhikshus, a practitioner is aware of body as body, when, thanks to having put aside the Five Desires, a feeling of bliss arises during his concentration and saturates every part of his body. This feeling of bliss which arises during concentration reaches every part of his body. Like the bath attendant who, after putting powdered soap into a basin, mixes it with water until the soap paste has water in every part of it, so the practitioner feels the bliss which is born when the desires of the sense realms are put aside, saturate every part of his body. This is how the practitioner is aware of body as body, from both within and from without, and establishes mindfulness in the body with recognition, insight, clarity, and realization. This is called being aware of body as body.

"Further, bhikshus, a practitioner who is aware of body as body feels the joy which arises during concentration that saturates every part of his body. There is no part of his body this feeling of joy, born during concentration, does not reach. Like a spring within a mountain whose clear water flows out and down all sides of that mountain and bubbles up in places where water has not previously entered, saturating the entire mountain, in the same way, joy, born during concentration, permeates the whole of the practitioner's body; it is present everywhere. This is how the practitioner is aware of body as body, from both within and from without, and establishes mindfulness in the body with recognition, insight, clarity, and realization. This is called being aware of body as body.

"Further, bhikshus, a practitioner who is aware of body as body experiences a feeling of happiness which arises with the disappearance of the feeling of joy and permeates his whole body. This feeling of happiness which arises with the disappearance of the feeling of joy reaches every part of his body. Just as the different species of blue, pink, red, and white lotus which grow up from the bottom of a pond of clear water and appear on the surface of that pond have their tap roots, subsidiary roots, leaves, and flowers all full of the water of that pond, and there is no part of the plant which does not contain the water, so the feeling of happiness which arises with the disappearance of joy permeates the whole of the practitioner's body, and there is no part which it does not penetrate. This is how the practitioner is aware of body as body, from both within and from without, and establishes mindfulness in the body with recognition, insight, clarity, and realization, and that is called being aware of body as body.

"Further, bhikshus, a practitioner who is aware of body as body envelops the whole of his body with a clear, calm mind, filled with understanding. Just as someone who puts on a very long robe which reaches from his head to his feet, and there is no part of his body which is not covered by this robe, so the practitioner with a clear, calm mind envelops his whole body in understanding and leaves no part of the body untouched. This is how the practitioner is aware of body as body, from both within and from without, and establishes mindfulness in the body with recognition, insight, clarity, and realization. This is called being aware of body as body.

"Further, bhikshus, a practitioner who is aware of body as body is aware of clear light, knows how to welcome clear light, practice with and recall to mind clear light, whether it comes from in front to behind him or from behind to in front of him, day and night, above and below him, with a mind which is well-balanced and not hindered. He practices "the one way in" by means of clear light, and finally his mind is not obscured in darkness. This is how the practitioner is aware of body as body, from both within and from without, and establishes mindfulness in the body with recognition, insight, clarity, and realization. This is called being aware of body as body.

"Further, bhikshus, a practitioner who is aware of body as body knows how to use the meditational 'sign' skillfully and knows how to maintain the object of meditation skillfully. As someone sitting observes someone lying down and someone lying down observes someone sitting, so the practitioner knows how to recognize the meditational sign and use it skillfully and knows how skillfully to maintain the object of meditation. This is how the practitioner is aware of body as body, from both within and from without, and establishes mindfulness in the body with recognition, insight, clarity, and realization. This is called being aware of body as body.

"Further, bhikshus, a practitioner who is aware of the body knows very well that this body exists due to the interdependence of the parts of the body, from the top of the head to the soles of the feet. He sees that all the parts of the body are impure. In his body are the hairs of the head, the hairs of the body, the fingernails, teeth, hard skin, soft skin, flesh, sinews, bones, heart, kidneys, liver, lungs, large intestine, small intestine, gallbladder, stomach, excrement, brain, tears, sweat, sputum, saliva, pus, blood, grease, marrow, bladder, urine. He sees all these clearly as someone with good eyesight sees in a cask full of all sorts of grains that this is rice, this is millet, this is mustard seed, and so on. The practitioner who takes his attention throughout his body knows that it only exists in dependence on the true value of the parts out of which it is made, from the top of the head to the soles of the feet, and sees that all those parts are impure. This is how the practitioner is aware of body as body, from both within and from without, and establishes mindfulness in the body with recognition, insight, clarity, and realization. This is called being aware of body as body.

"Further, bhikshus, a practitioner who is aware of body as body observes the elements which comprise his body: 'In this very body of mine, there is the element earth, the element water, the element fire, the element air, the element space, and the element consciousness.' Just as a butcher, after killing the cow and skinning it, lays out the meat on the ground in six parts, so the practitioner observes the six elements of which the body is comprised: 'Here is the earth element in my body, here is the water element, here is the fire element, here is the air element, here is the space element, and here is the consciousness element.' This is how the practitioner is aware of body as body, from both within and from without, and establishes mindfulness in the body with understanding, insight, clarity, and realization. This is called being aware of body as body.

"Further, bhikshus, a practitioner who is meditating on body as body visualizes a corpse. It is one to seven days old and has been disemboweled by vultures and torn by wolves. It is either distended or rotting, having been thrown onto the charnel ground or buried in the earth. When the practitioner visualizes a corpse like this, he compares it with his own body: 'This body of mine will also undergo a state such as this. In the end, there is no way it can avoid this condition.' This is how the practitioner is aware of body as body, from both within and from without, and establishes mindfulness in the body with recognition, insight, clarity, and realization. This is called being aware of body as body.

"Further, bhikshus, a practitioner who meditates on body as body visualizes a bluish corpse, decayed and half-gnawed away, lying in a heap on the ground. When the practitioner visualizes a corpse like this, he compares it with his own body: 'This body of mine will also undergo a state such as this. In the end, there is no way it can avoid this condition.' This is how the practitioner is aware of body as body, from both within and from without, and establishes mindfulness in the body with recognition, insight, clarity, and realization. This is called being aware of body as body.

"Further, bhikshus, a practitioner who meditates on body as body visualizes a skeleton which has no skin, flesh, blood, or bloodstains. There are only the bones held together by sinews. When the practitioner visualizes a skeleton like this, he compares it with his own body: 'This body of mine will also undergo a state such as this. In the end, there is no way it can avoid this condition.' This is how the practitioner is aware of body as body, from both within and from without, and establishes mindfulness in the body with recognition, insight, clarity, and realization. This is called being aware of body as body.

"Further, bhikshus, a practitioner who meditates on body as body visualizes the bones scattered in different directions: foot bone, shin bone, thigh bone, clavicle, spinal column, shoulder blade, tarsus, skull—each one in a different place. When he visualizes them like this, he compares it with his own body: 'This body of mine will also undergo a state such as this. In the end, there is no way it can avoid this condition.' This is how the practitioner is aware of body as body, from both within and from without, and establishes mindfulness in the body with understanding, insight, clarity, and realization. This is called being aware of body as body.

"Further, bhikshus, a practitioner who meditates on body as body visualizes the bones bleached to the color of shells or the color of a dove, and the bones which have rotted down to form a powder. When he visualizes them like this, he compares it with his own body: 'This body of mine will also undergo a state such as this. In the end, there is no way it can avoid this condition.' This is how the practitioner is aware of body as body, from both within and from without, and establishes mindfulness in the body with recognition, insight, clarity, and realization. This is called being aware of body as body."

SECTION THREE

"What is the way to remain established in the meditation on feelings as feelings?

"When the practitioner has a pleasant feeling, he knows immediately that he has a pleasant feeling. When he has an unpleasant feeling, he knows immediately that he has an unpleasant feeling. When he has a neutral feeling, he knows immediately that he has a neutral feeling. When there is a pleasant feeling, an unpleasant feeling, or a neutral feeling in the body; a pleasant feeling, an unpleasant feeling, or a neutral feeling in the mind; a pleasant feeling, an unpleasant feeling, or a neutral feeling of this world; a pleasant feeling, an unpleasant feeling, or a neutral feeling not of this world; a pleasant feeling, an unpleasant feeling, or a neutral feeling associated with desire; a pleasant feeling, an unpleasant feeling, or a neutral feeling not associated with desire, he is clearly aware of this. This is how the practitioner is aware of feelings as feelings, from both within and from without, and establishes right mindfulness. If there are bhikshus and bhikshunis who meditate on feelings as feelings, according to these instructions, then they are capable of dwelling in the meditation on feelings as feelings."

SECTION FOUR

"What is the way to remain established in the meditation on mind as mind?

"When the practitioner's mind is attached to something, he knows it is attached to something. When the practitioner's mind is not attached, he knows it is not attached. When the practitioner's mind hates something, he knows that it hates something. When his mind is not hating, he knows it is not hating. When his mind is confused, he knows it is confused. When it is not confused, he knows it is not confused. When his mind is defiled, he knows it is defiled. When his mind is not defiled, he knows it is not defiled. When it is distracted, he knows it is distracted. When it is not distracted, he knows it is not distracted. When his mind has obstacles, he knows it has obstacles. When it has no obstacles, he knows it has no obstacles. When it is tense, he knows it is tense. When it is not tense, he knows it is not tense. When it is boundless, he knows it is boundless. When it is bound, he knows it is bound. When his mind is concentrating, he knows it is concentrating. When it is not concentrating, he knows it is not concentrating. When his mind is not liberated, he knows it is not liberated. When it is liberated, he knows it is liberated. That is how the practitioner is aware of mind as mind, from both within and from without, and establishes mindfulness in the mind with recognition, insight, clarity, and realization, and that is called being aware of mind as mind. If bhikshus or bhikshunis meditate on mind as mind according to the details of these instructions, then they know how to dwell in the practice of observing mind as mind."

SECTION FIVE

"What is the way to remain established in the meditation on objects of mind as objects of mind?

"When the practitioner realizes that his eyes in contact with form give rise to an internal formation, then he knows without any doubt that an internal formation is being formed. If there is no internal formation, he knows without any doubt that there is no internal formation. If an internal formation that had not arisen formerly now arises, he knows this. If an internal formation that had arisen formerly now comes to an end and will not arise again, he knows this. The same is true with all the other sense organs: ears, nose, tongue, body, and mind. When these sense organs are in contact with an external object and bring about an internal formation, then the practitioner knows without any doubt that there is an internal formation. If an internal formation which had not arisen formerly now arises, he knows this. If an internal formation which had arisen formerly now comes to an end and will not arise again, he knows this. This is how the practitioner is aware of objects of mind as objects of mind, from both within and from without, and establishes mindfulness in the object of mind with recognition, insight, clarity, and realization. This is called being aware of objects of mind as objects of mind. If bhikshus or bhikshunis meditate on objects of mind as objects of mind according to these instructions, then they know how to dwell in the practice of observing objects of mind as objects of mind with regard to the six realms of consciousness.

"Further, bhikshus, when the practitioner is meditating on objects of mind as objects of mind, if he sees sensual desire in himself, he knows without any doubt that sensual desire is there. If he sees no sensual desire in himself, he knows without any doubt that no sensual desire is there. If a sensual desire that had not arisen formerly now arises, he knows this without any doubt. If a sensual desire that had arisen formerly now comes to an end, he also knows this without any doubt. The same is true of the four other obstacles: anger, torpor, agitation, and doubt. If there is doubt in his mind, he knows for certain that there is doubt. If there is no doubt in his mind, he knows for certain that there is no doubt. When a formally nonexistent doubt arises, he knows that for certain. When an already arisen doubt comes to an end, he also knows that for certain. That is how the practitioner is aware of objects of mind as objects of mind, from both within and from without, and establishes mindfulness in the object of mind with recognition, insight, clarity, and realization, and that is called being aware of objects of mind as objects of mind. If bhikshus or bhikshunis meditate on objects of mind as objects of mind according to the details of these instructions, then they know how to dwell in the practice of observing objects of mind as objects of mind with regard to the Five Obstacles.

"Further bhikshus, when the practitioner is meditating on objects of mind as objects of mind, if he sees in his mind the Factor of Awakening, mindfulness, he knows without any doubt that mindfulness is there. When mindfulness is not present, he knows without a doubt that mindfulness is not present. When mindfulness which had formerly not been present is now present, the practitioner also knows this without any doubt. When mindfulness has arisen and is still present, is not lost, does not decline but actually increases, the practitioner is also aware of all this. The same is true of all the other Factors of Awakening—the investigation of dharmas, energy, joy, ease, concentration, and letting go. When letting go is present in his mind, he knows without a doubt that letting go is present. When letting go is not present, he knows without a doubt that letting go is not present. When letting go that had formerly not been present is now present, the practitioner also knows this without any doubt. When letting go has arisen and is still present, is not lost, does not decline, but actually increases, the practitioner is also aware of all this. This is how the practitioner is aware of objects of mind as objects of mind, from both within and from without, and establishes mindfulness in the object of mind with understanding, insight, clarity, and realization, and that is called being aware of objects of mind as objects of mind. If bhikshus or bhikshunis meditate on objects of mind as objects of mind according to these instructions, then they know how to dwell in the practice of meditating on objects of mind as objects of mind with regard to the Seven Factors of Awakening."

SECTION SIX

"Any bhikshu or bhikshuni who practices being established in the Four Grounds of Mindfulness for seven years will certainly realize one of two fruits—either attaining in this very life the highest understanding or the fruit of Arhat with some residue of ignorance. And not just seven, or six, or five, or four, or three, or two years, or one year. A bhikshu or a bhikshuni who practices being established in the Four Grounds of Mindfulness for seven months will certainly realize one of two fruits— either attaining in this very life the highest understanding or the fruit of Arhat with some residue from former deeds. And not just seven months, or six, five, four, three, two months, or one month. A bhikshu or a bhikshuni who practices being established in the Four Grounds of Mindfulness for seven days and seven nights will certainly realize one of two fruits—either attaining in this very life the highest understanding or the fruit of Arhat with some residue from former deeds. Not to mention seven days and seven nights, six days and nights, five days and nights, four days and nights, three days and nights, two days and nights, or one day and night, a bhikshu or a bhikshuni who practices being established in the Four Grounds of Mindfulness for just a few hours, if she begins the practice in the morning, by the evening there will have been progress, and if she begins in the afternoon, by nightfall there will have been progress."

After the Lord Buddha had spoken, the bhikshus and bhikshunis who heard him teach were delighted to carry out the Buddha's teachings.

VERSION THREE:
THE ONE WAY IN SUTRA

Yi Ru Dao Jing (Mahasanghika) from Ekottara Agama, chapter 12. Translated by Dharmanandi from Sanskrit into Chinese, and by Thich Nhat Hanh and Annabel Laity into English.

SECTION ONE

I heard these words of the Buddha one time when he was staying in the Jeta Grove in the town of Shravasti. The Lord addressed the assembly of monks:

"There is a way to practice which purifies the actions of living beings, eradicates all sorrow, anxiety, and the roots of afflictions, and leads to the highest understanding and the realization of nirvana. It is a path which destroys the Five Obstacles. It is the path of the Four Ways of Stopping and Concentrating the Mind. Why is it called 'the one way in?' Because it is the way to the oneness of mind. Why is it called a way? Because it is the Noble Eightfold Path, the way of Right View, right contemplation, right action, right livelihood, right practice, right speech, right mindfulness, and right concentration. This explains the expression 'the one way in.'

"What then are the Five Obstacles? They are attachment, aversion, agitation, torpor, and doubt. These are the obstacles which need to be removed.

"What are the Four Ways of Stopping and Concentrating the Mind? The practitioner meditates on the body in the body from within to end unwholesome thoughts and remove anxiety, and he meditates on the body in the body from without to end unwholesome thoughts and remove anxiety. The practitioner meditates on the feelings in the feelings from within and from without in order to be at peace and have joy, and he meditates on the feelings in the feelings from both within and from without in order to be at peace and have joy. The practitioner meditates on the mind in the mind from within, and he meditates on the mind in the mind from without in order to be at peace and have joy, and he meditates on the mind in the mind from both within and from without in order to be at peace and have joy. The practitioner meditates on the objects of mind in the objects of mind from within, and he meditates on the objects of mind in the objects of mind from without in order to be at peace and have joy, and he meditates on the objects of mind in the objects of mind from both within and from without in order to be at peace and have joy."

SECTION TWO

"How does the practitioner meditate on the body from within so as to realize peace and joy in himself?

"In this case, the practitioner meditates on the nature and functions of the body. When he examines it from head to toes or from toes to head, he sees that it is composed of impure constituents, and he is unable to be attached to it. He observes that this body has hair of the head and hair of the body, nails, teeth, skin, flesh, sinews, bones, marrow, sweat, pus, stomach, small intestine, large intestine, heart, liver, spleen, kidneys. He observes and recognizes urine, excrement, tears, saliva, blood vessels, grease, and observing and knowing them all, he is unattached and regrets nothing. This is the way the practitioner observes the body in order to realize peace and joy and be able to end unwholesome thoughts and remove anxiety and sorrow.

"Further, the practitioner meditates on this body in order to see the Four Elements of earth, water, fire, and air, and he distinguishes these Four Elements. Just like a skillful butcher or his apprentice might lay out the different parts of a slaughtered cow and distinguish the leg, heart, torso, and head, the practitioner observing his own body distinguishes the Four Elements just as clearly, seeing that this is earth, this is water, this is fire, and this is air. Thus, the practitioner meditates on the body in the body in order to end attachment.

"Further, bhikshus, one should observe this body as having many openings from which many impure substances flow. Just as we look at bamboo or reeds and see the joints in the canes, so the practitioner observes the body with many openings from which impure substances flow.

"Further, bhikshus, the practitioner meditates on the corpse of one who has died one day ago or one week ago. It is distended, fetid, impure. Then he meditates on his own body and sees that his own body is no different. This very body of his will not be able to escape death. The practitioner observes this corpse being seen and pecked at by vultures, being discovered and gnawed at by all sorts of wild creatures like tigers, panthers, and wolves, and then comes back to observing his own body and sees that it is no different. 'This very body of mine will not be able to escape that condition.' This is how the practitioner meditates on the body to realize peace and joy.

"Further, bhikshus, the practitioner visualizes a corpse, which has lain on the ground for a year. It is half-eaten, fetid, and impure. Then he comes back to meditating on his own body and sees that his own body is no different. 'This very body of mine will not be able to escape that condition.' This is how the practitioner meditates on the body.

"Further, bhikshus, the practitioner visualizes the corpse from which the skin and flesh has shriveled away. All that is left are the bones stained with blood. Then he comes back to meditating on his own body and sees that his own body is no different. 'This very body of mine will not be able to escape that condition.' This is how the practitioner meditates on the body.

"Further, bhikshus, the practitioner visualizes a skeleton, which is just bones held together by some ligaments. Then he comes back to meditating on his own body and sees that his own body is no different. 'This very body of mine will not be able to escape that condition.' This is how the practitioner meditates on the body.

"Further, bhikshus, the practitioner visualizes a corpse which has become a collection of scattered bones, all in different places: the hand bone, leg bone, ribs, shoulder blades, spinal column, kneecap, and skull. Then he comes back to meditating on his own body and sees that his own body is no different. 'This very body of mine will not be able to escape that condition.' His body will also decay in that way. This is how the practitioner meditates on the body in order to realize peace and joy.

"Further, bhikshus, the practitioner visualizes a corpse which has become a collection of bones bleached like shells. Then he comes back to meditating on his own body and sees that his own body is no different. 'This very body of mine will not be able to escape that condition.' His body will also decay in that way. This is how the practitioner meditates on the body.

"Further, bhikshus, the practitioner visualizes a corpse which has become a collection of yellowing bones, to which there is nothing worth being attached, or bones that have become the color of ash and are no longer distinguishable from the earth. Thus the practitioner meditates on his own body, abandoning unwholesome thoughts and removing sorrow and anxiety, observing, 'This body is impermanent, it is something which decomposes.' A practitioner who observes himself like this from within or from without, or both from within and without the body together understands that there is nothing which is eternal."

Section Three

"How does the practitioner meditate on the feelings in the feelings?

"When the practitioner has a pleasant feeling, he knows that he has a pleasant feeling. When he has a painful feeling, he knows that he has a painful feeling. When his feelings are neutral, he knows that his feelings are neutral. When he has a pleasant, painful, or neutral feeling with a material basis, he knows that he has a pleasant, painful, or neutral feeling with a material basis. When he has a pleasant, painful, or neutral feeling with a nonmaterial basis, he knows he has a pleasant, painful, or neutral feeling with a nonmaterial basis. This is how the practitioner meditates on the feelings in the feelings by his own insight.

"Further, bhikshus, when the practitioner has a pleasant feeling, then there is not a painful feeling, and the practitioner knows there is a pleasant feeling. When there is a painful feeling, then there is not a pleasant feeling, and the practitioner knows that there is a painful feeling. When there is a neutral feeling, then there is neither a pleasant feeling nor a painful feeling, and the practitioner is aware that the feeling is neither pleasant nor painful. The practitioner is aware of the arising of all dharmas and the disappearance of all dharmas in such a way that, by his own insight, he realizes peace and joy. As feelings arise, the practitioner recognizes and is aware of them and their roots, and he is not dependent on them and does not give rise to feelings of attachment to the world. At that time there is no fear, and having no fear, he liberates himself forever from illusion and realizes nirvana. Birth and death are no longer. The holy life has been lived. What needs to be done has been done. There will be no more rebirth. He understands this directly. This is how the practitioner is aware of the feelings in the feelings to end dispersed thinking and remove sorrow and anxiety. Such is the meditation on the inside of the feelings and the outside of the feelings."

SECTION FOUR

"What is meant by meditating on the mind in the mind in order to realize peace and joy?

"When the practitioner has desire in his mind, he knows that he has desire in his mind. When he does not have desire, he knows that he does not have desire. When he has hatred in his mind, he knows that he has hatred in his mind. When he does not have hatred, he knows that he does not have hatred. When he has confusion in his mind, he knows that he has confusion in his mind. When he does not have confusion, he knows that he does not have confusion. When he has craving in his mind, he knows that he has craving in his mind. When he does not have craving, he knows that he does not have craving. When there is mastery of his mind, he knows that there is mastery of his mind. When there is no mastery, he knows there is no mastery. When there is dispersion, he knows that there is dispersion. When there is no dispersion, he knows that there is no dispersion. When there is inattention, he knows that there is inattention. When there is no inattention, he knows that there is no inattention. When there is universality, he knows that there is universality. When there is no universality, he knows that there is no universality. When there is extensiveness, he knows that there is extensiveness. When there is not extensiveness, he knows that there is not extensiveness. When there is boundlessness, he knows that there is boundlessness. When there is not boundlessness, he knows that there is not boundlessness. When there is concentration, he knows that there is concentration. When there is no concentration, he knows that there is no concentration. When he has not yet realized liberation, he knows that he has not yet realized liberation. When he has realized liberation, he knows that he has realized liberation.

"This is how the practitioner is mindful of the mind in the mind. He observes the arising of dharmas, observes the destruction of dharmas, or observes both the arising and destruction of dharmas; being mindful of dharmas in order to realize peace and joy. He is able to see, know, and observe what is not observable, and he does not become dependent on the object and does not give rise to worldly thoughts. Because there are no thoughts of attachment to the world, there is no fear. Because there is no fear, there is no residue of affliction. When there is no residue of affliction, nirvana arises, and birth and death are no more, the holy life is realized, what needs to be done has been done, and there will be no more rebirth. The practitioner knows all this to be true. Thus in his own person the practitioner observes mind in mind, both from within and from without, in order to remove uncontrolled thought and cut off all anxiety."

SECTION FIVE

"What is meant by 'meditating on the objects of mind in the objects of mind?'

"When the practitioner practices the first factor of awakening, mindfulness, it is in reliance on the initial application of thought, on no-craving, on destroying the unwholesome mind and abandoning the unwholesome dharmas. He practices the factors of awakening, investigation of dharmas, energy, joy, concentration, and letting go, in reliance on applied thought, in reliance on no-craving, in reliance on destroying the unwholesome dharmas. This is how he practices meditating on the objects of mind in the objects of mind.

"Further, bhikshus, having been liberated from sensual attachment, having abandoned unwholesome dharmas, with initial application of thought and sustained thought, with joy, he delights to dwell in the first dhyana in order to have joy in his own person. This is how the practitioner meditates on the objects of mind in the objects of mind.

"Further, bhikshus, with the passing of applied thought and sustained thought, a joy arises in his mind which leads to the oneness of mind. When there is no more initial application of thought and sustained thought, the practitioner, maintaining joy, enters the second dhyana that has peace as well as joy. This is how the practitioner meditates on the objects of mind in the objects of mind.

"Further, bhikshus, with the passing of thought and the constant practice of letting go of applied thought, he enjoys for himself that state which the holy ones long for, where mindfulness in letting go is fully purified, and he enters the third dhyana. This is how the practitioner meditates on the objects of mind in the objects of mind.

"Further, bhikshus, with the absence of joy, when anxiety about joy and elation as well as pleasure and pain are no longer, and his mindfulness in letting go is fully purified, he enters the fourth dhyana, and that is to meditate on the objects of mind in the objects of mind. He meditates on the arising of dharmas and the passing of dharmas in order to arrive at peace and joy. He realizes right mindfulness in the present moment. He is able to see, know, and abandon dispersion. He is no longer dependent on anything. He does not give rise to thoughts of the world. Because he does not have worldly thoughts, he is not afraid. When there is no fear, birth and death no longer exist, and the holy life has been accomplished, what needs to be done has been done, there is no more rebirth, and everything is known in its true nature."

SECTION SIX

"Bhikshus, relying on this one way of entering the path, living beings are purified, freed from sorrow and anxiety, their minds no longer subject to agitation, their understanding stable, and they are able to realize nirvana. This one way in is the destruction of the Five Hindrances and practice of the Four Ways of Stopping and Concentrating the Mind." The bhikshus who heard the Buddha teach thus, applied themselves joyfully at that time to the practice.

SUMMARY COMPARISON OF THE THREE VERSIONS

SECTION ONE

This section is about the circumstances under which the sutra was delivered, the importance of the sutra, and the subject matter of the sutra, namely the Four Establishments of Mindfulness.

In the first and second versions, it says that the sutra was delivered at Kammassadhamma, in the land of the Kuru people. The third version says that the sutra was delivered in Jetavana Monastery in Shravasti.

In this section, all three versions use the term, *ekayana* (the One Vehicle). The third version uses this term in the title of the sutra. The first and second versions use the term, "nian chu" (Establishments of Mindfulness) in the title.

A literal translation of the first sentence following the description of the location in the first version of the sutra would say, "This one way, O bhikkhus, is the way" or "This only way, O bhikkhus, is the way" (*ekayano ayam bhikkhave maggam*). The second version says, "O bhikkhus, there is a way." The third version says, "There is the 'one way in.' Why should it be called 'one way'? Because it refers to our single-mind concentration."

The first section of the first version is short and concise. The second version adds that all the Tathagatas of the three times, thanks to their practice of the Four Establishments of Mindfulness, were able to overcome the Five Obstacles and realize the path. The third version also mentions the Five Obstacles and says what they are. It also says that the Noble Eightfold Path is a path for practicing the Four Establishments of Mindfulness. In The One Way In Sutra, the Four Establishments of Mindfulness are called the "Four Practices to Stop and Concentrate the Mind." As previously discussed, there is some question whether the translator of the third version is Gautama Sanghadeva or Dharmanandi. If the translator had been Sanghadeva, it is likely he would have used the term "Four Establishments of Mindfulness," as he did in version two.

SECTION TWO

This section expounds the ways of observing the body in the body. In the first version, six ways of observing the body are taught:

1. Observing the breathing
2. Observing the positions of the body
3. Observing movements and functions of the body
4. Observing the parts of the body
5. Observing the elements in the body
6. Observing a corpse

In the second version, these six ways of observing the body are also taught, but breathing is offered third following the positions and functions of the body. In the observation of a corpse, only five parts are given to this observation instead of the nine in the first version.

The third version teaches only three ways of observing the body. It does not include observing the breathing, the positions, or the functions of the body. There are eight parts to the meditation on observing a corpse.

The unique feature of the second version is that, after the six teachings on how to observe the movements and functions of the body, there is a section that deals with unwholesome thoughts. This section has two parts: how to use a wholesome mind to deal with an unwholesome mind and how to use the mind to restrain the mind, like a strong wrestler holding down a weak man. Both of these ideas come from Vitakkasanthana Sutta (Majjhima Nikaya 20). We can say with certainty that this part was added at a later date, and in fact was added in an inappropriate place in the sutra, because at this point, the Buddha is discussing the practice of observing the body in the body and has not yet reached the Establishment of Mind. Other differences in the second version are teachings on the kind of concentration that gives birth to joy and happiness, which is equivalent to the first *jhana*, and a concentration that abandons joy but maintains happiness, which is equivalent to the second jhana, as well as meditations on purity, clear light, and signs. All this is evidence that the practice of the Four Jhanas had already begun to infiltrate the Sutra Pitaka, although discreetly. By the time of the third version, the practice of the jhanas is mentioned quite openly, by name. The meditation that observes the clear light can be seen as announcing the first steps in the formation of Pure Land Buddhism, and the meditation on the sign will be developed in the use of the *kasina*, a symbolic image visualized as a point of concentration.

When it comes to the section that teaches observing mindfully the different elements that constitute the body, the second version mentions six elements as opposed to the usual four elements of the first and third versions. The six elements are earth, water, air, fire, emptiness, and consciousness.

The third version has an additional practice that is the observation of impure elements pouring out from the apertures of the body (not as a part of the Nine Contemplations of the corpse).

In the third version, the phrase most often repeated is, "to arrive at peace and joy." The equivalent phrases most repeated in the first and second versions are as follows:

Version One:
This is how a practitioner observes the body in the body. He observes the body from within or from without, or from both within and without. He observes the process of coming-to-be in the body or the process of dissolution in the body or both the process of coming-to-be and the process of dissolution. Or he is mindful of the fact, 'There is a body here,' until understanding and full awareness come about. He maintains the observation, free, not caught up in any worldly consideration. That is how to practice observation of the body in the body.

Version Two:
This is how the practitioner is aware of body as body, both inside the body and outside the body, and establishes mindfulness in the body with recognition, insight, clarity, and realization. This is called being aware of body as body.

These paragraphs are repeated in the sections of the sutra teaching observation of the feelings, the mind, and the dharmas, substituting the words feelings, mind, or dharmas for the word body. If we are bothered by questions such as "How can there be an inside of the feelings or an outside of the feelings?" when we read, "mindfully observing the feelings in the feelings, observation of the feelings from within or from without, or from both within and without," we must remember that repetition, though not always relevant, is a mark of oral transmission. The second version uses the phrase, "observes the body as the body" (Chinese: *guan shen ru shen*) instead of the phrase, "observes the body in the body" (Pali: *kaye kayanupassana*).

Section Three

This section concerns the practice of observing the feelings in the feelings. "Feelings" is the translation from the Pali *vedana* in the first version. In the second version the Chinese word used to translate vedana is *jue*, while in the third version the word used is *tong*. Why does the third version use tong instead of jue? The original meaning of tong is "painful." Perhaps the translator had been strongly influenced by the doctrine that every single feeling is suffering. In this third section, the third version emphasizes that when there is a painful feeling, there cannot be a pleasant feeling, and when there is a pleasant feeling, there cannot be a painful feeling. It also emphasizes the necessity of observing mindfully the arising and disappearing of feelings and knowing their source in order not to be imprisoned in them or afraid of them. This is a positive point in the third version.

The following is a quotation from the third version: "Because he is not afraid, he is able to realize nirvana. Birth and death are no more, the holy life has been realized, what needs to be done has been done, there will be no more births." This quotation, which is not found in the first and second versions, appears three times in the third version. It is a sentence that is found over and over again in the sutras, and most probably during the course of oral transmission it was added here.

Section Four

This section deals with observing the mind in the mind. The third version does not mention mindfulness of the process of the arising and disappearing of psychological phenomena as do the first and second versions. In the third version, it is mentioned that we observe the dharmas that we can know, see, and observe as well as dharmas that we cannot observe. The word "observe" here has the meaning of practicing mindful observation. Observing dharmas that cannot be observed is a strange idea, equivalent to the teaching of the Sutra of Forty-Two Chapters, "Our practice is the practice which is non-practice," which has a strong Mahayana flavor.

An additional quotation of interest from the third version is: "The practitioner does not rely on anything at all, does not give rise to thoughts of the world. Because there is no arising of such thoughts, there is no more fear. Because there is no more fear, no residue of the afflictions is left, and nirvana is realized." The latter part of this quotation is nearly equivalent to the Prajñaparamita Hrdaya Sutra: "Having no obstacles, they overcome fear, liberating themselves forever from illusion and realizing perfect nirvana."

Section Five

This part deals with the practice of observing dharmas in dharmas. In the first version, we have the practices of observing the Five Obstacles, the Five Skandhas, the Twelve Realms of Sense Organs and Sense Objects, the Seven Factors of Awakening, and the Four Noble Truths. The first version (in its form in the Digha Nikaya) develops a teaching on the mindful observation of the Four Noble Truths and the Noble Eightfold Path, and this development is what gives it its name Maha ("great") Satipatthana. The second version only teaches mindful observation of the Twelve Realms, the Five Obstacles, and the Seven Factors of Awakening.

The third version only teaches the Seven Factors of Awakening. (It has already dealt with the Five Obstacles in its first section.) Possibly because of carelessness on the part of the copyist, only six of the Seven Factors of Awakening are mentioned: mindfulness, investigation of dharmas, energy, joy, concentration, and equanimity. The third version teaches the Four Jhanas. The terms *vitarka* and *vicara*, usually translated as "initial application" and "sustained attention" are translated into Chinese as *jue* ("perception") and *guan* ("observation"). In this fifth section, the third version repeats the phrases we have already seen in the second and fourth sections and that have been compared with part of the Prajñaparamita Hrdaya Sutra, and adds some words that make it seem even closer to the Prajñaparamita. These words are equivalent to "liberating themselves forever from illusion" of the Prajñaparamita.

SECTION SIX

This section deals with the length of time the practitioner needs to realize the fruits of the practice, and it identifies what those fruits are. The first version says that the fruit known as the highest understanding can be reached in this very life, if the practitioner practices the Establishments of Mindfulness. The sutra says that practicing for seven years, five years, down to one month, and half a month, and, finally, seven days, can also result in the highest understanding.

The second version goes farther, saying that to practice mindfulness for one day and night can lead to highest awakening, or that if we begin to practice in the morning, by the afternoon the practice will already have results. The third version does not mention the period of time necessary for realizing the fruits of the practice.

THE SUTRA ON KNOWING THE
BETTER WAY TO LIVE ALONE

BHADDEKARATTA SUTTA

Contents

Our appointment with life is in the present moment.
The place of our appointment is right here, in this very place.
—Thich Nhat Hanh

The Elder Sutra[38]

THERANAMO SUTTA

I heard these words of the Buddha one time when the Lord was staying at the monastery in the Jeta Grove, in the town of Shravasti. At that time there was a monk named Thera (Elder), who always preferred to be alone. Whenever he could, he praised the practice of living alone. He sought alms alone and sat in meditation alone.

One time a group of bhikshus came to the Lord. They paid their respect by prostrating at his feet, stepped to one side, sat down at a distance, and said, "Blessed One, there is an elder by the name of Thera who only wants to be alone. He always praises the practice of living alone. He goes into the village alone to seek alms, returns home from the village alone, and sits in meditation alone."

The Lord Buddha told one of the bhikshus, "Please go to the place where the monk Thera lives and tell him I wish to see him."

The bhikshu obeyed. When the monk Thera heard the Buddha's wish he came without delay, prostrated at the feet of the Buddha, stepped to one side, and sat down at a distance. Then the Blessed One asked the monk Thera, "Is it true that you prefer to be alone, praise the life of solitude, go for alms alone, come back from the village alone, and sit in meditation alone?"

The monk Thera replied, "It is true, Blessed One."

Buddha asked the monk Thera, "How do you live alone?"

The monk Thera replied, "I live alone; no one else lives with me. I praise the practice of being alone. I go for alms alone, and I come back from the village alone. I sit in meditation alone. That is all."

The Buddha taught the monk as follows. "It is obvious that you like the practice of living alone. I do not want to deny that, but I want to tell you that there is a more wonderful and profound way to be alone.

It is the way of deep observation to see that the past no longer exists and the future has not yet come, and to dwell at ease in the present moment, free from desire. When a person lives in this way, he has no hesitation in his heart. He gives up all anxieties and regrets, lets go of all binding desires, and cuts the fetters which prevent him from being free. This is called 'the better way to live alone.' There is no more wonderful way of being alone than this."

Then the Blessed One recited this gatha:

> Observing life deeply,
> it is possible to see clearly all that is.
> Not enslaved by anything,
> it is possible to put aside all craving,
> resulting in a life of peace and joy.
> This is truly to live alone.

Hearing the Lord's words, the monk Thera was delighted. He prostrated respectfully to the Buddha and departed.

The Sutra on Knowing
the Better Way to Live Alone[39]

BHADDEKARATTA SUTTA

I heard these words of the Buddha one time when the Lord was staying at the monastery in the Jeta Grove, in the town of Shravasti. He called all the monks to him and instructed them, "Bhikkhus!"[40]

And the bhikkhus replied, "We are here."

The Blessed One taught, "I will teach you what is meant by 'knowing the better way to live alone.' I will begin with an outline of the teaching, and then I will give a detailed explanation. Bhikkhus, please listen carefully."

"Blessed One, we are listening."

The Buddha taught:

"Do not pursue the past.
Do not lose yourself in the future.
The past no longer is.
The future has not yet come.
Looking deeply at life as it is
in the very here and now,
the practitioner dwells
in stability and freedom.
We must be diligent today.
To wait till tomorrow is too late.
Death comes unexpectedly.
How can we bargain with it?
The sage calls a person who
dwells in mindfulness
night and day

'the one who knows
   the better way to live alone.'

"Bhikkhus, what do we mean by 'pursuing the past'? When some-one considers the way her body was in the past, the way her feelings were in the past, the way her perceptions were in the past, the way her mental formations were in the past, the way her consciousness was in the past; when she considers these things and her mind is burdened by and attached to these things which belong to the past, then that person is pursuing the past.

"Bhikkhus, what is meant by 'not pursuing the past'? When someone considers the way her body was in the past, the way her feelings were in the past, the way her perceptions were in the past, the way her mental formations were in the past, the way her consciousness was in the past; when she considers these things but her mind is neither enslaved by nor attached to these things which belong to the past, then that person is not pursuing the past.

"Bhikkhus, what is meant by 'losing yourself in the future'? When someone considers the way his body will be in the future, the way his feelings will be in the future, the way his perceptions will be in the future, the way his mental formations will be in the future, the way his consciousness will be in the future; when he considers these things and his mind is burdened by and daydreaming about these things which belong to the future, then that person is losing himself in the future.

"Bhikkhus, what is meant by 'not losing yourself in the future'? When someone considers the way his body will be in the future, the way his feelings will be in the future, the way his perceptions will be in the future, the way his mental formations will be in the future, the way his consciousness will be in the future; when he considers these things but his mind is not burdened by or daydreaming about these things which belong to the future, then he is not losing himself in the future.

"Bhikkhus, what is meant by 'being swept away by the present'? When someone does not study or learn anything about the Awakened One, or the teachings of love and understanding, or the community that lives in harmony and awareness, when that person knows nothing about the noble teachers and their teachings, does not practice these teachings, and thinks, 'This body is myself, I am this body; these feel-ings are myself, I am these feelings; this perception is myself, I am this perception; this mental formation is myself, I am this mental formation;

this consciousness is myself, I am this consciousness,' then that person is being swept away by the present.

"Bhikkhus, what is meant by 'not being swept away by the present'? "When someone studies and learns about the Awakened One, the teachings of love and understanding, and the community that lives in harmony and awareness, when that person knows about noble teachers and their teachings, practices these teachings, and does not think, 'This body is myself, I am this body; these feelings are myself, I am these feelings; this perception is myself, I am this perception; this mental formation is myself, I am this mental formation; this consciousness is myself, I am this consciousness,' then that person is not being swept away by the present.

"Bhikkhus, I have presented the outline and the detailed explanation of knowing the better way to live alone."

Thus, the Buddha taught, and the bhikkhus were delighted to put his teachings into practice.

COMMENTARY

1: What Does It Mean to Live Alone?

The Sutra on Knowing the Better Way to Live Alone is called the Bhaddekaratta Sutta in Pali. It is number 131 in the Majjhima Nikaya. This important sutra is one of the oldest written teachings on how to live in the present moment.

"Knowing how to live alone" doesn't mean you have to live in solitude in a cave, separated from other people. If we sit alone in a cave, lost in our thinking, we aren't really living alone. "Living alone" means living to have sovereignty over ourselves, to have the freedom that comes from not being dragged away by the past, not living in fear of the future, and not being pulled around by strong emotions caused by the circumstances of the present. When we are master of ourselves, we can grasp the situation as it is, and we're in the best position to handle whatever may arise. When we dwell in mindfulness day and night, then we are truly practicing "the better way to live alone." This is true whether we are surrounded by friends and family, or when we are living a solitary life.

If a doctor tells you, "You have cancer and probably only have six months to live," you will likely feel completely overwhelmed. The fear, the idea that "I'm going to die in six months," can take away your peace and joy. Before the doctor told you about the cancer you could sit and enjoy your tea, eat your meal, or watch the moon, while now your fear takes away all your joy and freedom.

But the doctor's words can be a bell of mindfulness. We all have six months left to live, or seven months, or ten years. If we can know and accept that death is something that comes to everybody, we will not suffer so much. The doctor who tells us we have six months left to live will also die. Maybe the doctor will die before us. We may be lucky to have six months to live. If we look deeply, we see things that we can't otherwise see. We can get back our freedom from fear and, with that freedom and non-fear, we may live those six months happily.

We are all equal as far as life and death are concerned. Everyone has to die. But before we die, can we live properly? If we live properly, the quality of our last six months can be higher than if we were to live six or sixty more years. If we're caught in the fetters of suffering, our lives don't have the same meaning they would if we lived in freedom. Knowing that we have to die, we can become determined to live our lives properly and deeply. If we're not able to live with peace, joy, and freedom, then we live as if we're already dead.

In the Sutra on Knowing the Better Way to Live Alone, the Buddha teaches that we must struggle to get back our freedom, to be able to live the moments of our daily lives deeply. If in the moments of our daily lives we can have peace and joy, then we can heal the suffering we have in our bodies and our minds. Living deeply in each moment of our lives we can be in touch with the wonderful things of life; we can nourish our bodies and minds with these wonderful elements, and we can embrace and transform our suffering. To live each day of our lives deeply is to live a life of wonder, nourishment, and healing. Living like this we can revive our freedom, experience life deeply, give rise to the truth, and have awakened understanding. Our fears, anxieties, sufferings, and sadness will evaporate, and we will become a source of joy and life for ourselves and those around us.

LIVING ALONE IN THE PRESENT MOMENT

There are people who can't see the happiness of the present and think that life was more beautiful in the past. Many of us are caught in this way of thinking. The past is no longer there, but we compare it with the present. Even when we were living those moments in the past we didn't really value them at the time, because in the past we also weren't able to live in the present moment.

There are other people who pursue the past because the past made them suffer. We have all suffered in the past, and those heavy wounds are calling us back: "Come back to the past. You cannot escape me." We can become like sheep running back to the past for it to enclose and imprison us, and make us suffer.

Sometimes when we're sitting with a friend, we can feel abandoned by that friend, because our friend is drowning in the past. He is sitting next to us, but he's not really there. Suppose we find a way to free our friend from the past. We might ask him what he is thinking, or touch him gently in some way to remind him of the present moment. Then our friend may wake up and smile, and be free from the prison of the past.

Sometimes we don't want to go back into the past, but the past grabs hold of us and pulls us back. We have to look directly into the past, smile at it and say, "You can no longer oppress me. I am free of you." The past is just a ghost. We know that the past is a ghost, but we allow the ghost to imprison us.

Some of us run to pursue the future. But the future is another ghost. Why are we afraid of the future? Fear comes from our worry that this or that will or won't happen tomorrow. But the future is something that is not yet here. The future is never here. Once it's here, it's the present.

When we live with a ghost we're not living alone, we're living with another. We eat a meal, but we have the ghost sitting alongside us. When we see a friend sitting with a ghost we can say, "Who are you sitting with?" and perhaps that person will wake up. It's not just the ghosts of the past and the future that like to sit with us. In the present we have infatuations, attachments, feelings of sadness, and projects that take us away from the joy of the present moment. When we live with these things, we are not living alone; we are living with ghosts.

The ghosts of the past and the future take away a lot of our freedom. We can become their slaves. They follow us and condition our lives, and order us about. But if we know how to deal with them, we will never fall under their influence. We only have to smile at them. We only need to breathe and come back to our awareness of the present moment and say, "Oh, I know you are a ghost."

Being aware in the present moment does not preclude our thinking about the past or the future. But we must still dwell in the present moment whenever we look deeply into the past or the future, so that we can be aware of any fear or sadness without being overwhelmed by it. According to the teachings of interbeing, the past makes the present, and the present makes the future. Being in touch with the present, we are already in touch with the past and the future.

We're caught by the ghosts of the past and the future because we don't know they're ghosts. We think the past is still right here with us, and we dwell in it. But if we can smile to the ghost of the past, and acknowledge that the past was there, but that now it is gone, then we can have the smile of enlightenment. When we smile like that, it shows we have love for ourselves. We know the past and the future are not our enemies. We know how to live in this moment we are in right now. We need to live our daily moments deeply, as they occur. When we live and know that we are living, this is freedom.

2: Great Peace in Solitude

During the time of the Buddha, there was a bhikkhu named Ekavihariya, who liked to live alone. Literally, his name means "One" (*eka*) "Living" (*vihariya*). The Buddha once praised him with this short *gatha* that appears in the Dhammapada:

> Sitting alone, resting alone,
> going forth alone, without laziness;
> he who understands deeply
> the roots of suffering
> enjoys great peace,
> while dwelling in solitude.

The monk Ekavihariya was well loved and respected by his fellow practitioners.[41] There was another monk, named Thera (Elder), who also liked to live alone and often spoke highly of the solitary life. However this monk was not praised by his fellow practitioners or by the Buddha. Perhaps Thera wanted to emulate other solitary monks or perhaps he just wanted to practice living alone. But he lived the solitary life only according to the outer form, and his fellow practitioners noticed there was something unbalanced about it. They told the Buddha about him, and the Buddha invited Thera to come see him. The Elder Sutra comes from that encounter.

When Thera presented himself, the Buddha questioned him about his daily life and then offered to show him a much more enjoyable way to live alone, a way that was much more deep and wonderful.

Then the Buddha taught him, "Let go of what is past. Let go of what is not yet. Observe deeply what is happening in the present moment, but do not be attached to it. This is the most wonderful way to live alone."[42]

The title of the sutra in Pali, Theranamo, means "The One Named Thera." It is possible that after the Buddha taught Thera the contents of this sutra, the other monks, out of respect for him, began to refer to him in the sutra as the Elder, rather than by his prior name.

As the Buddha taught, a person who knows the better way to live alone does not necessarily live isolated from society. To put society at a distance and to live isolated in the forest is no guarantee of being alone. When we are surrounded by the past, worries about the future, or distractions of the present, our vision is muddled and we are never alone. One who knows the better way to live alone can see clearly, even in a crowd of people.

The Buddha discussed the importance of living alone in many sutras, including Migajala Sutra.[43] In this sutra, a monk named Migajala had heard about the teaching of the better way to live alone and came to ask the Buddha about it.

The Buddha instructed Migajala, "The forms and images which are the objects of our vision can be pleasant, enjoyable, and memorable, and can lead to craving and desire. If a monk is attached to them, then he is bound by them, and he is not alone. He is always with another."

The expression "being with another" is translated from the Pali word sadutiyavihari. It is the opposite of "living alone." But when the Buddha used this word, he did not mean that the monk was living with other people. He meant that a monk who is bound by any objects, even objects of consciousness, is actually living with those objects.

The Buddha added, "Indeed, Migajala, if a monk is bound by any fetter like this, even if he lives deep in the forest, in a deserted place without others, and without any outer disturbance, he still lives with another. Why? Because he still has not thrown off the fetters that bind him. Those fetters are the ones with whom he lives."

The Buddha taught Migajala that a person who knows the better way to live alone is someone who lives at ease, not bound by the internal formations which are based on the objects of the six senses: form, sound, smell, taste, touch, and the objects of the mind.

The Buddha concluded, "Migajala, if a monk lives like this, even in the center of a village; with monks, nuns, or lay practitioners; among royalty, or high-ranking officials; or with those who practice another way, he is still someone who knows the better way to live alone. He can be said to be living alone because he has freed himself from all attachments."

The Bhaddekaratta gatha was composed by the Buddha to summarize what he had taught Thera and Migajala. The Buddha read this gatha to the monks in the Jetavana Monastery and later commented on it for them. The opening paragraphs of the sutra depict the occasion on which the Sutra On Knowing the Better Way to Live Alone was delivered.

The people who were able to hear the Buddha that day were limited to the monks who were present in the Jetavana Monastery. Because of the importance of the subject, monks and nuns living elsewhere gradually came to know about the "Knowing the Better Way to Live Alone" gatha. The God of the Forest Hot Springs Sutra tells us, "At that time the Buddha was staying in Rajagriha at the Venuvana Monastery. The monk Samiddhi was residing in the nearby forest. One morning after bathing in the hot springs Samiddhi was putting on his robe when a beautiful god appeared, prostrated before him, and asked him if he had ever heard and practiced the "Knowing the Better Way to Live Alone" gatha, saying, 'Venerable Samiddhi, you should ask the Buddha to teach us this gatha so that we can put it into practice. I have heard that this gatha contains the deepest meaning of the Buddha's teachings, that it is the basis for the enlightened life, and that it can lead to awakened understanding and nirvana.' After the god had spoken, he joined his palms and walked clockwise three times around the monk to show his respect.

The monk Samiddhi went to the Buddha. After prostrating to the Awakened One, he told about his encounter with the god and asked the Buddha to teach him the "Knowing the Better Way to Live Alone" gatha. The Buddha asked Samiddhi if he knew who the god was. When Samiddhi replied that he did not, the Buddha told him the god's name and that he came from the thirty-third heaven. Then Samiddhi and the monks who were present asked the Buddha again to teach them the gatha. The Buddha recited it for them:

Do not pursue the past.
Do not lose yourself in the future.
The past no longer is.
The future has not yet come.
Looking deeply at life as it is
in the very here and now,
the practitioner dwells

in stability and freedom.
We must be diligent today.
To wait until tomorrow is too late.
Death comes unexpectedly.
How can we bargain with it?
The sage calls a person who
dwells in mindfulness
night and day
"the one who knows
the better way to live alone."

After reciting the gatha, the Buddha left his seat and returned to his hut to meditate. The monks, including Samiddhi, wished to hear an explanation of it, so they went to the elder Kaccana, a senior disciple of the Buddha, recited the gatha to him, and asked if he would comment on it. The monk Kaccana was known to have many excellent qualities. He was often praised by the Buddha for his intelligence, and the monks thought he would be able to offer a penetrating explanation. At first Kaccana hesitated. He suggested that the monks go directly to the Buddha, so that the commentary was from the Teacher himself. But in the end, because the bhikkhus insisted, he agreed to explain the gatha to them. This elder's commentary is the essential content of The God of the Forest Hot Springs Sutra.

After offering his explanation of the gatha, the elder told the monks that if the opportunity presented itself, they should ask the Buddha to explain it directly, because his own insight could never be as profound as the insight of the Awakened One.

The bhikkhus, including Samiddhi, did have another audience with the Buddha, and they told the Buddha the explanation of the "Knowing the Better Way to Live Alone" gatha that they had heard from Kaccana. The Buddha began by speaking in praise of the elder: "Excellent. Among my disciples there are those who grasp the meaning of the Dharma and understand its significance. If the teacher recites a gatha and does not have a chance to comment on it, then it is the disciples who must penetrate the meaning of the gatha and give a fuller explanation of the teaching. The Elder Kaccana is a senior bhikkhu. The commentary he gave you shows the true meaning of the gatha and is in accord with the truth of the way things are. You should use it and make it part of your practice."

This exchange took place in Rajagriha, the capital city of Magadha, on the right bank of the Ganges. The account that follows took place further north and west, in the town of Shravasti, the capital of the kingdom of Koshala, on the left bank of the Ganges. That account is given in the Shakyan Hermitage Sutra.

The Shakyan Hermitage had been built by members of the Shakyan clan in the hills not far from Shravasti. This hermitage also had the name "No Problems" or "At Peace." At that time, the bhikkhu Lomasakangiya was staying in the hermitage. One night shortly before daybreak, he stepped outside and spread out a cloth on one of the string cots under the trees. As soon as he began to sit on the cot in the lotus position, a very beautiful god appeared, prostrated before him, and asked if he knew the "Knowing the Better Way to Live Alone" gatha and if he had ever heard a commentary on it. The monk in turn asked the god the same question, and the god replied that he had heard the gatha but he had not yet had the chance to hear the commentary explaining the deep meaning of the gatha. The elder asked, "How is it that you have heard the gatha but have not yet heard the commentary?"

The god explained that at one time, when the Buddha was residing in Rajagriha, he had heard the Buddha recite the gatha, but the Buddha had given no commentary.

Then the god recited the gatha and advised the monk to go and ask the Buddha to explain it. The gatha in this sutra is identical to the one in The God of the Forest Hot Springs Sutra.

After that, the bhikkhu Lomasakangiya went to the Buddha and told him what had happened. At that time, the Buddha was staying in the Jetavana Monastery in Shravasti. Having heard the account, the Buddha told Lomasakangiya that the name of the god who had appeared to him was Candana (Sandalwood) and that he came from the thirty-third heaven. Then bhikkhu Lomasakangiya requested the Buddha to explain the gatha.

That day, there were many bhikkhus present. The Buddha's commentary on the gatha forms the essence of the Shakyan Hermitage Sutra.[44]

Another sutra related to the Sutra on Knowing the Better Way to Live Alone is the Sutra Spoken by Ananda.[45] The Buddha delivered this discourse at Shravasti. One night the Venerable Ananda asked the monks to assemble in the main Dharma hall of the Jetavana Monastery, and he recited and explained the "Knowing the Better Way to Live

Alone" gatha. Early the next day, one of the bhikkhus went to see the Buddha and told him about Ananda's Dharma talk. The sutra does not say that the bhikkhu expressed any lack of confidence in the Venerable Ananda, but the sutra does say that after the Buddha heard about the Dharma talk, he sent the bhikkhu to invite Ananda to join them.

When Ananda arrived in the Buddha's room, the Buddha asked him, "Is it true that you recited and gave a talk on the gatha, 'Knowing the Better Way to Live Alone' last night?"

Ananda replied that it was true, and the Buddha asked, "Can you recite it for me and tell me your commentary on it?"

After Ananda recited the gatha and told the Buddha his explanation of it, the Buddha asked Ananda several more questions. The main part of the Sutra Spoken by Ananda is comprised of the answers given by Ananda to the Buddha's questions. When he heard Ananda's answers, he praised him saying, "Excellent! Among my disciples there are those who have the insight to understand the essential significance of the teachings."

The Buddha praised Ananda in the way that he had praised Kaccana. On that day there were many bhikkhus present, among them the bhikkhu who had told the Buddha about Ananda's Dharma talk. Perhaps the Buddha spoke those words to assure the monks that the Venerable Ananda's grasp of the Dharma was as firm as Kaccana's and that the bhikkhus could make Ananda's teachings a part of their practice.

3: Putting the Teachings of the Buddha into Practice

To live alone does not mean to reject the world and society. The Buddha said that living alone means living in the present moment, deeply observing what is happening. If we do that, we will not be dragged into the past or swept away into thoughts about the future. The Buddha said that if we cannot live in the present moment, even if we are alone in the deepest forest, we are not really alone. He said that if we are fully alive in the present moment, even if we are in a crowded urban area, we can still be said to be living alone.

It is important to practice in a community. A Vietnamese proverb goes: "Soup is to a meal what friends are to the practice." When we practice in a community, we can learn from its members, and take refuge in our communal practice. We need to discover the way of being alone in a practice community.

The monk Thera was part of a practice community, but he was determined to live alone. He believed in the idea of a solitary life, because he had at some time heard the Buddha praising the practice of living alone. So he kept his distance from everyone else. He begged for alms alone, he returned alone, he ate alone, and he meditated alone. He was like a drop of oil in a bowl of water, unable to mix with his fellow practitioners. The other monastics felt something was not right with his practice, and they expressed their concern to the Buddha.

The Buddha was very kind. He did not criticize Thera. He only said that Thera's way of living alone was not the best way of doing so. Because there were many other monks present at the time and they could benefit from the teaching, the Buddha took the opportunity to teach Thera that the better way of living alone is to associate with the other monastics, to learn from them and take refuge in them.

There were bhikkhus who were the opposite of Thera, who would always gather in small groups and fritter away their time chatting and joking. Their conversations were not about the teachings, and the Buddha frequently reprimanded them. There are stories throughout the sutras in which the Buddha advises or chides the bhikkhus who act in a noisy and undisciplined way, not knowing how to keep body and mind in check, not knowing how to spend their time usefully in practicing walking and sitting meditation and observing deeply things as they are in the present moment.[46]

When I first became a monk, my master gave me a copy of the book *Encouraging Words of Master Guishan*. I will never forget the sentences in which Master Guishan reprimands practitioners who, after the midday meal, gather in small groups and talk about meaningless things. Guishan's words of advice have often come back to me and served as a reminder:

> When you receive food offered by donors, wouldn't it be better to meditate on the food than to think that as a monk you deserve to receive it? When you finish eating, if you sit around talking idly, it will increase everyone's suffering later on. How many lifetimes do you plan to chase after worldly matters without looking deeply at where your life is going? Time flies like an arrow, yet you are still attached to the pleasure of the offerings you receive, and you still think that money and possessions will provide you security. The Buddha taught his monks to be satisfied with just enough food, clothing, and shelter. Why would a monk or a nun spend so much time craving these things? By the time you wake up, your hair will be white. Listen to the wise ones. They did not become monks and nuns just to have some food to eat and a robe to wear.[47]

When we live in a practice community, there should always be at least one or two people who serve as role models. Sometimes we only need to watch them standing, walking, speaking, or smiling in mindfulness, and we feel steady in our own practice. The fact that we know "the better way to live alone" does not prevent us from enjoying and benefitting from the presence of such people. On the contrary, it is because we know "the better way to live alone" that we have the ability to observe them deeply and appreciate them.

To be in touch does not mean just to talk with the other person. When we are in touch with the blue sky, for example, the white clouds, the green willow, or the rose, we do not communicate with them only in words. We recognize and accept these things, and feel their warmth. Confidence springs up in us, and we learn a lot from their presence. In this way we are able to profit from the third jewel, the practice community.

If we practice "the better way of living alone," and we spend most of our time quietly practicing walking and sitting meditation, our presence will make a real contribution to the community. Unlike the monk Thera or the monks who gather after meals to talk about things that are not important, every step we make adds to the quality and stability of the practice in the community. We are like Shariputra, Kashyapa, Badhya, or Kimbila—all students of the Buddha. Seeing us, the Buddha will be satisfied and smile. The Buddha knows that if every individual in the community knows how to live alone, the quality of life in the community will be excellent. When all the members of the community contribute to that quality, the community has a strong foundation, and many people can benefit from it. To live alone means to live in mindfulness. It does not mean to isolate oneself from society. If we know the better way to live alone, we can be in real touch with people and society, and we will know what to do and what not to do to be of help.

AWAKE AND ALONE

If we live in forgetfulness, if we lose ourselves in the past or in the future, if we allow ourselves to be tossed about by our desires, anger, and ignorance, we will not be able to live each moment of our lives deeply. We will not be in contact with what is happening in the present moment, and our relations with others will become shallow and impoverished.

Some days we may feel hollow, exhausted, and joyless, not really our true selves. On such days, even if we try to be in touch with others, our efforts will be in vain. The more we try, the more we fail. When this happens, we should stop trying to be in touch with what is outside of ourselves and come back to being in touch with ourselves. We should "be alone." This is a time to practice conscious breathing, observing deeply what is going on inside and around us. We can accept all the phenomena we observe, say hello to them, and smile at them. We do well to do simple things, like walking or sitting meditation, washing our clothes, cleaning the floor, making tea, and cleaning the bathroom in mindfulness. If we do these things, we will restore the richness of our spiritual lives.

The Buddha was someone who lived an awakened life, dwelling constantly in the present moment in a relaxed and steady way. There was always a richness about him—a richness of freedom, joy, understanding, and love. Whether he was seated on a rocky crag of Vulture Peak, in the shade of the bamboo groves of Venuvana Monastery, or under the thatched roof of his hut in Jetavana, Buddha was Buddha, unagitated, content, and of few words. Everyone could see that his presence contributed greatly to the harmony and stability of the community. The monks and nuns were affected just by knowing he was nearby. Many students of the Buddha, including hundreds of senior disciples, inspired similar confidence in those who observed them. King Prasenajit of Koshala once told the Buddha that what gave him so much confidence in the Buddha was the unhurried, calm, and joyful way of life of the monks and nuns who were practicing under his guidance.

If we live in mindfulness, we are no longer poor, because our practice of living in the present moment makes us rich in joy, peace, understanding, and love. Even when we encounter someone poor in spirit, we can look deeply and discover that person's rich layers.

When we watch a documentary or read a book or look at someone's painting or sculpture, if we are already poor in heart and mind, and weak in mindfulness, what we are reading or looking at may irritate us and make us feel even more poor. But if we are rich in mindfulness, we will discover what lies in the depths of that art. We may be able to see deeply into the inner world of the person who made it. Looking with the eyes of an art critic, we can see things that most people do not see, and even a bad movie or book or sculpture can teach us. Maintaining full awareness of each detail of the present moment, we are able to profit from it. This is the better way to live alone.

TIED UP INSIDE

The "Knowing the Better Way To Live Alone" gatha begins with the line: "Do not pursue the past." To "pursue the past" means to regret what has already come and gone. We regret the loss of the beautiful things of the past that we can no longer find in the present. Buddha commented on this line as follows: "When someone thinks how his body was in the past, how his feelings were in the past, how his perceptions were in the past, how his mental formations were in the past, how his consciousness was in the past, when he thinks like that and gives rise to a mind which is enslaved by those things which belong to the past, then that person is pursuing the past."

Buddha taught that we should not pursue the past "because the past no longer is." When we are lost in thoughts about the past, we lose the present. Life exists only in the present moment. To lose the present is to lose life. The Buddha's meaning is very clear: we must say goodbye to the past so that we may return to the present. To return to the present is to be in touch with life.

What dynamics in our consciousness compel us to go back and live with the images of the past? These forces are made up of internal formations (Sanskrit: *samyojana*), mental formations that arise in us and bind us. Things we see, hear, smell, taste, touch, imagine, or think can all give rise to internal formations—desire, irritation, anger, confusion, fear, anxiety, suspicion, and so on. Internal formations are present in the depths of the consciousness of each of us.

Internal formations influence our consciousness and our everyday behavior. They cause us to think, say, and do things that we may not even be aware of. Because they compel us in this way, they are also called fetters, because they bind us to acting in certain ways.

The commentaries usually mention nine kinds of internal formations: desire, hatred, pride, ignorance, stubborn views, attachment, doubt, jealousy, and selfishness. Among these, the fundamental internal formation is ignorance, the lack of clear seeing. Ignorance is the raw material out of which the other internal formations are made. Although there are nine internal formations, because "desire" is always listed first, it is often used to represent all the internal formations. In the Kaccana-Bhaddekaratta, the monk Kaccana explains:

> My friends, what is meant by dwelling in the past? Someone
> thinks, "In the past my eyes were like that and the form (with

which my eyes were in contact) was like that," and thinking like this, he is bound by desire. Bound by desire, there is a feeling of longing. This feeling of longing keeps him dwelling in the past.

Kaccana's commentary could make us think that the only internal formation holding one in the past is desire. But when Kaccana refers to "desire," he is using it to represent all the internal formations—hatred, doubt, jealousy, and so forth. All of these tie us and hold us back in the past.

Sometimes we only have to hear the name of someone who has wronged us in the past, and our internal formations from that time automatically take us back into the past, and we relive the suffering. The past is the home ground of both painful and happy memories. Being absorbed in the past is a way of being dead to the present moment. It is not easy to drop the past and return to living in the present. When we try to do it, we have to resist the force of the internal formations in us. We have to learn to transform our internal formations, so that we will be free to be attentive to the present moment.

STANDING FIRMLY

The present contains the past. When we understand how our internal formations cause conflicts in us, we can see how the past is in the present moment, and we will no longer be overwhelmed by the past. When the Buddha said, "Do not pursue the past," he was telling us not to be overwhelmed by the past. He did not mean that we should stop looking at the past in order to observe it deeply. When we review the past and observe it deeply, if we are standing firmly in the present, we are not overwhelmed by it. The materials of the past that make up the present become clear when they express themselves in the present. We can learn from them. If we observe these materials deeply, we can arrive at a new understanding of them. That is called "looking again at something old in order to learn something new."

If we know that the past also lies in the present, we understand that we are able to change the past by transforming the present. The ghosts of the past, which follow us into the present, also belong to the present moment. To observe them deeply, recognize their nature, and transform them, is to transform the past. The ghosts of the past are very real. They are the internal formations in us, which are sometimes quietly asleep, while at other times they awaken suddenly and forcefully. There is the Sanskrit term *anushaya*. *Anu* means "along with." *Shaya* means "lying down." We could translate anushaya as "latent tendency." The internal formations continue to be with us, but they are lying asleep in the depths of our consciousness. We call them ghosts, but they are present in a very real way. According to the Vijñanavada school of Buddhism, anushaya are seeds that lie in everyone's subconscious (*alaya*). An important part of the work of observation meditation is to be able to recognize the anushaya when they manifest, observe them deeply, and transform them.

FUTURE GHOSTS

Sometimes, because the present is so difficult, we give our attention to the future, hoping that the situation will improve in the future. Imagining the future will be better, we are better able to accept the suffering and hardship of the present. But at other times, thinking about the future may cause us a lot of fear and anxiety, and yet we cannot stop doing it. The reason we continue to think about the future, even when we do not want to, is due to the presence of internal formations. Although not yet here, the future is already producing ghosts that haunt us. In fact, these ghosts are not produced by the future or the past. It is our consciousness that creates them. The past and the future are creations of our consciousness.

The energies behind our thinking about the future are our hopes, dreams, and anxieties. Our hopes can be the result of our sufferings and failures. Because the present does not bring us happiness, we allow our minds to travel into the future. We hope that in the future, the situation will be brighter: "When someone considers how his body will be in the future, how his feelings will be in the future, how his mental formations will be in the future, how his consciousness will be in the future . . ." Thinking in this way can give us the courage to accept failure and suffering in the present. The poet Tru Vu said that the future is the vitamin for the present. Hope brings us back some of the joys of life that we have lost.

We all know that hope is necessary for life. But according to

Buddhism, hope can be an obstacle. If we invest our minds in the future, we will not have enough mental energy to face and transform the present. Naturally we have the right to make plans for the future, but making plans for the future does not mean to be being swept away by daydreams. While we are making plans, our feet are firmly planted in the present. We can only build the future from the raw materials of the present.

The essential teaching of Buddhism is to be free of all desire for the future in order to come back with all our hearts and minds into the present. To realize awakening means to arrive at a deep and full insight into reality, which is in the present moment. In order to return to the present and to be face to face with what is happening, we must look deeply into the heart of what is and experience its true nature. When we do so, we experience the deep understanding that can release us from suffering and darkness.

According to Buddhism, hell, paradise, *samsara*, and *nirvana* are all here in the present moment. To return to the present moment is to discover life and to realize the truth. All the Awakened Ones of the past have come to Awakening in the present moment. All the Awakened Ones of the present and the future will realize the fruit of Awakening in the present also. Only the present moment is real: "The past no longer is, and the future has not yet come."

If we do not stand firmly in the present moment, we may feel ungrounded when we look at the future. We may think that in the future we will be alone, with no place of refuge and no one to help us. "When someone considers how his body will be in the future, how his feelings will be in the future, how his mental formations will be in the future, how his consciousness will be in the future . . ." Such concerns about the future bring about unease, anxiety, and fear, and do not help us at all in taking care of the present moment. They just make our way of dealing with the present weak and confused. There is a Confucian saying that a person who does not know how to plan for the distant future will be troubled and perplexed by the near future. This is meant to remind us to care for the future, but not to be anxious and fearful about it. The best way of preparing for the future is to take good care of the present, because we know that if the present is made up of the past, then the future will be made up of the present. All we need to be responsible for is the present moment. Only the present is within our reach. To care for the present is to care for the future.

SMILING WITHIN

When we think about the past, feelings of regret or shame may arise. When we think about the future, feelings of desire or fear may come up. But all of these feelings arise in the present moment, and they all affect the present moment. Most of the time, their effect does not contribute to our happiness or joy. We have to learn how to face these feelings. The main thing we need to remember is that the past and the future are both in the present, and if we take hold of the present moment, then we also transform the past and the future.

How can we transform the past? In the past we may have said or done something destructive or harmful, and now we regret it. According to Buddhist psychology, regret is an "indeterminate emotion." This means that it can be either constructive or destructive. When we know that something we have said or done has caused harm, we may give rise to a mind of repentance, vowing that in the future we will not repeat the same mistake. In this case, our feelings of regret have a wholesome effect. If, on the other hand, the feelings of regret continue to disturb us, making it impossible for us to concentrate on anything else, taking all the peace and joy out of our lives, then those feeling of regret have an unwholesome effect.

When regret becomes unwholesome, we should first distinguish whether the cause was based on something we did or said, or on something we failed to do or say. If in the past, we said or did something destructive, we can call that an "error of commission." We did or said something with a lack of mindfulness, and it caused harm. Sometimes we commit an "error of omission." We did harm by not saying or doing what needed to be said or done, and that brought us regret and sorrow. Our lack of mindfulness was there, and its results are still present. Our pain, shame, and regret are an important part of that result. If we observe the present deeply and take hold of it, we can transform it. We do so by means of mindfulness, determination, and correct actions and speech. All these come about in the present moment. When we transform the present in this way, we also transform the past, and at the same time, we build the future.

If we say that all is lost, everything is destroyed, or the suffering has already happened, we do not see that the past has become the present. Of course, the suffering has already been caused and the wound of that suffering can touch our very soul, but instead of lamenting about or suffering from what we have done in the past, we should take hold of the present and transform it. The traces of a bad drought can only be erased by a bountiful rainfall, and rain can only fall in the present moment.

Buddhist repentance is based on the understanding that wrongdoing originates in the mind. There is a gatha of repentance:

> All wrongdoing arises from the mind.
> If mind is purified, what trace of wrong is left?
> After repentance, my heart is light
> like the white clouds that have always floated over
> the ancient forest in freedom.

Because of our lack of mindfulness, because our minds were obscured by desire, anger, and jealousy, we acted wrongly. That is what is meant by "All wrongdoing arises from the mind." But if the wrongdoing arose from our minds, it can also be transformed within our minds. If our minds are transformed, then the objects perceived by our minds will also be transformed. Such transformation is available if we know how to return to the present moment. Once we have transformed our minds, our hearts will be as light as floating clouds, and we will become a source of peace and joy for ourselves and others. Yesterday, perhaps out of foolishness or anger, we said something that made our mothers sad. But today our minds are transformed and our hearts light, and we can see our mothers smiling at us, even if they are no longer alive. If we can smile within ourselves, our mother can also smile with us.

If we can transform the past, we can also transform the future. Our anxieties and fears for the future make the present dark. There is no doubt that the future will be black too, because we know that the future is made up of the present. Taking care of the present is the best way to take care of the future. Sometimes, because we are so concerned about what will happen the next day, we toss and turn all night, unable to sleep. We worry that if we cannot sleep during the night, we will be tired the next day and unable to perform to the best of our ability. The more we worry, the more difficult it is for us to sleep. Our worries and fears for the future destroy the present. But if we stop thinking about tomorrow and just stay in bed and follow our breathing, really enjoying the opportunity we have to rest, not only will we savor the moments of peace and joy under the warm blankets, but we will fall asleep quite easily and naturally. That kind of sleep is a big help for making the next day a success.

When we hear that the forests of our planet are diseased and dying so rapidly, we may feel anxious. We are concerned for the future, because we are aware of what is happening in the present moment. Our awareness can motivate us to do something to halt the destruction of our environment. Obviously, our concern for the future is different from worry and anxiety, which only drain us. We have to know how to enjoy the presence of beautiful, healthy trees in order to be able to do something to protect and preserve them.

When we throw a banana peel into the compost heap, if we are mindful, we know that the peel will become compost and be reborn as a tomato or as lettuce in just a few months. But when we throw a plastic bag into the garbage, thanks to our awareness, we know that a plastic bag will not become a tomato or a salad very quickly. Some kinds of garbage need four or five hundred years to decompose. Nuclear waste needs a quarter of a million years before it stops being harmful and returns to the soil. Living in the present moment in an awakened way, looking after the present moment with all our heart, we will not do things that destroy the future. That is the most concrete way to do what is constructive for the future.

In our everyday life, we may also produce poisons for our minds, and these poisons destroy not only us but also those who live with us, in the present and in the future too. Buddhism talks about three poisons: desire, hatred, and ignorance. In addition, there are other poisons whose capacity to do harm is very great: jealousy, prejudice, pride, suspicion, and obstinacy.

In our day-to-day relationships with ourselves, others, and our environment, any or all of these poisons can manifest, blaze up, and destroy our peace and joy, as well as the peace and joy of those around us. These poisons can linger and pollute our minds, causing bitter consequences in the future. So to live in the present moment is also to accept and face these poisons as they arise, manifest, and return to the unconscious, and to practice observation meditation in order to transform them. This is a Buddhist practice. To live in the present is also to see the wonderful and wholesome things in order to nourish and protect them. Happiness is the direct result of facing things and being in touch. That happiness is the material from which a beautiful future is constructed.

LIFE IS A PATH

To return to the present is to be in contact with life. Life can be found only in the present moment, because "the past no longer is" and "the future has not yet come." Buddhahood, liberation, awakening, peace, joy, and happiness can only be found in the present moment. Our appointment with life is in the present moment. The place of our appointment is right here, in this very place.

According to the Avatamsaka Sutra, time and space are not separate. Time is made up of space, and space is made up of time. When we speak about spring, we usually think of time, but spring is also space. When it is spring in Europe, it is winter in Australia.

When we have a tea mediation, those who attend breathe in and out and recite the following gatha together before taking the first sip of tea:

> This cup of tea in my two hands—
> mindfulness is held uprightly.
> My mind and body dwell
> in the very here and now.

When we drink tea in mindfulness, we practice coming back to the present moment to live our lives right here. When our minds and our bodies are fully in the present moment, then the steaming cup of tea appears clearly to us. We know it is a wonderful aspect of existence. At that time we are really in contact with the cup of tea. It is only at times like this that life is really present.

Peace, joy, liberation, awakening, happiness, Buddhahood, the source—everything we long for and seek after can only be found in the present moment. To abandon the present moment in order to look for these things in the future is to throw away the substance and hold on to the shadow. In Buddhism, aimlessness (*apranihita*) is taught as a way to help the practitioner stop pursuing the future and return wholly to the present. Aimlessness is sometimes called wishlessness, and it is one of the "three doors of liberation." (The other two are emptiness and signlessness.) To be able to stop pursuing the future allows us to realize that all the wonderful things we seek are present in us, in the present moment. Life is not a particular place or a destination. Life is a path. To practice walking meditation is to go without needing to arrive.

Every step can bring us peace, joy, and liberation. That is why we walk in the spirit of aimlessness. There is no way to liberation, peace, and joy; peace and joy are themselves the way. Our appointment with the Buddha, with liberation, with happiness, is here and now. We should not miss this appointment.

Buddhism teaches a way of breathing that gives us the capacity of making body and mind one in order to be face to face with life. This is called "oneness of body and mind." That is why every meditator begins by practicing the Sutra on the Full Awareness of Breathing (Anapanasati Sutta).

But to come back to the present does not mean to be carried away by what is happening in the present. The sutra teaches us to observe life deeply and be in touch with the present moment, and see all the sufferings and the wonders of the present. Yet we must do so in mindfulness, maintaining a high degree of awareness in order not to be carried away by, or caught in, desire for or aversion to what is happening in the present.

> Looking deeply at life as it is
> in the very here and now,
> the practitioner dwells
> in stability and freedom.

"Stability and freedom" refer to the contentment and tranquility of not being carried away by anything whatsoever. Stability and ease are two characteristics of nirvana. The Pali version of this verse uses two terms, *asamkuppam* and *asamhiram*. Asamkuppam means "unwavering, unshakable, immovable, unexcitable." Sanghadeva, the monk and translator of the Madhyama Agama, translates it as "firm and unwavering." The monk Dharmapala translates it as "stable." Asamhiram means, literally, "not folded together, not restrained, not collected, not carried away by anything." Sanghadeva translated asamhiram into Chinese as "non-existing" (*wu yu*), that is not exact. Dharmapala, in The Elder Sutra, translated asamhiram as "not fettered." "Fettered" here means "imprisoned." So "not fettered" means "not caught" or "in freedom."

Being in contact with life in the present moment, we observe deeply what is. Then we are able to see the impermanent and selfless nature of all that is. Impermanence and selflessness are not negative aspects of life but the very foundations on which life is built. Impermanence is the constant transformation of things. Without impermanence, there can be no life. Selflessness is the interdependent nature of all things. Without interdependence, nothing could exist. Without the sun, the clouds, and the Earth, the tulip could not be. We often feel sad about the impermanence and selflessness of life, because we forget that without impermanence and selflessness, life cannot be. To be aware of impermanence and selflessness does not take away the joy of being alive. On the contrary, it adds healthiness, stability, and freedom. It is because people cannot see the impermanent and selfless nature of things that they suffer. They take what is impermanent as permanent and what is selfless as having a self.

Looking deeply into a rose, we can see its impermanent nature quite clearly. At the same time, we can see its beauty and value its preciousness. Because we perceive its fragile and impermanent nature, we may see that flower as even more beautiful and precious. The more fragile something is, the more beautiful and precious it is—for example, a rainbow, a sunset, a cereus cactus flowering by night, a falling star. Looking at the sun rising over Vulture Peak, at the town of Vesali, at a field of ripe, golden rice, the Buddha saw their beauty and told Ananda so.

Seeing deeply the impermanent nature of those beautiful things, their transformation and disappearance, the Buddha did not suffer or despair. We, too, by observing deeply and seeing impermanence and selflessness in all that is, can overcome despair and suffering and experience the preciousness of the miracles of everyday life—a glass of clear water, a cool breeze, a step taken in ease and freedom. These are wonderful things, although they are impermanent and selfless.

Life is suffering, but it is also wonderful. Sickness, old age, death, accidents, starvation, unemployment, and natural disasters cannot be avoided in life. But, if our understanding is deep and our minds free, we can accept these things with tranquility, and the suffering will already be greatly lessened. This is not to say we should close our eyes before suffering. By being in contact with suffering, we give rise to and nourish our natural love and compassion. Suffering becomes the element that nourishes our love and compassion, and so we are not afraid of it. When our heart is filled with love and compassion, we will act in ways to help relieve the suffering of others.

If the human species has been able to make any progress, it is because of our heart of love and compassion. We need to learn from compassionate beings how to develop the practice of deep observation for the sake of others. Then others will be able to learn from us the way to live in the present and see the impermanent and selfless nature of all that is. This insight will lighten suffering.

Fear of the unexpected leads many people to live a constricted and anxious life. No one can know in advance the misfortunes that may happen to us and our loved ones, but if we learn to live in an awakened way, living deeply every moment of our lives, treating those who are close to us with gentleness and understanding, then we will have nothing to regret when something happens to us or to them. Living in the present moment, we are able to be in touch with life's wonderful, refreshing, and health-giving phenomena, which allow us to heal the wounds in ourselves. Every day we become more wonderful, fresh, and healthy.

PEACE, FREEDOM, AND JOY

To practice a life of deep observation according to the teachings of the Buddha is to have a life of peace, freedom, and joy, and to realize complete liberation. The "Knowing the Better Way to Live Alone" gatha reminds us that we cannot avoid death and advises us to be diligent in the practice today, for tomorrow it will be too late. Death comes unexpectedly, and there is no way to bargain with it. If we live observing everything deeply in the present moment, we learn to live in peace and joy with freedom and stability. If we continue to practice diligently in this way, peace, joy, and stability will grow every day until we realize complete liberation. When there is complete liberation, death can no longer harm us.

A life like this will bring joy to our dear ones and others. The material of stability and release is also the element of liberation. Liberation is the fruit of deep observation, which leads to the realization of the impermanent and selfless nature of all that is. By observing at a deep level, we can defeat death, because the observation of impermanence can lead us to transcend the boundaries of birth and death. When we look at all that is in the universe and all those dear to us, we see that there is nothing eternal and unchanging that we can call "I" or "self."

TRANSCENDING BIRTH AND DEATH

We often think that birth means that what did not exist comes into existence, and that death means that which exists ceases to exist. When we look deeply at things, we see that this idea about birth and death is mistaken in many respects. No phenomenon whatsoever can come into existence out of nothing, and no phenomenon that exists can become nothing. Things are ceaselessly transforming. The cloud does not die; it only becomes rain. The rain is not born; it is only the transformation and continuation of the cloud. Leaves, a pair of shoes, joy, and sorrow all conform to this principle of no-birth and no-death. To think that after death we no longer exist is a narrow view, which in Buddhism is called the "nihilistic view." The narrow view, that after death we continue to exist without changing is called the "view of permanence." Reality transcends both permanence and annihilation.

The Buddha taught us to look directly into the elements that combine together to constitute our bodies, in order to see the nature of these elements and transcend the idea of "self"—whether it is the idea of a permanent, indestructible self, or the idea of a self subject to complete annihilation after we die. The sutra says: "Someone who studies and learns about the Awakened One, the teachings of love and understanding, and the community that lives in harmony and awareness, who knows about noble teachers and their teachings, practices these teachings, and does not think, 'This body is myself, I am this body; these feelings are myself, I am these feelings; this perception is myself, I am this perception; this mental formation is myself, I am this mental formation; this consciousness is myself, I am this consciousness'— then that person does not go back to the past, does not think ahead to the future, and is not being swept away by the present."

The five elements that combine together to become the thing we call self are form (the body), feelings, perceptions, mental formations, and consciousness. If we look penetratingly into the substance of these elements and see their impermanent and interdependent nature, we naturally see that there is no entity we can call "self." All five elements are constantly transforming. They are never born and never die. There is no element that goes from nothingness into existence, nor any element that goes from existence into nothingness. The thing which we think of as "I" is not born and does not die. We do not identify "I" with the body, whether that body is developing or degenerating, nor with the feelings that change at every moment. Similarly, we do not identify with our perceptions and our consciousness. We are not bound or limited by these five elements. We see that if these elements really are not born or destroyed, then we need no longer be oppressed by death. This insight enables us to transcend birth and death.

When the sutra refers to someone who "practices according to the teachings of the Noble Ones," it means someone who lives in the present and observes deeply in order to see life's impermanent and selfless nature. The Buddha taught that "we must practice diligently today, for tomorrow will be too late; death comes unexpectedly and there is no bargaining with it." Observing deeply, we can realize the birthless and deathless nature of things, and there is nothing more that can frighten us, not even death. We directly overcome birth and death when, by deep observation and realization of impermanence and selflessness, we pierce through false ideas about the nature of existence. Once we overcome death, we no longer need to "bargain with death." We can smile, take the hand of death, and go for a walk together.

The life called the "brahma-faring life" of a monk or a nun can lead to the realization of the birthless and deathless nature of all that is. That realization is the substance of liberation. That is why in the Kaccana-Bhaddekaratta Sutra it is emphasized that the practice of living alone is the basis of the brahma-faring life of a monk or a nun. It is also the basis of life for all of us.

4: The Bhaddekaratta Gatha in Other Sutras

The Bhaddekaratta gatha became well known and is found in many other sutras in both the Pali Canon and the Chinese Canon.

In the Pali Canon, I have come across four suttas with the "Bhaddekaratta" gatha, all in the Majjhima Nikaya. The first is the Bhaddekaratta Sutta (no. 131). The second is the Ananda-Bhaddekaratta Sutta (no. 132), which is the equivalent of the Sutra Spoken by Ananda. The third is the Mahakaccana-Bhaddekaratta Sutta (no. 133), equivalent to The God of the Forest Hot Springs Sutra. The fourth is the Lomasakangiya-Bhaddekaratta Sutta (M134), equivalent to the Shakyan Hermitage Sutra.

Besides the four Pali suttas and Chinese sutras mentioned above, the subject of living alone is referred to in many other places in the canons, in detail in the Theranamo and the Migajala sutras, although the Bhaddekaratta gatha is not specifically quoted.

The terms *ekavihari* (one who lives alone) and *sadutiyavihari* (one who lives with another) in the Migajala Sutta are easy to understand and accept. But the term *bhaddekaratta* is difficult to translate. Dharmanandi, who translated the Samyukta Agama into Chinese, did not understand this compound word, so he just transcribed it into Chinese characters and used it as the title of the gatha.[48]

A number of Buddhist masters of the Southern Tradition understand *ekaratta* as "one night" and translate Bhaddekaratta as "A Good Night for Meditation." Judging from the content of the sutra, I believe this translation is not correct. *Bhadda* means "good" or "ideal." *Eka* means "one" or "alone." *Ratta* means "to like." The contemporary Buddhist scholar Bhikkhu Nanananda translates the title as "The Ideal Lover of Solitude." After much reflection, I think that "Knowing the Better Way to Live Alone" is closer to the original meaning of the sutra.

THE BHADDEKARATTA GATHA IN THE CHINESE CANON

In the Madhyama Agama there are three sutras that quote this gatha. The first is The God of the Forest Hot Springs Sutra (no. 165), in which the poem is quoted four times. The second is The Shakyan Hermitage Sutra (no. 166), in which the gatha is quoted three times. The third sutra is the Sutra Spoken by Ananda (no. 167), in which the gatha is quoted once. The following is the translation of the gatha as it appears in the three sutras:

> Do not think of the past.
> Do not worry about the future.
> Things of the past have died.
> The future has not arrived.
> What is happening in the present
> should be observed deeply.
> The Wise Ones live according to this
> and dwell in stability and freedom.
> If one practices the teachings
> of the Wise Ones,
> why should one be afraid of death?
> If we do not understand this,
> there is no way to avoid
> the great pain of the final danger.
> To practice diligently day and night,
> one should regularly recite
> the Bhaddekaratta Gatha.

The following Bhaddekaratta Gatha is seen in the translation of the Great Reverence Sutra, which is number 77 in the Taisho Revised Tripitaka.

> Not thinking about the past,
> not seeking something in the future—
> the past has already died,
> the future is not in our hands—
> we should observe deeply
> and contemplate

what is in the present moment.
The person who constantly practices
the way of the wise ones
has awakened understanding.
Diligently practicing,
without wavering, and
released from care,
what does he fear at the time of death?
If he does not practice diligently,
how can he overcome death and its armies?
Truly we should practice
according to this wonderful gatha.

THE SUTRA ON KNOWING
THE BETTER WAY TO CATCH A SNAKE

ALAGADDUPAMA SUTTA

Contents

The Sutra on Knowing the Better Way to Catch a Snake

I heard these words one time when the Buddha was staying at the Ana-thapindika Monastery in the Jeta Park, near Shravasti. At that time, the Bhikshu Arittha, who before being ordained had been a vulture trainer, had the wrong view that according to the teachings of the Buddha, sense pleasures are not an obstacle to the practice.[49] After hearing this, many bhikshus went to Arittha and asked, "Brother Arittha, do you really believe that the Buddha teaches that sense pleasures are not an obstacle to the practice?"

Arittha replied, "Yes, friends, it is true that I believe the Buddha does not regard sense pleasures as an obstacle to the practice."

The bhikshus scolded him, "Brother Arittha, you misrepresent the Buddha's teachings and even slander him. The Lord has never said that sense pleasures are not an obstacle to the practice. In fact, he uses many examples to teach that sense pleasures *are* an obstacle to the practice. You should abandon your wrong view." Although the bhikshus counseled Arittha in this way, he was not moved to change his view. Three times they asked him to abandon his wrong view, and three times he refused, continuing to say that he was right and the others were wrong.

So the bhikshus went to the hut of the Buddha, prostrated at the Lord's feet, sat to one side, and addressed him respectfully, "World-Honored One, the Bhikshu Arittha says that according to the teachings of the Lord, sense pleasures are not an obstacle to the practice. We asked him three times to abandon his wrong view, but he continues to hold to this view. So we have come to you, Lord. What should we do?"

Hearing this, the Buddha asked one of the bhikshus to invite Arittha to come to his hut. The bhikshu stood up, prostrated himself, circumambulated the Buddha three times, and went to Bhikshu Arittha. When Arittha heard that the Lord wanted to see him, he came right away, prostrated before the Buddha, and sat to one side. The Buddha said, "Arittha, is it true you have been saying that I teach that sense pleasures are not an obstacle to the practice?"

Arittha replied, "Yes, Lord—I do believe that according to the spirit of your teachings, sense pleasures are not an obstacle to the practice."

The Lord admonished him. "Arittha, what could have led you to that view? When did you ever hear me teach that sense pleasures are not an obstacle to the practice? Who has said that I teach that? Arittha, you are not correct. Your brothers in the Dharma have advised you to drop your wrong view, and you should." The Buddha then asked the other monks, "Bhikshus, have you ever heard me teach that sense pleasures are not an obstacle to the practice?"

The bhikshus replied, "No, Lord, we have not."

The Buddha then asked, "What have you heard me teach?"

The bhikshus replied, "We have heard the Lord teach that sense pleasures are an obstacle to the practice. Lord, you have said that sense pleasures are like a skeleton, a piece of raw meat, a straw torch, a pit of burning charcoal, a poisonous snake, a dream, borrowed belongings, or a tree laden with fruit.⁵⁰ The Lord said, "Bhikshus, that is correct. I have always taught that sense pleasures are an obstacle to the practice. Sense pleasures are like a skeleton, a piece of raw meat, a straw torch, a pit of burning charcoal, a poisonous snake, a dream, borrowed belongings, or a tree laden with fruit. Bhikshu Arittha, you have misunderstood both the letter and the spirit of my teachings. You have presented my teachings as the opposite of what I intended. You have misrepresented and even slandered me, and, at the same time, you have done harm to yourself and others. This is a serious transgression that will cause noble teachers and sincere practitioners much sadness." Hearing the Lord's reprimand, Bhikshu Arittha bowed his head in silence. He was hurt and upset and could think of nothing at all to say.

After admonishing Arittha this way, the Buddha taught all of the bhikshus, "Monks, it is important to understand my teachings thoroughly before you teach or put them into practice. If you have not understood the meaning of any teaching I give, please ask me or one of the elder brothers in the Dharma or one of the others who is excellent in the practice about it. There are always some people who do not understand the letter or the spirit of a teaching and, in fact, take it the opposite way of what was intended, whether the teachings are offered in the form of verse or prose, predictions, verse summaries, interdependent origination, similes, spontaneous utterances, quotations, stories of previous births, wonderful occurrences, detailed commentaries, or clarifications with definitions.[51] There are always some people who study only to satisfy their curiosity or win arguments, and not for the sake of liberation. With such a motivation, they miss the true spirit of the teaching. They may go through much hardship, endure difficulties that are not of much benefit, and eventually exhaust themselves.

"Bhikshus, a person who studies that way can be compared to a man trying to catch a poisonous snake in the wild. If he reaches out his hand, the snake may bite his hand, leg, or some other part of his body. Trying to catch a snake that way has no advantages and can only create suffering.

"Bhikshus, understanding my teaching in the wrong way is the same. If you do not practice the Dharma correctly, you may come to understand it as the opposite of what was intended. But if you practice intelligently, you will understand both the letter and the spirit of the teachings and will be able to explain them correctly. Do not practice just to show off or argue with others. Practice to attain liberation, and if you do, you will have little pain or exhaustion.

"Bhikshus, an intelligent student of the Dharma is like a man who uses a forked stick to catch a snake. When he sees a poisonous snake in the wild, he places the stick right below the head of the snake and grabs the snake's neck with his hand. Even if the snake winds itself around the man's hand, leg, or another part of his body, it will not bite him. This is the better way to catch a snake, and it will not lead to pain or exhaustion.

"Bhikshus, a son or daughter of good family who studies the Dharma needs to apply the utmost skill to understanding the letter and the spirit of the teachings. He or she should not study with the aim of boasting, debating, or arguing, but only to attain liberation. Studying in this way, with intelligence, he or she will have little pain or exhaustion.

"Bhikshus, I have told you many times the importance of knowing when it is time to let go of a raft and not hold on to it unnecessarily. When a mountain stream overflows and becomes a torrent of floodwater carrying debris, a man or woman who wants to get across might think, 'What is the safest way to cross this floodwater?' Assessing the situation, she may decide to gather branches and grasses, construct a raft, and use it to cross to the other side. But, after arriving on the other side, she thinks, 'I spent a lot of time and energy building this raft. It is a prized possession, and I will carry it with me as I continue my journey.' If she puts it on her shoulders or head and carries it with her on land, bhikshus, do you think that would be intelligent?"

The bhikshus replied, "No, World-Honored One."

The Buddha said, "How could she have acted more wisely? She could have thought, 'This raft helped me get across the water safely. Now I will leave it at the water's edge for someone else to use in the same way.' Wouldn't that be a more intelligent thing to do?"

The bhikshus replied, "Yes, World-Honored One."

The Buddha taught, "I have given this teaching on the raft many times to remind you how necessary it is to let go of all the true teachings, not to mention teachings that are not true."

"Bhikshus, there are six bases for views.[52] This means that there are six grounds of wrong perception that we need to drop. What are the six?

"First, there is the body. Whether belonging to the past, the future, or the present, whether they are our own bodies or the body of someone else, whether subtle or gross, ugly or beautiful, near or far, the body is not mine, is not me, is not the self. Bhikshus, please look deeply so that you can see the truth concerning the body.

"Second, there are feelings.

"Third, there are perceptions.

("Fourth, there are mental formations.)[53] Whether these phenomena belong to the past, the future, or the present, whether they are our own or someone else's, whether they are subtle or gross, ugly or beautiful, near or far, such phenomena are not mine, are not me, are not the self.

"Fifth, there is consciousness. Whatever we see, hear, perceive, know, mentally grasp, observe, or think about at the present time or any other time is not ours, is not us, is not the self.

"Sixth, there is the world. Some people think, 'The world is the self. The self is the world. The world is me. I will continue to exist without changing even after I die. I am eternal. I will never disappear.' Please meditate so you can see that the world is not mine, is not me, is not the self. Please look deeply so you can see the truth concerning the world."[54]

Upon hearing this, one bhikshu stood up, bared his right shoulder, joined his palms respectfully, and asked the Buddha, "World-Honored One, can fear and anxiety arise from an internal source?"[55]

The Buddha replied, "Yes, fear and anxiety can arise from an internal source. If you think, 'Things that did not exist in the past have come to exist, but now no longer exist,' you will feel sad or become confused and despairing. This is how fear and anxiety can arise from an internal source."

The same bhikshu then asked, "World-Honored One, can fear and anxiety from an internal source be prevented from arising?"

The Buddha replied, "Fear and anxiety from an internal source can be prevented from arising. If you do not think, 'Things that did not exist in the past have come to exist, but now no longer exist,' you will not feel sad or become confused and despairing. This is how fear and anxiety from an internal source can be prevented from arising."

"World-Honored One, can fear and anxiety arise from an external source?"

The Buddha taught, "Fear and anxiety can arise from an external source. You may think, 'This is a self. This is the world. This is myself. I will exist forever.' Then if you meet the Buddha or a disciple of the Buddha who has the understanding and intelligence to teach you how to let go of all views of attachment to the body, the self, and the objects of the self with a view to giving up pride, internal formations, and energy leaks, and you think, 'This is the end of the world. I have to give up everything. I am not the world. I am not me. I am not the self. I will not exist forever. When I die, I will be completely annihilated. There is nothing to look forward to, to be joyful about, or to remember,' you will feel sad and become confused and despairing. This is how fear and anxiety can arise from an external source."[56]

"World-Honored One, can fear and anxiety from an external source be prevented from arising?"

The Buddha taught, "Fear and anxiety from an external source can be prevented from arising if you do not think, 'This is the self. This is the world. This is myself. I will exist forever.' Then if you meet the Buddha or a disciple of the Buddha who has the understanding and intelligence to teach you how to let go of all views of attachment to the body, the self, and the objects of the self with a view to giving up pride, internal formations, and energy leaks, and you do not think, 'This is the end of the world. I have to give up everything. I am not the world. I am not me. I am not the self. I will not exist forever. When I die I will be completely annihilated. There is nothing to look forward to, to be joyful about, or to remember,' you will not feel sad or become confused and despairing. This is how fear and anxiety from an external source can be prevented from arising."

Hearing these words, the bhikshu praised and thanked the Buddha, completely accepted the Lord's teaching, and then kept silent.

The Buddha asked, "Bhikshus, do you think the Five Aggregates and the self are permanent, changeless, and not subject to destruction?"

"No, reverend teacher."

"Is there anything you can hold on to with attachment that will not cause anxiety, exhaustion, sorrow, suffering, and despair?"

"No, reverend teacher."

"Is there any view of self in which you can take refuge that will not cause anxiety, exhaustion, sorrow, suffering, and despair?"

"No, reverend teacher."

"Bhikshus, you are quite correct. Whenever there is an idea of self, there is also an idea of what belongs to the self. When there is no idea of self, there is no idea of anything that belongs to the self. Self and what belongs to the self are two views that are based on trying to grasp things that cannot be grasped and to establish things that cannot be established.[57] Such wrong perceptions cause us to be bound by internal formations that arise the moment we are caught by ideas that cannot be grasped or established and have no basis in reality. Do you see that these are wrong perceptions? Do you see the consequences of such wrong perceptions in the case of Bhikshu Arittha?"

The bhikshus replied, "Yes, reverend teacher. These are wrong perceptions, and the consequences of such wrong perceptions can be seen in the case of Bhikshu Arittha."

The Buddha continued, "If, when he considers the six bases for wrong views, a bhikshu does not give rise to the idea of 'I' or 'mine,' he is not caught in the chains of this life.[58] Since he is not caught in the chains of this life, he has no fear. To have no fear is to arrive at nirvana. Such a person is no longer troubled by birth and death; the holy life has been lived; what needs to be done has been done; there will be no further births or deaths; and the truth of things as they are is known. Such a bhikshu has filled in the moat, crossed the moat, destroyed the enemy citadel, unbolted the door, and is able to look directly into the mirror of highest understanding.

"What is meant by 'filling in the moat'? 'Filling in the moat' means to know and clearly understand the substance of ignorance. Ignorance has been uprooted and shattered and cannot arise anymore.

"What is meant by 'crossing the moat'? 'Crossing the moat' means to know and clearly understand the substance of becoming and craving.[59] Becoming and craving have been uprooted and shattered and cannot arise anymore.

"What is meant by 'destroying the enemy citadel'? 'Destroying the enemy citadel' means to know and clearly understand the substance of the cycle of birth and death. The cycle of birth and death has been uprooted and shattered and cannot arise anymore.

"What is meant by 'unbolting the door'? 'Unbolting the door' means to know and clearly understand the substance of the five dull internal formations.[60] "What is meant by 'looking directly into the mirror of highest understanding'? 'Looking directly into the mirror of highest understanding' means to know and understand clearly the substance of pride. Pride has been uprooted and shattered and cannot arise anymore.

"Bhikshus, that is the Way of the Tathagata and those who have attained liberation. Indra, Prajapati, Brahma, and the other gods in their entourage, however hard they look, cannot find any trace or basis for the consciousness of a Tathagata.[61] The Tathagata is a noble fount of freshness and coolness. There is no great heat and no sorrow in this state. When recluses and brahmans hear me say this, they may slander me, saying that I do not speak the truth, that the monk Gautama proposes a theory of nihilism and teaches absolute nonexistence, while in fact living beings do exist. Bhikshus, the Tathagata has never taught the things they say. In truth, the Tathagata teaches only the ending of suffering in order to attain the state of non-fear. If the Tathagata is blamed, criticized, defamed, or defeated, he does not care. He does not become angry, walk away in hatred, or do anything in revenge. If someone blames, criticizes, defames, or defeats the Tathagata, how does he react? The Tathagata thinks, 'If someone respects, honors, or makes offerings to a Tathagata, the Tathagata would not on that account feel pleased. He would think only that someone is doing this because the Tathagata has attained the fruits of awakening and transformation.'

"Bhikshus, if people blame, criticize, defame, or defeat you, or respect, honor, or make offerings to you, there is no need on either account to feel angry or pleased, nor to do anything in revenge. Why? If you look deeply, you will see that there is no 'I' and no 'mine.' If someone were to walk around the grounds of this monastery and pick up the dead branches and dried grass to take home and burn or use in some other way, should we think that it is we ourselves who are being taken home to be burned or used in some way?"

"No, reverend teacher."

"It is the same when someone praises, honors, or makes offerings to us, or blames, criticizes, or defames us. We should not rejoice or become angry. Why? It is because there are no such things as 'I' or 'mine.'

"The true teachings have been illuminated and made available in the worlds of humans and gods, with nothing lacking. If someone with right understanding penetrates these teachings, the value will be immeasurable. If, at the time of passing from this life, someone has been able to transform the five dull internal formations, in the next life he or she will attain nirvana. That person will arrive at the state of Non-Returner and will not reenter the cycle of birth and death. If, at the time of passing from this life, someone has been able to transform the three internal formations of attachment, aversion, and ignorance, he or she will be born only one more time in the worlds of humans or gods in order to be liberated. If, at the time of passing from this life, someone has been able to attain the fruit of Stream-Enterer, he or she will not fall again into states of extreme suffering and will surely go in the direction of right awakening. After being born seven times in the worlds of humans or gods, he or she will come to the place of liberation. If, at the time of passing from this life, someone has faith in understanding the teachings, he or she will be born in a blessed world and will continue to progress on the path to the highest awakening."

Having heard the Buddha speak thus, the bhikshus, with great joy, put the teachings into practice.

COMMENTARY

1: Thundering Silence

In the Sutra on Knowing the Better Way to Catch a Snake, the Buddha urges us to study and practice his teachings in an intelligent way so we will not be caught by notions and words. The sutra reminds us that if we are skillful and careful in learning and practicing the Buddha's teachings, then we can experience peace and joy right in this present moment. For those of us new to Buddhism and practice, it is a wonderful beginning. For experienced practitioners, the sutra can bring space and fresh air back into our practice. The Buddha encourages us to be like a person who can catch a snake without being bitten by it. Before reading this sutra, I'd never before heard anyone compare his or her teaching to a snake or say that it can be dangerous to learn and practice.

There are two different versions of this sutra, the Pali version from the Tamrashatiya school and the Chinese version from the Sarvastivada school. By comparing the two, we can discover something close to the original words of the Buddha. It is wonderful to receive these teachings.

Although his teachings are deep, the Buddha likes to present them in a simple way. While describing the interdependent-origination nature of reality, for example, he simply says, "This is, because that is." This may not sound difficult, but it is very profound and easy to misunderstand. The Buddha taught the Sutra on Knowing the Better Way to Catch a Snake because many people, including many monks and nuns in the Buddha's own time, misinterpreted or misrepresented his teachings. One example of this is the teaching of the Three Dharma Seals of impermanence, no-self, and nirvana. These three insights are wonderful keys for unlocking the door to reality, but they continue to be misunderstood from generation to generation.

Many people think that the Buddha believed in nonbeing, annihilation, the destruction of all feelings and intentions, and the dissolution of identities. This isn't so. The Buddha taught that we must go beyond pairs of opposites such as being and nonbeing, becoming and annihilation. This sutra is full of openness, playfulness, and nonattachment from views. In reminding us to use great care and skill while studying and practicing his teachings, the Buddha uses another wonderful parable. He reminds us that if we use a raft to cross a river, we need to give up the raft when we've made it to the other shore. Instead of continuing to carry it with us, we leave it on the shore for others to use.

In the Mahayana tradition there is a saying of the Buddha: "During forty-five years, I have not said anything." This statement is truly the roar of a great lion. In the Vimalakirti Nirdesha Sutra (Taisho no. 475), the silence of the layman Vimalakirti is praised by the Bodhisattva Manju shri as a "thundering silence" that echoes far and wide, having the power to break the bonds of attachment and bring about liberation. It is the same as the lion's roar that proclaims, "It is necessary to let go of all the true teachings, not to mention teachings that are not true." This is the spirit we need if we want to understand the Buddha's teachings. May the Sutra on Knowing the Better Way to Catch a Snake sweep away the fog of words and notions in us so that the sun of the true teaching can shine brightly on the field of our understanding mind.

2: About the Sutra

In the Southern tradition, this sutra is recorded in Pali as the Alagaddu-pama Sutta, which means "Snake Simile." It's number 22 in the Majj-hima Nikaya of the Pali Canon. In the Northern tradition, the same sutra is recorded in Chinese as the Arittha Sutra. The Chinese version is number 220 in the Madhyama Agama. In the Taisho Revised Tripitaka, the Madhyama Agama is number 26. This sutra was translated from Sanskrit into Chinese by Gautama Sanghadeva in the years 397–398.

The Buddha spoke these words when one of his disciples, Arittha, had been telling his fellow monks that he understood the Buddha's teachings to say that sense pleasures are not an obstacle to the practice. After telling Arittha that he had misunderstood his teachings, the Buddha taught Arittha and the other bhikshus the Sutra on Knowing the Better Way to Catch a Snake.

3: Arittha's Misunderstanding

Bhikshu Arittha had been saying that according to the teaching of the Buddha, sense pleasures are not an obstacle to the practice. Why was it that even though all the other bhikshus understood that sense pleasures bring suffering and the bonds of attachment, Bhikshu Arittha continued to say that sense pleasures are not an obstacle to the practice? Should we surmise that Arittha lacked intelligence to such an extent that he was incapable of understanding this simple and basic teaching? Or should we think that he wanted to distort the teaching or advocate the opposite of what the Buddha taught?

Who was Bhikshu Arittha? We are told that before becoming a monk, he had been a vulture trainer. In the Arittha Sutta that is found in the Samyutta Nikaya (Vol. V, pp. 314–315) of the Pali Canon, the Buddha asks some monks whether they practice mindfulness of breathing. Arittha says that he does, and he explains to the Buddha the way he practices. The Buddha does not comment on what he says but goes on to teach the bhikshus several practices to further increase their concentration.

In the Vinaya Pitaka of the Southern tradition, we read how Bhikshu Arittha, after being asked by other bhikshus three times to refrain from speaking the wrong view presented in this sutra, was accused of a *pacittaya* offense by the Sangha in Chabbaggiya, a place not far from Shravasti, and we are told that he received the penalty of *ukkhepaniya kamma*, suspension from the order (Vinaya Vol. II, pp. 25–28).[62] We see that during the time of his suspension, a number of bhikshus and a bhikshuni, Thullananda (Vinaya Vol. IV, p. 218), stayed in contact with him and, as a result, were also suspended (Vinaya Vol. IV, p. 137). In reading the Sutra on Knowing the Better Way to Catch a Snake, I have the feeling that although Bhikshu Arittha was willful, he was not unintelligent. From other sources, we see that his views as well as his personality were able to influence other bhikshus and bhikshunis. So we need to examine how it was that he misunderstood this teaching of the Buddha and continued to hold to his view.

In my opinion, Arittha's misunderstanding stems from his failure to see the difference between attachment to sense pleasures and the joy and happiness that arise from a peaceful mind. On many occasions, the Buddha taught that joy and happiness are nourishing to us, while indulging in sense pleasures can cause us suffering. What is the difference? Let us first discuss what is meant by the joy and happiness of a mindful and peaceful person.

Many people think that to undergo spiritual discipline is to practice asceticism and austerities. But the practice of the Dharma does not exclude the enjoyment of the fresh air, the setting sun, a glass of cool water, and an appreciation of family and friends. Enjoying things in moderation doesn't bring us suffering or tie us with the bonds of attachment. Once we recognize that all of these things are impermanent, we have no problem enjoying them. In fact, real peace and joy are only possible when we see clearly into the nature of impermanence.

The Buddha often revealed himself as someone who was able to appreciate these kinds of simple joys. When Mahanama, the King of Kapilavastu, offered the Sangha a delicious lunch, the Buddha knew it was a good meal and expressed appreciation for it. When he was standing with Ananda on a hill overlooking an expanse of golden rice fields, the Buddha told Ananda how beautiful he found the scene. And when they climbed Vulture Peak together or visited the city of Vaishali, the Buddha asked Ananda, "Vulture Peak is beautiful, is it not, Ananda?" "Isn't Vaishali beautiful, Ananda?" Details like these are found in the texts and show us that the Buddha never repudiated the joy and happiness of a peaceful mind or said that joy and happiness are obstacles to the practice. Wholesome feelings of joy and happiness can nourish the well-being of our bodies and minds and help us go far on the path of practice. Siddhartha gave up the practice of self-mortification after he remembered the joy he had experienced while meditating under a rose-apple tree as a young boy. We all need joy and happiness. We only have to be aware that all things are impermanent and subject to change, including the cool breeze, the setting sun, Vulture Peak, and Vaishali.

But the Buddha did speak of the five sense pleasures (money, sex, fame, overeating, and sleeping too much) as obstacles to the practice. If we get a reasonable amount of sleep every night, that cannot harm our practice. In fact, deep and refreshing sleep will help our practice. But if we spend a large part of each day sleeping, that is an obstacle. Joy and happiness, in this case, have become an indulgence in a sense pleasure. In the same way, a simple, well-prepared, nourishing meal, eaten slowly and mindfully so that we remain in deep contact with the food, is not an obstacle to the practice. But an obsession with food, spending much of our time seeking special foods, is an obstacle to the practice. Again, this is to turn the joy and happiness of a peaceful mind into an indulgence. The same is true of the remaining three sense pleasures—if we are caught or obsessed by them, they will present obstacles on our path of practice.

It is possible that Bhikshu Arittha was unable to draw a line between the joy and happiness of a peaceful mind and indulging in sense pleasures. If that is the case, he may just have been trying to express the idea that feelings of joy are not harmful for the practice. We know that he himself had never broken the most grave of precepts, such as the precept forbidding a monk to have sexual intercourse, because we read in the Vinaya that he was not subjected to the penalty for breaking a *parajika* ("defeat") precept: permanent expulsion from the Sangha. He was only suspended temporarily for a less grave offense.

The bhikshus in Chabbaggiya were unable to persuade Bhikshu Arittha to give up his wrong view, perhaps because they were not able to explain clearly enough the difference between the joy and happiness of a peaceful mind and indulging in sense pleasures. Trying to get him to give up his view by finding him guilty of an offense, they disciplined him. But apparently, he never really submitted, as we read that a number of bhikshus and one bhikshuni stayed with him during his time of suspension, and, as a result, were also suspended.

In the end, a number of monks from Chabbaggiya had to go to the Jeta Grove near Shravasti to report this matter to the Buddha. Arittha's attitude and misunderstanding were probably shared by some other members of the Chabbaggiya Sangha. It is regrettable that the sutra does not tell us more about Arittha's ideas, apart from his idea that "sense pleasures are not an obstacle to the practice."

4: Sense Pleasures as Disasters

The disasters that, according to this sutra, are brought about by indulging in sense pleasures, are also listed in many other sutras: (1) Sense pleasures are a skeleton, bare bones thrown to a hungry dog that do nothing to appease its hunger. We do not receive nourishment or lasting contentment from indulging in sense pleasures. (2) Sense pleasures are a piece of raw flesh, a piece of waste meat of a butchered animal that a bird might pick up in its beak. If the bird does not let go of it when a larger bird comes along, there will be a fight and the smaller bird may be killed. Sense pleasures, in this sense, can kill us. (3) Sense pleasures are a burning torch. Its flame might burn the hand of the person holding the torch if the wind shifts suddenly. (4) Sense pleasures are a pit of burning charcoal into which we may be pushed and burn to death. (5) Sense pleasures are a poisonous snake, dangerous beyond measure. (6) Sense pleasures are a dream, short-lived and not real. (7) Sense pleasures are borrowed possessions. They do not belong to us, and we cannot hold on to them. (8) Sense pleasures are a tree laden with fruit. Its leaves and branches will be destroyed by those who come to pick the fruit. (9) Sense pleasures are an impaling stick, a sharp weapon that pierces the flesh. (10) Sense pleasures are a slaughterhouse, a place where lives are lost.

The idea that sense pleasures are a disaster and an obstacle to the practice must have been quite familiar to the bhikshus and bhikshunis. When we are obsessed by sense pleasures, we lose our freedom. This was taught by the Buddha, and it is also why we need the precepts to protect us from getting caught in sense pleasures. But we have to distinguish between indulging in sense pleasures and the joy and happiness that we experience when we are mindful and at peace. Indulging in sense pleasures is harmful, but enjoying peace and happiness is absolutely necessary for our physical and spiritual well-being, and for our practice on the path. Sense pleasures can bring about suffering and entanglement—both in the present moment and the future, for ourselves and others. The joy and happiness of a peaceful mind bring neither suffering nor attachment in the present or in the future, for ourselves or others. We practitioners need to develop our capacity for peace and joy if we want to realize the fruits of the practice. Nirvana is the highest peace and joy we can attain. If we practice only grimly and austerely, we will not be able to handle the peace and joy of nirvana. In the Sutra on Knowing the Better Way to Catch a Snake, the Buddha says that the Tathagata is a noble, cool, and fresh state, free of the discomfort of heat or sorrow. This is the state of nirvana.

5: Catching a Snake

Arittha must have heard the Buddha talk about the joy and happiness of a mind at peace, but he seems not to have understood the difference between indulging in sense pleasures and the joy and happiness of a peaceful mind. We shouldn't think Bhikshu Arittha was unique in this misunderstanding. It is probably the case that a number of other monks also did not see the difference between the joy and happiness of a peaceful mind and indulging in sense pleasures, although most of the others probably erred in the opposite direction, being afraid of both sense pleasures and the joy and happiness of a peaceful mind. Today there are still practitioners of Buddhism who are afraid of joy and happiness, who do not dare to appreciate the beautiful and wonderful things of life because they have heard that all things are impermanent and contain suffering. They are even afraid to appreciate the beauty of a newly blossomed flower or a magnificent sunset, although they could do so in the full awareness that things are impermanent, subject to suffering, and without a separate self. Bhikshu Arittha must have come into contact with monks who had attitudes like this and, unable to draw the line between indulging in sense pleasures and the joy and happiness of a peaceful mind, he went to the other extreme, saying that sense pleasures are not an obstacle to the practice. Because he went too far, the Buddha had to correct him. The Buddha taught:

> "Monks, it is important to understand my teachings thoroughly before you teach or put them into practice. If you have not understood the meaning of any teaching I give, please ask me or one of the elder brothers in the Dharma or one of the others who is excellent in the practice about it."

"Elder brothers in the Dharma" are those who have realized the practice and not those who simply have a vast store of knowledge. "Excellent in the practice" is a translation of *brahmacarya*, which means those whose lives are exemplary, pure, and clear. It does not mean those who live a harsh, austere life.

There are two reasons why someone might understand a teaching of the Buddha in the opposite way to which it was intended. One is the lack of insight or skillfulness due to inaccurately perceiving the letter or the spirit of the teachings. The other is a motivation that focuses on being able to win disputes or enhance one's reputation. Those who study the sutras in order to win arguments have lost sight that the practice is intended to be liberating. But this is not to suggest that all who study the sutras with a view to liberation are on the right path. They may be going in the right direction, but they still need insight and skillfulness if they are to understand the meaning of the sutra. Without insight and skill, they too will

> "endure difficulties that are not of much benefit, and eventually exhaust themselves." The Buddha taught, "If you practice intelligently, you will understand both the letter and the spirit of the teachings and will be able to explain them correctly. Do not practice just to show off or argue with others. Practice to attain liberation, and if you do, you will have little pain or exhaustion."

Skillfulness in receiving the letter and the spirit of the teachings without distorting the meaning is the correct way to study the Dharma. Here skillfulness is accompanied by intelligence, and the meaning of intelligence is understanding. Without skill and intelligence, we can easily misunderstand the teachings.

At this point, the Buddha presents the simile of catching a snake. He says that a skillful, intelligent snake catcher always uses a forked stick to pin the snake just below the head so that the snake cannot turn around and bite him. This comparison is extremely apt:

> "Bhikshus, a person who studies that way can be compared to a man trying to catch a poisonous snake in the wild. If he reaches out his hand, the snake may bite his hand, leg, or

some other part of his body. Trying to catch a snake that way has no advantages and can only create suffering.

"Bhikshus, understanding my teaching in the wrong way is the same. If you do not practice the Dharma correctly, you may come to understand it as the opposite of what was intended. But if you practice intelligently, you will understand both the letter and the spirit of the teachings and will be able to explain them correctly. Do not practice just to show off or argue with others. Practice to attain liberation, and if you do, you will have little pain or exhaustion.

"Bhikshus, an intelligent student of the Dharma is like a man who uses a forked stick to catch a snake. When he sees a poisonous snake in the wild, he places the stick right below the head of the snake and grabs the snake's neck with his hand. Even if the snake winds itself around the man's hand, leg, or another part of his body, it will not bite him. This is the better way to catch a snake, and it will not lead to pain or exhaustion.

"Bhikshus, a son or daughter of good family who studies the Dharma needs to apply the utmost skill to understanding the letter and the spirit of the teachings. He or she should not study with the aim of boasting, debating, or arguing, but only to attain liberation. Studying in this way, with intelligence, he or she will have little pain or exhaustion."

There are probably not many teachers who would compare their own teachings to a poisonous snake. There must not be many who would say that their teachings can be dangerous if not understood and practiced correctly. The Buddha never said that his teachings were the absolute truth. He called them skillful means to guide us in the practice. The way to make use of these teachings is with our own intelligence and skill.

The Buddha described himself at other times as a doctor whose teachings are a kind of medicine. If the medicine is used correctly, it can help cure sickness. But if it is misused, it can threaten a patient's life. We have accounts of several occasions during the Buddha's lifetime on which his teachings were misunderstood and practiced incorrectly. During one rainy-season retreat, in the great forest near Vaishali, a number of monks took their own lives after hearing teachings on the foulness of the body, impermanence, no-self, and emptiness. These bhikshus heard the teachings from the Buddha and yet completely misunderstood the meaning. If it is possible to hear the teachings from the Buddha himself and still misconstrue them, how much more dangerous is it for those of us who are hearing the teachings after many centuries of oral and written transmission and interpretation? We have to use our own skill and intelligence to determine the Buddha's true intention in offering any teaching, and we must be humble when we do.

6: The Raft is Not the Shore

The snake simile is used to convey the danger we risk when we study the sutras without skill and intelligence. In the Sutra on Knowing the Better Way to Catch a Snake, there is another excellent simile, that of the raft. It shows how we can get caught by the teachings.

"Bhikshus, I have told you many times the importance of knowing when it is time to let go of a raft and not hold on to it unnecessarily. When a mountain stream overflows and becomes a torrent of floodwater carrying debris, a man or woman who wants to get across might think, 'What is the safest way to cross this floodwater?' Assessing the situation, she may decide to gather branches and grasses, construct a raft, and use it to cross to the other side. But, after arriving on the other side, she thinks, 'I spent a lot of time and energy building this raft. It is a prized possession, and I will carry it with me as I continue my journey.' If she puts it on her shoulders or head and carries it with her on land, bhikshus, do you think that would be intelligent?"

The bhikshus replied, "No, World-Honored One."

The Buddha said, "How could she have acted more wisely? She could have thought, 'This raft helped me get across the water safely. Now I will leave it at the water's edge for someone else to use in the same way.' Wouldn't that be a more intelligent thing to do?"

The bhikshus replied, "Yes, World-Honored One."

The Buddha taught, "I have given this teaching on the raft many times to remind you how necessary it is to let go of all the true teachings, not to mention teachings that are not true."

"It is necessary to let go of all the true teachings, not to mention teachings that are not true." This mighty proclamation can be compared to the roar of a lion. The same proclamation is made in its entirety in the Diamond (Vajracchedika Prajñaparamita) Sutra.[63] This lion's roar has the power to help the practitioner give up the attitude of clinging even if he or she has had it for many thousands of lifetimes. The shout of Chan Master Linji is simply the echo of this lion's roar of the Buddha. The Buddha teaches impermanence, no-self, emptiness, and nirvana not as theories, but as skillful means to help us in our practice. If we take these teachings and use them as theories, we will be trapped. In the time of the Buddha and also today, many people study Buddhism only with a view to satisfying the thirst of their intellect. They pride themselves on their understanding of Buddhist systems of thought and use them in debates and discussions as a kind of game or amusement. It is quite different from a Dharma discussion, when we discuss the teachings with co-practitioners in order to shed light on the path of practice.

The teachings of impermanence, no-self, and emptiness were offered by the Buddha to help us liberate ourselves from our psychological prisons and pains. If someone studies and practices these teachings and does not find release from attachment and pain, he or she has not understood the letter and spirit of these teachings. He or she is caught in the form and has not been in touch with the substance. The simile of the raft is offered to help us see what it is to be caught in form. Instead of just using the raft to transport ourselves and others across the river, we want to carry it with us on our heads or shoulders.

Just as a raft that is not used to carry people is not performing its proper function, teachings that are used for speculative purposes are not able to release people from their sufferings and attachments.

Teachings received in the wrong way are, as the sutra says, "teachings that are not true" (or "non-teachings," in Chinese, *fei fa*). True teachings can be used as a raft to cross the river; teachings that are not true cannot. Being caught in the true teachings is harmful enough. Being caught by the teachings that are not true is much worse. With teachings that are not true, we can never arrive at the other shore. Anyone who has arrived at the other shore has used the raft of true teachings, and he or she is advised not to be attached to the raft. We must be free even from true teachings, not to mention non-teachings. This is the meaning of the parable. Even if we undertake the crossing, if we are attached to what we learn, we have not understood it properly, we have been bitten by the snake. In this case, a true raft is not available to us, and therefore we cannot cross the river. We may not even realize the importance of crossing to the other shore. The sutra warns us against this.

Nirvana is the release from the prisons of attachment, above all from the attachment to ideas, including ideas of impermanence, no-self, emptiness, and nirvana. In the Maharatnakuta Sutra, the Buddha says: "It is better to be caught in the idea that everything exists than to be caught in the idea of emptiness. Someone who is caught in the idea that everything exists can still be disentangled, but it is difficult to disentangle someone who is caught in the idea of emptiness." This is also true of the teachings of impermanence, no-self, nirvana, and every other teaching. All teachings are offered as skillful means to help us along on the path. They are not absolute truth. If we do not know how to use these teachings skillfully, we will be enslaved by them. Instead of helping us, they will only cause us harm. If we put our rafts on our shoulders as we walk, we will only strain ourselves and, when we are ready to cross over to the other shore or make our rafts available to others, we will not be able to do so.

THE FINGER POINTING AT THE MOON

The Surangama Sutra (Taisho 945) tells us, "If someone uses a finger to point out the moon to another person, if that person takes the finger to be the moon, he will not only fail to see the moon, but he will also fail to see the finger." The Lankavatara Sutra (Taisho 640) says, "All the teachings in the sutras are fingers pointing to the moon." These pointing fingers are not the moon itself, just as the raft is not the other shore. The teachings of the Buddha are not in themselves the experience of enlightenment, just as a map of Paris is not the city of Paris itself.

Master Tai Hsu, a well-known Chinese teacher of the 1920s and 1930s, distinguished between "essence teachings" and "image teachings." The former are the essence of enlightenment, the Buddha's realization under the Bodhi tree that cannot be expressed in words or concepts. When the Buddha began teaching in the Deer Park, image teachings were given, and these belong to the realms of concepts and spoken words. Image teachings are a shadow of the truth; they are not truth itself. If we study the image teachings and see that they are just shadows, they can help us touch the essence teachings, just as we can follow a tree's shadow to find and touch the tree itself.

THE PHEASANT

In the Sutra of One Hundred Parables (Taisho 209), the Buddha tells a story about words and concepts. A foolish man became ill, and when the doctor came to see him, he said that only pheasant could cure his disease. After the doctor left, the patient repeated the word "pheasant" hour after hour and day after day. Months passed, but he still was not cured. One day, a friend came to visit, and hearing the man repeat the word "pheasant" over and over, asked him why. The sick man told him what the doctor had said, and taking pity on him, his friend took a pencil and drew a pheasant. He showed it to the foolish man and told him, "This is what a pheasant looks like. You have to eat it if you want to cure your disease. Just repeating the word 'pheasant' is not enough." As soon as his friend left, the foolish man put the drawing of the pheasant in his mouth, chewed, and swallowed it. When he did not get well as a result of this, he hired an artist to draw hundreds more pheasants, and he chewed and swallowed all of them, but his illness only worsened, and, eventually, he contacted the doctor again.

When the doctor saw what had happened, great pity welled up in him. He took the foolish man's hand and walked with him to the market. There he bought two pheasants, accompanied the man home, helped him prepare them for eating, and asked the man to eat them before his eyes. After that, the foolish man was cured.

When we hear this story, we may think how incredibly stupid that man was. But when we look more deeply, we may see that we ourselves are not much better. Because we lack intelligence and skill, we study the Dharma and discuss it for amusement or merely to show off. We are not determined enough to liberate ourselves from our deepest suffering. We remain attached to words and ideas, both in our study and our practice. The way we count our breaths, practice loving kindness meditation, or recite mantras can also lack intelligence and skill. We can get caught in the forms. It is not easy to give rise to awakened understanding.

7: Breaking the Bonds

The Sutra on Knowing the Better Way to Catch a Snake does not aim at expounding the harm of sense pleasures or explaining concepts of no-self, nirvana, or Tathagata, although the sutra does mention these concepts. The main purpose of the sutra is to demonstrate the necessity of breaking the bonds of attachment. The Buddha shows us why it is a hindrance to be attached to anything, including his own teachings. That is why he says to "let go of all the true teachings, not to mention teachings that are not true." This is the quintessence of this sutra and of all Buddhist teachings. The word translated as "teachings" in this sentence is "Dharma." This spirit—this way of breaking through the bonds of attachment—is the foremost element of the Buddhist teachings.

Breaking the bonds of attachment is the most skillful and intelligent way to practice. We study the Dharma to understand and practice it, not to accumulate knowledge. Knowledge not used skillfully is an obstacle to understanding. "Knowledge" in Sanskrit is *jñeya* ("the object to be known"). Obstacles produced by our knowing something are called *jñeya avarana*. We might call them prejudices or obstinacy. If we can let go of our knowledge, we are free to reach a deeper understanding. It is like climbing a ladder—if we cannot let go of the fifth rung, we will never be able to step up to the sixth. If we think that the fifth rung is the highest rung possible, this will be the end of our climbing. This attitude is an obstacle produced by knowledge.

In the Sutra of One Hundred Parables, the Buddha tells this story. One day, while a young father was absent from his home in a rural village, a band of robbers came, stole all of the villagers' possessions, burned their houses to the ground, and kidnapped all the children, including his son. When the father returned to the village, he was stricken with grief. Seeing the charred corpse of a child in the ashes of what had been his house, he wept, beat his chest, and performed funeral rites for his son. Then he put the ashes into an embroidered pouch, which he carried around his neck wherever he went. Some months later, after the village had been completely rebuilt, the man's son was able to escape from the robbers and find his way home. That night, at about midnight, he knocked on his father's door, but the father, holding the pouch with the ashes, his face bathed in tears, was determined not to let the boy in. The child told him his name, but the man was certain that his son had been killed and that the boy at the door must be mocking his grief. In the end, the boy had to give up, and father and son were separated forever. If we are caught by the obstacle of knowledge, even if truth comes knocking at our door, we will refuse to let it in.

8: No-self

In the Samyutta Nikaya, we read about the ascetic Vacchagotta's visit to the Buddha. Vacchagotta asked, "Reverend Gautama, please tell me, is there a self?" The Buddha did not say anything. Vacchagotta asked again, "Then you do not think there is a self?" The Buddha remained silent. Eventually, Vacchagotta left.

Afterwards, Ananda asked the Buddha, "Venerable Sir, when you give us Dharma teachings you often speak about no-self. Why did you not reply to Vacchagotta's questions concerning the self?" The Buddha replied, "The teaching of no-self that I give the bhikshus is a means to guide you to look deeply in your meditation. It is not an ideology. If you make it into an ideology, you will be caught in it. I believe the ascetic Vacchagotta was looking for an ideology and not for a teaching to help him in the practice. So I remained silent. I did not want him to be caught by the teachings. If I had told him there is a self, that would not have been correct. If I told him there is no self, he would have clung to that dogmatically and made it into a theory, and that would not have been helpful either. That is why I kept silent."

The first precept of the Order of Interbeing represents the same spirit: "Aware of the suffering created by fanaticism and intolerance, we are determined not to be idolatrous about or bound to any doctrine, theory or ideology, even Buddhist ones. Buddhist teachings are guiding means to help us learn to look deeply and to develop our understanding and compassion. They are not doctrines to fight, kill, or die for."[64]

Teachings that are received as doctrines or theories are no longer teachings. They do not liberate, and the person receiving them is caught. In most precept texts, the first precept is not to take life. Not taking life, however, is not unique to Buddhism. In the Jainism of the naked ascetic Nirgantha, for example, restrictions concerning the taking of life were far more severe than in Buddhism. But in the spirit of breaking the bonds of attachment to ideology, the practice of the precept not to kill goes much further in Buddhism. A person caught in a doctrine or a system of thought can sacrifice millions of lives in order to put into practice his theory, which he considers the absolute truth, the unique path that can lead humankind to happiness. With a gun in hand, a person can kill one, five, or even ten people. But holding on to a doctrine or a system of thought, one can kill tens of thousands of people. Therefore, unless the precept not to take life is understood in terms of breaking the bonds of attachment to ideology, it is not truly the precept taught by the Buddha.

The teaching of no-self is one of the teachings of Buddhism most likely to be misunderstood. The Buddha refers to this teaching in the Sutra on Knowing the Better Way to Catch a Snake as an example of how many people have misunderstood his teachings, including brahmans. There is a simple and general way to explain no-self, which is that there is no single entity whose identity is changeless. All things are constantly changing. Nothing endures forever or contains a changeless element called a "self."

The Buddha refers to the six bases of views that are the ground for the idea of a self. "Ground" means the place in which we can take refuge, and when we take refuge in views, the term "view-refuge" is also used (Pali: *ditthi-nissaya*). The six bases are form (the body), feelings, perceptions (or ideas), mental formations, consciousness, and the world. The Buddha taught in many of his discourses, "The body, whether a body of the past, a body in the present moment, whether they are our own bodies or someone else's, subtle or gross, whether beautiful or ugly, near or far, is not mine, is not me, is not the self. A practitioner should meditate on this to be able to see the truth concerning a body."

The Buddha taught that there are three categories of wrong view of self: (1) *This body is mine.* This means that we see the body not as ourselves but as something that belongs to us, with an independent existence outside of, or apart from, ourselves. (2) *This body is me.* This body and I are one. This body is exactly the same as me. (3) *This body is the self.* This body is the *atman*, a spiritual first principle, a basic constituent of the universe present in every species and every thing. The body is not the possession of a separate, individual self, or one and the same as a separate, individual self. It is the spiritual essence of the whole universe.

In the Buddha's lifetime there were many theories concerning the self. Both Vedic and Upanishadic literature speak about it in various ways. In ancient Brahmanism, we find a belief similar to pantheism. According to this point of view, the self (atman) is found everywhere and *Brahman* is the permanent and absolute element at the beginning and end of everything in the universe. Sometimes Brahman is called "Great Self" (*mahatman*) or "True Self" (*paratman*). Within every species and every individual there is a piece of this Great Self that can be called "self" or "small self." This element is unchanging and absolute. It is not born and does not die. Liberation takes place when this small "self" returns to and merges with the Great Self. This is an oversimplification, but it conveys the essence of this belief. In Vedic and Upanishadic literature there are many more theories about the self, some quite complex. The Brahmajala Sutta (Digha Nikaya, Sutta no. 1) deals with sixty-three of these. When the Buddha proclaims that this body is not the self, it must be understood in the context of the Brahmanic beliefs of his time.

This body is not mine, is not me, and is not the self. These feelings are not mine, are not me, and are not the self. The same is true of perceptions, mental formations, and consciousness. Each aggregate of personality is like that, and the Five Aggregates combined are also like that.

> "Whatever we see, hear, perceive, know, mentally grasp, observe, or think about at the present time or any other time is not ours, is not us, is not the self." After discussing the selfless nature of the fifth aggregate, consciousness, the Buddha goes on to discuss the sixth ground of views, the world: "Some people think, 'The world is the self. The self is the world. The world is me. I will continue to exist without changing even after I die. I am eternal. I will never disappear.' Please meditate so you can see that the world is not mine, is not me, is not the self. Please look deeply so you can see the truth concerning the world."

It is very clear from this quotation that the Buddha is referring to the Brahmanic belief in the self as the basic, unchanging, unfading constituent of the universe. In the Brahmajala Sutta, the Buddha says,

"There are ascetics and brahmans who belong to the school of thought professing eternalism, which holds that the self and the universe are one—permanent and unchanging (*sassatavada sassatam attananca lokañca paññapenti*)."

Usually it is enough for the Buddha to speak of five grounds only, the Five Aggregates of personality, because according to the Buddhist way of seeing things, the world is all included within the Five Aggregates. The world is an object of consciousness and, therefore, it is consciousness. An object of consciousness is called a dharma, and all dharmas constitute the world. The reason the Buddha adds the sixth ground here is to have an opportunity to discuss in detail being caught in the view of an atman as the spiritual basis of the whole universe. In the Pali version of the Sutra on Knowing the Better Way to Catch a Snake, we read "*so loko, so atto...*" which literally means "This is the world, this is the self." This can also be understood as, "The world is the self, the self is the world."

In the Sutra on the Sign of No-Self (Anattalakkhana Sutta, Samyutta Nikaya, Vol. III, p. 66), the second discourse the Buddha gave after his enlightenment, it is taught that because there is not a self, the Five Aggregates of personality are not enduring and do not have sovereignty. Our Five Aggregates may want to be eternal, unchanging, and beautiful, but they cannot be as our minds want them to be. This is one of the ways of explaining the teaching on no-self. In the same sutra, the Buddha also says, "Bhikshus, the body is not self. If the body were self, it would not be a cause of afflictions and we could say to the body, 'You should be like this,' or 'You should not be like this.' The same is true of the other four aggregates of personality: feelings, perceptions, mental formations, and consciousness." In this passage, the Buddha is thinking about self as an absolute entity with sovereignty. Because there is no sovereignty within the Five Aggregates of personality, it can be said that there is no self present within the Five Aggregates of personality.

DITTHI-NISSAYA (VIEW-REFUGE)

To establish peace of mind, to be free of the fear of annihilation (nihilism), human beings tend to cling to the idea of a self. This is a universal human need. Even the busiest person cannot avoid reflecting on the matter of life and death once in a while. Perhaps our death will be sudden and unexpected, or perhaps it will be prolonged. Will we just turn into nothingness? Because we human beings are afraid of nothingness, we cling to the belief in a permanent, indestructible self. Sometimes we look for explanations why there must be a self. "I think, therefore I am," Descartes' position, is an expression of this need.

We also have a need to identify the self with something, whether it is the body, feelings, perceptions, mental formations, consciousness, or the world. Believing that the world will last forever, that the world is the self, and that the self will persist with the world are ways of clinging to the self. According to the teachings of Buddhism, everything is impermanent. The Five Aggregates are impermanent and the world is also impermanent. To look for an eternal self is a fruitless endeavor, like taking refuge in a sand castle. Sooner or later, sand castles must collapse, and, in the end, searching for an eternal self only brings us anxiety, exhaustion, sorrow, suffering, and despair. Let us read this passage from the Sutra on Knowing the Better Way to Catch a Snake.

> "Bhikshus, do you think the Five Aggregates and the self are permanent, changeless, and not subject to destruction?"
>
> "No, reverend teacher."
>
> "Is there anything you can hold on to with attachment that will not cause anxiety, exhaustion, sorrow, suffering, and despair?"
>
> "No, reverend teacher."
>
> "Is there any view of self in which you can take refuge that will not cause anxiety, exhaustion, sorrow, suffering, and despair?"
>
> "No, reverend teacher."

A place where one takes refuge in a view of self is called *ditthi nissaya* in Pali, "view-refuge." As long as we continue to take refuge in views, we continue to experience fear, suffering, and despair. Therefore, it is best to give up all view-refuges. To believe in an eternal self is fruitless and dangerous. When one day we lose that belief for one reason or another, we will plummet into the depths of confusion and despair. From the extreme of being caught in a view of the self as eternal, we will fall into the abyss of nihilism, the other extreme, and our suffering and confusion will be boundless. The following passage from the sutra refers to this danger:

Upon hearing this, one bhikshu stood up, bared his right shoulder, joined his palms respectfully, and asked the Buddha, "World-Honored One, can fear and anxiety arise from an internal source?"

The Buddha replied, "Yes, fear and anxiety can arise from an internal source. If you think, 'Things that did not exist in the past have come to exist, but now no longer exist,' you will feel sad or become confused and despairing. This is how fear and anxiety can arise from an internal source."

"Things" refers to the self: "In the past, before my mother gave birth to me, I did not exist. After my mother gave birth to me, naturally I existed. I believed I existed. Despite that, today I see that I do not exist. I am nothing at all." This is to go from being caught in existence to being caught in nonexistence, from being caught in permanence to being caught in nihilism. These are all extreme views. The insight of the Buddha goes beyond these extremes so that we remain in the Middle Way, which is neither existence nor nonexistence, permanence nor annihilation.

A suggestion was made by one commentator that "things" refers to the material offerings made to the bhikshus. This is incorrect and indicates this scholar has caught the snake by the wrong end. "Things" refers to the self to which we cling. "Things" could also be the belief in a soul or in heaven. Without such a belief, we may feel confused, and with it, we may feel comfort, so we cling to that belief. But our clinging is also accompanied by anxiety or longing, and if some day we experience upheaval or loss, our faith will be undermined and our suffering will be unbearable. We will "feel sad and become completely confused and despairing." The Buddha asks, "Is there anything you can hold on to with attachment that will not cause anxiety, exhaustion, sorrow, suffering, and despair?"

THE WAY TO PRACTICE THE TEACHINGS OF NO-SELF

When we realize the true nature of no-self, we can let go of all of the grounds of view. We no longer need to cling to or identify ourselves with anything, and we will no longer fall into states of confusion, anxiety, or sorrow. To receive the teachings of no-self requires us to use our full intelligence and skillfulness. If we do not, these same teachings can cause us confusion, anxiety, and sorrow, especially during times of upheaval and loss in our lives. If we receive the teachings of no-self incorrectly, we may think they are about nihilism and destruction, and feelings of despair may overwhelm us. If we believe the world is a self, that we are that self, and that we will endure as long as the world endures, when we hear the Buddhist teaching of no-self and we are not ready for it, we will immediately fall into a state of confusion. From being caught in a view that everything exists, we will descend into a view that nothing exists. From being caught in a view that everything is permanent, we will descend into a view that everything is nonexistent. Even though the teachings on no-self are not theories of nihilism or destruction, if we receive them as if they were, we have caught the snake by the tail. A brahman could fall into this condition. From his belief in self, he could descend into the confusion of nihilism and nonbeing:

> "World-Honored One, can fear and anxiety arise from an external source?" The Buddha taught, "Fear and anxiety can arise from an external source. You may think, 'This is a self. This is the world. This is myself. I will exist forever.' Then if you meet the Buddha or a disciple of the Buddha who has the understanding and intelligence to teach you how to let go of all views of attachment to the body, the self, and the objects of the self with a view to giving up pride, internal formations, and energy leaks, and you think, 'This is the end of the world. I have to give up everything. I am not the world. I am not me. I am not a self. I will not exist forever. When I die, I will be completely annihilated. There is nothing to look forward to, to be joyful about, or to remember,' you will feel sad and become confused and despairing. This is how fear and anxiety can arise from an external source."

We can lose faith in the presence of a self for reasons that are within ourselves, and when we hear the teachings of no-self, we can lose that faith for reasons that are outside ourselves. If we lose faith in the self from hearing the teachings, we are like one who is bitten by a snake while trying to catch it. This is the theme of this sutra.

Reading the sutra this far, we understand how many people have misunderstood the teachings of no-self. We have learned that among the Five Aggregates of personality and the world, there is nothing that is not subject to change. But we should note that the Buddha never taught that the Five Aggregates and the world are nonexistent. The coming together of the Five Aggregates is an existence, although it is an impermanent and selfless existence. This existence is impermanent and selfless, therefore in its essence it cannot be described as being or not being, eternal or subject to annihilation. The Five Aggregates and the world transcend the four categories of being (*bhava*), nonbeing (*abhava*), permanence (*sassata*), and annihilation (*uccheda*). This is the Buddha's teaching of the Middle Way. It is offered in many sutras of both the Northern and Southern Traditions. The following passage from the Sutra on the Middle Way elucidates this point:

"When someone observes the coming-to-be of the world, he is not caught in the idea that the world does not exist. When someone observes the fading away of the world, he is not caught in the idea that the world exists. Kaccayana, in the world there are two extreme views: the view of being and the view of non-being. The Tathagata is not caught by either view. He teaches the Dharma of the Middle Way" (Samyukta Agama, Sutra No. 301, equivalent to Kaccanagotta Sutta, Samyutta Nikaya, Vol. II, pp. 16–17).

9: The Non-achieved and the Non-expressed

In the Sutra on Knowing the Better Way to Catch a Snake, the teachings on no-self are described in the context of the Brahmanic belief of self (atman). Within the Buddhist community, the Buddha usually spoke of self in terms of the three different ways of being caught in the view of self: (1) self (me, I), (2) object of self (mine), and (3) self within something or something within self. To understand this, let us look at the example of the body:

1. *I am this body.* We identify ourselves with our bodies. "I am the body. The body is me."
2. *This body is mine.* The body and I are not identical. The body is my possession, like my name, my belongings, or my bank account.
3. *I am in this body, this body is in me.* The body is not me, but I am present in the body. I am not the body, but the body is in me. The self lies in the body and the body lies in the self. In Chinese this is called xiang zai, "mutual inter-containing." This view is the most subtle and is linked to the idea, developed by a few later Buddhist schools, that the self is not the Five Aggregates, but without the Five Aggregates, the self cannot exist.

These three categories (of being caught in the view of self) are mentioned in many sutras, especially in the Samyutta Agama and the Samyutta Nikaya. They are three traps we may fall into. When we are free of the first two traps, we may still fall into the third, which is more subtle. Among Buddhists in many traditions, there are always people looking for a ground of views so they can establish a subtle sense of self, because, as we have already seen, the need to cling to a self is a powerful one. The Sutra on Knowing the Better Way to Catch a Snake is unique in that it mentions the sixth ground of views, "the world is self," which is a fourth trap, after the view of xiang zai, or mutual inter-containing. The Buddha teaches that the idea of "I" or "me" arises on the basis of the idea of "mine," and the idea of "mine" arises on the basis of the idea of "I" or "me." Both are wrong perceptions, with no basis, so they cannot be established or grasped. If we try to establish and hold on to an idea of self, we just bring suffering and despair on ourselves. Thus, the four traps, or ways of establishing a self, are only a smoke screen of wrong perceptions—internal formations that are responsible for our present and future suffering. This is the Buddha's teaching:

> "Whenever there is an idea of self, there is also an idea of what belongs to the self. When there is no idea of self, there is no idea of anything that belongs to the self. Self and what belongs to the self are two views that are based on trying to grasp things that cannot be grasped, and to establish things that cannot be established. Such wrong perceptions cause us to be bound by internal formations that arise the moment we are caught by ideas that cannot be grasped or established and have no basis in reality."

The Five Aggregates and the world have their own suchness. Our ideas about the Five Aggregates arise within the framework of notions of existence, nonexistence, permanence, destruction, and so on. These notions cannot contain or hold reality, just as a net cannot contain or hold space. That is what is meant by "cannot be grasped" and "cannot be established." Such teachings are important in Buddhism. The Sanskrit term for "ungraspable" is anupalabhya. Here it is translated as "cannot be grasped" and "cannot be established." Despite the inestimable importance of this teaching it was never developed to its fullest by either the Sarvastivada or Tamrashatiya schools of Buddhism.

10: Impermanence

The Buddha described the world as impermanent, ever-changing. Hearing this, we may get a notion about impermanence. But a notion is not yet an insight. It's only an idea that has come from listening to a talk or reading a book. Ideas about impermanence are not yet useful, only the insight, the wisdom of impermanence is useful. We may all have an idea about impermanence, but few of us have the insight of impermanence. The sutra is trying to help liberate us from such concepts as impermanence, nonself, and nirvana, but the sutra still has to use concepts. So we need to be artists whenever we speak, listen, or study a sutra. We need to be intelligent and skillful so we're not caught in notions, concepts, and words.

We all agree that everything is impermanent, yet we still behave as though things were permanent. Intellectually you know that your beloved one is impermanent, that one day she will have to die. But in your daily life you behave as though she's going to be there forever. If you truly knew that she is impermanent, you'd do whatever you could do today to make her happy. Knowing that she is impermanent and that you are also impermanent, you wouldn't wait for tomorrow, you'd cherish her presence. But you don't treat her well, because deep down you believe that she is permanent and that you are permanent also. That is the trouble. Intellectually we can accept impermanence as a truth, but in our everyday lives, we still behave as if things were permanent. So impermanence needs to be a practice and not just an idea.

Impermanence is not a notion or a philosophy; it is an insight. We gain that insight not by studying books or listening to Dharma talks, but by using our mindfulness and concentration to observe. If we know how to observe the things inside and outside of us every day, then one day we will gain the insight of impermanence. Once the insight is gained, we will be free. When the Buddha taught about impermanence he could only give us a hint about impermanence, a concept of impermanence. The teaching of impermanence is not the reality of impermanence. The teaching is only an idea. An idea cannot liberate us. It is the insight that liberates us.

Whatever you look at, listen to, touch, you have to touch its nature of impermanence. When you look at the cloud, touch its nature of impermanence. When you look at your beloved one, you should be able to touch her nature of impermanence. Impermanence is a *samadhi*, a concentration. That is, we maintain the insight of impermanence alive and never lose sight of it. Whatever you come in touch with, including yourself, know it is impermanent. When the insight of impermanence is there, you act wisely and refrain from doing harm. Living like this, you won't have any regrets. All you have to do to avoid regret is take care of the present moment.

If we use our intelligence and insight, we can see how crucial impermanence is to life. If everything were permanent, nothing would be possible. Impermanence is vital for everything to be. Impermanence allows us to transform and move in a better direction. If things weren't impermanent, your situation couldn't change, a child couldn't grow up, a grain of corn would never become an ear of corn to eat. So we shouldn't complain about impermanence. It's not a negative note of music, it's rather positive, because thanks to impermanence, everything is possible. Your disease can be cured, a regime characterized by dictatorship can change, we can do something to reverse the course of global warming—otherwise global warming would be there forever. Because of impermanence, there is hope.

Even the blocks of pain, sorrow, and despair hidden in the depths of our consciousness are impermanent. If we know how to practice, we can bring about deep self-transformation. We have learned that there are two ways to transform our pain. The first way is to invite it up and look deeply into its nature. The second way is to water the seeds of the opposite nature, and know that they will bring about transformation at the base of our consciousness.

So instead of complaining about impermanence, we must say: "long live impermanence!" Touching the nature of interbeing, emptiness, no-self, we can have hope, we know that we can change and transform. The insight of impermanence can liberate us from much of our fear, sorrow, anger, and our feelings of separation. Knowing that everything is impermanent, we're less attached to it. Flowers are beautiful, but when a flower dies, we don't cry a lot. We know that flowers are impermanent. So awareness of the nature of the impermanence of things is important to us. When we practice that awareness, we suffer much less. And we enjoy being alive much more. Knowing that things are impermanent, we will cherish them in the present moment.

Our bodies are also impermanent. Birth and death take place in every moment in our bodies. Not a single cell is permanent. My body of this moment is no longer my body of the previous moment. When you review all your bodily and mental formations, you see that everything is impermanent, especially what we call the "self." We know this, yet we fear that we are nothing without a permanent self, and yet we continue to believe that we have a separate, permanent self. We are not satisfied with our Five Aggregates. We want more. We want to live forever. But everything, from form to feelings, perceptions, mental formations, and consciousness is impermanent. "Experiencing my body, I breathe in." Touching impermanence during our in-breath, we touch the nature of impermanence in the whole cosmos. Touching one thing, we touch everything.

Scientifically, we can't find anything that is permanent. Everything is always changing. We have to confront the fact that everything is impermanent, that nothing stays the same in two consecutive moments. Therefore, there's no permanent entity that can be called a self.

Impermanence is the manifestation of reality from the point of view of time. No-self is the manifestation of reality from the point of view of space. No-self is impermanence. Time is not a separate entity. In order to be it has to inter-be with everything else, including space, consciousness, and so on. Einstein showed us that time is not possible without space. Time is space. It is like the wave and the particle in physics. Sometimes reality manifests itself as a wave, and sometimes as a particle. Sometimes reality manifests itself as time, and sometimes as space. It looks like two things, but it is not. It is not one thing, either. The notions of one and two are not applicable to reality.

II: Nirvana

Nirvana is another teaching that is easily misunderstood. The basic meaning of nirvana is "extinction," or "to blow out a flame." It means to blow out the flame of afflictions, suffering, and hatred. It also means the extinction of ideas of existence, nonexistence, permanence, destruction, impermanence, no-self, Middle Way, ungraspable, samsara, and even nirvana itself. In spite of this, many people continue to understand nirvana as a state of nothingness and annihilation. The snake of the teachings on nirvana is frequently grasped by the tail. In the Sutra on Knowing the Better Way to Catch a Snake we read,

> "If, when he considers the six bases for wrong views, a bhik-shu does not give rise to the idea of 'I' or 'mine,' he is not caught in the chains of this life. Since he is not caught in the chains of this life, he has no fear. To have no fear is to arrive at nirvana. Such a person is no longer troubled by birth and death; the holy life has been lived; what needs to be done has been done; there will be no further births or deaths; and the truth of things as they are is known."

Here "nirvana" is defined as:

1. To have realized in practice the teachings of no-self (*"the holy life has been lived; what needs to be done has been done"*).
2. To arrive at right understanding (*"the truth of things as they are is known"*).
3. To be able to put an end to the cycle of birth and death (*"Such a person is no longer troubled by birth and death"*).
4. To have no fear (*"he has no fear"*).

After defining nirvana, the Buddha says a little more about its characteristics:

> "Such a bhikshu has filled in the moat, crossed the moat, destroyed the enemy citadel, unbolted the door, and is able to look directly into the mirror of highest understanding."

Here nirvana is described as a struggle for liberation, a victory, and the complete satisfaction of the one who has arrived at full understanding.

Let us read on:

> "What is meant by 'filling in the moat'? 'Filling in the moat' means to know and clearly understand the substance of ignorance. Ignorance has been uprooted and shattered and cannot arise anymore.
>
> "What is meant by 'crossing the moat'? 'Crossing the moat' means to know and clearly understand the substance of becoming and craving. Becoming and craving have been uprooted and shattered and cannot arise anymore.
>
> "What is meant by 'destroying the enemy citadel'? 'Destroying the enemy citadel' means to know and clearly understand the substance of the cycle of birth and death. The cycle of birth and death has been uprooted and shattered and cannot arise anymore.
>
> "What is meant by 'unbolting the door'? 'Unbolting the door' means to know and clearly understand the substance of the five dull internal formations. The five dull internal formations have been uprooted and shattered and cannot arise anymore.
>
> "What is meant by 'looking directly into the mirror of highest understanding'? 'Looking directly into the mirror of highest understanding' means to know and understand clearly the substance of pride. Pride has been uprooted and shattered and cannot arise anymore."

Pride is produced by being caught in a view of self. "Looking directly into the mirror of highest understanding" means liberation from being caught by a view of self.

TATHAGATA

Even though the Buddha described nirvana in very concrete terms, as above, he was often misunderstood, and nihilistic views and ideas of non-continuation were attributed to him. People misunderstood because they thought that once nirvana was attained, everything ceased to exist—that a leaf was no longer a leaf, a flower no longer a flower, a person no longer a person. Everything dissolved into empty space, losing all delineation. But the Buddha never said that nirvana was a huge gap of nothingness. To realize nirvana means not to be caught by ideas of birth and death, existence and nonexistence, one and many, coming and going. Someone who abides in nirvana is a Tathagata.

The concept "tathagata" is deep and wonderful. This is not stressed or developed in the Sarvastivada and Tamrashatiya traditions. According to the Vajracchedika Prajñaparamita Sutra (Taisho 235) the Tathagata is someone who does not come from anywhere and does not go anywhere. Elsewhere, it is said that the Tathagata is one who comes from suchness and returns to suchness. This is another way of saying that the Tathagata does not come and does not go, because he or she realizes the path and abides in nirvana.

In the Sutra on Knowing the Better Way to Catch a Snake, the Buddha says,

"The Tathagata is a noble fount of freshness and coolness.
There is no great heat and no sorrow in this state."

The Tathagata has the joy of peace, freedom, and happiness. The Tathagata, just like nirvana, cannot be confined to categories like birth and death, existence and nonexistence, one and many, coming and going. One will never find the Tathagata in concepts, even if the one searching is Indra, the king of the gods, Prajapati, or Brahma.

In the Mahayana scriptures, beginning with the Prajñaparamita and Maharatnakuta Sutras and continuing in the Avatamsaka and Vimalakirti Nirdesha Sutras, there is an effort to present the teachings of the Middle Way to help people not be caught in the ideas of nothingness and non-continuation. The Madhyamaka Shastra, by Nagarjuna, has the same aim when explaining the eight characteristics that are not the Middle Way: birth, death, permanence, non-continuation, oneness, otherness, coming, and going.

In the Anuradha Sutta (Samyutta Nikaya, Vol. III, pp. 116–119), a small group of wandering ascetics met the Bhikshu Anuradha and asked him whether, after death, the Tathagata (1) continues to exist, (2) ceases to exist, (3) both continues and ceases to exist, or (4) neither continues nor ceases to exist. Anuradha said that none of the four propositions expressed the truth about the Tathagata. The ascetics thought that he was either unintelligent or new to the practice, and they left him. When he returned to the monastery, Bhikshu Anuradha told the Buddha what had happened and asked for his response. The Buddha asked Anuradha if he could find the Tathagata in the body, feelings, perceptions, mental formations, or consciousness. The bhikshu replied that he could not. The Buddha asked him if he could find the Tathagata outside of the body, feelings, perceptions, mental formations, or consciousness, and Anuradha again said no. The Buddha said, "Bhikshu Anuradha, if you cannot find the Tathagata while the Tathagata is still here, how can you expect to find the Tathagata within these four propositions after he is dead?"

In the Chinese version of the Sutra on Knowing the Better Way to Catch a Snake, the Buddha says, "Indra, Prajapati, Brahma, and the other gods in their entourage, however hard they look, cannot find any trace or basis for the consciousness of a Tathagata." The Pali version states, "I say that right here and now it is impossible to find any trace of the Tathagata" (*ditth' ev' aham, bhikkhave, dhamme Tathagatam ananuvejjo 'ti vadami*). In the Pali version, the Buddha concludes, "In former times and still today, the Tathagata teaches only about suffering and the path to transform suffering." The Buddha did not want to waste time looking for ideas and categories of reality. He maintained that such a search could not be of help to anyone, and, in any case, no conclusion could be reached. The eight "noes" of the Middle Way cited by Nagarjuna are already clearly expressed in these early Buddhist sutras.[65]

So that people do not fall into the abyss of nothingness and non-continuation, the Mahaparinirvana Sutra says that permanence, joy, sovereignty, and purity are the four characteristics of nirvana. These four notions had been considered the four basic wrong perceptions, called the four perverted views, but we are taught otherwise in the Mahaparinirvana Sutra in order to heal ideas of nothingness and non-continuation, a kind of medicine to heal snakebites.

12: Treating Wrong Understanding

In every age and every place, there are people who misunderstand the teachings of the Buddha. How can one respond to these kinds of misunderstandings? The Buddha addresses this in the last part of the sutra.

> "When recluses and brahmans hear me say this, they may slander me, saying that I do not speak the truth, that the monk Gautama proposes a theory of nihilism and teaches absolute nonexistence, while in fact living beings do exist. Bhikshus, the Tathagata has never taught the things they say."

Although the Buddha said clearly that he did not support theories of nihilism and non-continuation, for twenty-six hundred years there have always been people who accuse him of exactly that.

It is because the teachings of the Buddha are so deep that they are easily misunderstood. Although the Buddha never said that living beings do not exist, because of some of the things he did say, some people always understand him to be teaching that living beings do not exist. In the Vajracchedika Prajñaparamita Sutra, for example, the Buddha says, "If a bodhisattva thinks there really are sentient beings, he is not yet an authentic bodhisattva." Here, the Buddha was giving the teaching of no-self. In light of interdependent co-origination, sentient beings can only exist because of non-sentient species. To think that sentient beings can possibly exist in isolation from the non-sentient world is a mistake. The Buddha is trying to help us transcend the idea of an independent, separate living being, which is one of the four notions: self, living being, person, and life span. But he only had to open his mouth to be misunderstood. That is why in the Mahayana tradition, we hear this saying of the Buddha, "In forty-five years I have never said anything." It means, "Please do not get caught by any of my words." The Buddha's silent response to Vacchagotta's questions is the same.

How can we face people who falsely accuse, reprimand, or slander us? The Buddha suggests we practice the teaching of no-self. When we practice no-self, false accusations, reprimands, and slander cannot hurt us. When we are in touch with and see the nature of no-self, we are always aware of the principle of interdependent co-origination, because interdependent co-origination and no-self are one. All things arise because of their interdependence, and that is why nothing has a separate, independent identity. It is because of our ignorance and hatred that we accuse, reprimand, or slander one another. Each of us is a product of our family, environment, friends, education, culture, and society. These conditions lead to a certain way of seeing things and a certain way of responding to things. When we see this, we have compassion for everyone, including ourselves. We see that if we want someone to change, we also have to help change his or her family, environment, friends, education, culture, and society. We are responsible, directly or indirectly, for each person's consciousness and attitudes. When we see the conditions that have led to that person's consciousness and attitudes, we will know how to help that person. We won't feel angry, or blame him. On the contrary, we will try to find ways to help him be free from the constrictions of environment and so forth that have produced his consciousness in that way.

With this kind of insight, we cannot help but feel compassion and accept others. How could we continue to see ourselves as the object of false accusations, reprimands, or slander? Even if we are beaten or murdered, when we see deeply and feel compassion like this, we will have a heart of love and will not feel the slightest anger, hatred, or vengeance. If we do not identify ourselves with the Five Aggregates of body, feelings, perceptions, mental formations, and consciousness, others' false accusations, reprimands, or slander will not touch us. The Buddha says,

> "If someone were to walk around the grounds of this monastery and pick up the dead branches and dried grass to take home and burn or use in some other way, should we think that it is we ourselves who are being taken home to be burned or used in some way?"

If criticism, false accusations, and slander are not able to make us angry or vindictive, what about offerings, adoration, praise, and respect? Will they make us proud or arrogant? The answer is still no—not if we are free of the ideas of "I" and "mine."

The Buddha taught,

> "If someone respects, honors, or makes offerings to a Tathagata, the Tathagata would not on that account feel pleased. He would think only that someone is doing this because the Tathagata has attained the fruits of awakening and transformation."

Among the "eight winds"—gain, loss, dishonor, praise, flattery, disgrace, pain, and joy—not one can knock down a person who has realized the teaching of no-self. In the final section of the sutra, the Buddha says,

> "The true teachings have been illuminated and made available in the worlds of humans and gods, with nothing lacking. If someone with right understanding penetrates these teachings, the value will be immeasurable. If, at the time of passing from this life, someone has been able to transform the five dull internal formations, in the next life he or she will attain nirvana. That person will arrive at the state of Non-Returner and will not reenter the cycle of birth and death. If, at the time of passing from this life, someone has been able to transform the three internal formations of attachment, aversion, and ignorance, he or she will be born only one more time in the worlds of humans or gods in order to be liberated. If, at the time of passing from this life, someone has been able to attain the fruit of Stream-Enterer, he or she will not fall again into states of extreme suffering and will surely go in the direction of right awakening. After being born seven times in the worlds of humans or gods, he or she will come to the place of liberation. If, at the time of passing from this life, someone has faith in understanding the teachings, he or she will be born in a blessed world and will continue to progress on the path to highest awakening."

13: Living Wisdom

The teachings of the Buddha are offered not as views or notions for us to grasp at, but as instruments of practice. If we get caught in views and notions, we lose the true teachings. The Sutra on Knowing the Better Way to Catch a Snake is a kind of bell of mindfulness, reminding us to be very careful, attentive, and open when we receive the teaching of the Buddha, so that we understand it in such a way that we can make use of it to transform ourselves and help ourselves and others to have more peace, enlightenment, and freedom.

We practice to have joy and happiness. We practice to bring relief to a difficult situation. But when mindfulness is powerful enough, our concentration will be significant and can help us gain insight, understanding, and wisdom that can liberate us from our pain, sorrow, and fear. The ultimate purpose of Buddhist practice is to gain insight in order to have liberation from our afflictions—our fear, anger, craving, and despair. Bringing relief is okay, we suffer less; but the problem still remains. Only when we get insight can we truly be liberated. In Buddhism we speak of emancipation or salvation by means of insight, not by grace. Yet insight is a kind of grace. In appearance it seems contradictory, but if we look deeply, we see that insight is a kind of grace—the greatest kind of grace, because it helps to liberate. The Buddha said that if we're not attentive, if we don't bring all our hearts and minds, our whole being, into studying the sutras and listening to the Dharma, we may understand them in the wrong way. Liberation is only possible when we are capable of correcting our impressions.

Teachings, ideas, are like a match. The match brings about the flame, which is insight. A teaching, a notion, is not the insight. But if we practice, we can produce the living insight, the living wisdom. Many of us, including quite a few Buddhist scholars, are caught by words and concepts. We stick to the words, the doctrine, the teaching, and we are not free; we become dogmatic. But once we have the insight, it burns away our ideas and notions, just as the flame burns the match that brought it into being.

We should never consider any teaching or ideology to be the absolute truth; it is only a means to gaining insight. We should not kill or be killed because of an idea. If we become dogmatic, we can become a dictator, wanting everyone to accept what we say, believing that we have the truth and that whoever doesn't agree with us is our enemy. This creates more war, conflict, and discrimination. Most wars have been born from fanaticism, being caught in religion or ideologies. This teaching of the Buddha, nonattachment to views, is a deep practice of peace. We are ready to release our view in order to gain the insight. That is also the spirit of science. If a scientist is attached to a finding and thinks it to be the absolute truth, he has no hope of finding something deeper, something higher. We have to burn up all notions in order for the insight to be there. A true practitioner is never dogmatic, never clings to ideas and notions, but makes use of them to produce insight, Right View.

This sutra reminds us that practices like The Three Dharma Seals—impermanence, no-self, and nirvana—are helpful, with the condition that you know how to learn about them. If not, these notions become very dangerous, and once you are caught in them, it's very difficult to get out. There are so many Buddhists who are caught in ideas, words, and concepts. They lose Buddhism, though they claim to be true Buddhists. This sutra is a big mindfulness bell for all of us, reminding us to be careful, to be open, and not to be dogmatic and narrow-minded, so that we have a chance to understand and receive the true teaching of the Buddha.

The teachings of impermanence, no-self, and nirvana are common to all schools of Buddhism. These teachings are deep enough: If we practice intelligently, we can use these notions to gain the insight that we need. I think this is the greatest gift of the Buddha. To be able to receive it or not depends on each of us. Buddhism is not a philosophy or a description of reality. Buddhism is only devices, skillful means that help us to practice and get the insight we need for our own liberation and release from our afflictions. If we can arrange to be less busy, we'll have a better chance of deepening our understanding of the Dharma and putting it into practice. In Buddhism we say: liberation is possible by means of insight. Impermanence, no-self, and nirvana are like tools given us to clear the ground and plant vegetation. The tool isn't to be put on the altar to worship; it has to be used. The Sutra on Knowing the Better Way to Catch a Snake is a gentle yet effective reminder that the teachings of the Buddha are wonderful tools to help bring us deeper into the heart of reality.

THE DIAMOND SUTRA

Vajracchedika Prajñaparamita Sutra

Contents

The Diamond Sutra

SECTION ONE

This is what I heard one time when the Buddha was staying in the monastery in Anathapindika's park in the Jeta Grove near Shravasti with a community of 1,250 bhikshus, fully ordained monks.

That day, when it was time to make the round for alms, the Buddha put on his sanghati robe and, holding his bowl, went into the city of Shravasti to seek alms food, going from house to house. When the almsround was completed, he returned to the monastery to eat the midday meal. Then he put away his sanghati robe and his bowl, washed his feet, arranged his cushion, and sat down.

SECTION TWO

At that time, the Venerable Subhuti stood up, bared his right shoulder, put his knee on the ground, and, folding his palms respectfully, said to the Buddha, "World-Honored One, it is rare to find someone like you. You always support and show special confidence in the bodhisattvas.

"World-Honored One, if sons and daughters of good families want to give rise to the highest, most fulfilled, awakened mind, what should they rely on and what should they do to master their thinking?"

The Buddha replied, "Well said, Subhuti! What you have said is absolutely correct. The Tathagata always supports and shows special confidence in the bodhisattvas. Please listen with all of your attention and the Tathagata will respond to your question. If daughters and sons of good families want to give rise to the highest, most fulfilled, awakened mind, they should rely on the following and master their thinking in the following way."

The Venerable Subhuti said, "Lord, we are so happy to hear your teachings."

SECTION THREE

The Buddha said to Subhuti, "This is how the bodhisattva mahasattvas master their thinking. However many species of living beings there are—whether born from eggs, from the womb, from moisture, or spontaneously; whether they have form or do not have form; whether they have perceptions or do not have perceptions; or whether it cannot be said of them that they have perceptions or that they do not have perceptions—we must lead all these beings to the ultimate nirvana so that they can be liberated. And when this innumerable, immeasurable, infinite number of beings has become liberated, we do not, in truth, think that a single being has been liberated.

"Why is this so? If, Subhuti, a bodhisattva holds on to the idea that a self, a person, a living being, or a life span exists, that person is not an authentic bodhisattva."

SECTION FOUR

"Moreover, Subhuti, when a bodhisattva practices generosity, he does not rely on any object—that is to say he does not rely on any form, sound, smell, taste, tactile object, or dharma—to practice generosity. That, Subhuti, is the spirit in which a bodhisattva should practice generosity, not relying on signs. Why? If a bodhisattva practices generosity without relying on signs, the happiness that results cannot be conceived of or measured. Subhuti, do you think that the space in the Eastern Quarter can be measured?"

"No, World-Honored One."

"Subhuti, can space in the Western, Southern, and Northern Quarters, above and below be measured?"

"No, World-Honored One."

"Subhuti, if a bodhisattva does not rely on any concept when practicing generosity, then the happiness that results from that virtuous act is as great as space. It cannot be measured. Subhuti, the bodhisattvas should let their minds dwell in the teachings I have just given."

SECTION FIVE

"What do you think, Subhuti? Is it possible to grasp the Tathagata by means of bodily signs?"

"No, World-Honored One. When the Tathagata speaks of bodily signs, there are no signs being talked about."

The Buddha said to Subhuti, "In a place where there is something that can be distinguished by signs, in that place there is deception. If you can see the signless nature of signs, then you can see the Tathagata."

SECTION SIX

The Venerable Subhuti said to the Buddha, "In times to come, will there be people who, when they hear these teachings, have real faith and confidence in them?"

The Buddha replied, "Do not speak that way, Subhuti. Five hundred years after the Tathagata has passed away, there will still be people who enjoy the happiness that comes from observing the precepts. When such people hear these words, they will have faith and confidence that here is the truth. We should know that such people have sown seeds not only during the lifetime of one buddha, or even two, three, four, or five buddhas, but have, in truth, planted wholesome seeds during the lifetimes of tens of thousands of buddhas. Anyone who, for only a second, gives rise to a pure and clear confidence upon hearing these words of the Tathagata, the Tathagata sees and knows that person, and he or she will attain immeasurable happiness because of this understanding. Why?

"Because that kind of person is not caught up in the idea of a self, a person, a living being, or a life span. They are not caught up in the idea of a dharma or the idea of a non-dharma. They are not caught up in the notion that this is a sign and that is not a sign. Why? If you are caught up in the idea of a dharma, you are also caught up in the ideas of a self, a person, a living being, and a life span. If you are caught up in the idea that there is no dharma, you are still caught up in the ideas of a self, a person, a living being, and a life span. That is why we should not get caught up in dharmas or in the idea that dharmas do not exist. This is the hidden meaning when the Tathagata says, 'Bhikshus, you should know that all of the teachings I give to you are a raft.' All teachings must be abandoned, not to mention non-teachings."

SECTION SEVEN

"What do you think, Subhuti, has the Tathagata arrived at the highest, most fulfilled, awakened mind? Does the Tathagata give any teaching?"

The Venerable Subhuti replied, "As far as I have understood the Lord Buddha's teachings, there is no independently existing object of mind called the highest, most fulfilled, awakened mind, nor is there any independently existing teaching that the Tathagata gives. Why? The teachings that the Tathagata has realized and spoken of cannot be conceived of as separate, independent existences and therefore cannot be described. The Tathagata's teaching is not self-existent nor is it nonself-existent. Why? Because the noble teachers are only distinguished from others in terms of the unconditioned."

SECTION EIGHT

"What do you think, Subhuti? If someone were to fill the three thousand chiliocosms with the seven precious treasures as an act of generosity, would that person bring much happiness by this virtuous act?"

The Venerable Subhuti replied, "Yes, World-Honored One. It is because the very natures of virtue and happiness are not virtue and happiness that the Tathagata is able to speak about virtue and happiness."

The Buddha said, "On the other hand, if there is someone who accepts these teachings and puts them into practice, even if only a gatha of four lines, and explains them to someone else, the happiness brought about by this virtuous act far exceeds the happiness brought about by giving the seven precious treasures. Why? Because, Subhuti, all buddhas and the dharma of the highest, most fulfilled, awakened mind of all buddhas arise from these teachings. Subhuti, what is called Buddhadharma is everything that is not Buddhadharma."

SECTION NINE

"What do you think, Subhuti? Does a Stream-Enterer think, 'I have attained the fruit of Stream-Entry.'?"

Subhuti replied, "No, World-Honored One. Why? Stream-Enterer means to enter the stream, but in fact there is no stream to enter. One does not enter a stream that is form, nor a stream that is sound, smell, taste, touch, or object of mind. That is what we mean when we say entering a stream."

"What do you think, Subhuti? Does a Once-Returner think, 'I have attained the fruit of Once-Returning'?"

Subhuti replied, "No, World-Honored One. Why? Once-Returner means to go and return once more, but in truth there is no going just as there is no returning. That is what we mean when we say Once-Returner."

"What do you think, Subhuti? Does a Non-Returner think like this, 'I have attained the fruit of No-Return.'?"

Subhuti replied, "No, World-Honored One. Why? No-Return means not to return to this world, but in fact there cannot be any Non-Returning. That is what we mean when we say Non-Returner."

"What do you think, Subhuti? Does an Arhat think like this, 'I have attained the fruit of Arhatship.'?"

Subhuti replied, "No, World-Honored One. Why? There is no separately existing thing that can be called Arhat. If an Arhat gives rise to the thought that he has attained the fruit of Arhatship, then he is still caught up in the idea of a self, a person, a living being, and a life span. World-Honored One, you have often said that I have attained the concentration of peaceful abiding and that in the community, I am the Arhat who has most transformed need and desire. World-Honored One, if I were to think that I had attained the fruit of Arhatship, you certainly would not have said that I love to dwell in the concentration of peaceful abiding."

SECTION TEN

The Buddha asked Subhuti, "In ancient times when the Tathagata practiced under Buddha Dipankara, did he attain anything?"

Subhuti answered, "No, World-Honored One. In ancient times when the Tathagata was practicing under Buddha Dipankara, he did not attain anything."

"What do you think, Subhuti? Does a bodhisattva create a serene and beautiful Buddha field?"

"No, World-Honored One. Why? To create a serene and beautiful Buddha field is not in fact creating a serene and beautiful Buddha field. That is why it is called creating a serene and beautiful Buddha field."

The Buddha said, "So, Subhuti, all the bodhisattva mahasattvas should give rise to a pure and clear intention in this spirit. When they give rise to this intention, they should not rely on forms, sounds, smells, tastes, tactile objects, or objects of mind. They should give rise to an intention with their minds not dwelling anywhere."

"Subhuti, if there were someone with a body as big as Mount Sumeru, would you say that his was a large body?"

Subhuti answered, "Yes, World-Honored One, very large. Why? What the Tathagata says is not a large body, that is known as a large body."

Section Eleven

"Subhuti, if there were as many Ganges Rivers as the number of grains of sand in the Ganges, would you say that the number of grains of sand in all those Ganges Rivers is very many?"

Subhuti answered, "Very many indeed, World-Honored One. If the number of Ganges Rivers were huge, how much more so the number of grains of sand in all those Ganges Rivers."

"Subhuti, now I want to ask you this: if a daughter or son of good family were to fill the three thousand chiliocosms with as many precious jewels as the number of grains of sand in all the Ganges Rivers as an act of generosity, would that person bring much happiness by her virtuous act?"

Subhuti replied, "Very much, World-Honored One."

The Buddha said to Subhuti, "If a daughter or son of a good family knows how to accept, practice, and explain this sutra to others, even if it is a gatha of four lines, the happiness that results from this virtuous act would be far greater."

Section Twelve

"Furthermore, Subhuti, any plot of land on which this sutra is proclaimed, even if only one gatha of four lines, will be a land where gods, men, and ashuras will come to make offerings just as they make offerings to a stupa of the Buddha. If the plot of land is regarded as that sacred, how much more so the person who practices and recites this sutra. Subhuti, you should know that that person attains something rare and profound. Wherever this sutra is kept is a sacred site enshrining the presence of the Buddha or one of the Buddha's great disciples."

SECTION THIRTEEN

After that, Subhuti asked the Buddha, "What should this sutra be called and how should we act regarding its teachings?"

The Buddha replied, "This sutra should be called The Diamond That Cuts through Illusion because it has the capacity to cut through all illusions and afflictions and bring us to the shore of liberation. Please use this title and practice according to its deepest meaning. Why? What the Tathagata has called the highest, transcendent understanding is not, in fact, the highest, transcendent understanding. That is why it is truly the highest, transcendent understanding."

The Buddha asked, "What do you think, Subhuti? Is there any dharma that the Tathagata teaches?"

Subhuti replied, "The Tathagata has nothing to teach, World-Honored One."

"What do you think, Subhuti? Are there many particles of dust in the three thousand chiliocosms?"

"Very many, World-Honored One."

"Subhuti, the Tathagata says that these particles of dust are not particles of dust. That is why they are truly particles of dust. And what the Tathagata calls chiliocosms are not in fact chiliocosms. That is why they are called chiliocosms."

"What do you think, Subhuti? Can the Tathagata be recognized by the possession of the thirty-two marks?"

The Venerable Subhuti replied, "No, World-Honored One. Why? Because what the Tathagata calls the thirty-two marks are not essentially marks and that is why the Tathagata calls them the thirty-two marks."

"Subhuti, if as many times as there are grains of sand in the Ganges a son or daughter of a good family gives up his or her life as an act of generosity and if another daughter or son of a good family knows how to accept, practice, and explain this sutra to others, even if only a gatha of four lines, the happiness resulting from explaining this sutra is far greater."

SECTION FOURTEEN

When he had heard this much and penetrated deeply into its significance, the Venerable Subhuti was moved to tears. He said,

"World-Honored One, you are truly rare in this world. Since the day I attained the eyes of understanding, thanks to the guidance of the Buddha, I have never before heard teachings so deep and wonderful as these. World-Honored One, if someone hears this sutra, has pure and clear confidence in it, and arrives at insight into the truth, that person will realize the rarest kind of virtue. World-Honored One, that insight into the truth is essentially not insight. That is what the Tathagata calls insight into the truth.

"World-Honored One, today it is not difficult for me to hear this wonderful sutra, have confidence in it, understand it, accept it, and put it into practice. But in the future, in five hundred years, if there is someone who can hear this sutra, have confidence in it, understand it, accept it, and put it into practice, then certainly the existence of someone like that will be great and rare. Why? That person will not be dominated by the idea of a self, a person, a living being, or a life span. Why? The idea of a self is not an idea, and the ideas of a person, a living being, and a life span are not ideas either. Why? Buddhas are called buddhas because they are free of ideas."

The Buddha said to Subhuti, "That is quite right. If someone hears this sutra and is not terrified or afraid, he or she is rare. Why? Subhuti, what the Tathagata calls *paramaparamita*, the highest transcendence, is not essentially the highest transcendence, and that is why it is called the highest transcendence.

"Subhuti, the Tathagata has said that what is called transcendent endurance is not transcendent endurance. That is why it is called transcendent endurance. Why? Subhuti, thousands of lifetimes ago when my body was cut into pieces by King Kalinga, I was not caught in the idea of a self, a person, a living being, or a life span. If, at that time, I had been caught up in any of those ideas, I would have felt anger and ill will against the king.

"I also remember in ancient times, for five hundred lifetimes, I practiced transcendent endurance by not being caught up in the idea of a self, a person, a living being, or a life span. So, Subhuti, when a bodhisattva gives rise to the unequalled mind of awakening, he has to give up all ideas. He cannot rely on forms when he gives rise to that mind, nor on sounds, smells, tastes, tactile objects, or objects of mind. He can only give rise to that mind that is not caught up in anything.

"The Tathagata has said that all notions are not notions and that all living beings are not living beings. Subhuti, the Tathagata is one who speaks of things as they are, speaks what is true, and speaks in accord with reality. He does not speak deceptively or to please people. Subhuti, if we say that the Tathagata has realized a teaching, that teaching is neither graspable nor deceptive.

"Subhuti, a bodhisattva who still depends on notions to practice generosity is like someone walking in the dark. He will not see anything. But when a bodhisattva does not depend on notions to practice generosity, he is like someone with good eyesight walking under the bright light of the sun. He can see all shapes and colors.

"Subhuti, if in the future there is any daughter or son of good family who has the capacity to accept, read, and put into practice this sutra, the Tathagata will see that person with his eyes of understanding. The Tathagata will know that person, and that person will realize the measureless, limitless fruit of her or his virtuous act."

SECTION FIFTEEN

"Subhuti, if on the one hand, a daughter or son of a good family gives up her or his life in the morning as many times as there are grains of sand in the Ganges as an act of generosity, and gives as many again in the afternoon and as many again in the evening, and continues doing so for countless ages; and if, on the other hand, another person listens to this sutra with complete confidence and without contention, that person's happiness will be far greater. But the happiness of one who writes this sutra down, receives, recites, and explains it to others cannot be compared.

"In summary, Subhuti, this sutra brings about boundless virtue and happiness that cannot be conceived or measured. If there is someone capable of receiving, practicing, reciting, and sharing this sutra with others, the Tathagata will see and know that person, and he or she will have inconceivable, indescribable, and incomparable virtue. Such a person will be able to shoulder the highest, most fulfilled, awakened career of the Tathagata. Why? Subhuti, if one is content with the small teachings, if he or she is still caught up in the idea of a self, a person, a living being, or a life span, he or she will not be able to listen, receive, recite, and explain this sutra to others. Subhuti, any place this sutra is found is a place where gods, men, and ashuras will come to make offerings. Such a place is a shrine and should be venerated with formal ceremonies, circumambulations, and offerings of flowers and incense."

SECTION SIXTEEN

"Furthermore, Subhuti, if a son or daughter of good family, while reciting and practicing this sutra, is disdained or slandered, his or her misdeeds committed in past lives, including those that could bring about an evil destiny, will be eradicated, and he or she will attain the fruit of the most fulfilled, awakened mind. Subhuti, in ancient times before I met Buddha Dipankara, I had made offerings to and had been attendant of all eighty-four thousand multimillions of buddhas. If someone is able to receive, recite, study, and practice this sutra in the last epoch, the happiness brought about by this virtuous act is hundreds of thousands times greater than that which I brought about in ancient times. In fact, such happiness cannot be conceived or compared with anything, even mathematically. Such happiness is immeasurable.

"Subhuti, the happiness resulting from the virtuous act of a son or daughter of good family who receives, recites, studies, and practices this sutra in the last epoch will be so great that if I were to explain it now in detail, some people would become suspicious and disbelieving, and their minds might become disoriented. Subhuti, you should know that the meaning of this sutra is beyond conception and discussion. Likewise, the fruit resulting from receiving and practicing this sutra is beyond conception and discussion."

SECTION SEVENTEEN

At that time, the Venerable Subhuti said to the Buddha, "World-Honored One, may I ask you again that if daughters or sons of good family want to give rise to the highest, most fulfilled, awakened mind, what should they rely on and what should they do to master their thinking?"

The Buddha replied, "Subhuti, a good son or daughter who wants to give rise to the highest, most fulfilled, awakened mind should do it in this way: 'We must lead all beings to the shore of awakening, but, after these beings have become liberated, we do not, in truth, think that a single being has been liberated.' Why is this so? Subhuti, if a bodhisattva is still caught up in the idea of a self, a person, a living being or a life span, that person is not an authentic bodhisattva. Why is that?

"Subhuti, in fact, there is no independently existing object of mind called the highest, most fulfilled, awakened mind. What do you think, Subhuti? In ancient times, when the Tathagata was living with Buddha Dipankara, did he attain anything called the highest, most fulfilled, awakened mind?"

"No, World-Honored One. According to what I understand from the teachings of the Buddha, there is no attaining of anything called the highest, most fulfilled, awakened mind."

The Buddha said, "Right you are, Subhuti. In fact, there does not exist the so-called highest, most fulfilled, awakened mind that the Tathagata attains. Because if there had been any such thing, Buddha Dipankara would not have predicted of me, 'In the future, you will come to be a Buddha called Shakyamuni.' This prediction was made because there is, in fact, nothing that can be attained that is called the highest, most fulfilled, awakened mind. Why? Tathagata means the suchness of all things (*dharma*s). Someone would be mistaken to say that the Tathagata has attained the highest, most fulfilled, awakened mind since there is not any highest, most fulfilled, awakened mind to be attained. Subhuti, the highest, most fulfilled, awakened mind that the Tathagata has attained is neither graspable nor elusive. This is why the Tathagata has said, 'All dharmas are Buddhadharma.' What are called all dharmas are, in fact, not all dharmas. That is why they are called all dharmas.

"Subhuti, a comparison can be made with the idea of a great human body."

Subhuti said, "What the Tathagata calls a great human body is, in fact, not a great human body."

"Subhuti, it is the same concerning bodhisattvas. If a bodhisattva thinks that she has to liberate all living beings, then she is not yet a bodhisattva. Why? Subhuti, there is no independently existing object of mind called bodhisattva. Therefore, the Buddha has said that all dharmas are without a self, a person, a living being, or a life span. Subhuti, if a bodhisattva thinks, 'I have to create a serene and beautiful Buddha field,' that person is not yet a bodhisattva. Why? What the Tathagata calls a serene and beautiful Buddha field is not in fact a serene and beautiful Buddha field. And that is why it is called a serene and beautiful Buddha field. Subhuti, any bodhisattva who thoroughly understands the principle of nonself and non-dharma is called by the Tathagata an authentic bodhisattva."

SECTION EIGHTEEN

"Subhuti, what do you think? Does the Tathagata have the human eye?"

Subhuti replied, "Yes, World-Honored One, the Tathagata does have the human eye."

The Buddha asked, "Subhuti, what do you think? Does the Tathagata have the divine eye?"

Subhuti said, "Yes, World-Honored One, the Tathagata does have the divine eye."

"Subhuti, what do you think? Does the Tathagata have the eye of insight?"

Subhuti replied, "Yes, World-Honored One, the Tathagata does have the eye of insight."

"Subhuti, what do you think? Does the Tathagata have the eye of transcendent wisdom?"

"Yes, World-Honored One, the Tathagata does have the eye of transcendent wisdom."

The Buddha asked, "Does the Tathagata have the Buddha eye?"

"Yes, World-Honored One, the Tathagata does have the Buddha eye."

"Subhuti, what do you think? Does the Buddha see the sand in the Ganges as sand?"

Subhuti said, "World-Honored One, the Tathagata also calls it sand."

"Subhuti, if there were as many Ganges Rivers as the number of grains of sand of the Ganges and there was a Buddha land for each grain of sand in all those Ganges Rivers, would those Buddha lands be many?"

"Yes, World-Honored One, very many."

The Buddha said, "Subhuti, however many living beings there are in all these Buddha lands, though they each have a different mentality, the Tathagata understands them all. Why is that? Subhuti, what the Tathagata calls different mentalities are not in fact different mentalities. That is why they are called different mentalities.

"Why? Subhuti, the past mind cannot be grasped, neither can the present mind or the future mind."

SECTION NINETEEN

"What do you think, Subhuti? If someone were to fill the three thousand chiliocosms with precious treasures as an act of generosity, would that person bring great happiness by his virtuous act?"

"Yes, very much, World-Honored One."

"Subhuti, if such happiness were conceived as an entity separate from everything else, the Tathagata would not have said it to be great, but because it is ungraspable, the Tathagata has said that the virtuous act of that person brought about great happiness."

SECTION TWENTY

"Subhuti, what do you think? Can the Tathagata be perceived by his perfectly formed body?"

"No, World-Honored One. What the Tathagata calls a perfectly formed body is not in fact a perfectly formed body. That is why it is called a perfectly formed body."

"What do you think, Subhuti? Can the Tathagata be perceived by his perfectly formed physiognomy?"

"No, World-Honored One. It is impossible to perceive the Tathagata by any perfectly formed physiognomy. Why? Because what the Tathagata calls perfectly formed physiognomy is not in fact perfectly formed physiognomy. That is why it is called perfectly formed physiognomy."

SECTION TWENTY-ONE

"Subhuti, do not say that the Tathagata conceives the idea 'I will give a teaching.' Do not think that way. Why? If anyone says that the Tathagata has something to teach, that person slanders the Buddha because he does not understand what I say. Subhuti, giving a Dharma talk in fact means that no talk is given. This is truly a Dharma talk."

Then, Insight-Life Subhuti said to the Buddha, "World-Honored One, in the future, will there be living beings who will feel complete confidence when they hear these words?"

The Buddha said, "Subhuti, those living beings are neither living beings nor non-living beings. Why is that? Subhuti, what the Tathagata calls non-living beings are truly living beings."

SECTION TWENTY-TWO

Subhuti asked the Buddha, "World-Honored One, is the highest, most fulfilled, awakened mind that the Buddha attained the unattainable?"

The Buddha said, "That is right, Subhuti. Regarding the highest, most fulfilled, awakened mind."

SECTION TWENTY-THREE

"Furthermore, Subhuti, that mind is everywhere equally. Because it is neither high nor low, it is called the highest, most fulfilled, awakened mind. The fruit of the highest, most fulfilled, awakened mind is realized through the practice of all wholesome actions in the spirit of nonself, non-person, non-living being, and non-life span. Subhuti, what are called wholesome actions are in fact not wholesome actions. That is why they are called wholesome actions."

SECTION TWENTY-FOUR

"Subhuti, if someone were to fill the three thousand chiliocosms with piles of the seven precious treasures as high as Mount Sumeru as an act of generosity, the happiness resulting from this is much less than that of another person who knows how to accept, practice, and explain the Vajracchedika Prajñaparamita Sutra to others. The happiness resulting from the virtue of a person who practices this sutra, even if it is only a gatha of four lines, cannot be described by using examples or mathematics."

SECTION TWENTY-FIVE

"Subhuti, do not say that the Tathagata has the idea, 'I will bring living beings to the shore of liberation.' Do not think that way, Subhuti. Why? In truth there is not one single being for the Tathagata to bring to the other shore. If the Tathagata were to think there was, he would be caught in the idea of a self, a person, a living being, or a life span. Subhuti, what the Tathagata calls a self essentially has no self in the way that ordinary persons think there is a self. Subhuti, the Tathagata does not regard anyone as an ordinary person. That is why he can call them ordinary persons."

SECTION TWENTY-SIX

"What do you think, Subhuti? Can someone meditate on the Tathagata by means of the thirty-two marks?"

Subhuti said, "Yes, World-Honored One. We should use the thirty-two marks to meditate on the Tathagata."

The Buddha said, "If you say that you can use the thirty-two marks to see the Tathagata, then the Cakravartin is also a Tathagata?"

Subhuti said, "World-Honored One, I understand your teaching. One should not use the thirty-two marks to meditate on the Tathagata."

Then the World-Honored One spoke this verse:

> Someone who looks for me in form
> or seeks me in sound
> is on a mistaken path
> and cannot see the Tathagata.

SECTION TWENTY-SEVEN

"Subhuti, if you think that the Tathagata realizes the highest, most fulfilled, awakened mind and does not need to have all the marks, you are wrong. Subhuti, do not think in that way. Do not think that when one gives rise to the highest, most fulfilled, awakened mind, one needs to see all objects of mind as nonexistent, cut off from life. Please do not think in that way. One who gives rise to the highest, most fulfilled, awakened mind does not contend that all objects of mind are nonexistent and cut off from life."

SECTION TWENTY-EIGHT

"Subhuti, if a bodhisattva were to fill the three thousand chiliocosms with the seven precious treasures as many as the number of sand grains in the Ganges as an act of generosity, the happiness brought about by his or her virtue is less than that brought about by someone who has understood and wholeheartedly accepted the truth that all dharmas are of selfless nature and are able to live and bear fully this truth. Why is that, Subhuti? Because a bodhisattva does not need to build up virtue and happiness."

Subhuti asked the Buddha, "What do you mean, World-Honored One, when you say that a bodhisattva does not need to build up virtue and happiness?"

"Subhuti, a bodhisattva gives rise to virtue and happiness but is not caught in the idea of virtue and happiness. That is why the Tathagata has said that a bodhisattva does not need to build up virtue and happiness."

Section Twenty-Nine

"Subhuti, if someone says that the World-Honored One comes, goes, sits, and lies down, that person has not understood what I have said. Why? The meaning of Tathagata is 'does not come from anywhere and does not go anywhere.' That is why he is called a Tathagata."

Section Thirty

"Subhuti, if a daughter or son of a good family were to grind the three thousand chiliocosms to particles of dust, do you think there would be many particles?"

Subhuti replied, "World-Honored One, there would be many indeed. Why? If particles of dust had a real self-existence, the Buddha would not have called them particles of dust. What the Buddha calls particles of dust are not, in essence, particles of dust. That is why they can be called particles of dust. World-Honored One, what the Tathagata calls the three thousand chiliocosms are not chiliocosms. That is why they are called chiliocosms. Why? If chiliocosms are real, they are a compound of particles under the conditions of being assembled into an object. That which the Tathagata calls a compound is not essentially a compound. That is why it is called a compound."

"Subhuti, what is called a compound is just a conventional way of speaking. It has no real basis. Only ordinary people are caught up in conventional terms."

Section Thirty-One

"Subhuti, if anyone says that the Buddha has spoken of a self view, a person view, a living-being view, or a life span view, has that person understood my meaning?"

"No, World-Honored One. Such a person has not understood the Tathagata. Why? What the Tathagata calls a self view, a person view, a living-being view, or a life span view is not in essence a self view, a person view, a living-being view, or a life span view. That is why he or she is called a self view, a person view, a living-being view, or a life span view."

"Subhuti, someone who gives rise to the highest, most fulfilled, awakened mind should know that this is true of all dharmas, should see that all dharmas are like this, should have confidence in the understanding of all dharmas without any conceptions about dharmas. Subhuti, what is called a conception of dharmas, the Tathagata has said is not a conception of dharmas. That is why it is called a conception of dharmas."

SECTION THIRTY-TWO

"Subhuti, if someone were to offer an immeasurable quantity of the seven treasures to fill the worlds as infinite as space as an act of generosity, the happiness resulting from that virtuous act would not equal the happiness resulting from a son or daughter of a good family who gives rise to the awakened mind and reads, recites, accepts, and puts into practice this sutra, and explains it to others, even if only a gatha of four lines. In what spirit is this explanation given? Without being caught up in signs, just according to things as they are, without agitation. Why is this?

> All composed things are like a dream,
> a phantom, a drop of dew, a flash of lightning.
> That is how to meditate on them,
> that is how to observe them.

After they heard the Lord Buddha deliver this sutra, the Venerable Subhuti, the bhikshus and bhikshunis, laymen and laywomen, and gods and ashuras, filled with joy and confidence, undertook to put these teachings into practice.

1: How to Read the Diamond Sutra

Please read The Diamond That Cuts through Illusion with a serene mind, a mind free from views. It's the basic sutra for the practice of meditation. Late at night, it's a pleasure to recite the Diamond Sutra alone, in complete silence. The sutra is so deep and wonderful. It has its own language. The first Western scholars who obtained the text thought it was talking nonsense. Its language seems mysterious, but when you look deeply, you can understand.

The sutra's full name is The Diamond That Cuts through Illusion, Vajracchedika Prajñaparamita in Sanskrit. *Vajracchedika* means "the diamond that cuts through afflictions, ignorance, delusion, or illusion." In China and Vietnam, people generally call it the Diamond Sutra, emphasizing the word "diamond," but, in fact, the phrase "cutting through" is the most important. *Prajñaparamita* means "perfection of wisdom," "transcendent understanding," or "the understanding that brings us across the ocean of suffering to the other shore." Studying and practicing this sutra can help us cut through ignorance and wrong views and transcend them, transporting ourselves to the shore of liberation.

2: The Dialectics of Prajñaparamita

1. THE SETTING

> This is what I heard one time when the Buddha was staying in the monastery in Anathapindika's park in the Jeta Grove near Shravasti with a community of 1,250 bhikshus, fully ordained monks.

The first sentence of the sutra tells us that the Buddha gave this discourse to 1,250 monks. It does not say that innumerable bodhisattvas from different worlds gathered to hear the Buddha. This detail demonstrates that The Diamond That Cuts through Illusion is among the earliest of the prajñaparamita sutras. Although the Buddha mentions bodhisattvas in this sutra, the audience at the time was almost entirely *shravaka*s, his noble disciples.

> That day, when it was time to make the round for alms, the Buddha put on his sanghati robe and, holding his bowl, went into the city of Shravasti to seek alms food, going from house to house. When the almsround was completed, he returned to the monastery to eat the midday meal. Then he put away his sanghati robe and his bowl, washed his feet, arranged his cushion, and sat down.

This activity was repeated day after day by the monks in the Anathapindika Monastery, as well as in all of the Buddha's monasteries. The Buddha taught his monks and nuns not to distinguish between rich and poor homes when going for alms food, just to go from one dwelling to the next. Seeking alms food is a way to cultivate nondiscriminating mind and also to be in touch with different classes of people to guide them in the practices taught by the Buddha. Even if a monk knew that the people in a particular house would be unkind and not offer him food, he still had to go there and stand still for a few minutes before moving along to the next house.

2. SUBHUTI'S QUESTION

> At that time, the Venerable Subhuti stood up, bared his right shoulder, put his knee on the ground, and, folding his palms respectfully, said to the Buddha, "World-Honored One, it is rare to find someone like you. You always support and show special confidence in the bodhisattvas."

The student, Subhuti, begins this discourse by praising his teacher and then asking an important question. He says that it is rare to find someone like the Buddha, who always gives full support and shows special confidence in the bodhisattvas.

Bodhisattvas are compassionate people whose intention is to relieve their own suffering and the suffering of their fellow beings. Just like a young Vietnamese student who always makes the effort to succeed so that he can take care of his parents and siblings who are still in Vietnam, the bodhisattvas practice not only for themselves, but for their families, communities, and the entire society. One Vietnamese college student in Bordeaux has a sign on his desk that says, "I clench my teeth in order to succeed." There are so many temptations and distractions, and he knows that if he is carried away by any of them, he will ruin his parents' hopes and expectations. Because of his firm determination, he is like a bodhisattva and those on the path of practice. When we meet someone like this, compassion wells up in us. We want to help and support him. It is a waste of energy to support those who live only for themselves and forget about others. In the mind and heart of the bodhisattva there exists a great energy called *bodhicitta*. This is why the Buddha gives special attention and offers care and support to those with the mind and heart of a bodhisattva, those who have a great vow and a great aspiration. It is not because he is discriminating, but because he knows that it is a good investment. Someone who has a great aspiration can help many people.

I always invest in young people. It is not that I discriminate against older people, but, in my country, after many long and painful wars, the minds of the older people are wounded and confused, and it is safer to invest in the young people. Our people are less beautiful than they were in the past. There is so much suspicion, hatred, and misunderstanding. Weeds and thorns have grown everywhere in the soil of their minds. If we sow healthy seeds in such depleted soil, perhaps a few will sprout, but if we sow the same seeds in the fertile minds of young people whose wounds of war are relatively few, most of them are likely to sprout. This is a good investment. Of course, we should also support the older people, but since our time and energy are limited, sowing seeds in the most fertile land has to be our priority.

In the Pali Canon, a layman asks the Buddha why he gives more care and attention to monks and nuns than to laypersons. The Buddha answers that he does so because monks and nuns spend all of their time and energy practicing the way. Their spiritual land is richer, so the Buddha invests more of his time in cultivating it. Subhuti, an elder monk with the title Mahathera, "Great Elder," notices that the Buddha has been paying special attention to the bodhisattvas, and he asks him about it. The Buddha confirms that he does give special support to those whose determination is to help all living beings, and he also gives them a lot of responsibility.

> "World-Honored One, if sons and daughters of good families want to give rise to the highest, most fulfilled, awakened mind, what should they rely on and what should they do to master their thinking?"
>
> The Buddha replied, "Well said, Subhuti! What you have said is absolutely correct. The Tathagata always supports and shows special confidence in the bodhisattvas. Please listen with all of your attention and the Tathagata will respond to your question. If daughters and sons of good families want to give rise to the highest, most fulfilled, awakened mind, they should rely on the following and master their thinking in the following way."
>
> The Venerable Subhuti said, "Lord, we are so happy to hear your teachings."

Bodhi means "awake." *Sattva* means "living being." A bodhisattva is an awakened being who helps other beings wake up. Humans are only one kind of living being. Other living beings also have the potential to awaken. When we enter the path of awakening, our minds are determined to practice. To give rise to a bodhisattva mind, that is, to the deepest understanding and the greatest ability to help others, where should our minds take refuge and how can we master our thinking? The Diamond Sutra is a response to this question.

3. THE FIRST FLASH OF LIGHTNING

> The Buddha said to Subhuti, "This is how the bodhisattva mahasattvas master their thinking. 'However many species of living beings there are—whether born from eggs, from the womb, from moisture, or spontaneously; whether they have form or do not have form; whether they have perceptions or do not have perceptions; or whether it cannot be said of them that they have perceptions or that they do not have perceptions—we must lead all these beings to the ultimate nirvana so that they can be liberated.'"

The word *maha* means "great," so *mahasattva* means "a great being." Liberation here means arriving at *nirvana*, "extinction," a joyful, peaceful state in which all causes of afflictions have been uprooted and we are totally free. The mahasattvas take the great vow to relieve the suffering of all living beings, to bring all to absolute nirvana where they can realize ultimate peace and joy. Absolute nirvana is also called "nirvana without residue of affliction," as compared to nirvana with some residue of afflictions. Some commentators explain that nirvana with some residue of afflictions is a state in which the body of the Five Aggregates (form, feelings, perceptions, mental formations, and consciousness) still exists. They regard the body as a residue of the afflictions of our previous lives. After we die, they say, the body of the Five Aggregates disintegrates completely, and we enter "nirvana without residue of affliction," leaving no trace behind.

I do not fully agree. It is true that once we put an end to the causes of suffering and transform them, we will not bring about new consequences of suffering in the future. But what has existed for a long time, even after it is cut off, still has momentum and will continue for a while before stopping completely. When an electric fan is switched off, although the current has been cut, the blades keep moving for a while longer. Even after the cause has been cut off, the consequence of this past cause continues for a while. The residue of afflictions is the same. What comes to a stop is the creation of new causes of suffering, not the body of the Five Aggregates. One day, Devadatta threw a rock at the Buddha, and his foot was wounded. The Buddha was no longer creating new karma, but he experienced this karmic consequence as the result of a past action that had some energy left over before it could stop. This does not mean that the Buddha had not realized complete extinction after he passed away.

The Mahayana sutras say that bodhisattvas ride on the waves of birth and death. Riding on the waves of birth and death means that although birth and death are there, they are not drowned by them. While traveling in the ocean of birth and death, the bodhisattvas are in perfect nirvana, that is, nirvana without any residue of afflictions—not in the imperfect nirvana that has some residue of afflictions. Although their bodies are there and they are riding on birth and death, they do not suffer. Therefore, the residues of afflictions in the imperfect nirvana are not the Five Aggregates themselves, but rather the afflictions that remain as the karmic consequence of past actions.

> "However many species of living beings there are—whether born from eggs, from the womb, from moisture, or spontaneously; whether they have form or do not have form; whether they have perceptions or do not have perceptions; or whether it cannot be said of them that they have perceptions or that they do not have perceptions—we must lead all these beings to the ultimate nirvana so that they can be liberated."

The World-Honored One answers him directly, saying that an authentic bodhisattva is one who embodies two factors in his being: the first is the great aspiration to bring all beings to the shore of liberation; the second is the wisdom of nondiscrimination. This sentence exemplifies the bodhisattva's Great Vow. It is the prerequisite of becoming a bodhisattva, an awakened person, a person for whom the work for enlightenment is his or her life work, a person who is called a great being, a person to whom the Buddha gives special support and attention. This vow is not only the basic condition of being a bodhisattva, it is also the primary condition. It is the foundation of the highest, most fulfilling wish of a bodhisattva.

When we read this passage, we must look at ourselves and ask, "Is this vow at all related to my life and the life of my community? Are we practicing for ourselves or for others? Do we only want to uproot our own afflictions, or is our determination to study and practice to bring happiness to other living beings?" If we look at ourselves, we will see if we are among the bodhisattvas the Buddha is addressing, supporting, and investing in. If we study and practice with a heart like this, we won't have to wait several years for others to notice. They will see it right away by the way we treat the cat, the caterpillar, or the snail. When we wash the dishes, do we put the leftover food aside to feed the birds? These kinds of small acts show our love for all living beings. The great heart of a bodhisattva mahasattva can be seen throughout his or her daily life. While studying the bodhisattva's actions in the Mahayana sutras, we should also practice looking at ourselves—the way we drink tea, eat our food, wash the dishes, or tend our garden. If we observe ourselves in this way, we will see whether we have the understanding of a bodhisattva, and our friends will also know.

The living beings mentioned in this sutra are not only remote strangers. They are the brothers and sisters with whom we study and practice the Dharma. They too have joy and pain, and we must see them and be open to them. If we are only an independent island, living in a community but not seeing or smiling with the community, we are not practicing as a bodhisattva. Besides just our Dharma brothers and sisters, there are also other species of animals, as well as the plants in the garden and the stars in the sky. This sutra is addressing all of them, and explaining how all are related to our daily lives and our practice. If we are mindful, we will see.

> "And when this innumerable, immeasurable, infinite number
> of beings has become liberated, we do not, in truth, think
> that a single being has been liberated."

This is the first flash of lightning. The Buddha goes directly to the heart of the prajñaparamita, presenting the principle of formlessness. He tells us that a true practitioner helps all living beings in a natural and spontaneous way, without distinguishing between the one who is helping and the one who is being helped. When the left hand is injured, the right hand takes care of it right away. It doesn't stop to say, "I am taking care of you. You are benefiting from my compassion." The right hand knows very well that the left hand is also the right hand. There is no distinction between them. This is the principle of interbeing—coexistence, or mutual interdependence. "This is because that is." With this understanding—the right hand helping the left hand in a formless way—there is no need to distinguish between the right hand and the left hand.

For a bodhisattva, the work of helping is natural, like breathing. When her brother suffers, she offers care and support. She does not think that she has to help him in order to practice the Dharma or because her teacher says she should. It isn't necessary to have an idea of helping. We feel the need to do it, and we do it. This is easy to understand. If we act in this spirit of formlessness, we will not say, later on, "When my brother was sick, I took care of him every day. I made him soup and did many other things for him, and now he is not at all grateful." If we speak like that, our actions were done in the spirit of form. That is not what is called a good deed according to the teaching of prajñaparamita. Formlessness is something concrete that we can put into practice here and now.

If someone in your community is lazy and does not work hard when everyone else does, you may think, "She is awful. She stays in her room and listens to music while I have to work hard." The more you think about her, the more uncomfortable you become. In that state, your work does not bring happiness to you or anyone else. You should be able to enjoy what you are doing. Why should the absence of one person affect your work so? If, when you are working, you do not distinguish between the person who is doing the work and the one who is not, that is truly the spirit of formlessness. We can apply the practice of prajñaparamita into every aspect of our lives. We can wash the dishes or clean the bathroom in exactly the way the right hand puts a Band-Aid on the left hand, without discrimination.

When the Buddha says, "When innumerable, immeasurable, infinite beings become liberated, we do not think that a single being has been liberated," these are not empty words. The Buddha is encouraging us to support and love all living beings. It would be wonderful if those who study Buddhism understood this one sentence. The teaching here is so complete and profound.

"Why is this so? If, Subhuti, a bodhisattva holds on to the idea that a self, a person, a living being, or a life span exists, that person is not an authentic bodhisattva."

A person has to get rid of the four notions of self, a person, a living being, and a life span in order to have the wisdom of nondiscrimination. "Self" refers to a permanent, changeless identity, but since, according to Buddhism, nothing is permanent and what we normally call a self is made entirely of nonself elements, there is really no such entity as a self. Our concept of self arises when we have concepts about things that are not self. Using the sword of conceptualization to cut reality into pieces, we call one part "I" and the rest "not I."

The concept of "person," like the concept of self, is made only of non-person elements—sun, clouds, wheat, space, and so on. Thanks to these elements, there is something we call a person. But erecting a barrier between the idea of person and the idea of non-person is erroneous. If we say, for example, that the cosmos has given birth to humankind and that other animals, plants, the moon, the stars, and so forth, exist to serve us, we are caught up in the idea of person. These kinds of concepts are used to separate self from nonself and person from non-person, and they are erroneous.

We put a lot of energy into advancing technology in order to serve our lives better, and we exploit the non-human elements, such as the forests, rivers, and oceans, in order to do so. But as we pollute and destroy nature, we pollute and destroy ourselves as well. The results of discriminating between human and non-human are global warming, pollution, and the emergence of many strange diseases. In order to protect ourselves, we must protect the non-human elements. This fundamental understanding is needed if we want to protect our planet and ourselves.

The concept of "living being," arises the moment we separate living from non-living beings. The French poet Alphonse de Lamartine once asked, "Inanimate objects, do you have a soul?" to challenge our popular understanding. But what we call non-living makes what we call living beings possible. If we destroy the non-living, we also destroy the living.

In Buddhist monasteries, during the Ceremony of Beginning Anew, each monk and nun recites, "I vow to practice wholeheartedly so that all beings, living and non-living, will be liberated." In many ceremonies, we bow deeply to show our gratitude to our parents, teachers, friends, and numerous beings in the animal, plant, and mineral worlds. Doing this helps us realize that there is no separation between the living and the so-called non-living. Vietnamese composer Trinh Cong Son wrote, "How do we know the stones are not suffering? Tomorrow the pebbles will need one another." When we really understand love, our love will include all beings, living and so-called non-living.

We usually think of "life span" as the length of our lives, beginning the moment we are born and ending when we die. We believe that we are alive during that period, not before or after. And while we are alive, we think that everything in us is life, not death. Once again, the sword of conceptualization is cutting reality into pieces, separating one side, life, from the other side, death. But to think that we begin our lives at the moment we are born and end them the moment we die is an erroneous view, called the "view of life span."

According to prajñaparamita, life and death are one. We are born and die during every second of our lives. During one so-called life span, there are millions of births and millions of deaths. Cells in our body cease to be every day—brain cells, skin cells, blood cells, and many, many others. Our planet is also a body, and we are each a cell in that body. Must we cry and organize a funeral every time one cell of our bodies or one cell of the Earth's body dies? Death is necessary for life to be. In the Samyutta Nikaya, the Buddha says, "When causes and conditions are sufficient, eyes are present. When causes and conditions are not sufficient, eyes are absent. The same is true of body and consciousness." We love life and grasp it tightly. We dread death and want to hide from it. Doing this brings us much worry and anxiety and is caused entirely by our view of life span.

The Sanskrit word for "perception" is *samjña*.[66] According to the Vijñanavada school of Buddhist psychology, perception has two components: a subject and an object of cognition. Walking in the woods at night, if we see a snake, we will probably feel very frightened. But if we shine a flashlight on it and see that it is just a rope, we will feel a great relief. Seeing the snake was an erroneous perception, and the Buddha teaches us that the four notions (self, person, sentient being, and life span) are four erroneous perceptions at the root of our suffering.

We all enjoy leaving the city and going to the countryside. The trees are so beautiful; the air is so fresh. For me, this is one of the great pleasures of life. In the countryside, I like to walk slowly in the woods, look deeply at the trees and flowers, and, when I have to urinate, I can do so right in the open air. The fresh air is so much more pleasant than any bathroom in the city, especially some very smelly public restrooms. But I have to confess that for years I was uneasy about urinating in the woods. The moment I approached a tree, I felt so much respect for its beauty and grandeur that I couldn't bring myself to urinate right in front of it. It seemed impolite, even disrespectful. So I would walk somewhere else, but there was always another tree or bush, and I felt equally disrespectful there.

We usually think of our bathrooms at home, made of wood, tile, or cement, as inanimate and we have no problem urinating there. But after I studied the Diamond Sutra and I saw that wood, tile, and cement are also marvelous and animate, I began to even feel uncomfortable using my own bathroom. Then I had a realization. I realized that urinating is also a marvelous and wondrous reality, our gift to the universe. We only have to urinate mindfully, with great respect for ourselves and whatever surroundings we are in. So now I can urinate in nature, fully respectful of the trees, the bushes, and myself. Through studying the Diamond Sutra, I solved this dilemma, and I enjoy being in the countryside now more than ever.

4. The Greatest Gift

> "Moreover, Subhuti, when a bodhisattva practices generosity, he does not rely on any object—that is to say he does not rely on any form, sound, smell, taste, tactile object, or dharma—to practice generosity."

Why does the Buddha go from talking about the four notions to talking about the practice of generosity? Getting rid of notions is the practice of prajñaparamita, also called insight or the perfection of wisdom. It's the last of the Six Paramitas, the six bodhisattva practices for crossing to the other shore. The others are generosity (*danaparamita*), mindfulness trainings (*shilaparamita*), endurance (*kshantiparamita*), diligence (*viryaparamita*), and meditation (*dhyanaparamita*).

Generosity is the first practice, so the Buddha uses it as an example for the other five. He does mention endurance in section 14, but not the other three practices. However, the nature of all six practices is prajñaparamita, wisdom; otherwise it's not the highest practice of generosity. If you practice generosity without being caught by the four notions, then it's the highest practice of generosity. It's the same with the other five practices. When we practice the Six Paramitas, we need to maintain our insight of nondiscrimination.

I think you already understand this sentence from the sutra, even if you are hearing it for the first time. While working to relieve the suffering of others, you do it in the spirit of signlessness, not distinguishing between yourself and others. You do not base your work on the perception of a self, a person, a living being, or a life span. This spirit can be manifested in any act of generosity, practicing the precepts, endurance, energy, concentration, or understanding.

There are three kinds of gifts: material resources, the Dharma, and non-fear. In the Heart Sutra, Avalokita Bodhisattva offers us the gift of non-fear, or security. When traveling on the high seas, many Vietnamese boat people bring with them only a copy of the Heart Sutra. When we recite this prajñaparamita text with our full attention, we become fearless. Avalokita's gift to us is the greatest act of generosity one can offer.

When a bodhisattva practices generosity, he or she always does so in the spirit of fearlessness, not bound by the four wrong perceptions. In fact, the moment we are not imprisoned by the four erroneous perceptions, we are already in the world of non-fear. Erroneous perceptions arise because of our ignorance about the nature of perception. We do not see the true nature of the forms, sounds, smells, tastes, tactile objects, and objects of mind, and we are caught by them. If, on the other hand, we see someone who is hungry and offer him or her food without asking a lot of other questions or saying that we are practicing generosity, we are truly in the spirit of prajñaparamita and free from misperceptions.

Many of us want to help other people and practice generosity. But when we're caught by the four notions, the happiness that results from our generosity is not very great. We're still angry, jealous, sad; we still suffer because we still believe in the idea of our separate self, person, living being, and life span. If we practice generosity according to the spirit of the Diamond Sutra, using the wisdom of nondiscrimination as fuel for our practice, then the happiness that results is great.

People usually think that forms are stable and real, but according to the Buddha and modern science, form is made only of empty space. Any mass of matter, whether rock, iron, or wood, is composed of countless molecules which are, in turn, composed of countless atomic and subatomic particles, all of which are held together by electromagnetic and nuclear forces. Atoms are vast, empty spaces in which infinitely small particles—protons, electrons, neutrons, and so on—are in perpetual motion at enormous speeds. When we look deeply into matter, we see that it is like a beehive moving at a very great speed. Electrons travel around their nucleus at 300,000 kilometers per second. How erroneous was our concept of form! Physicists say that when they enter the world of atomic particles, they can see clearly that our conceptualized world is an illusion. The Buddha uses the image of a bubble to make it clear that there is space in matter, and he says the same is true of sounds, smells, tastes, tactile objects, and objects of mind. Due to our wrong perceptions about these six sense objects, we develop erroneous perceptions of a self, a person, a living being, and a life span. Therefore, while practicing generosity, we must go beyond our wrong perceptions and be free from them, not holding on to anything. If we take refuge in things that collapse easily, we too will collapse easily.

A meditation center, for example, is only a form. In our daily lives we need forms, but we do not need to cling to them. We can study and practice meditation anywhere. If Plum Village were not here, we could go somewhere else. Once we see that, we become peaceful and fearless and are able to use the objects of our six senses freely. We know their true nature and are not their slaves. We do not feel more faith when they come together, and we do not feel less faith when they dissolve.

It is not correct to think that it is only possible to practice generosity when we have money. We can always offer others our peace and happiness. Many young people tell me, "Thây, I must get a job with a good salary because I want to help others." They study to become doctors or engineers, and studying takes most of their time now, so they do not have time to practice generosity. Then, after they become doctors or engineers, they are even busier and still do not have the time to practice generosity, even to themselves.

"That, Subhuti, is the spirit in which a bodhisattva should practice generosity, not relying on signs. Why? If a bodhisattva practices generosity without relying on signs, the happiness that results cannot be conceived of or measured. Subhuti, do you think that the space in the Eastern Quarter can be measured?"

"No, World-Honored One."

"Subhuti, can space in the Western, Southern, and Northern Quarters, above and below be measured?"

"No, World-Honored One."

"Subhuti, if a bodhisattva does not rely on any concept when practicing generosity, then the happiness that results from that virtuous act is as great as space. It cannot be measured. Subhuti, the bodhisattvas should let their minds dwell in the teachings I have just given."

The happiness that results from practicing generosity without relying on signs is boundless. We often say that the fruits of practice are peace and liberation. If we are washing dishes and thinking of others who are enjoying themselves doing nothing, we cannot enjoy washing the dishes. We may have a few clean dishes afterwards, but our happiness is smaller than one teaspoon. If, however, we wash the dishes with a serene mind, our happiness will be boundless. This is already liberation. The words in the sutra are very much related to our daily lives.

5. SIGNLESSNESS

"What do you think, Subhuti? Is it possible to grasp the Tathagata by means of bodily signs?"

"No, World-Honored One. When the Tathagata speaks of bodily signs, there are no signs being talked about."

The Buddha said to Subhuti, "In a place where there is something that can be distinguished by signs, in that place there is deception. If you can see the signless nature of signs, then you can see the Tathagata."

Is it possible to grasp the Tathagata by the eighty signs of beauty or the thirty-two marks of a great person? Perceptions have signs as their object, and our perceptions are often inaccurate and sometimes quite erroneous. The accuracy of our perceptions depends on our insight. When we achieve insight, our knowledge is no longer based simply on perceptions, and we call this knowledge prajña, wisdom or understanding beyond signs.

In this passage, we encounter the dialectics of prajñaparamita. Our usual way of perceiving is according to the principle of identity: "A is A" and "A is not B." However, in this passage, Subhuti says, "A is not A." As we continue to study the Diamond Sutra, we will see many other sentences like this.

When the Buddha sees a rose, does he recognize it as a rose in the same way that we do? Of course he does. But before he says the rose is a rose, the Buddha has seen that the rose is not a rose. He has seen that it is made of non-rose elements, with no clear demarcation between the rose and those elements that are not the rose. When we perceive things, we generally use the sword of conceptualization to cut reality into pieces, saying, "This piece is A, and A cannot be B, C, or D." But when A is looked at in light of dependent co-arising, we see that A is comprised of B, C, D, and everything else in the universe. "A" can never exist by itself alone. When we look deeply into A, we see B, C, D, and so on. Once we understand that A is not just A, we understand the true nature of A and are qualified to say "A is A," or "A is not A." But until then, the A we see is just an illusion of the true A.

Look deeply at the one you love (or at someone you do not like at all!) and you will see that she is not herself alone. "She" includes her education, society, culture, heredity, parents, and all the things that contribute to her being. When we see that, we truly understand her. If she makes us unhappy, we can see that she did not intend to but that unfavorable conditions made her do it. To protect and cultivate the good qualities in her, we need to know how to protect and cultivate the elements outside of her, including ourselves, that make her fresh and lovely. If we are peaceful and pleasant, she too will be peaceful and pleasant.

If we look deeply into A and see that A is not A, we see A in its fullest flowering. At that time, love becomes true love, generosity becomes true generosity, practicing the precepts becomes truly practicing the precepts, and support becomes true support. This is the way the Buddha looks at a rose, and it is why he is not attached to the rose. When we are still caught in signs, we are still attached to the rose. A Chinese Zen master once said, "Before practicing Zen, mountains are mountains and rivers are rivers. While practicing Zen, mountains are no longer mountains and rivers are no longer rivers. After practicing, mountains are mountains again and rivers are rivers again." These are the dialectics of prajñaparamita.

You know that monks and nuns are very much associated with signs. Their shaved heads, their robes, the way they walk, stand, sit, and lie down, are different from others, and, because of these signs, we can recognize them as monks and nuns. But some monks and nuns practice only for the form, so we cannot pass any judgments, positive or negative, based on signs. We must be able to see through the form in order to be in touch with the substance. Recognizing the Tathagata by means of the thirty-two marks or the eighty signs of beauty is dangerous, because Mara and the Wheel-Turning Kings (*cakravarti-raja*) also have the same signs. "Do not look for the Tathagata by means of bodily signs," the Buddha said. He also said, "Where there is sign, there is illusion." That is, when there is perception, there is deception. The substance of any perception is its sign. Our task is to practice until signs no longer deceive us and our perceptions become insight and understanding.

Tathagata is the true nature of life, wisdom, love, and happiness. Only when we can see the signless nature of signs do we have a chance of seeing the Tathagata. When we look at a rose without being caught by its signs, we see the nature of non-rose and therefore we begin to see the Tathagata in the rose. If we look into a pebble, a tree, or a child in this way, we also see the Tathagata in them. Tathagata means coming from nowhere and going nowhere, showing no sign of coming and no sign of going, no sign of being and no sign of non-being, no sign of birth and no sign of death.

Before continuing, please read the first five sections of the sutra again. All of the essentials have been presented, and if you reread these sections, you will come to understand the meaning of The Diamond That Cuts through Illusion. Once you understand, you may find the Diamond Sutra like a piece of beautiful music. Without straining at all, the meaning will just enter you.

3: The Language of Nonattachment

6. A Rose is Not a Rose

The Venerable Subhuti said to the Buddha, "In times to come, will there be people who, when they hear these teachings, have real faith and confidence in them?"

The Buddha replied, "Do not speak that way, Subhuti. Five hundred years after the Tathagata has passed away, there will still be people who enjoy the happiness that comes from observing the precepts. When such people hear these words, they will have faith and confidence that here is the truth. We should know that such people have sown seeds not only during the lifetime of one Buddha, or even two, three, four, or five Buddhas, but have, in truth, planted wholesome seeds during the lifetimes of tens of thousands of Buddhas."

The Venerable Subhuti understands deeply what the Buddha has already explained. But he is concerned that those in the future will not, since these teachings appear to contradict common sense. It may not be difficult to understand the teachings of the Buddha while he is alive, but five hundred years after he has passed away, those who hear these teachings may have doubts. So the Buddha reassures Subhuti that there will still be people in the future who are able to derive happiness from following the precepts, and that these people, when they hear the teaching of The Diamond That Cuts through Illusion, will accept these teachings just as Subhuti has accepted them. In fact, more than two thousand years have passed since the Buddha has entered parinirvana, and there are still many people who practice the precepts and accept these teachings.

In Buddhism, we often say that the mind is like a field, and every time we do something wholesome or joyful, we sow a Buddha seed in that field. In this passage, the Buddha says that people who understand his teachings have planted wholesome seeds during the lifetimes of tens of thousands of buddhas.

> "Anyone who, for only a second, gives rise to a pure and clear confidence upon hearing these words of the Tathagata, the Tathagata sees and knows that person, and he or she will attain immeasurable happiness because of this understanding."

There are two very important words in this sentence: "see" and "know." If, for one second, a person is confident about these teachings, the Buddha will see and know that person. To be seen and known by the Buddha is a great inspiration and support for anyone on the path of practice. If we have one close friend who can understand us and know our aspirations, we feel greatly supported. A good friend does not have to do much. He or she only needs to see us and know that we are here, and we feel greatly encouraged. Imagine if our friend is the Buddha!

This sentence in the Diamond Sutra became clear to me one day several years ago as I was reading a poem I had written in 1967 for the brothers and sisters of the School of Youth for Social Service. It was a pleasant surprise to have insight into a sutra by reading or doing something else. I discovered that reading a sutra is like planting a tree inside our being. When we walk, look at the clouds, or read something else, the tree grows and it may reveal itself to us.

By 1967, the war in Vietnam had become so terrifying and destructive that many of the young social workers, monks, and nuns in the School of Youth for Social Service had to evacuate villagers even as the bombs were dropping. Already in exile, I received news from time to time that a brother or a sister of our school had been killed while doing this work. Neither the communists nor the anticommunists accepted our Buddhist movement. The communists thought that we were backed by the CIA, and the pro-American side suspected that we were communists. We would not accept the killing by either side. We only wanted reconciliation.

One evening, five young brothers were shot and four died. The one survivor told Sister Chan Khong that the killers had taken them to the riverbank, asked if they were members of the School of Youth for Social Service, and, when they said "Yes," said, "We are very sorry, but we have to kill you."

When I heard the news, I cried. A friend asked me, "Why do you cry? You are the commander-in-chief of a nonviolent army working for love. There are certain losses every army has to take. You are not taking the lives of people; you are saving lives. Even for warriors of love in a nonviolent army, casualties are inevitable."

I told him, "I am not a commander-in-chief. I am just a person. These young people joined the school in response to my call, and now they are dead. Of course I cry."

I wrote a poem for the brothers and sisters at the school and asked them to read it carefully. In that poem I told them never to look at anyone with hatred, even if they hate you, suppress you, kill you, or step on your life as if you were a wild plant or an insect. If you die because of violence, you must meditate on compassion in order to forgive those who killed you. The title of the poem is "Recommendation." Our only enemies are greed, violence, and fanaticism. When you die realizing this state of compassion, you are truly a child of the Awakened One. Before immolating herself to call for a cease-fire between the warring sides, my disciple, Sister Nhat Chi Mai, read the same poem into a cassette recorder and left the tape for her parents.

Promise me,
promise me this day,
promise me now,
while the sun is overhead
exactly at the zenith,
promise me:

Even as they
strike you down
with a mountain of hatred and violence;
even as they step on you and crush you
like a worm,
even as they dismember and disembowel you,
remember, brother,
remember:
man is not our enemy.

The only thing worthy of you is compassion—
invincible, limitless, unconditional.
Hatred will never let you face
the beast in man.

One day, when you face this beast alone,
with your courage intact, your eyes kind,
untroubled
(even as no one sees them),
out of your smile
will bloom a flower.
And those who love you
will behold you
across ten thousand worlds of birth and dying.

Alone again,
I will go on with bent head,
knowing that love has become eternal.
On the long, rough road,
the sun and the moon
will continue to shine,
guiding my way.

Even if you are dying in oppression, shame, and violence, if you can
smile with forgiveness, you have a great power. When I was rereading
these lines, I suddenly understood the Diamond Sutra: "Your courage
intact, your calm eyes full of love, even if no one knows of your smile,
blossoming as a flower in solitude and great pain, those who love you
will still see you, while traveling through a thousand worlds of birth
and death." If you die with compassion in your mind, you are a torch
lighting our path.

"Alone again, I will go on with my head bent down in order to
see you, know you, remember you. Your love has become eternal.
Although the road is long and difficult, the light of the sun and the
moon is still there to guide my steps." When there is a mature relationship between people, there is always compassion and forgiveness. In our
lives, we need others to see and recognize us so that we feel supported.
How much more do we need the Buddha to see us! On our path of
service, there are moments of pain and loneliness, but when we know

that the Buddha sees and knows us, we feel a great surge of energy and a firm determination to carry on.

> "Why? Because that kind of person is not caught up in the idea of a self, a person, a living being, or a lifespan. They are not caught up in the idea of a dharma or the idea of a non-dharma. They are not caught up in the notion that this is a sign and that is not a sign. Why? If you are caught up in the idea of a dharma, you are also caught up in the ideas of a self, a person, a living being, and a life span. If you are caught up in the idea that there is no dharma, you are still caught up in the ideas of a self, a person, a living being, and a life span."

Sign here means concept. When we have a concept about something, its image appears within that concept. For example, when we have a concept of a table, we see an image of that table, but we must remember that our concept is not the thing itself. It is just our perception, which might in fact be very different from the table. A termite, for example, may perceive a table as a feast, and a physicist may perceive it as a mass of rapidly moving particles. Those of us on the path of Buddhist practice, because we have been practicing looking deeply, might have fewer erroneous views and our perceptions might be closer to being complete and true, but they are still perceptions.

In Buddhism, a dharma is commonly defined as any phenomenon that can maintain its unique characteristics and not be mistaken for another phenomenon. Anger, sadness, worry, and other psychological phenomena are called *citta dharmas*. Chairs, tables, houses, mountaintops, rivers, and other physical phenomena are called *rupa dharmas*. Phenomena that are neither psychological nor physical, such as gain, loss, being, and nonbeing, are classified as *cittaviprayukta-samskara dharmas*. Phenomena that are not conditioned by anything are called *asamskrita dharmas*.

According to the Sarvastivada school of Buddhism, space is an asamskrita dharma. It has a birthless and deathless nature and is not formed by anything. But this was just a way for them to offer an example. In fact, space is made of such things as time and consciousness and is, therefore, not really an unconditioned dharma. The Sarvastivadins also call "suchness" an unconditioned dharma, but if we look deeply, we can see that suchness is not an unconditioned dharma either. The concept of "suchness" exists because we have the concept of "non-suchness." If we think that suchness is different from all other dharmas, our concept of suchness is born from our concept of non-suchness. When there is above, there is below; when there is inside, there is outside; when there is permanence, there is impermanence. According to the law of relativity, our views are always defined by their opposites.

In the dialectics of prajñaparamita, however, we have to say the opposite: "Because this is not what it is, it really is what it is." When we look into a dharma and see everything that is not that dharma, we begin to see that dharma. Therefore, we must not be bound to the concept of any dharma or even to the concept of non-dharma.

I am introducing the idea of non-dharma to help us go beyond the idea of dharma, but please do not get caught by the concept of non-dharma. When we see a rose, we know that the rose is a dharma. To avoid being caught by the concept "rose," we must remember that this rose cannot exist as a completely separate, independent entity but is made up only of non-rose elements. We know that rose is not a separate dharma, but once we leave behind the concept of a rose that can exist independently, we can be caught by the idea of non-rose. We must also be free from the concept of non-dharma.

In the dialectics of prajñaparamita, there are three stages: (1) A rose is (2) not a rose, therefore (3) it is a rose. The third rose is very different from the first. The notion "empty of emptiness" (shunyata) in the teaching of prajñaparamita aims at helping us be free from the concept of emptiness.

Before practicing meditation, we see that mountains are mountains. When we start to practice, we see that mountains are no longer mountains. After practicing for a while, we see that mountains are again mountains. Now the mountains are very free. Our minds are still with the mountains, but they are no longer bound to anything. The mountains in the third stage are not the same as those in the first. In the third stage, the mountains reveal themselves freely, and we call this "true being." It is beyond being and nonbeing. The mountains are there in their wonderful presence, not as an illusion.

When the Buddha sees a rose, the rose he sees is a miracle. It is the rose of true being. The rose that you and I see may be one of being, still full of conceptualizations. The notion of emptiness in the prajña-paramita literature is very deep. It goes beyond the illusory world of being and nonbeing, yes and no. It is called "true emptiness." True emptiness is not emptiness. True emptiness is true being.

When we dwell in the world of duality, we are conditioned by it. When we say, "My friend has passed away," and we cry, we are enslaved by the world of coming and going. The world of conditions is filled with erroneous views. It is only by learning to look deeply into the nature of things that we become free of the concepts of being and nonbeing and arrive in a world where such concepts as coming and going, existence and non-existence, birth and death, one and many, and above and below vanish. Once we are free, this world is still around us and inside us, but it is now the world of true emptiness. The principle of identity is at the top of the tree, but the world of true being is at the root. The principle of identity is the basis of the concept of self. Therefore, we have to break through the nets of both dharma and non-dharma and go beyond perceptions and non-perceptions.

> "That is why we should not get caught up in dharmas or in the idea that dharmas do not exist. This is the hidden meaning when the Tathagata says, 'Bhikshus, you should know that all of the teachings I give to you are a raft.' All teachings must be abandoned, not to mention non-teachings."

The first sentence means that we should not get caught up in being or nonbeing, because both are illusory. When we no longer cling to these erroneous ideas, we arrive at the wondrous world of true emptiness.

At this point, the Diamond Sutra repeats what was said in the Alaggadupama Sutta, The Snake Simile. There the Buddha tells us that his teachings are like a raft that needs to be abandoned when we reach the other shore. The words "hidden meaning" are found only in the Sanskrit version, not in the Chinese one. When the Buddha offers teachings, it is possible that his listeners will cling to these teachings even after they are no longer appropriate or necessary. Listening to the teachings of the Buddha is like catching a dangerous snake. If you don't know how to do it, you might take hold of the tail first and the snake might turn around and bite you. If you know how to catch a snake, you will use a two-pronged stick to stop it, and then you will pick the snake up by the neck so that it cannot bite you. The same is true of the teachings of the Buddha—you can get hurt if you are unskillful. You must be careful not to get caught by the teachings. The ideas of emptiness, impermanence, and selflessness are extremely helpful, but if you use them without understanding them deeply and clearly, you can suffer and cause harm to others.

7. ENTERING THE OCEAN OF REALITY

"What do you think, Subhuti, has the Tathagata arrived at the highest, most fulfilled, awakened mind? Does the Tathagata give any teaching?"

The Venerable Subhuti replied, "As far as I have understood the Lord Buddha's teachings, there is no independently existing object of mind called the highest, most fulfilled, awakened mind, nor is there any independently existing teaching that the Tathagata gives. Why? The teachings that the Tathagata has realized and spoken of cannot be conceived of as separate, independent existences and therefore cannot be described. The Tathagata's teaching is not self-existent nor is it nonself-existent. Why? Because the noble teachers are only distinguished from others in terms of the unconditioned."

The Buddha is testing Subhuti to see if he understands what he has said concerning the dialectics of prajñaparamita. In answering the question whether the Tathagata has arrived at the highest, most fulfilled, awakened mind and if there is any teaching that the Tathagata gives, Subhuti demonstrates his understanding by using the language of prajñaparamita. He goes on to explain that the teachings of the Tathagata can neither be grasped nor described. This is a very wise reply.

The Buddha has already explained these points, and now Subhuti repeats them in his own way by saying, "There is no independently existing object of mind called the highest, most fulfilled, awakened mind." If we say that there is a dharma called the highest, most fulfilled awakened mind, we are using the sword of conceptualization to slice out a piece of reality and call it the highest, most fulfilled, awakened mind. We should also be able to see the non-highest, non-most fulfilled, non-awakened mind just as we saw the non-rose elements while looking at a rose.

When Subhuti says that there is no independently existing object of mind called "the highest, most fulfilled, awakened mind," he means that what is called "the highest, most fulfilled, awakened mind" has no separate existence. Just as the rose cannot be separated from clouds, sun, soil, and rain, the teaching of the Buddha cannot be found outside of daily life. No dharma—not "the highest, most fulfilled, awakened mind," suchness, nirvana, Tathagata, a rose, eating a meal, washing the dishes, Subhuti, a friend, a house, a horse, or the teachings the Tathagata has realized—can be grasped or described.

The notion that things can exist independently of one another comes from the perception that they have a beginning and an end. But it is impossible to find the beginning or end of anything. When you look at your close friend, you may think that you understand her completely, but that is difficult because she is a river of reality. In every moment, dharmas that are not her enter and leave her. You cannot take hold of her. By observing her form, feelings, perceptions, mental formations, and consciousness, you can see that she is here sitting next to you, and she is elsewhere at the same time. She is in the present, the past, and the future. Your friend, the Tathagata, Subhuti, and the rose cannot be grasped because they have no beginning and no end. Their presence is deeply connected to all dharmas, all objects of mind in the universe.

When we practice Zen, we may be assigned the koan "What was your face before your parents were born?" We cannot grasp or describe this because it transcends forms. We have only our concepts, and we cannot grasp these dharmas through our perceptions. It is like trying to hold on to the air with our hands. The air slips out. This is why Subhuti said, "The teachings that the Tathagata has realized and spoken of cannot be conceived of as separate, independent existences and therefore cannot be described. The Tathagata's teaching is not self-existent nor is it nonself-existent." It is not correct to call the Tathagata's teaching a dharma, since by doing so we put it into a box, a pattern, and isolate it from other things. But saying it is not a dharma is also not correct, because it really is a dharma—not one that can be isolated but one that transcends all perceptions.

Then Subhuti says that the noble teachers can be distinguished from others only in terms of the unconditioned. "Noble teachers" is a translation of the Sanskrit term *aryapudgala*. *Arya* means honor. *Pudgala* means person. Aryapudgala are those who have attained the status of "Stream-Enterer" (*sotapatti-phala*), "Once-Returner" (*sakadagami-phala*), "Never-Returner" (*anagami-phala*), or "the one who is free from craving and rebirth" (*arhat*). Asamskrita dharmas are uncondi-tioned. They transcend all concepts. The noble teachers are liberated. They are distinguished from others because they are in touch with and realize the unconditioned dharmas. They are no longer imprisoned by forms and concepts.

This section of the sutra shows that all dharmas are without form and transcend conceptual knowledge. When we realize the suchness of all dharmas, we are freed from our conceptual prisons. In daily life, we usually use our conceptual knowledge to grasp reality. But this is impossible. Meditation aims at breaking through all conceptual limita-tions and barriers so that we can move freely in the boundless ocean of reality.

8. Nonattachment

> "What do you think, Subhuti? If someone were to fill the three thousand chiliocosms with the seven precious treasures as an act of generosity, would that person bring much hap-piness by this virtuous act?"
>
> The Venerable Subhuti replied, "Yes, World-Honored One. It is because the very natures of virtue and happiness are not virtue and happiness that the Tathagata is able to speak about virtue and happiness."

Chiliocosm comes from two Greek words: *chilioi*, meaning "a thou-sand," and *kosmos*, meaning "universe." Three thousand chiliocosms means an innumerable number of universes. The Buddha asks, "If someone were to fill the three thousand chiliocosms with the seven precious treasures as an act of generosity, would that person bring much happiness by this virtuous act?" Subhuti replies, "Yes," and goes on to show the Buddha that he is not confined by language. Aware that there are no separate objects of mind called "virtue" or "happiness," Subhuti is no longer imprisoned by words and therefore can use them without any harm. But if we do not see the nature of interbeing implied in each word, they can be a kind of attachment or imprisonment. We have to use words in a way that they do not enslave us. This is why the Buddha is giving us The Diamond That Cuts through Illusion.

The Buddha said, "On the other hand, if there is someone who accepts these teachings and puts them into practice, even if only a gatha of four lines, and explains them to someone else, the happiness brought about by this virtuous act far exceeds the happiness brought about by giving the seven precious treasures."

The happiness brought about by this virtuous act is boundless. It is the utmost, unconditioned emancipation, not merely an accumulation of conditioned happinesses.

"Why? Because, Subhuti, all Buddhas and the dharma of the highest, most fulfilled, awakened mind of all Buddhas arise from these teachings."

This remarkable proclamation embraces the notion that prajña, understanding, is the mother of all buddhas and bodhisattvas.

"Subhuti, what is called Buddhadharma is everything that is not Buddhadharma."

Those who bring Buddhist practice to the West should do so in this spirit. Since Buddhism is not yet known to most Westerners, the essence of Buddhism won't have much chance to blossom in the West if the teachings emphasize form too much. If you think that the teachings of Buddhism are completely separate from the other teachings in your society, that is a big mistake. When I travel in the West to share the teachings of Buddhism, I often remind people that there are spiritual values in Western culture and tradition—Judaism, Islam, and Christianity—that share the essence of Buddhism. When you look deeply into your culture and tradition, you will discover many beautiful spiritual values. They are not called Buddhadharma, but they are really Buddhadharma in their content.

In his last meal, for example, Jesus held up a piece of bread and shared it with his students, saying, "Friends, eat this bread which is my flesh. I offer it to you." When he poured the wine, he said, "Here is my blood. I offer it to you. Drink it." Many years ago, when I met Cardinal Danielou in Paris, I told him, "I think Lord Jesus was teaching his students the practice of mindfulness." In our lives, we eat and drink many times a day, but while doing so, our minds are usually wandering elsewhere, and what we really eat are our worries, thoughts, and anxieties. Eating in mindfulness is to be in touch with life. Jesus spoke the way he did so that his students would really eat the bread. The Last Supper was a mindfulness meal. If the disciples could pierce through their distractions and eat one piece of bread in the present moment with their whole being, isn't that Buddhadharma? Words like "mindfulness" or "meditation" may not have been used, but the fact that thirteen people were sitting and eating together in mindfulness is surely the practice of Buddhism. Vietnamese King Tran Nhan Tong once said that eating a meal, drinking water, and using the toilet are all Buddhadharma. Buddhadharma is not something different from so-called non-Buddhadharma.

The Diamond Sutra is not difficult to understand, although it may sound strange until you get used to this kind of language. It also may seem repetitive, but if you read it carefully, you will find something new in every sentence. Moreover, the Diamond Sutra helps us sow many wholesome seeds into our consciousness, so when a similar thought is repeated, good seeds are sown into our store consciousness (*alaya vijñana*). In teaching the Diamond Sutra, the Buddha is training Subhuti how to use the language of nonattachment. As we become conversant in this language, we are able to develop our deepest understanding.

4: The Answer is the Question

9. DWELLING IN PEACE

"What do you think, Subhuti? Does a Stream-Enterer think, 'I have attained the fruit of Stream-Entry.'?"

Subhuti replied, "No, World-Honored One. Why? Stream-Enterer means to enter the stream, but in fact there is no stream to enter. One does not enter a stream that is form, nor a stream that is sound, smell, taste, touch, or object of mind. That is what we mean when we say entering a stream."

According to traditional Buddhism, Stream-Entry is the first of the four fruits of the practice. When you become a Stream-Enterer, you enter the stream of awakened mind, which always flows into the ocean of emancipation. Is that stream a dharma that exists independently from other dharmas? Subhuti's reply is very much in the language of the dialectics of prajñaparamita.

"What do you think, Subhuti? Does a Once-Returner think, 'I have attained the fruit of Once-Returning.'?"

Subhuti replied, "No, World-Honored One. Why? Once-Returner means to go and return once more, but in truth there is no going just as there is no returning. That is what we mean when we say Once-Returner."

The nature of all dharmas is neither coming nor going. There is no point in space from which they come, and there is no point in space to which they go. They reveal themselves only when conditions are sufficient. When conditions are insufficient, they are latent. The same is true of human beings. According to the traditional definition, a Once-Returner is a person who, after death, will return to the cycle of birth and death just one more time before realizing the fruit of Arhatship (no birth, no death). But in truth, we come from nowhere and we go nowhere. That is why we say such a person is a Once-Returner.

> "What do you think, Subhuti? Does a Non-Returner think like this, 'I have attained the fruit of No-Return.'?"
> Subhuti replied, "No, World-Honored One. Why? No-Return means not to return to this world, but in fact there cannot be any Non-Returning. That is what we mean when we say Non-Returner."

Those who realize the fruit of never returning do not return after this life to this world. It is said that they go to another world to practice until they realize the fruit of Arhatship. Once again, Subhuti applies the language of the dialectics of prajñaparamita. He says that the idea of returning is already illusory, much less the idea of non-returning.

> "What do you think, Subhuti? Does an Arhat think like this, 'I have attained the fruit of Arhatship.'?"
> Subhuti replied, "No, World-Honored One. Why? There is no separately existing thing that can be called Arhat. If an Arhat gives rise to the thought that he has attained the fruit of Arhatship, then he is still caught up in the idea of a self, a person, a living being, and a life span. World-Honored One, you have often said that I have attained the concentration of peaceful abiding and that in the community, I am the Arhat who has most transformed need and desire. World-Honored One, if I were to think that I had attained the fruit of Arhatship, you certainly would not have said that I love to dwell in the concentration of peaceful abiding."

Arana means the absence of struggle. Subhuti is well known throughout the Buddha's community as someone who likes to dwell in the practice of arana, peaceful abiding. He has no wish to compete with anyone. He is regarded as an Arhat, one who has transformed all afflictions and desires. Because Subhuti is not caught by the idea that he has attained the fruit of Arhatship, he is truly an Arhat. At Plum Village, we eat vegetarian food without thinking of ourselves as vegetarians. This is the essence of non-action or formlessness. Because Subhuti practices non-action, he is praised by the World-Honored One as a disciple who loves to dwell in peace.

10. Creating a Formless Pure Land

> The Buddha asked Subhuti, "In ancient times when the Tathagata practiced under Buddha Dipankara, did he attain anything?"
>
> Subhuti answered, "No, World-Honored One. In ancient times when the Tathagata was practicing under Buddha Dipankara, he did not attain anything."
>
> "What do you think, Subhuti? Does a bodhisattva create a serene and beautiful Buddha field?"
>
> "No, World-Honored One. Why? To create a serene and beautiful Buddha field is not in fact creating a serene and beautiful Buddha field. That is why it is called creating a serene and beautiful Buddha field."

Upon attaining enlightenment, all Buddhas and bodhisattvas open a new world for people on the path of realization who want to study and practice with them. Every Buddha creates a pure land as a practice center. A pure land is a fresh, beautiful place where people are happy and peaceful. Creating a pure land is called "setting up a serene and beautiful Buddha field." Teachers and students work together to make such a place beautiful, pleasant, and fresh, so that many people can go there to live and practice. The greater their power of awakening and peace, the more pleasant is their pure land.

Amitabha Buddha has a Pure Land in the Western Paradise. Akshobya Buddha has a place called Wondrous Joy. After a period of practice, if you have some attainment and peace, you may wish to share them with others and establish a small practice community. But this should always be done in the spirit of formlessness. Do not be bound by the practice center you establish. "To create a serene and beautiful Buddha field is not in fact creating a serene and beautiful Buddha field" means to do so in the spirit of formlessness. Do not let yourself be devoured by your Buddha field or you will suffer. Do not allow yourself to be burnt out in the process of setting up a practice center.

> The Buddha said, "So, Subhuti, all the bodhisattva mahasattvas should give rise to a pure and clear intention in this spirit. When they give rise to this intention, they should not rely on forms, sounds, smells, tastes, tactile objects, or objects of mind. They should give rise to an intention with their minds not dwelling anywhere."

Not dwelling anywhere means not relying on anything. Giving rise to an intention means having the wish to attain the highest awakening. Relying on forms, sounds, smells, tastes, tactile objects, and objects of mind means being caught by perceptions, ideas, and concepts. In section two of this sutra, the first question Subhuti asked the Buddha was, "If sons and daughters of good families want to give rise to the highest, most fulfilled, awakened mind, what should they rely on and what should they do to master their thinking?" This passage is the Buddha's answer.

> "Subhuti, if there were someone with a body as big as Mount Sumeru, would you say that his was a large body?"
> Subhuti answered, "Yes, World-Honored One, very large. Why? What the Tathagata says is not a large body, that is known as a large body."

The word "body" is a translation of the Sanskrit word *atmabhava*, not the word *kaya*. Mount Sumeru is the king of all mountains. In this paragraph, the teacher and his student are still using the language of the dialectics of prajñaparamita. When the Buddha asks, "Would you say that his was a large body?" Subhuti answers, "Very large," because he understands clearly the Buddha's language. He is aware that the Buddha says "large" because he is free of the concepts of large and small. If we are aware of the way the Buddha uses words, we will not be caught by any of his words. The teacher is important, the director of the practice center is important, but if the idea of being important becomes an obstacle for the teaching and the practice, then the meaning will be lost.

11. The Sand in the Ganges

"Subhuti, if there were as many Ganges Rivers as the number of grains of sand in the Ganges, would you say that the number of grains of sand in all those Ganges Rivers is very many?"

Subhuti answered, "Very many indeed, World-Honored One. If the number of Ganges Rivers were huge, how much more so the number of grains of sand in all those Ganges Rivers."

"Subhuti, now I want to ask you this: if a daughter or son of good family were to fill the three thousand chiliocosms with as many precious jewels as the number of grains of sand in all the Ganges Rivers as an act of generosity, would that person bring much happiness by her virtuous act?"

Subhuti replied, "Very much, World-Honored One."

The Buddha said to Subhuti, "If a daughter or son of a good family knows how to accept, practice, and explain this sutra to others, even if it is a gatha of four lines, the happiness that results from this virtuous act would be far greater."

The number of grains of sand in the Ganges means a quantity that cannot be reached using mathematics. If one were to fill the three thousand chiliocosms with as many precious jewels as there are grains of sand in the Ganges as an act of generosity, the happiness that is brought about by this virtuous act would still be less than the happiness brought about by accepting, practicing, and explaining the Diamond Sutra. The happiness resulting from the study and practice of The Diamond That Cuts through Illusion is so great that it has become an object of worship, as can be seen in the next section of the sutra.

12. Every Land is a Holy Land

"Furthermore, Subhuti, any plot of land on which this sutra is proclaimed, even if only one gatha of four lines, will be a land where gods, men, and ashuras will come to make offerings just as they make offerings to a stupa of the Buddha. If the plot of land is regarded as that sacred, how much more so the person who practices and recites this sutra. Subhuti, you should know that that person attains something rare and profound. Wherever this sutra is kept is a sacred site enshrining the presence of the Buddha or one of the Buddha's great disciples."

Any ground on which this sutra, even one verse of four lines, is proclaimed is a holy land that is worthy of offerings by gods, men, and ashuras, as sacred and precious as any stupa of the Buddha's relics. If the plot of land is sacred, how much more so the person who practices and recites the sutra, for that means the sutra has penetrated into the flesh, soul, and life of that person. That person is now worthy of offerings by gods, men, and ashuras.

In 1963 in Saigon, the bodhisattva Thich Quang Duc immolated himself in order to awaken our country's dictators. When poet Vu Hoang Chuong visualized the ground on which Thich Quang Duc had sat, he knew that that ground was holy ground, and he said, "The place you sit has become an eternal chef d'œuvre, your compassion shines from the heart of invisibility." Vu Hoang Chuong may not have studied the Diamond Sutra, but he arrived at the same insight. When a person uses his body to save the lives of his fellow beings, his compassion can transform the ground on which he sits into a holy ground. Even though no statue or stupa is there, it is still truly a holy ground and should be considered a place for worship.

13. The Diamond That Cuts through Illusion

After that, Subhuti asked the Buddha, "What should this sutra be called and how should we act regarding its teachings?"

The Buddha replied, "This sutra should be called The Diamond That Cuts through Illusion because it has the capacity to cut through all illusions and afflictions and bring us to the shore of liberation. Please use this title and practice according to its deepest meaning. Why? What the Tathagata has called the highest, transcendent understanding is not, in fact, the highest, transcendent understanding. That is why it is truly the highest, transcendent understanding."

The Buddha asked, "What do you think, Subhuti? Is there any dharma that the Tathagata teaches?"

Subhuti replied, "The Tathagata has nothing to teach, World-Honored One."

"What do you think, Subhuti? Are there many particles of dust in the three thousand chiliocosms?"

"Very many, World-Honored One."

"Subhuti, the Tathagata says that these particles of dust are not particles of dust. That is why they are truly particles of dust. And what the Tathagata calls chiliocosms are not in fact chiliocosms. That is why they are called chiliocosms."

"What do you think, Subhuti? Can the Tathagata be recognized by the possession of the thirty-two marks?"

The Venerable Subhuti replied, "No, World-Honored One. Why? Because what the Tathagata calls the thirty-two marks are not essentially marks and that is why the Tathagata calls them the thirty-two marks."

"Subhuti, if as many times as there are grains of sand in the Ganges a son or daughter of a good family gives up his or her life as an act of generosity and if another daughter or son of a good family knows how to accept, practice, and explain this sutra to others, even if only a gatha of four lines, the happiness resulting from explaining this sutra is far greater."

Subhuti asks what this sutra should be called and how we should practice its teachings, and the Buddha answers that it should be called The Diamond That Cuts through Illusion. A diamond has the capacity to cut through all ignorance and afflictions. He also says that we should practice in an intelligent way, that we should learn to look deeply so that we will realize that even transcendent understanding is not an independently existing dharma and that his teaching has no separate nature. That is why Subhuti says, "The Tathagata has nothing to teach."

If someone were to grind the three thousand chiliocosms into dust, these particles of dust would be very, very many. We should look deeply into the concepts of "many" and "chiliocosms" with the eye of transcendent understanding if we want to avoid being caught by these concepts. The same is true of the concepts of "dust" and "thirty-two marks." Although such words are used, we should not be caught by them. If someone were to accept, practice, and explain these teachings, even if only one verse of four lines, the happiness resulting from this would be far greater than the happiness that would result from any other virtuous act. Because the practice of nonattachment as it is taught in the sutra can liberate us completely from wrong views, the happiness that results from this practice is far greater than any kind of happiness. Virtuous acts still based on the ground of self, person, living being, and life span may bring some happiness, but compared to the happiness of true liberation, it is still quite small. When a person is absolutely free from wrong views, his or her actions will greatly benefit the world. The practice of The Diamond That Cuts through Illusion is thus the basis for all meaningful action.

14. Abiding in Non-abiding

When he had heard this much and penetrated deeply into its significance, the Venerable Subhuti was moved to tears. He said, "World-Honored One, you are truly rare in this world. Since the day I attained the eyes of understanding, thanks to the guidance of the Buddha, I have never before heard teachings so deep and wonderful as these. World-Honored One, if someone hears this sutra, has pure and clear confidence in it, and arrives at insight into the truth, that person will realize the rarest kind of virtue. World-Honored One, that insight into the truth is essentially not insight. That is what the Tathagata calls insight into the truth.

"World-Honored One, today it is not difficult for me to hear this wonderful sutra, have confidence in it, understand it, accept it, and put it into practice. But in the future, in five hundred years, if there is someone who can hear this sutra, have confidence in it, understand it, accept it, and put it into practice, then certainly the existence of someone like that will be great and rare. Why? That person will not be dominated by the idea of a self, a person, a living being, or a life span. Why? The idea of a self is not an idea, and the ideas of a person, a living being, and a life span are not ideas either. Why? Buddhas are called buddhas because they are free of ideas."

When he had heard this much and penetrated deeply into its significance, the Venerable Subhuti was moved to tears. Hearing something
so profound or seeing a view so beautiful, we too may be moved to
tears of happiness. Then Subhuti says, "Since the day I attained the
eyes of understanding, I have never before heard teachings so deep
and wonderful as these." The eyes of understanding mentioned here
are not yet the eyes of the deepest, all-embracing understanding of a
Buddha. They are only the eyes of an Arhat. This means that Subhuti
is beginning to see things more deeply after hearing this much of the
Diamond Sutra.

If someone hears this sutra, has confidence in it, and arrives at insight
into the truth, that person will have pure, clear, and stable confidence
without questions or doubts. The Diamond That Cuts through Illusion came into existence five hundred years after the Buddha entered
nirvana. This sutra is difficult to understand because what is said is
contrary to the common perceptions of people. Therefore, anyone who
can understand the Diamond Sutra, at any time, should know that he
or she is of a very rare nature.

Subhuti goes on to say, "The idea of a self is not an idea, and the ideas
of a person, a living being, and a life span are not ideas either. Why?
Buddhas are called buddhas because they are free of ideas." The English
word "view" is actually closer to the Chinese character used here than
the word "idea," although views themselves are ideas or perceptions.
Any perception has two parts: a viewer (subject) and that which is being
viewed (object). A self view, a person view, a living-being view, and a life
span view are all objects of perception. They are neither independently
existing nor permanent. Like everything else, they are of the nature of
interbeing. The last line is a powerful statement: "Buddhas are called
buddhas because they are free of ideas."

> The Buddha said to Subhuti, "That is quite right. If some-
> one hears this sutra and is not terrified or afraid, he or she
> is rare. Why? Subhuti, what the Tathagata calls parama-
> paramita, the highest transcendence, is not essentially the
> highest transcendence, and that is why it is called the highest
> transcendence.
>
> "Subhuti, the Tathagata has said that what is called tran-
> scendent endurance is not transcendent endurance. That
> is why it is called transcendent endurance. Why? Subhuti,

thousands of lifetimes ago when my body was cut into pieces by King Kalinga, I was not caught in the idea of a self, a person, a living being, or a life span. If, at that time, I had been caught up in any of those ideas, I would have felt anger and ill-will against the king."

The Buddha uses transcendent endurance, one of the Six Paramitas, as an example of the spirit of deep understanding. According to the Prajñaparamita (known as the "Mother of all Buddhas") Sutras, prajñaparamita is the clay pot that contains all the other paramitas. If the clay has not been fired properly, liquids stored in it will gradually leak out. That is why prajñaparamita is the very foundation. The Buddha was able to practice transcendent endurance because he had attained transcendent understanding, prajñaparamita.

Thousands of lifetimes ago, when his body was cut to pieces by King Kalinga, the bodhisattva who was to become the Buddha was able not to get angry because he already had transcendent understanding, that is, he was not caught up in views. He was not caught up in the idea of a self, a person, a living being, or a life span. If the bodhisattva had still been caught up in views, he would have had ill will against the king and would not have succeeded.

We can see that what is called transcendent endurance is, in fact, not only transcendent endurance. It is, at the same time, transcendent generosity and observing the precepts, as well as everything else that is not transcendent endurance. Just as a rose is not just a rose, transcendent endurance cannot exist independently of the other five paramitas. With this understanding, we can call it transcendent endurance. As we begin to follow the Buddha's reasoning, we can see why he talks about transcendent endurance in order to teach about prajñaparamita, transcendent understanding.

"I also remember in ancient times, for five hundred lifetimes, I practiced transcendent endurance by not being caught up in the idea of a self, a person, a living being, or a life span. So, Subhuti, when a bodhisattva gives rise to the unequalled mind of awakening, he has to give up all ideas. He cannot rely on forms when he gives rise to that mind, nor on sounds, smells, tastes, tactile objects, or objects of mind. He can only give rise to that mind that is not caught up in anything."

A mind that still relies on one thing does not abide in stillness. That is why the Buddha always says that the bodhisattva should not rely on form to practice generosity. In order to really benefit living beings, the bodhisattva practices generosity without relying on anything. In this section, the Buddha repeats what he has already said several times in this sutra: A mind that does not rely on anything is not caught by forms, sounds, smells, tastes, tactile objects, or objects of mind. When we take refuge in something that is changing, we can never have peace. We need to abide in what is stable. All objects of our six senses are conditioned and continuously changing. If we abide in them, we will not have stability.

Today, throughout the world, many single parents are trying to raise children by themselves. It is difficult, and many of them are not at peace. They are working hard to give up the idea of needing a partner so they can just rely on themselves. In the past they may have relied on someone who lacked stability, and their relationship fell apart. But I know that many of them still wish to find another person to rely on.

There are many stable things we can rely on—the earth, the air, the Buddha, the Dharma, the Sangha. It is always best to take refuge in something that is stable. Otherwise, if the object of our refuge changes or falls apart, we too may fall apart. It's most stable to abide in non-abiding. Before Vietnamese Dhyana master Van Hanh passed away, he asked his disciples, "Where do you abide, my students? I abide in neither abiding nor non-abiding." A mind that abides in anything, ultimately, cannot have peace. That is why the Buddha often tells the bodhisattvas not to rely on form to practice generosity. Because they truly wish to benefit other beings, the bodhisattvas practice generosity in this spirit.

> "The Tathagata has said that all notions are not notions and that all living beings are not living beings. Subhuti, the Tathagata is one who speaks of things as they are, speaks what is true, and speaks in accord with reality. He does not speak deceptively or to please people. Subhuti, if we say that the Tathagata has realized a teaching, that teaching is neither graspable nor deceptive.
>
> "Subhuti, a bodhisattva who still depends on notions to practice generosity is like someone walking in the dark. He will not see anything. But when a bodhisattva does not

depend on notions to practice generosity, he is like someone
with good eyesight walking under the bright light of the sun.
He can see all shapes and colors.

"Subhuti, if in the future there is any daughter or son of
good family who has the capacity to accept, read, and put
into practice this sutra, the Tathagata will see that person
with his eyes of understanding. The Tathagata will know that
person, and that person will realize the measureless, limitless
fruit of her or his virtuous act."

The Buddha is saying that the truth he has realized is not what we
generally think it is. It lies in the Middle Way, which is beyond the idea
of graspable and the idea of deceptive. We should understand this in
light of the teaching of the raft given earlier. The raft is to help us cross
over to the other shore. It is a wonderful, even necessary instrument.
But we should use the raft in an intelligent way. We should not cling
to it or carry it on our backs after we are done with it. The teaching
is to help us, not to be possessed by us. It is not meant to deceive us,
but we may be deceived by it because of our own way of clinging to
it. The finger that is pointing to the moon is not the moon. We need
the finger to see the moon. The finger is not deceiving us, but if we
cling to it, we may miss the moon and feel that we have been deceived
by the finger.

As long as we are still caught up in ideas and signs, we are blinded by
them. When we walk in the dark, we cannot see reality as it is. But when
we are free of the concepts of signs—of forms, sounds, smells, tastes,
tactile objects, and objects of mind—we are like those with perfect
vision walking in the midday sun. We can see directly into the world of
"wondrous reality," where everything reveals its true nature.

15. GREAT DETERMINATION

"Subhuti, if on the one hand, a daughter or son of a good
family gives up her or his life in the morning as many times
as there are grains of sand in the Ganges as an act of generosity, and gives as many again in the afternoon and as many
again in the evening, and continues doing so for countless
ages; and if, on the other hand, another person listens to this

sutra with complete confidence and without contention, that person's happiness will be far greater. But the happiness of one who writes this sutra down, receives, recites, and explains it to others cannot be compared.

"In summary, Subhuti, this sutra brings about boundless virtue and happiness that cannot be conceived or measured. If there is someone capable of receiving, practicing, reciting, and sharing this sutra with others, the Tathagata will see and know that person, and he or she will have inconceivable, indescribable, and incomparable virtue. Such a person will be able to shoulder the highest, most fulfilled, awakened career of the Tathagata. Why? Subhuti, if one is content with the small teachings, if he or she is still caught up in the idea of a self, a person, a living being, or a life span, he or she will not be able to listen, receive, recite, and explain this sutra to others. Subhuti, any place this sutra is found is a place where gods, men, and ashuras will come to make offerings. Such a place is a shrine and should be venerated with formal ceremonies, circumambulations, and offerings of flowers and incense."

Please take note of the phrase "writes down" towards the end of the first paragraph. For more than five hundred years, the texts of the Canon were transmitted orally. They were not written on palm leaves until the first century BCE. It was in that period, perhaps twenty or thirty years earlier, that The Diamond That Cuts through Illusion made its appearance.

In this section, the Buddha mentions the "small teachings." These small teachings are authentic teachings of the Buddha, but they are not his most profound ones. The Buddha's teachings can be seen as a house with an outer room and many inner rooms. If we stay in the outer room, we may only benefit from a table, a chair, and a few other small comforts. We may have come to the Buddha with the intention of relieving our most profound suffering, but if we are content to stay in this outer room, we will obtain only minimal relief. When we feel calm enough, we may open the door and go further into the inner rooms of the Buddha's house. We will discover many precious gems and treasures in these rooms. As the heirs of the Buddha, we should make the effort to receive his most precious gifts. They can provide us with the energy and determination to help many other people. These gifts are called the "great Dharma." The great Dharma is the heart of a bodhisattva. "Small teachings" here means the teachings offered only to shravakas and not to bodhisattvas.

16. The Last Epoch

"Furthermore, Subhuti, if a son or daughter of good family, while reciting and practicing this sutra, is disdained or slandered, his or her misdeeds committed in past lives, including those that could bring about an evil destiny, will be eradicated, and he or she will attain the fruit of the most fulfilled, awakened mind. Subhuti, in ancient times before I met Buddha Dipankara, I had made offerings to and had been attendant of all eighty-four thousand multimillions of buddhas. If someone is able to receive, recite, study, and practice this sutra in the last epoch, the happiness brought about by this virtuous act is hundreds of thousands times greater than that which I brought about in ancient times. In fact, such happiness cannot be conceived or compared with anything, even mathematically. Such happiness is immeasurable."

"Disdain" and "slander" are translations of the Sanskrit word *parimuta*. This paragraph gives us the impression that even as the Diamond Sutra was being written down, it was already being condemned by some who probably criticized these teachings as not being the original words of the Buddha. Those who were reciting this sutra were probably also being denigrated, so right in the sutra it says that if anyone maintains confidence in these teachings, their study and practice will give rise to immeasurable virtue and happiness—their misdeeds from the past will be absolved, including those that could bring them to the three evil realms of hell-beings, hungry ghosts, and animals, and they will attain the highest, most fulfilled, awakened mind.

Today, Mahayana Buddhism has become a tradition, and the number of people who condemn these teachings is relatively few. But during that period, after a sutra like this appeared, studying, reciting, practicing, copying, and spreading it could make you a target for attack. So the

Buddha offers an example that in ancient times, before he met Buddha Dipankara, he had already made offerings to and had been attendant of eighty-four thousand multimillions of buddhas, yet the happiness brought about by these virtuous acts was far less than the virtue generated by someone who will be born at the end of the last epoch who studies and practices this sutra. "The end of the last epoch" means the time when the deepest teachings of the Buddha will not have a chance to spread anymore.

> "Subhuti, the happiness resulting from the virtuous act of a son or daughter of good family who receives, recites, studies, and practices this sutra in the last epoch will be so great that if I were to explain it now in detail, some people would become suspicious and disbelieving, and their minds might become disoriented. Subhuti, you should know that the meaning of this sutra is beyond conception and discussion. Likewise, the fruit resulting from receiving and practicing this sutra is beyond conception and discussion."

In the Ekottara Agama, the Buddha lists four things that can neither be conceived of nor explained: (1) the virtue of a Buddha, (2) the state of a person dwelling in concentration, (3) the notions of karma and consequence, and (4) the origin of the universe. Anyone who thinks, "I have already explained this sutra thoroughly and completely," has not really understood this sutra. Studying and practicing The Diamond That Cuts through Illusion will result in the kind of peace, joy, and action that will have the power to change the world. The happiness it produces is beyond all conception and discussion.

Even if we are only washing dishes, the peace and joy experienced from the practice of the sutra while washing the dishes cannot be described—they are beyond conception and discussion. The merit produced by washing dishes will be immeasurable.

17. The Answer is in the Question

> At that time, the Venerable Subhuti said to the Buddha, "World-Honored One, may I ask you again that if daughters

or sons of good families want to give rise to the highest, most fulfilled, awakened mind, what should they rely on and what should they do to master their thinking?"

The Buddha replied, "Subhuti, a good son or daughter who wants to give rise to the highest, most fulfilled, awakened mind should do it in this way: 'We must lead all beings to the shore of awakening, but, after these beings have become liberated, we do not, in truth, think that a single being has been liberated.' Why is this so? Subhuti, if a bodhisattva is still caught up in the idea of a self, a person, a living being or a life span, that person is not an authentic bodhisattva. Why is that?

"Subhuti, in fact, there is no independently existing object of mind called the highest, most fulfilled, awakened mind. What do you think, Subhuti? In ancient times, when the Tathagata was living with Buddha Dipankara, did he attain anything called the highest, most fulfilled, awakened mind?"

"No, World-Honored One. According to what I understand from the teachings of the Buddha, there is no attaining of anything called the highest, most fulfilled, awakened mind."

The Buddha said, "Right you are, Subhuti. In fact, there does not exist the so-called highest, most fulfilled, awakened mind that the Tathagata attains. Because if there had been any such thing, Buddha Dipankara would not have predicted of me, 'In the future, you will come to be a Buddha called Shakyamuni.' This prediction was made because there is, in fact, nothing that can be attained that is called the highest, most fulfilled, awakened mind. Why? Tathagata means the suchness of all things (dharmas). Someone would be mistaken to say that the Tathagata has attained the highest, most fulfilled, awakened mind since there is not any highest, most fulfilled, awakened mind to be attained. Subhuti, the highest, most fulfilled, awakened mind that the Tathagata has attained is neither graspable nor elusive. This is why the Tathagata has said, 'All dharmas are Buddha-dharma.' What are called all dharmas are, in fact, not all dharmas. That is why they are called all dharmas."

Here the Buddha repeats what was said in the beginning of the sutra to help water the seeds that were sown in our consciousness at that time. There are things in this passage that are already clear, but certain things still need to be reviewed.

Tathagata means suchness, the suchness of all objects of mind, of all dharmas. All objects of mind have their outer appearance, which is called "illusory sign." When our minds hold on to this illusory form, they make an "erroneous perception." The concepts of birth and death, high and low, many and one are all erroneous. If we can break through all erroneous perceptions and penetrate directly into the true nature of all objects of mind, we will be in touch with suchness. To be in touch with the suchness of all dharmas is to see the Tathagata, and to see the Tathagata is to be in touch with the suchness of all dharmas. The Tathagata is the suchness of all objects of mind.

"Someone would be mistaken to say that the Tathagata has attained the highest, most fulfilled, awakened mind since there is not any highest, most fulfilled, awakened mind to be attained." When we think that we have something now that we did not have before, we are caught up in the ideas of having and not having, and we still do not see suchness. Through the prism of our erroneous perceptions, we see being and nonbeing, gain and loss, attainment and non-attainment, and we fail to see the suchness of all dharmas.

"Subhuti, the highest, most fulfilled, awakened mind that the Tathagata has attained is neither graspable nor elusive." We may think that birth and death, one and many, and gain and loss are erroneous but that suchness is true. But suchness is free of all concepts like true and false, graspable and deceptive. If we say that other objects of mind are deceptive but that suchness is not deceptive, that too is a mistake. Like all concepts, deceptive and not deceptive are wrong perceptions and are not at all related to suchness. This is why the Tathagata can say, "All dharmas are Buddhadharma."

As the Zen Master King Tran Nhan Tong said, "Eating, drinking, and going to the toilet are all Buddhadharma." Because Buddhadharma is made of non-Buddhadharma elements, Buddhadharma cannot be found outside of non-Buddhadharma. This is explained clearly in the Ratnakuta Sutra. Those who bring Buddhism to the West should understand this well. They should be able to go into the world of Western culture and see many values of the West as elements of Buddhadharma. Drug addiction, alcoholism, and sexual misconduct are ruining the lives of many young people, but we can look deeply and see into their true nature, we can transform them into Buddhadharma. When we look directly into the suffering, we will find answers. One philosopher said that a true question already contains the answer in it. When a teacher gives you a good math problem, the answer is already there.

When we say, "What gave birth to the cosmos?" no answer is possible because we have not asked a true question. In it is the assumption that the cosmos was born of a single cause, and no phenomenon was ever born of a single cause. Everything comes from innumerable causes. In a flower, there are soil, clouds, compost, consciousness, rain, and sun. Because "Who gave birth to the cosmos?" is not a true question, the answer cannot be found in it. If the sufferings of people due to drug addiction, alcoholism, and sexual misconduct can be correctly formed into a question, the answers will be found in it. When there is a true question, Buddhadharma is already there. The art of posing a question is very important.

If those who teach Buddhism in the West keep in mind that all dharmas are Buddhadharma, they will not feel like a drop of oil in a glass of water. If Westerners bring into their society an exotic expression of Buddhism, thinking that this particular form of Buddhism is the only true Buddhism, the oil will never dissolve into the water. Buddhism will only succeed here if it is built from your own experiences and with your own cultural ingredients. If you practice in exactly the same way we practice in Vietnam, Tibet, Thailand, Burma, Sri Lanka, Japan, or Korea, the oil drops will always remain separate from the water. As Western Buddhists, please use the many elements of your own culture to weave the fabric of Buddhadharma.

Although this part of the sutra sounds like the previous sections, when we read it carefully we find many new elements. "All dharmas are Buddhadharma" is a short sentence, but it reveals the deepest teachings of the Buddha.

"Subhuti, a comparison can be made with the idea of a great human body."

Subhuti said, "What the Tathagata calls a great human body is, in fact, not a great human body."

"Subhuti, it is the same concerning bodhisattvas. If a bodhisattva thinks that she has to liberate all living beings, then she is not yet a bodhisattva. Why? Subhuti, there is no independently existing object of mind called bodhisattva. Therefore, the Buddha has said that all dharmas are without a self, a person, a living being, or a life span. Subhuti, if a bodhisattva thinks, 'I have to create a serene and beautiful Buddha field,' that person is not yet a bodhisattva. Why? What the Tathagata calls a serene and beautiful Buddha field is not in fact a serene and beautiful Buddha field. And that is why it is called a serene and beautiful Buddha field. Subhuti, any bodhisattva who thoroughly understands the principle of nonself and non-dharma is called by the Tathagata an authentic bodhisattva."

The Buddha says that all objects of mind are concepts, even the object of mind called bodhisattva. When we use the language of the dialectics of prajñaparamita, we practice according to the principles of nonself and non-dharma. All schools of Buddhism talk about nonself. The Sarvastivada school said it this way, "Even though the self does not exist, dharmas do exist." The existence of these objects of mind (dharmas) gives the impression that the self exists. Mahayana Buddhism opens a different door and proclaims that even what we call objects of mind or dharmas are of a selfless nature. The teaching of no-self is applied not only to humans and so-called living beings but also to other objects such as a table or a house. Self and dharma are just concepts. They are like a game. We should begin meditation practice by looking deeply into things and not letting the mind entrap us in games of words, reasoning, or speculation.

Not only is emptiness the nature of human beings and other so-called living beings, but it is also the nature of those things we call dharmas, things, or inanimate objects. A true bodhisattva is one who sees no demarcations between organic and non-organic, self and nonself, living beings and non-living beings, bodhisattvas and non-bodhisattvas.

5: Mountains and Rivers Are Our Own Bodies

18. REALITY IS A STEADILY FLOWING STREAM

"Subhuti, what do you think? Does the Tathagata have the human eye?"

Human eye is the eye we all have that can see flowers, the blue sky, and the white clouds. Does the Buddha, the Awakened One, have the ordinary human eye?

Subhuti replied, "Yes, World-Honored One, the Tathagata does have the human eye."
The Buddha asked, "Subhuti, what do you think? Does the Tathagata have the divine eye?"

"Divine eye" is the eye of gods that sees very near and very far and also sees in darkness and through obstacles.

Subhuti said, "Yes, World-Honored One, the Tathagata does have the divine eye."
"Subhuti, what do you think? Does the Tathagata have the eye of insight?"

The "eye of insight" is the eye that can see the true nature of nonself in living beings and the impermanent nature of all objects of mind. It is the eye of the shravakas and *pratyeka buddhas.*

Subhuti replied, "Yes, World-Honored One, the Tathagata does have the eye of insight.

"Subhuti, what do you think? Does the Tathagata have
the eye of transcendent wisdom?"

The "eye of transcendent wisdom" is the eye of the bodhisattvas that
can see the true nature of the emptiness of all objects of mind. It can
see the nature of awakened mind and of the great vow. A bodhisattva
with the eye of transcendent wisdom sees that he or she and all beings
share the same nature of emptiness, and therefore his or her liberation
is one with the liberation of all beings.

"Yes, World-Honored One, the Tathagata does have the eye
of transcendent wisdom."
The Buddha asked, "Does the Tathagata have the Bud-
dha eye?"
"Yes, World-Honored One, the Tathagata does have the
Buddha eye."

"The Buddha eye" is the eye that can see clearly the past, the present,
and the future, as well as the minds of all living beings in the past, the
present, and the future.
These five questions and answers state that the Buddha has not only
the Buddha eye, but also the eyes of the bodhisattvas, shravakas, gods,
humans, and all other living beings. The fact that the Buddha has a
human eye gives us a pleasant feeling. It makes us feel closer to the
Buddha. It means that what the Buddha accomplished, we too have
the ability to accomplish.

"Subhuti, what do you think? Does the Buddha see the sand
in the Ganges as sand?"
Subhuti said, "World-Honored One, the Tathagata also
calls it sand."
"Subhuti, if there were as many Ganges Rivers as the number of grains of sand of the Ganges and there was a Buddha
land for each grain of sand in all those Ganges Rivers, would
those Buddha lands be many?"
"Yes, World-Honored One, very many."
The Buddha said, "Subhuti, however many living beings
there are in all these Buddha lands, though they each have a
different mentality, the Tathagata understands them all. Why

is that? Subhuti, what the Tathagata calls different mentalities are not in fact different mentalities. That is why they are called different mentalities."

Here, the Buddha begins to talk about the mind. This teaching is developed more extensively in the Ratnakuta Sutra, which made its appearance between the second and third centuries, particularly in the chapter named "The Manifestations of Consciousness." It also talks about the human eye, the divine eye, the eye of insight, the eye of transcendent wisdom, and the Buddha eye.

This section of the Diamond Sutra briefly explains the Buddha eye as the eye that can see into the minds of all living beings. The Buddha has a very profound insight into the mentality of all of these beings. The Buddha says that if there were as many Ganges Rivers as the number of grains in the sand of the Ganges and if the number of worlds were as many as those grains of sand, he knows the mentalities of all living beings in all of these worlds. This means that the Buddha has a profound understanding of the mind. The mind here includes the mind understood by contemporary psychology as well as the roots and nature of all psychological phenomena, which are not conditioned by the birth and death of psychological phenomena.

Modern psychology only studies psychological phenomena at their surface level. In Buddhism, the study of the mind begins at the roots, so the Buddha sees both the phenomenal aspect of the different mentalities and also their true nature. The Tathagata understands all these different mentalities because what we call different mentalities are not, in fact, only different mentalities.

"Why? Subhuti, the past mind cannot be grasped, neither can the present mind or the future mind."

How can we have a true understanding of the mind if we keep going after different psychological phenomena trying to grasp them? This is why it is difficult for modern psychology to truly grasp the mind. In the practice of Buddhism, by means of direct experience, one is able to be in touch with the true mind. Psychological studies, research, theories, and comparisons of different mental phenomena cannot really grasp the mind, since the past mind cannot be grasped, neither can the present mind or the future mind. As soon as any mind arises, it immediately dissolves.

In this sutra, we learn how to deal with words and concepts. Words are used to name or describe concepts, but as soon as we see things as they are, we understand that both words and concepts are not the things themselves. Words and concepts are rigid and motionless, but reality is a steadily flowing stream. It is impossible to contain a living reality in a rigid framework. We should always bear this in mind when we are trying to describe anything. There is always some distance between our words or concepts and that which is being described.

There is a famous story of a monk in China who was on his way to visit Zen Master Sung Tin in Long Dam. He stopped at the foot of the Zen master's mountain to spend the night in a small inn that was run by an old lady. The monk arrived holding a copy of the Diamond Sutra, and the old lady, who was well versed in the sutra, noticed it.

After a night's rest, the monk said, "Good morning, madam. May I have something to point my mind?" ("Pointing the mind" was the Chinese expression for breakfast.)

The old woman asked back, "What kind of mind do you want to point—the past mind, the present mind, or the future mind?"

The monk was unable to answer. Feeling ashamed of himself, he gave up his journey to meet the master and headed back home. He felt that if he could not even answer the question of an old innkeeper, how could he confront a true master.

If she had asked me the same question, I would have answered something like this: "I do not need past mind, present mind, or future mind. I am hungry and only want something to eat." I could have touched my empty stomach as I spoke. The idea that the past mind, present mind, and future mind cannot be grasped is an excellent idea, but it is still just an idea. We need to eat. This is a living reality. When you are hungry, you need your breakfast. Why should you be impressed by a talkative innkeeper?

19. GREAT HAPPINESS

"What do you think, Subhuti? If someone were to fill the three thousand chiliocosms with precious treasures as an act of generosity, would that person bring great happiness by his virtuous act?"

"Yes, very much, World-Honored One."

"Subhuti, if such happiness were conceived as an entity separate from everything else, the Tathagata would not have said it to be great, but because it is ungraspable, the Tathagata has said that the virtuous act of that person brought about great happiness."

This is to confirm the fact that it is possible to use words and concepts for true communication, as long as you are not caught by words and concepts. The way to avoid being caught by words and concepts is to see the nature of interbeing in everything.

20. THIRTY-TWO MARKS

"Subhuti, what do you think? Can the Tathagata be perceived by his perfectly formed body?"

"No, World-Honored One. What the Tathagata calls a perfectly formed body is not in fact a perfectly formed body. That is why it is called a perfectly formed body."

"What do you think, Subhuti? Can the Tathagata be perceived by his perfectly formed physiognomy?"

"No, World-Honored One. It is impossible to perceive the Tathagata by any perfectly formed physiognomy. Why? Because what the Tathagata calls perfectly formed physiognomy is not in fact perfectly formed physiognomy. That is why it is called perfectly formed physiognomy."

According to legend, the Buddha's perfect physiognomy consists of thirty-two special marks. But the Buddha and Subhuti both say that the Tathagata cannot be perceived by any bodily form. As with all other forms, bodily forms are given a name, but both names and forms are framed by ideas and concepts and therefore cannot contain the living, boundless reality. The same teaching concerning the use of words and concepts is found in the following sections.

21. INSIGHT-LIFE

"Subhuti, do not say that the Tathagata conceives the idea 'I will give a teaching.' Do not think that way. Why? If anyone says that the Tathagata has something to teach, that person slanders the Buddha because he does not understand what I say. Subhuti, giving a Dharma talk in fact means that no talk is given. This is truly a Dharma talk."

Then, Insight-Life Subhuti said to the Buddha, "World-Honored One, in the future, will there be living beings who will feel complete confidence when they hear these words?"

The Buddha said, "Subhuti, those living beings are neither living beings nor non-living beings. Why is that? Subhuti, what the Tathagata calls non-living beings are truly living beings."

When we can see the non-rose elements when looking at a rose, it is safe for us to use the word "rose." When we look at A and see that A is not A, we know that A is truly A. Then A is no longer a dangerous obstacle for us.

"Insight-life" is a title given to noble teachers who have attained transcendent understanding, such as Insight-Life Subhuti, Insight-Life Shariputra, and so on. If we keep in mind that reality cannot be framed by words, concepts, speech, or symbols, we can easily understand the Buddha's teachings in these sections of the sutra.

22. THE SUNFLOWER

Subhuti asked the Buddha, "World-Honored One, is the highest, most fulfilled, awakened mind that the Buddha attained the unattainable?"

The Buddha said, "That is right, Subhuti. Regarding the highest, most fulfilled, awakened mind, I have not attained anything. That is why it is called the highest, most fulfilled, awakened mind."

Here we come to the notion of non-attainment. If we think that the Buddha has achieved an independently existing attainment, this attainment cannot be called the highest, most fulfilled awakened mind. The moment the concept of highest, most fulfilled, awakened mind arises, the essence of highest, most fulfilled, awakened mind vanishes. This is why the Buddha says, "I have not attained anything."

Many years ago I wrote a poem about a sunflower. The sunflower here is prajñaparamita, transcendent understanding.

> Come dear, with your innocent eyes,
> look at the clear, blue ocean of the Dharmakaya,
> and look at the green color,
> the manifestation of suchness.
>
> Even if the world is shattered,
> your smile will never vanish.
> What did we gain yesterday?
> And what will we lose today?
>
> Come dear, look right into existence,
> adorned by illusion.
> Since the sunflower is already there,
> all flowers turn toward it and contemplate.

23. THE MOON IS JUST THE MOON

"Furthermore, Subhuti, that mind is everywhere equally. Because it is neither high nor low, it is called the highest, most fulfilled, awakened mind. The fruit of the highest, most fulfilled, awakened mind is realized through the practice of all wholesome actions in the spirit of nonself, non-person, non-living being, and non-life span. Subhuti, what are called wholesome actions are in fact not wholesome actions. That is why they are called wholesome actions."

Now we come to the nature of equality, *samata* in Sanskrit. Equality means "neither this nor that," neither liberating nor being liberated, neither I nor others, neither many nor few, neither high nor low. All objects of mind are equal and share the same nature of interbeing.

The "highest, most fulfilled, awakened mind" cannot exist independently of what is not the highest, most fulfilled, awakened mind. There is no teapot that exists independently of non-teapot elements. Clouds are oceans; oceans are clouds. Clouds do not exist independently of oceans, and vice versa. Because all objects of mind are neither high nor low, this is called "the highest, most fulfilled, awakened mind." In our thoughts, the moon may be full or new, bright or dim, present or not present, but the moon itself has none of those characteristics. The moon is just the moon. All objects of the mind are equal.

24. THE MOST VIRTUOUS ACT

"Subhuti, if someone were to fill the three thousand chiliocosms with piles of the seven precious treasures as high as Mount Sumeru as an act of generosity, the happiness resulting from this is much less than that of another person who knows how to accept, practice, and explain the Vajracchedika Prajñaparamita Sutra to others. The happiness resulting from the virtue of a person who practices this sutra, even if it is only a gatha of four lines, cannot be described by using examples or mathematics."

This section repeats the idea expressed in section 19. Please refer to the commentaries offered in that section.

25. ORGANIC LOVE

"Subhuti, do not say that the Tathagata has the idea, 'I will bring living beings to the shore of liberation.' Do not think that way, Subhuti. Why? In truth there is not one single being for the Tathagata to bring to the other shore. If the Tathagata were to think there was, he would be caught in the idea of a self, a person, a living being, or a life span."

Reflection is necessary for insight. The Diamond That Cuts through Illusion has many repetitions such as the ones above, and the more we chant or read this sutra, the more deeply we penetrate its profound significance. If we read it only once, we may think we understand all of it, but this can be dangerous. Reading a sutra is like doing massage. Time and energy are necessary for success.

The Tathagata uses words and ideas in the same way as others—a flower is a flower, garbage is garbage, awakening is awakening, illusion is illusion, afflictions are afflictions—but the Tathagata does not get caught in names or ideas. We, on the other hand, are in the habit of looking at these things as fixed entities, and we may get caught up in our views. So the Tathagata chooses language that can help us look deeply and, gradually, become liberated.

Sometimes the Buddha speaks in a way that sounds as if there is a self. For example, he said, "Ananda, would you like to go up to Vulture Peak with me?" When he uses the word "Ananda," the idea of a person is used. In the sentence, "Would you like to go up to Vulture Peak with me?" the idea of a self is used. Although the Tathagata uses words and ideas like others, he is not caught by the words and ideas.

"Subhuti, what the Tathagata calls a self essentially has no self in the way that ordinary persons think there is a self. Subhuti, the Tathagata does not regard anyone as an ordinary person. That is why he can call them ordinary persons."

This is a very deep and beautiful sentence. A person is called an ordinary person but is, at the same time, a buddha. By calling him or her an ordinary person, the Buddha is not being condescending. We say the word Buddha with respect and admiration. We never imagine that there could be an impure element in the body of a buddha or a bodhisattva, because we do not want to be disrespectful. But the teachings of prajñaparamita say that the Buddha's Five Aggregates are also of an organic nature. The Buddha is made of non-Buddha elements. The pure is made of the impure.

In Buddhism, nonduality is the essential characteristic of love. In love, the person who loves and the person being loved are not two. Love has an organic characteristic. In light of interbeing, all problems of the world and of humankind should be solved according to the principles of organic love and nondual understanding. These principles can be applied to solve the problems of the Middle East and the former Soviet Union. The suffering of one side is also the suffering of the other side. The mistakes of one side are also the mistakes of the other side. When one side is angry, the other side suffers, and vice versa. These principles can also be applied to solve environmental problems, such as climate change and the environmental degradation. Rivers, oceans, forests, mountains, earth, and rocks are all the body. To protect the living environment is also to protect ourselves. This is the organic, nondualistic nature of the Buddhist way of looking at conflicts, the environment, and love.

26. A Basket Filled with Words

> "What do you think, Subhuti? Can someone meditate on the Tathagata by means of the thirty-two marks?"
>
> Subhuti said, "Yes, World-Honored One. We should use the thirty-two marks to meditate on the Tathagata."
>
> The Buddha said, "If you say that you can use the thirty-two marks to see the Tathagata, then the Cakravartin is also a Tathagata?"
>
> Subhuti said, "World-Honored One, I understand your teaching. One should not use the thirty-two marks to meditate on the Tathagata."

In Buddhism there are many different methods of meditation. One is the meditation on the image of the Buddha. According to this method, one visualizes the Buddha with thirty-two serene and beautiful marks. Sometimes the name of the Buddha is called so that the image of the Buddha can appear more clearly in the mind of the practitioner, who then feels peaceful and calm. The monks were accustomed to this practice and did it whenever they wanted to see the image of the Tathagata. That is why Subhuti answers quickly, "Yes, World-Honored One. We should use the thirty-two marks to meditate on the Tathagata."

A Cakravartin is a king who keeps the wheel of righteousness turning throughout his reign. He, too, was said to have the thirty-two marks of a great person. In light of the Diamond Sutra, we should not identify the body of thirty-two marks with the Buddha. In fact, we should make just as great an effort to look for the Buddha where the thirty-two marks are absent—in stagnant water and in beggars who have leprosy. When we can see the Buddha in these kinds of places, we have a signless view of the Buddha. This is not to say that the meditation on the Buddha through the thirty-two marks is erroneous. To a new practitioner, this meditation can bring confidence, stability, and peace of mind.

> The precious lotus is blooming on the throne of awakening.
> The Buddha's light reaches in the ten directions.
> His understanding envelops the realm of all dharmas.
> His love penetrates mountains and rivers.
> On seeing the image of the Awakened One, I feel all my
>   afflictions vanish.
> I praise his boundless merit and vow to study and practice in
>   order to attain the fruit of awakening.

While going through difficult moments in life, if we contemplate the Buddha with the thirty-two marks, we feel fresh and relaxed. The Diamond Sutra does not tell us not to do that. It just teaches us to look more deeply and to also meditate on the Buddha outside of the thirty-two marks. The Buddha will suffocate if we grasp him too firmly. One Zen master stopped using the word "Buddha" because people overused the word so. He told his community, "From now on, every time I use the word 'Buddha,' I will go to the river and wash my mouth out three times." His statement is completely in accord with the dialectics of prajñaparamita, but when people heard his words, they thought he was being disrespectful. Only one honored guest in the community understood. He stood up and said, "Venerable sir, I deeply appreciate your words. Every time I hear you say the word 'Buddha,' I will have to go to the river and wash out my ears three times." How wonderful! Both men were free of empty words. Those of us who use Buddhist terms without conveying the teaching of the Buddha should wash out our mouths and ears. We must be cautious. The Vietnamese musician Pham Duy wrote these words in his song "Man Is Not Our Enemy":

> Our enemy wears the colors of an ideology.
> Our enemy wears the label of liberty.
> Our enemy has a huge appearance.
> Our enemy carries a big basket filled with words.

Then the World-Honored One spoke this verse:

"Someone who looks for me in form
or seeks me in sound
is on a mistaken path
and cannot see the Tathagata."

When we first learn to meditate, we may visualize the Buddha with his thirty-two special marks. We may even see the Buddha in our dreams. But once our wounds are healed, we should leave those images and see the Buddha in birth, sickness, old age, and death. Nirvana is made of the same substance as attachment, and awakening of the same substance as ignorance. We should be able to sow the seeds of awakening right here on Earth and not just in empty space. The beautiful lotus grows out of the mud. Without afflictions and suffering, we cannot make a Buddha.

This section of the sutra has taught us not to be bound by the idea of the thirty-two marks. We may come to think that the thirty-two marks are of no value, but, in truth, the practice of mindfulness always gives birth to beautiful marks. The fruits of practice—serenity, peace, and happiness—are truly there, but they cannot be seen in collections of views. They reveal themselves only in the wondrous reality.

27. NOT CUT OFF FROM LIFE

"Subhuti, if you think that the Tathagata realizes the highest, most fulfilled, awakened mind and does not need to have all the marks, you are wrong. Subhuti, do not think in that way. Do not think that when one gives rise to the highest, most fulfilled, awakened mind, one needs to see all objects of mind as nonexistent, cut off from life. Please do not think in that way. One who gives rise to the highest, most fulfilled, awakened mind does not contend that all objects of mind are nonexistent and cut off from life."

"Nonexistent" and "cut off from life" are also attachments. When we look at a table, a flower, or the highest, most fulfilled, awakened mind, if we see that they exist independently of other objects of mind, we are caught in the view of permanence. On the other hand, if we think that everything is nonexistent, we are caught in the view of annihilation. The Middle Way taught by the Buddha is a way free of these two views. Liberation is not to cut ourselves off from life or to try to reach nonbeing.

28. VIRTUE AND HAPPINESS

"Subhuti, if a bodhisattva were to fill the three thousand chiliocosms with the seven precious treasures as many as the number of sand grains in the Ganges as an act of generosity, the happiness brought about by his or her virtue is less than that brought about by someone who has understood and wholeheartedly accepted the truth that all dharmas are of selfless nature and is able to live and bear fully this truth. Why is that, Subhuti? Because a bodhisattva does not need to build up virtue and happiness."

Subhuti asked the Buddha, "What do you mean, World-Honored One, when you say that a bodhisattva does not need to build up virtue and happiness?"

"Subhuti, a bodhisattva gives rise to virtue and happiness but is not caught in the idea of virtue and happiness. That is why the Tathagata has said that a bodhisattva does not need to build up virtue and happiness."

Whatever a bodhisattva thinks, says, and does can give rise to limitless virtue and happiness, but he or she is not caught in this. This is why the Buddha says that the bodhisattvas do not need to accumulate virtue and happiness. When we volunteer to wash the dishes, if we think that our work will bring us some happiness or merit in the future, we are not true bodhisattvas. We only need to live joyfully in each moment while we wash them. After they are washed, we don't need to tell everyone that we have just finished washing their dishes. If we do that, our work will have been a waste of time. Washing the dishes just to wash the dishes, on the other hand, brings us inestimable virtue and happiness.

We all know people who cannot bear great suffering, but we do not realize that to fully enjoy great happiness also requires great strength and endurance. The Sanskrit word for endurance is *kshanti*. It is one of the Six Paramitas. Only those who can bear great truth and great happiness are called mahasattvas. That is why in this section of the sutra we see the phrase: "[someone] who is able to live and bear fully this truth."

29. NEITHER COMING NOR GOING

"Subhuti, if someone says that the World-Honored One comes, goes, sits, and lies down, that person has not understood what I have said. Why? The meaning of Tathagata is 'does not come from anywhere and does not go anywhere.' That is why he is called a Tathagata."

Sometimes the Tathagata is defined as coming from suchness and going to suchness. This is meant to show us the nature of no coming and no going of all things. The ideas of coming and going cannot be applied to suchness. Suchness is suchness. How can suchness come and go?

So far the Buddha has talked about equality, nonduality, attachment to the view of permanence, and attachment to the view of annihilation. Now he tells us that reality is neither coming nor going. This truth does not apply only to the Tathagata. It applies also to all dharmas, all objects of mind.

30. THE INDESCRIBABLE NATURE OF ALL THINGS

"Subhuti, if a daughter or son of a good family were to grind the three thousand chiliocosms to particles of dust, do you think there would be many particles?"

Subhuti replied, "World-Honored One, there would be many indeed. Why? If particles of dust had a real self-existence, the Buddha would not have called them particles of dust. What the Buddha calls particles of dust are not, in essence, particles of dust. That is why they can be called particles of dust. World-Honored One, what the Tathagata calls the three thousand chiliocosms are not chiliocosms. That is why they are called chiliocosms. Why? If chiliocosms are real, they are a compound of particles under the conditions of being assembled into an object. That which the Tathagata calls a compound is not essentially a compound. That is why it is called a compound."

"Subhuti, what is called a compound is just a conventional way of speaking. It has no real basis. Only ordinary people are caught up in conventional terms."

This passage is very important. At the time of the Buddha, it was thought that matter was formed by the coming together of atoms. Most people still think that way. Under proper conditions, atoms come together to form a table or a teapot. When we perceive a table or a teapot, we have an image in our minds of atoms coming together. That image is called a compound. Compound and atom thus become two opposite concepts. Only by seeing that atoms and compounds are not in themselves really atoms and compounds can we be freed from our erroneous concepts. If we think that anything is really a self-existent composite, we are caught by our attachment to that object of mind.

We cannot make any statement about the true nature of reality. Words and ideas can never convey reality. This passage of the sutra describes the indescribable nature of all things. If we base our understanding of reality on our concepts of particles, atoms, or composites we are stuck. We must go beyond all concepts if we want to be in touch with the true nature of things.

31. TORTOISE HAIR AND RABBIT HORNS

"Subhuti, if anyone says that the Buddha has spoken of a self view, a person view, a living being view, or a life span view, has that person understood my meaning?"

"No, World-Honored One. Such a person has not understood the Tathagata. Why? What the Tathagata calls a self view, a person view, a living being view, or a life span view are not in essence a self view, a person view, a living being view, or a life span view. That is why they are called a self view, a person view, a living being view, or a life span view."

"Subhuti, someone who gives rise to the highest, most fulfilled, awakened mind should know that this is true of all dharmas, should see that all dharmas are like this, should have confidence in the understanding of all dharmas without any conceptions about dharmas. Subhuti, what is called a conception of dharmas, the Tathagata has said is not a conception of dharmas. That is why it is called a conception of dharmas."

Those who have not penetrated deeply into the meaning of the Diamond Sutra may think that the ideas of a self, a person, a living being, and a life span are the enemies of understanding, suchness, and the Tathagata. Because of that, they may want to eliminate these four ideas from reality. In this section, the Buddha gives us an antidote to that kind of dualistic thinking. He says that all dharmas—including self, person, living being, life span, nonself, non-person, non-living being, and non-life span—are concepts. We should not let go of one set of concepts just to be caught by another. The idea of nonself is born from the idea of self, just as a rose needs non-rose elements in order to exist.

When we look deeply into the concept of self, we can see the concept of nonself. Tortoise hair and rabbit horns do not exist in reality, but the ideas of tortoise hair and rabbit horns do. They are born from the ideas of hair, horns, tortoises, and rabbits. It is possible to look deeply into the reality of the ideas of tortoise hair and rabbit horns to see the true nature of the world, the true nature of suchness, and the true nature of the Tathagata.

The Buddha teaches us not to discriminate against the concepts of self, person, living being, and life span. These concepts are as valuable as the concepts of emptiness, suchness, Tathagata, and the highest, most fulfilled, awakened mind. All concepts co-arise and are empty of a separate self. If the highest, most fulfilled, awakened mind is empty, then the ideas of self, person, living being, and life span are also empty. So why should we discriminate or be afraid of them? All concepts are dharmas, objects of mind, signs. The Buddha tells us that whenever there is a sign, there is deception. The sign of self, person, suchness, or Tathagata all are subject to deception.

In light of the teachings of interbeing and dependent co-origination, all dharmas depend on one another to be born and develop. Look deeply into one dharma, and you will see all dharmas. This is explained in the Avatamsaka Sutra. Please keep in mind that to discriminate against the concepts of self, person, living being, and life span is to go after the opposite concepts. Once we understand that a concept is just a concept, we can go beyond that concept and be free of the dharma that concept represents. Then we can begin to have a direct experience of the wondrous reality that is beyond concepts.

32. TEACHING THE DHARMA

"Subhuti, if someone were to offer an immeasurable quantity of the seven treasures to fill the worlds as infinite as space as an act of generosity, the happiness resulting from that virtuous act would not equal the happiness resulting from a son or daughter of a good family who gives rise to the awakened mind and reads, recites, accepts, and puts into practice this sutra, and explains it to others, even if only a gatha of four lines. In what spirit is this explanation given? Without being caught up in signs, just according to things as they are, without agitation. Why is this?"

The Buddha is telling us how to teach this sutra to others. He says that we should explain it according to the way things are, without encouraging the listeners to be caught up in signs. He adds that we should stay calm, not agitated, while we teach.

If we observe someone who is sharing the sutra, we can usually tell whether he or she is doing it in the spirit of signlessness. By being observant, we can hear and feel whether the explanations have in them the idea that "I am the one who is teaching the sutra, and you are the listeners." In this way, we can tell to what extent the instructor is still caught in the concepts of self, person, living being, and life span. If he or she is heavily caught by those four concepts, their insights about the Diamond Sutra cannot be authentic. The spirit of the transcendent understanding can only be revealed by someone who is free of signs.

To explain the Diamond Sutra, a teacher must be in touch with suchness, the nature of nonduality, the truth that cannot be described. Being in touch with suchness is like digging a well and reaching the point where the water forces its way up. Once we can drink directly from the well of understanding, we are no longer caught by the signs of a self, a person, a living being, or a life span. When we see that someone is free of those signs, even if it is not yet complete, we know his or her teaching is authentic. Even if such a teacher is criticized or accused of explaining the sutra incorrectly, he or she will remain happy and at peace, with no signs of anger or agitation.

The Buddha offers us this gatha to end the Diamond Sutra:

> All composed things are like a dream,
> a phantom, a drop of dew, a flash of lightning.
> That is how to meditate on them.
> That is how to observe them.

Composed things are all objects of mind that are conditioned to arise, exist for a while, and then disappear, according to the principle of dependent co-arising. Everything in life seems to follow this pattern, and, although things look real, they are actually more like the things a magician conjures up. We can see and hear them clearly, but they are not really what they appear to be. A bubble, *timira* in Sanskrit, is an image that we can use to describe appearances. Or if we rub our eyes vigorously and see many stars, we may think the stars are real, but they are not.

After reading this verse, we may think that the Buddha is saying that all dharmas are impermanent—like clouds, smoke, or a flash of lightning. The Buddha is saying, "All dharmas are impermanent," but he is not saying that they are not here. He only wants us to see the things in themselves. We may think that we have already grasped reality, but, in fact, we are only grasping its fleeting images. If we look deeply into things, we will be able to free ourselves from the illusion.

We can even use scientific research to prove, to some extent, some sentences in this sutra. A table that looks firm and real, for example, may be only space and electrons moving like a swarm of bees at close to the speed of light. Nuclear physicists have said that while going into the subatomic world, they find our common, daily perceptions funny. Regardless of that, a physicist lives his ordinary life as other people do. He drinks tea, and eats bread like the rest of us, even though he knows that his piece of bread is made up mostly of space and a very small number of particles of matter. The same is true of the Buddha. The Buddha knows that all things are like a dream, a phantom, a bubble, a flash of lightning, but he still lives his life normally. He still eats and drinks. The only difference is that the Buddha lives his life in the spirit of signlessness and nonattachment.

After they heard the Lord Buddha deliver this sutra, the Venerable Subhuti, the bhikshus and bhikshunis, laymen and laywomen, and gods and ashuras, filled with joy and confidence, undertook to put these teachings into practice.

Reciting the Diamond Sutra is one of several methods to practice and observe it. At night, you can sit quietly and recite this sutra. Recitation is a way to water the seeds of understanding that lie deep in the soil of our minds. If these seeds are watered infrequently, they will dry up. But if they are watered often, they will sprout and develop. Occasionally, in totally unexpected moments, you will come to a bright and profound realization. Don't be put off by the repetitive conversations between the Buddha and Subhuti. There are sayings that we need to repeat for ourselves throughout our lives. There are songs that need to be sung often. The more we sing them, the more we are penetrated by their meaning. I am sure you will discover new things in the sutra every time you study it.

6: Becoming a Modern Bodhisattva

Often people ask me how the teachings in the Diamond Sutra relate to our everyday lives and the current environmental crisis. I have learned the lesson of patience. Sometimes things and people need a lot of time for transformation. The important thing is to be planting good seeds. Sometimes a seed needs one hundred years to bloom as a flower. The Diamond Sutra is the most ancient text on deep ecology and the basic Buddhist teaching on the art of protecting ourselves and protecting the environment. It is a seed planted by the Buddha that is now beginning to blossom.

When the Venerable Subhuti asks the Buddha: "If good women and good men want to give rise to the highest awakened mind, what should they rely on, and what should they do to master their thinking?" He is asking, "If I want to use my whole being to protect life, what methods and principles should I use?" This is a very practical question that we are all struggling with today. How do we protect our health, the health of our loved ones, and the health of our planet?

The Buddha's answer to Subhuti's question is very direct: "We have to do our best to help every living being cross the ocean of suffering." Then he continues, "But if a bodhisattva holds onto the idea that a self, a person, a living being, a life span exists, that person is not an authentic bodhisattva." The essence of the Diamond Sutra is in this sentence. If we can understand this sentence about nondiscrimination then we can understand how to use the Diamond Sutra in our daily lives. It's like splitting bamboo; only the first part is difficult. Once we've made a crack, then the whole length of bamboo can be split easily. If we can understand this key sentence, understanding everything else in the sutra will come easily.

An authentic bodhisattva is someone who embodies two elements: the great aspiration to bring all beings to the shore of liberation, and the wisdom of nondiscrimination. The Diamond Sutra teaches us that there is no distinction between the one who saves and the living beings who are saved. This is a wonderful lesson for many who care about the environment! We don't take care of it out of any moral righteousness, but because there's no distinction between us and the plants, animals, and other sentient beings on the planet. The wisdom of nondiscrimination, *samatajñana*, is the wisdom that breaks the barrier of individualism. We have to learn to look at the world in this way.

PRACTICING NONSELF

All the media around us encourage us to focus on ourselves. What is self? It is our imagining. The barrier between self and nonself is created by deluded mind. How do we remove that barrier and liberate ourselves from the notion of self? The Buddha advises us to meditate on the nonself nature of things. Whenever we look at a leaf, a pebble, a cloud, a river, a baby, a society, or a human being, we look deeply into it to see its nonself nature, so we can liberate ourselves from the notion of self. The meditation on nonself needs to be practiced every day, in every moment of our daily lives. Whether we're eating, walking, sitting, working in the garden, whenever we look at other people, the clouds, the grass, we see that we are in those elements and those elements are in us; we are not separate.

We often forget that the human being is a creature that evolved from animals, plants, and minerals and that humans appeared only recently in the evolution of life on Earth. When we think we have the right to do anything we want, and that other animals, plants, and minerals are only the means for us to get what we want, then we have a very wrong notion about what it is to be a human being. We haven't understood that humans are made of non-human elements; that is the true nature of the human being. We need to remove the barrier between human beings and the non-human elements: animals, plants, and minerals. We know that human beings cannot survive without animals, plants, and minerals, yet we continue to discriminate and to destroy them, the elements of our environment.

In our daily lives, we can practice mindfulness in order to understand the relationship between the human and non-human. If we can protect the non-human elements, including the non-living beings, then we protect ourselves. We think of living beings as having feelings, perceptions, and so on, and that in this way they're different from non-living beings. But living beings are made of so-called non-living beings—of plants and minerals. We need to live our daily lives in a way that nourishes our understanding of the relationship between living and non-living beings. As human beings are made of non-human elements, so living beings are made of non-living beings.

Part of our misperception about how to help protect living and non-living beings comes out of the way we look at our own lives. We think our life span is seventy, eighty, or one hundred years. We think that we exist from the time we're born to the time we die, and that this is our life span. We think that before we're born we don't exist, and that after we die we're nothing. This is a very wrong notion. We have a great fear of being cut off from life, we have a fear of nothingness.

The notion of life span has to be removed in order for us to see that reality is free from all notions, including the notions of birth and death, being and nonbeing, and so on. The notion of life span is the basis for all the other notions. So if we look deeply into life span, we discover that this is only a manifestation. If we get caught in our perception, in the form, then we miss the whole thing. We're not seeing reality as it is: free from birth and death, coming and going, same and different. Our life span is not limited by time.

When we walk in autumn and see the dead leaves, we might have a feeling of sadness. But if we look deeply at the leaves we see that they're only pretending to die. The true nature of a leaf also goes beyond notions of birth and death, being and nonbeing, coming and going, permanence and annihilation. The leaf becomes the soil to later on become another leaf or a flower. We are like the leaf. We have to look deeply at being young, being old, being born, dying, coming, going, being, nonbeing, so we can see that all of these are just notions.

ACCEPTING OURSELVES

Because we can get stuck in the notion of self, when we look at ourselves, we often see many things we don't like and many behaviors we're not satisfied with. In each of us there's a judge and there's the person being judged. There are many of us who disagree with ourselves, cannot accept ourselves, and feel we are so bad, we have so many shortcomings. We are judgmental toward ourselves. We have so many weaknesses, and we don't want them. We want to transcend them, transform them, but we can't. So we start to despise ourselves.

If we can't accept ourselves, how can we accept others? How can we help change the world around us? We have to learn to accept ourselves first. The Buddha said that we will learn to accept ourselves by looking deeply at ourselves. We are made of elements that are not us. When we look deeply, we see the many elements that brought us into being. There are the many genetic elements we received from our parents, grandparents, and ancestors. There's our society, our traditions, the nation we live in, the people around us, our economic situation, and our educational background. When we see all these things, we see the many non-us elements in us. So we feel less judgmental and won't tend to criticize ourselves so much.

BECOMING A BODHISATTVA

We have to look deeply and ask: Are we growing every day? Are we happier every day? Are we more in harmony with ourselves and with the others around us every day, the unlovable people as well as the lovable people? We need to take care of ourselves and try our best to really help people. Becoming a bodhisattva, we make the vow to give rise to a lot of energy in order to transform our shortcomings and those of the people around us. Sometimes when we see someone's shortcomings, we point them out unskillfully and scold. Sometimes we behave in such a way as to create friction and anger around us. When we look deeply, we can see that the shortcomings of others are no different than the shortcomings in ourselves and we can respond in a skillful and compassionate way.

When our true mind can see there is no difference between self and other, then we're a bodhisattva, a fully awakened person. But usually it's our deluded mind that's in contact with the appearance, creating a wrong perception. Deluded mind is based on ignorance, *avidya*. When we're in this mind, many afflictions manifest. Greed, anger, and ignorance cloud our perception so that when we're in contact with something, we can't see it's real nature, and so we create an image of it. Therefore, when we're angry or upset, we're upset at our image and not the thing in itself.

We have the tendency to blame the other person. But if we look deeply, we can see the many elements in him that are not him. Then we can see why he behaves as he does, and we can accept him more easily and start to find a way to undo the difficulties and make peace. We can see that the other person has acted in such a way partly because of us. We have to see how much responsibility we have for the manifestation of that behavior and how much responsibility the other person has. When we look into ourselves and into the other person, we see the nonself elements in ourselves and in the other person. Even if only one of us is liberated from the notion of self, and is able not to be upset by what the other person does or says, then gradually the other person will change.

MAKING OUR HOME IN THE SANGHA

By ourselves we can get caught in laziness and our own negative habit energy. But in a Sangha, people remind us to practice mindfulness. In a Sangha, people reflect our negative energy back to us and remind us to let it go once, twice, three times, and then we have to try to transform. If we live alone and there is no one to reflect our energy back to us, our negative energy can grow stronger and stronger. Without a mindful community, a holy person can one day become a monster. The only way to help ourselves keep and strengthen our positive energy is to be with a Sangha.

In a healthy Sangha, everyone gives us a lot of happiness and we give everyone a lot of happiness without effort. If we're still jealous and still feel hurt by others, then it's because we've created a frontier, a boundary. If there's no effort it's because we have succeeded in dismantling the frontier between them and ourselves. Having the frontier, we feel hurt; not having the frontier, we're not hurt. Even if we can recite many sutras by heart or buy many books to read, that's not what others need from us. They only need our transformation, they only need that source of joy and peace radiating from us. If we have the habit of not being able to communicate with the people around us, we have to look deeply into ourselves to see why. The practice of the Diamond Sutra is to try to dismantle the shell that separates us from others in order to live happily with ourselves, happily with people around us, and happily with our planet.

BEING BODHISATTVAS IN A DIFFICULT SOCIETY

There are people whom we tend to think of as "bad," but we're also responsible to a certain degree for their actions and behaviors. If they're caught by drink or drugs, if they're caught up in crime, then we're also responsible, because we have organized society in such a way and taken care of our young generation in such a way that they turn to drugs, alcoholism, or crime. They may live in an environment in which people are violent, unkind, self-centered. If we had been born into such a situation, we would be exactly like them. If we look into those whom we think of as bad and see that they are us, they are our responsibility, then we will be able to love them and help change society.

In the Diamond Sutra, the Buddha doesn't call anyone a bad person even though they've behaved badly. So there is love, there is deep understanding, there is no discrimination, no blaming. We know that the person who is doing something wrong is ourselves.

We know that the problems with our environment cannot be fixed by ourselves alone, but they also cannot be fixed without us. One drop of water will not arrive at the ocean. One drop of water will evaporate along the way. But if the drop of water joins the river, then the whole river will go to the ocean. Alone, we cannot go anywhere. But if we have a community on the same path, a Sangha, then we can go anywhere. We can transform an ocean. We can transform the planet.

The Heart Sutra

Prajñaparamita Hrdaya Sutra

Contents

The Heart Sutra

The Bodhisattva Avalokita, while moving in the deep course
   of Perfect Understanding,
shed light on the Five Skandhas and found them equally empty.
After this penetration, he overcame ill-being.

"Listen, shariputra,
   form is emptiness, and emptiness is form.
Form is not other than emptiness, emptiness is not other than form.
The same is true with feelings, perceptions, mental formations,
   and consciousness.

"Listen, shariputra, all dharmas are marked with emptiness.
They are neither produced nor destroyed,
neither defiled nor immaculate,
neither increasing nor decreasing.
Therefore, in emptiness there is neither form, nor feelings,
   nor perceptions,
nor mental formations, nor consciousness.
No eye, or ear, or nose, or tongue, or body, or mind.
No form, no sound, no smell, no taste, no touch, no object of mind.
No realms of elements (from eyes to mind-consciousness),
no interdependent origins and no extinction of them
(from ignorance to death and decay).
No ill-being, no cause of ill-being, no end of ill-being, and no path.
No understanding and no attainment.

"Because there is no attainment,
   the Bodhisattvas, grounded in Perfect Understanding,

find no obstacles for their minds.
Having no obstacles, they overcome fear,
liberating themselves forever from illusion, realizing perfect Nirvana.
All Buddhas in the past, present, and future,
thanks to this Perfect Understanding,
arrive at full, right, and universal Enlightenment.

"Therefore, one should know
that Perfect Understanding is the highest mantra, the unequalled
     mantra,
the destroyer of ill-being, the incorruptible truth.
A mantra of Prajñaparamita should therefore be proclaimed:
Gate gate paragate parasamgate bodhi svaha."[67]

COMMENTARY

I: Interbeing

If you are a poet, you will see clearly that there is a cloud floating in this sheet of paper. Without a cloud, there will be no rain; without rain, the trees cannot grow; and without trees, we cannot make paper. The cloud is essential for the paper to exist. If the cloud is not here, the sheet of paper cannot be here either. We can say that the cloud and the paper inter-are. "Interbeing" is a word that is not in the dictionary yet, but if we combine the prefix "inter-" with the verb "to be," we have a new verb, inter-be.

If we look into this sheet of paper even more deeply, we can see the sunshine in it. If the sunshine is not there, the forest cannot grow. In fact, nothing can grow. Even we cannot grow without sunshine. and so, we know that the sunshine is also in this sheet of paper. The paper and the sunshine inter-are. And if we continue to look, we can see the logger who cut the tree and brought it to the mill to be transformed into paper. And we see the wheat. We know that the logger cannot exist without his daily bread, and therefore the wheat that became his bread is also in this sheet of paper. And the logger's father and mother are in it too. When we look in this way, we see that without all of these things, this sheet of paper cannot exist.

Looking even more deeply, we can see we are in it too. This is not difficult to see, because when we look at a sheet of paper, the sheet of paper is part of our perception. Your mind is in here and mine is also, so we can say that everything is in here in this sheet of paper. You cannot point out one thing that is not here—time, space, the earth, the rain, the minerals in the soil, the sunshine, the cloud, the river, the heat. Everything coexists with this sheet of paper. That is why I think the word inter-be should be in the dictionary. To be is to inter-be. You cannot just be by yourself alone. You have to inter-be with every other thing. This sheet of paper is, because everything else is.

Suppose we try to return one of the elements to its source. Suppose we return the sunshine to the sun. Do you think that this sheet of paper would be possible? No, without sunshine nothing can be. And if we return the logger to his mother, then we have no sheet of paper either. The fact is that this sheet of paper is made up only of "non-paper elements." And if we return these non-paper elements to their sources, then there can be no paper at all. Without non-paper elements, like mind, logger, sunshine, and so on, there will be no paper. As thin as this sheet of paper is, it contains everything in the universe in it.

But the Heart sutra seems to say the opposite. Avalokiteshvara tells us that things are empty. Let us look more closely.

2: Empty of What?

The Bodhisattva Avalokita,
while moving in the deep course of Perfect Understanding,
shed light on the Five Skandhas and found them equally empty.

Bodhi means being awake, and *sattva* means a living being, so bodhisattva means an awakened being. All of us are sometimes bodhisattvas, and sometimes not. Avalokita is the shorter name of the Bodhisattva Avalokiteshvara. Avalokita is neither male nor female and sometimes appears as a man and sometimes as a woman. In Chinese, Vietnamese, Korean, and Japanese, this bodhisattva's name is sometimes translated as Guanyin, Quan Am, Gwaneum, and Kannon, which means "the one who listens and hears the cries of the world in order to come and help." Avalokiteshvara also embodies the spirit of non-fear, as he himself has transcended fear. The Prajñaparamita Heart Sutra is his wonderful gift to us.

Perfect Understanding is *prajñaparamita* in Sanskrit. The word "wisdom" is usually used to translate *prajña*, but I think that wisdom is somehow not able to convey the meaning. Understanding is like water flowing in a stream. Wisdom and knowledge are solid and can block our understanding. In Buddhism, knowledge is regarded as an obstacle for understanding. If we take something to be the truth, we may cling to it so much that even if the truth comes and knocks at our door, we won't want to let it in. We have to be able to transcend our previous knowledge in the same way we climb up a ladder. If we are on the fifth rung and think that we are very high, there is no hope for us to step up to the sixth. We must learn to transcend our own views. Understanding, like water, can flow, can penetrate. Views, knowledge, and even wisdom are solid, and can block the way of understanding.

According to Avalokiteshvara, this sheet of paper is empty; but according to our analysis, it is full of everything. There seems to be a contradiction between our observation and his. Avalokita found the Five Skandhas empty. But, empty of what? The key word is *empty*. To be empty is to be empty of something.

If I am holding a cup of water and I ask you, "Is this cup empty?" you will say, "No, it is full of water." But if I pour out the water and ask you again, you may say, "Yes, it is empty." But empty of what? Empty means empty of something. The cup cannot be empty of nothing. "Empty" doesn't mean anything unless you know "empty of what?" My cup is empty of water, but it is not empty of air. To be empty is to be *empty of something*. This is quite a discovery. When Avalokita says that the Five Skandhas are equally empty, to help him be precise we must ask, "Mr. Avalokita, empty of what?"

The Five Skandhas, which may be translated into English as five heaps, or Five Aggregates, are the five elements that comprise a human being. These five elements flow like a river in every one of us. In fact, these are really five rivers flowing together in us: the river of form, which means our bodies; the river of feelings; the river of perceptions; the river of mental formations; and the river of consciousness. They are always flowing in us. So according to Avalokita, when he looked deeply into the nature of these five rivers, he suddenly saw that all five are empty.

And if we ask, "Empty of what?" he has to answer. And this is what he said: "They are empty of a separate self." That means none of these five rivers can exist by itself alone. Each of the five rivers has to be made by the other four. It has to coexist; it has to inter-be with all the others.

In our bodies we have lungs, heart, kidneys, stomach, and blood. None of these can exist independently. They can only coexist with the others. Your lungs and your blood are two things, but neither can exist separately. The lungs take in air and enrich the blood, and, in turn, the blood nourishes the lungs. Without the blood, the lungs cannot be alive, and without the lungs, the blood cannot be cleansed. Lungs and blood inter-are. The same is true with kidneys and blood, kidneys and stomach, lungs and heart, blood and heart, and so on.

When Avalokita says that our sheet of paper is empty, he means it is empty of a separate, independent existence. It cannot just be by itself. It has to inter-be with the sunshine, the cloud, the forest, the logger, the mind, and everything else. It is empty of a separate self. But, empty of a separate self means full of everything. So it seems that our observation and that of Avalokita do not contradict each other after all.

Avalokita looked deeply into the Five Skandhas of form, feelings, perceptions, mental formations, and consciousness, and he discovered that none of them can be by itself alone. Each can only inter-be with all the others. So he tells us that form is empty. Form is empty of a separate self, but it is full of everything in the cosmos. The same is true with feelings, perceptions, mental formations, and consciousness.

3: The Way of Understanding

After this penetration, he overcame ill-being.

Penetration means to enter something, not just to stand outside of it. When we want to understand something, we cannot just stand outside and observe it. We have to enter deeply into it and be one with it in order to really understand. If we want to understand a person, we have to feel their feelings, suffer their sufferings, and enjoy their joy. The sutra uses the word "penetration" to mean "full comprehension." The word "comprehend" is made up of the Latin roots *com*, which means "together in mind," and *prehendere*, which means "to grasp it or pick it up." So to comprehend something means to pick it up and be one with it. There is no other way to understand something. If we only look at the sheet of paper as an observer, standing outside, we cannot understand it completely. We have to penetrate it. We have to be a cloud, be the sunshine, and be the logger. If we can enter it and be everything that is in it, our understanding of the sheet of paper will be perfect. There is an Indian story about a grain of salt that wanted to know just how salty the ocean was, so it jumped in and became one with the water of the ocean. In this way, the grain of salt gained Perfect Understanding.

If we are concerned with peace and want to understand another country, we can't just stand outside and observe. We have to be one with a citizen of that country in order to understand her feelings, perceptions, and mental formations. Any meaningful work for peace must follow the principle of nonduality, the principle of penetration. This is our peace practice: to penetrate, to be one with, in order to really understand.

In the Sutra on the Four Establishments of Mindfulness, the Buddha recommended that we observe in a penetrating way. He said we should contemplate the body in the body, the feelings in the feelings, the mental formations in the mental formations. Why did he use this kind of repetition? Because you have to enter in order to be one with what you want to observe and understand. Nuclear scientists are beginning to say this also. When you enter the world of elementary particles you have to become a participant in order to understand something. You can no longer stand outside and remain just an observer. Today many scientists prefer the word "participant" to the word "observer."

In our effort to understand each other we should do the same. A husband and wife who wish to understand each other have to be in the skin of their partner in order to feel, otherwise they cannot really understand. In the light of Buddhist meditation, love is impossible without understanding. You cannot love someone if you do not understand him or her. If you don't understand and you love, that is not love; it is something else.

Avalokita's meditation was a deep penetration into the Five Skandhas. Seeing deeply into the rivers of form, feelings, perceptions, mental formations, and consciousness, he discovered the empty nature of all of them, and suddenly, he overcame all pain. All of us who would like to arrive at that kind of emancipation will have to look deeply in order to penetrate the true nature of emptiness.

4: Long Live Emptiness

Listen, Shariputra,
form is emptiness, and emptiness is form.
Form is not other than emptiness, emptiness is not other
  than form.
The same is true with feelings, perceptions, mental formations,
  and consciousness.

Form is the wave and emptiness is the water. To understand this, we have to think differently than many of us who were raised in the West were trained to think. In the West, when we draw a circle, we consider it to be zero, nothingness. But in India and many other Asian countries, a circle means totality, wholeness. The meaning is the opposite. So "form is emptiness, and emptiness is form" is like wave is water, water is wave. "Form is not other than emptiness, emptiness is not other than form. The same is true with feelings, perceptions, mental formations, and consciousness," because these contain each other. Because one exists, everything exists.

In the Vietnamese literary canon, there are two lines of poetry by a twelfth-century Zen master of the Ly dynasty that say:

If the cosmos exists, then the smallest speck of dust exists.
If the smallest speck of dust doesn't exist, then the whole
  cosmos doesn't exist.

The poet means that the notions of existence and nonexistence are just created by our minds. He also said that "the entire cosmos can be put on the tip of a hair," and "the sun and the moon can be seen in a mustard seed." These images show us that one contains everything, and everything is just one.

Because form is emptiness, form is possible. In form we find every-thing else—feelings, perceptions, mental formations, and conscious-ness. "Emptiness" means empty of a separate self. It is full of everything, full of life. The word "emptiness" should not scare us. It is a wonderful word. To be empty does not mean to be nonexistent. If the sheet of paper is not empty, how could the sunshine, the logger, and the forest come into it? How could it be a sheet of paper? The cup, in order to be empty, has to be there. Form, feelings, perceptions, mental forma-tions, and consciousness, in order to be empty of a separate self, have to be there.

Emptiness is the ground of everything. "Thanks to emptiness, every-thing is possible. "That is a declaration made by Nagarjuna, a Buddhist philosopher of the second century. Emptiness is quite an optimistic concept. If I am not empty, I cannot be here. And if you are not empty, you cannot be there. Because you are there, I can be here. This is the true meaning of emptiness. Form does not have a separate existence. Avalokita wants us to understand this point.

If we are not empty, we become a block of matter. We cannot breathe, we cannot think. To be empty means to be alive, to breathe in and to breathe out. We cannot be alive if we are not empty. Empti-ness is impermanence. It is change. We should not complain about impermanence, because without impermanence nothing is possible. A Buddhist who came to see me from Great Britain complained that life was empty and impermanent. (He had been a Buddhist for five years and had thought about emptiness and impermanence a great deal.) He told me that one day his fourteen-year-old daughter told him, "Daddy, please don't complain about impermanence. Without impermanence, how can I grow up?" Of course she was right.

When you have a kernel of corn and you entrust it to the soil, you hope that it will become a tall corn plant. If there is no impermanence, the kernel of corn will remain a kernel of corn forever and you will never have an ear of corn to eat. Impermanence is crucial to the life of everything. Instead of complaining about impermanence, we might say, "Long live impermanence!" Thanks to impermanence, everything is possible. That is a very optimistic note. And it is the same with empti-ness. Emptiness is important because without emptiness, nothing is possible. So we should also say, "Long live emptiness!" Emptiness is the basis of everything. Thanks to emptiness, life itself is possible. All the Five Skandhas follow this same principle.

5: Happy Continuation

Listen, Shariputra, all dharmas are marked with emptiness.
They are neither produced nor destroyed.

Dharmas in this line means "things." A human being is a dharma. A tree is a dharma. A cloud is a dharma. The sunshine is a dharma. Everything that can be conceived of is a dharma. So when we say, "All dharmas are marked with emptiness," we are saying, "Everything has emptiness as its own nature." And that is why everything can be. There is a lot of joy in this statement. It means nothing can be born, nothing can die. Avalokita has said something extremely important.

Every day in our lives, we see birth and we see death. When a person is born, a birth certificate is printed for them. After they die, a death certificate is made. These certificates confirm the existence of birth and death. But Avalokita said, "No, there is no birth and death." We have to look more deeply to see whether his statement is true. What is the date on which you were born, your birth date? Before that date, did you already exist? Were you already there before you were born? Let me help you. To be born means from nothing you become something. My question is, before you were born, were you already there?

Suppose a hen is about to lay an egg. Before she gives birth, do you think the egg is already there? Yes, of course. It is inside. You also were inside before you were outside. That means that before you were born, you already existed—inside your mother. The fact is that if something is already there, it does not need to be born. To be born means from nothing you become something. If you are already something, what is the use of being born?

So, your so-called birthday is really your Continuation day. The next time you celebrate, you can say, "Happy Continuation day." I think that we may have a better concept of when we were born. If we go back nine months to the time of our conception, we have a better date to put on our birth certificates. In China, and also in Vietnam, when you are born, you are already considered one year old. So we say we begin to be at the time of our conception in our mother's womb, and we write down that date on our birth certificate.

But the question remains: Even before that date, did you exist or not? If you say "yes," I think you are correct. Before your conception, you were there already, maybe half in your father, half in your mother. Because from nothing, we can never become something. Can you name one thing that was once a nothing? A cloud? Do you think that a cloud can be born out of nothing? Before becoming a cloud, it was water, maybe flowing as a river. It was not nothing. Do you agree?

We cannot conceive of the birth of anything. There is only continuation. Please look back even further and you will see that you not only exist in your father and mother, but you also exist in your grandparents and your great-grandparents. As I look more deeply, I can see that in a former life I was a cloud. This is not poetry; it is science. Why do I say that in a former life I was a cloud? Because I am still a cloud. Without the cloud, I cannot be here. I am the cloud, the river, and the air at this very moment, so I know that in the past I have been a cloud, a river, and the air. And I was a rock. I was the minerals in the water. This is not a question of belief in reincarnation. This is the history of life on Earth. We have been gas, sunshine, water, fungi, and plants. We have been single-celled beings. The Buddha said that in one of his former lives, he was a tree. He was a fish; he was a deer. These are not superstitious things. Every one of us has been a cloud, a deer, a bird, a fish, and we continue to be these things, not just in former lives.

This is not just the case with birth. Nothing can be born, and also nothing can die. That is what Avalokita said. Do you think that a cloud can die? To die means that from something you become nothing. Do you think that we can make something a nothing? Let us go back to our sheet of paper. We may have the illusion that to destroy it, all we have to do is light a match and burn it up. But if we burn a sheet of paper, some of it will become smoke, and the smoke will rise and continue to be. The heat that is caused by the burning paper will enter into the cosmos and penetrate other things. The heat is the next life of the paper. The ash that is formed will become part of the soil, and the sheet of paper, in his or her next life, might be a cloud and a rose at the same time. We have to be very careful and attentive in order to realize that this sheet of paper has never been born and it will never die. It can take on other forms of being, but we are not capable of transforming a sheet of paper into nothingness.

Everything is like that, even you and I. We are not subject to birth and death. A Zen master might give a student a subject of meditation like, "What was your face before your parents were born?" This is an invitation to go on a journey in order to recognize yourself. If you do well, you can see your former lives as well as your future lives. Please remember that we are not talking about philosophy; we are talking about reality. Look at your hand and ask yourself, "since when has my hand been around?" If I look deeply into my hand I can see it has been around for a long time, hundreds of thousands of years. I see many generations of ancestors in there, not just in the past, but in the present moment, still alive. I am only the continuation. I have never died once. If I had died even once, how could my hand still be here?

The French scientist Antoine Lavoisier (1743–1794) said, "Nothing is created, and nothing is destroyed." This is exactly the same as in the Heart Sutra. Even the best contemporary scientists cannot reduce something as small as a speck of dust or an electron to nothingness. One form of energy can only become another form of energy. Something can never become nothing, and this includes a speck of dust.

Usually we say that we humans come from dust and are going back to dust, and this does not sound very joyful. We don't want to return to dust. There is a discrimination here that humans are very valuable, and that dust has no value at all. But scientists do not even know what a speck of dust is! It is still a mystery. Imagine one atom of that speck of dust, with electrons speeding around its nucleus. It is very exciting. To return to a speck of dust will be quite an exciting adventure!

Sometimes we have the impression that we understand what a speck of dust is. We even pretend that we understand a human being—a human being who we say is going to return to dust. Because we have lived with a person for twenty or thirty years, we have the impression that we know everything about him. So, while driving in the car with that person sitting right next to us, we think about other things. We aren't interested in him anymore. What arrogance! The person sitting there beside us is really a mystery! We only have the impression that we know him, but we don't know anything yet. If we look with the eyes of Avalokita, we will see that even one hair of that person is the entire cosmos. One hair on his head can be a door opening to the ultimate reality. One speck of dust can be the Kingdom of God, the Pure Land. When you see that you, the speck of dust, and all things inter-are, you will understand that this is so. We must be humble. There is a Chinese proverb that says, "To say you don't know is the beginning of knowing."

One autumn day, I was in a park, absorbed in the contemplation of a very small but beautiful leaf in the shape of a heart. Its color was almost red, and it was barely hanging on the branch, nearly ready to fall down. I spent a long time with it, and I asked the leaf a lot of questions. I found out the leaf had been a mother to the tree. Usually we think that the tree is the mother and the leaves are just children, but as I looked at the leaf I saw that the leaf is also a mother to the tree. The sap that the roots take up is only water and minerals, not good enough to nourish the tree, so the tree distributes that sap to the leaves. The leaves take the responsibility of transforming that rough sap into refined sap and, with the help of the sun and gas, sending it back in order to nourish the tree. Therefore, the leaves are also the mother to the tree. And since the leaf is linked to the tree by a stem, the communication between them is easy to see.

We do not have a stem linking us to our mother anymore, but when we were in her womb we had a very long stem, an umbilical cord. The oxygen and the nourishment we needed came to us through that stem. Unfortunately, on the day we call our birthday, it was cut and we received the illusion that we are independent. That is a mistake. We continue to rely on our mother for a very long time, and we have several other mothers as well. The Earth is our mother. We have a great many stems linking us to our mother Earth. There is a stem linking us with the cloud. If there is no cloud, there is no water for us to drink. We are made of at least seventy percent water; the stem between the cloud and us is really there. This is also the case with the river, the forest, the logger, and the farmer. There are hundreds of thousands of stems linking us to everything in the cosmos, and therefore we can be. Do you see the link between you and me? If you are not there, I am not here; that is certain. If you do not see it yet, look more deeply and I am sure you will see. As I said, this is not philosophy. You really have to see.

I asked the leaf whether it was scared because it was autumn and the other leaves were falling. The leaf told me, "No. During the whole spring and summer I was very alive. I worked hard and helped nourish the tree, and much of me is in the tree. Please do not say that I am just this form, because this leaf form is only a tiny part of me. I am the whole tree. I know that I am already inside the tree, and when I go back to the soil, I will continue to nourish the tree. That's why I do not worry. As I leave this branch and float to the ground, I will wave to the tree and tell her, 'I will see you again very soon.'"

Suddenly I saw a kind of wisdom very much like the wisdom contained in the Heart Sutra. You have to *see* life. You shouldn't say, life *of* the leaf, but life *in* the leaf, and life *in* the tree. My life is just Life, and you can see it in me and in the tree. That day there was a wind blowing and, after a while, I saw the leaf leave the branch and float down to the soil, dancing joyfully, because as it floated it saw itself already there in the tree. It was so happy. I bowed my head, and I knew that we have a lot to learn from the leaf because it was not afraid—it knew that nothing can be born and nothing can die.

The cloud in the sky will also not be scared. When the time comes, the cloud will become rain. It is fun becoming rain, falling down, chanting, and becoming part of the Mississippi River, or the Amazon River, or the Mekong River, or falling onto vegetables and later becoming part of a human being. It is a very exciting adventure. The cloud knows that if it falls to the earth it might become part of the ocean. So the cloud isn't afraid. Only humans are afraid.

A wave on the ocean has a beginning and an end, a birth and a death. But Avalokiteshvara tells us that the wave is empty. The wave is full of water, but it is empty of a separate self. A wave is a form that has been made possible, thanks to the existence of wind and water. If a wave only sees its form, with its beginning and end, it will be afraid of birth and death. But if the wave sees that it is water and identifies itself with the water, then it will be emancipated from birth and death. Each wave is born and is going to die, but the water is free from birth and death.

When I was a child I used to play with a kaleidoscope. I took a tube and a few pieces of ground glass, turned it a little bit, and saw many wonderful sights. Every time I made a small movement with my fingers, one sight would disappear and another would appear. I did not cry at all when the first spectacle disappeared, because I knew that nothing was lost. Another beautiful sight always followed. If you are the wave and you become one with the water, looking at the world with the eyes of water, then you are not afraid of going up, going down, going up, going down. But please do not be satisfied with speculation, or with taking my word for it. You have to enter it, taste it, and be one with it yourself. And that can be done through meditation, not only in the meditation hall, but throughout your daily life.

While you cook a meal, while you clean the house, while you go for a walk, you can look at things and try to see them in their nature of emptiness. Emptiness is an optimistic word; it is not at all pessimistic. When Avalokita, in his deep meditation on Perfect Understanding, was able to see the nature of emptiness, he suddenly overcame all fear and pain. I have seen people die very peacefully, with a smile, because they see that birth and death are only waves on the surface of the ocean, just the spectacle in the kaleidoscope.

So you see there are many lessons we can learn from the cloud, the water, the wave, the leaf, and the kaleidoscope—and from everything else in the cosmos, too. If you look at anything carefully and deeply enough, you discover the mystery of interbeing, and once you have seen it you will no longer be subject to fear—fear of birth, or fear of death. Birth and death are only ideas we have in our minds, and these ideas cannot be applied to reality. It is just like the idea of above and below. We are very sure that when we point up, it is above, and when we point in the opposite direction, it is below. Heaven is above, and Hell is below. But the people who are sitting right now on the other side of the planet must disagree, because the idea of above and below does not apply to the cosmos, nor does the idea of birth and death.

So please continue to look back and you will see that you have always been here. Let us look together and penetrate into the life of a leaf, so we may be one with the leaf. Let us penetrate and be one with the cloud or with the wave, to realize our own nature as water and be free from our fear. If we look very deeply, we will transcend birth and death.

Tomorrow, I will continue to be. But you will have to be very attentive to see me. I will be a flower, or a leaf. I will be in these forms and I will say hello to you. If you are attentive enough, you will recognize me, and you may greet me. I will be very happy.

6: Roses and Garbage

Neither defiled nor immaculate . . .

Defiled or immaculate; dirty or pure; these are concepts we form in our minds. A beautiful rose we have just cut and placed in a vase is immaculate. It smells so good, so pure, so fresh. It supports the idea of immaculateness. The opposite is a garbage can. It smells horrible, and it is filled with rotten things. But that is only when you look on the surface. If you look more deeply you will see that in just five or six days, the rose will become part of the garbage. You do not need to wait five days to see it. If you just look at the rose, and you look deeply, you can see it now. And if you look into the garbage can, you see that in a few months its contents can be transformed into lovely vegetables, and even a rose. If you are a good organic gardener and you have the eyes of a bodhisattva, looking at a rose you can see the garbage, and looking at the garbage you can see a rose. Roses and garbage inter-are. Without a rose, we cannot have garbage; and without garbage, we cannot have a rose. They need each other very much. The rose and garbage are equal. The garbage is just as precious as the rose. If we look deeply at the concepts of defiled and immaculate, we return to the notion of interbeing.

In the Majjhima Nikaya, there is a very short passage on how the world has come to be. It is very simple, very easy to understand, and yet very deep: "This is, because that is. This is not, because that is not. This is like this, because that is like that." This is the Buddhist teaching of Genesis.

In the city of Manila there are many young prostitutes, some of them only fourteen or fifteen years old. They are very unhappy young people. They did not want to be prostitutes. Their families are poor and these young girls went to the city to look for some kind of job, like a street vendor, to make money to send back to their families. Of course this is not true only in Manila, but in Ho Chi Minh City in Vietnam, in Lagos in Nigeria, in New York City, and in Paris also. It is true that in the city you can make money more easily than in the countryside, so we can imagine how a young girl may have been tempted to go there to help her family. But after only a few weeks there, she was persuaded by a clever person to work for her and to earn perhaps one hundred times more money. Because she was so young and did not know much about life, she accepted and became a prostitute. Since that time, she has carried the feeling of being impure, defiled, and this causes her great suffering. When she looks at other young girls, dressed beautifully, belonging to good families, a wretched feeling wells up in her, and this feeling of defilement has become her hell.

But if she had an opportunity to meet with Avalokita, he would tell her to look deeply at herself and at the whole situation, and see that she is like this because other people are like that. "This is like this, because that is like that." So how can a so-called good girl, belonging to a good family, be proud? Because their way of life is like this, the other girl has to be like that. No one among us has clean hands. No one of us can claim it is not our responsibility. The girl in Manila is that way because of the way we are. Looking into the life of that young prostitute, we see the people who are not prostitutes. And looking at the people who are not prostitutes, and at the way we live our lives, we see the prostitute. This helps to create that, and that helps to create this.

Let us look at wealth and poverty. The affluent society and the society that is deprived of everything inter-are. The wealth of one society is made of the poverty of the other. "This is like this, because that is like that." Wealth is made of non-wealth elements, and poverty is made of non-poverty elements. It is exactly the same as with the sheet of paper. So we must be careful. We should not imprison ourselves in concepts. The truth is that everything is everything else. We can only inter-be, we cannot just be. And we are responsible for everything that happens around us. Avalokiteshvara would tell the young prostitute, "My child, look at yourself and you will see everything. Because other people are like that, you are like this. You are not the only person who is responsible, so please do not suffer." Only by seeing with the eyes of interbeing can that young girl be freed from her suffering. What else can you offer her to help her be free?

We are imprisoned by our ideas of good and evil. We want to be only good, and we want to remove all evil. But that is because we forget that good is made of non-good elements. Suppose I am holding a lovely branch. When we look at it with a nondiscriminating mind, we see this wonderful branch. But as soon as we distinguish that one end is the left and the other end is the right, we get into trouble. We may say we want only the left, and we do not want the right (as you hear very often), and there is trouble right away. If the rightist is not there, how can you be a leftist? Let us say that I do not want the right end of this branch, that I only want the left. So, I break off half of this reality and throw it away. But as soon as I throw the unwanted half away, the end that remains becomes the new right. Because as soon as the left is there, the right must be there also. If I become frustrated and do it again, breaking what remains of my branch in half, I will still have a right and a left.

The same may be applied to good and evil. You cannot be good alone. You cannot hope to remove evil, because thanks to evil, good exists, and vice versa. When you stage a play about a heroic figure, you have to provide an antagonist in order for the hero to be a hero. So, Buddha needs Mara to take the evil role so Buddha can be a Buddha. Buddha is as empty as the sheet of paper; Buddha is made of non-Buddha elements. If non-Buddhas like us are not here, how can a Buddha be? If the rightist is not there, how can there be a leftist?

In my tradition, every time I join my palms together to make a deep bow to the Buddha, I chant this short verse:

> The one who bows and the one who is bowed to
> are both, by nature, empty.
> Therefore, the communication between us
> is inexpressibly perfect.

It is not arrogant to say so. If I am not empty, how can I bow down to the Buddha? And if the Buddha is not empty, how can he receive my bow? The Buddha and I inter-are. Buddha is made of non-Buddha elements, like me. And I am made of non-me elements, like the Buddha. So the subject and object of reverence are both empty. Without an object, how can a subject exist?

In the West you have been struggling for many years with the problem of evil. How is it possible that evil should be there? It seems to be difficult for the Western mind to understand. But in the light of nonduality, there is no problem: as soon as the idea of good is there, the idea of evil is there. Buddha needs Mara in order to reveal himself, and vice versa. When you perceive reality in this way, you will not discriminate against the garbage in favor of the rose. You will cherish both. You need both right and left in order to have a branch. Do not take sides. If you take sides, you are trying to eliminate half of reality, which is impossible. For many years, the United States has been trying to describe various other countries as evil, from North Vietnam to the former Soviet Union, to Iran, Iraq, and North Korea. Some Americans even have the illusion that they can survive alone, without these other countries. Other countries may believe that they, too, can exist without us. The American imperialists, they might say, are on the bad side and must be eliminated for happiness to be possible. But that is the dualistic way of looking at things. It is the same as believing that the right side can exist without the left side.

If we look at the U.S. very deeply, we see Iran. And if we look deeply at Iran, we see the U.S. If we look deeply at the rose, we see the garbage; if we look deeply at the garbage, we see the rose. In international politics, each side pretends to be the rose and calls the other side the garbage. Recently, a young person asked me: "Why do we give different names to different things, since they're really together, they're really one?" That's a very good question. I replied: "That's the root of problems—names, the fact that we give names to everything. We give places different names, like America, Iran, Iraq. But in fact they all belong to the Earth; they shouldn't fight each other. Israel and Palestine are two hands of the same body. They continue to suffer because they haven't touched the wisdom of nondiscrimination that they have inside them."

Clearly, "this is, because that is." You have to work for the survival of the other side if you want to survive yourself. It is really very simple. Survival means the survival of humankind as a whole, not just a part of it. And we know now that this must be realized not only between the United States and the Middle East, but also between the East and West, the North and South. If the South cannot survive, then the North is going to crumble. If developing countries cannot pay their debts, everyone will suffer. If we do not take care of poorer countries, the well-being of richer countries is not going to last, and we will not be able to continue living in the way we have been for much longer.

Only when we can touch the wisdom of nondiscrimination in us can we all survive.

So do not hope that you can eliminate the evil side. It is easy to think that we are on the good side, and that the other side is evil. But wealth is made of poverty, and poverty is made of wealth. This is a very clear vision of reality. We do not have to look far to see what we have to do. The citizens of every country are human beings. we cannot study and understand a human being just through statistics. You can't leave the job to the governments or the political scientists alone. You have to do it yourself. If you arrive at an understanding of the fears and hopes of a citizen from Iraq or Sudan or Afghanistan, then you can understand your own fears and hopes. Only penetration into reality can save us. Fear cannot save us.

We are not separate. We are inextricably interrelated. The rose is the garbage, and the non-prostitute is the prostitute. The rich man is the very poor woman, and the Buddhist is the non-Buddhist. The non-Buddhist cannot help but be a Buddhist, because we inter-are. The emancipation of the young prostitute will come as she sees into the nature of interbeing. She will know that she is bearing the fruit of the whole world. And if we look into ourselves and see her, we bear her pain, and the pain of the whole world.

7: The Moon is Always the Moon

Neither increasing nor decreasing . . .

We worry because we think that, after we die, we will not be a human being anymore. We will go back to being a speck of dust. We think we will be somehow diminished.

But that is not true. A speck of dust contains the whole universe. If we were as big as the sun, we might look down at the Earth and see it as insignificant. As human beings, we look at dust in the same way. But the ideas of big and small are just concepts in our minds. Everything contains everything else; that is the principle of interpenetration. This sheet of paper contains the sunshine, the logger, the forest, everything, so the idea that a sheet of paper is small or insignificant is just an idea. We cannot destroy even one sheet of paper. We are incapable of destroying anything. Those who assassinated Mahatma Gandhi and Martin Luther King Jr. hoped to reduce them to nothingness. But these people continue to be with us, perhaps even more than before, because they continue in other forms. We, ourselves, continue their being. So let us not be afraid of diminishing. We are like the moon. We see the moon waxing and waning, but it is always the moon.

8: Buddha is Made of Non-Buddha Elements

Therefore, in emptiness there is neither form, nor feelings,
   nor perceptions,
nor mental formations, nor consciousness.
No eye, or ear, or nose, or tongue, or body, or mind.
No form, no sound, no smell, no taste, no touch, no object
   of mind.
No realms of elements (from eyes to mind consciousness),
no interdependent origins and no extinction of them
(from ignorance to death and decay).
No ill-being, no cause of ill-being, no end of ill-being,
   and no path.
No understanding and no attainment.

The first sentence is a confirmation that the Five Skandhas are all empty. They cannot exist by themselves. Each one has to inter-be with all the other skandhas.

The next part of the verse is an enumeration of the eighteen realms of elements (*dhatus*). First we have the six sense organs: eyes, ears, nose, tongue, body, and mind. Then there are the six sense objects: form, sound, smell, taste, touch, and object of mind. Form is the object of eyes, sound is the object of ears, and so on. Finally, the contact between these first twelve brings about the six consciousnesses: sight, hearing, smell, taste, touch, and the last is mind consciousness. So, with eyes as the first realm of elements and mind consciousness as the eighteenth, this part of the sutra is saying that not one of these realms can exist by itself, because each can only inter-be with every other realm.

The next part speaks of the twelve interdependent origins (*pratitya samutpada*), which begin with ignorance and end with old age and death. The meaning in the sutra is that none of these twelve can exist by itself. Each must rely on the being of the others in order for it to be. Therefore, all of them are empty, and because they are empty, they really exist. The same principle applies to the Four Noble Truths: "No ill-being, no cause of ill-being, no end of ill-being, and no path." The last line in this section is: "No understanding and no attainment." Understanding (*prajña*) is the essence of a Buddha. "No understanding" means understanding has no separate existence. Understanding is made of non-understanding elements, just as Buddha is made of non-Buddha elements.

I want to tell you a story about Buddha and Mara. One day the Buddha was in his cave, and Ananda, who was the Buddha's attendant, was standing outside near the door. Suddenly Ananda saw Mara coming. He was surprised. He didn't want that, and he wished Mara would get lost. But Mara walked straight up to Ananda and asked him to announce his visit to the Buddha.

Ananda said, "Why have you come here? Don't you remember that long ago you were defeated by the Buddha under the bodhi tree? Aren't you ashamed to come here? Go away! The Buddha will not see you. You are evil. You are his enemy."

When Mara heard this, he began to laugh and laugh. "Did you say your teacher told you he has enemies?" That made Ananda very embarrassed. He knew that his teacher had not said that he has enemies. So Ananda was defeated and had to go in and announce Mara, hoping that the Buddha would say, "Go and tell him that I am not here. Tell him that I am in a meeting."

But the Buddha was very excited when he heard that Mara, such a very old friend, had come to visit him. "Is that true? Is he really here?" the Buddha said, and he went out in person to greet Mara. Ananda was distressed. The Buddha went right up to Mara, bowed to him, and took his hands in his in the warmest way. The Buddha said, "Hello! How are you? How have you been? Is everything all right?"

Mara didn't say anything. So the Buddha brought him into the cave, prepared a seat for him to sit down, and told Ananda to go and make herb tea for both of them. "I can make tea for my master one hundred times a day, but making tea for Mara is not a joy," Ananda thought to himself. But since this was the order of his master, how could he refuse? So Ananda went to prepare some herb tea for the Buddha and his so-called guest, but while doing this he tried to listen to their conversation.

The Buddha repeated very warmly, "How have you been? How are things with you?" Mara said, "Things are not going well at all. I am tired of being a Mara. I want to be something else."

Ananda became very frightened. Mara said, "You know, being a Mara is not a very easy thing to do. If you talk, you have to talk in riddles. If you do anything, you have to be tricky and look evil. I am very tired of all that. But what I cannot bear is my disciples. They are now talking about social justice, peace, equality, liberation, nonduality, nonviolence, all of that. I have had enough of it! I think that it would be better if I hand them all over to you. I want to be something else."

Ananda began to shudder because he was afraid that the master would decide to take the other role. Mara would become the Buddha, and the Buddha would become Mara. It made him very sad.

The Buddha listened attentively and was filled with compassion. Finally, he said in a quiet voice, "Do you think it's fun being a Buddha? You don't know what my disciples have done to me! They put words into my mouth that I never said. They build garish temples and put statues of me on altars in order to attract bananas and oranges and sweet rice, just for themselves. And they package me and make my teaching into an item of commerce. Mara, if you knew what it is really like to be a Buddha, I am sure you wouldn't want to be one." And, thereupon, the Buddha recited a long verse summarizing the conversation.

9: Freedom

Because there is no attainment,
the Bodhisattvas, grounded in Perfect Understanding,
find no obstacles for their minds.
Having no obstacles, they overcome fear,
liberating themselves forever from illusion and realizing
    perfect Nirvana.
All Buddhas in the past, present, and future,
thanks to this Perfect Understanding,
arrive at full, right, and universal Enlightenment.

Obstacles are our ideas and concepts concerning birth and death, defilement, immaculateness, increasing, decreasing, above, below, inside, outside, Buddha, Mara, and so on. Once we see with the eyes of interbeing, these obstacles are removed from our minds and we overcome fear, liberating ourselves forever from illusion, and realizing perfect nirvana. Once the wave realizes that it is only water, that it is nothing but water, it realizes that birth and death cannot do it any harm. It has transcended all kinds of fear, and perfect nirvana is the state of non-fear. You are liberated, you are no longer subject to birth and death, defilement and immaculateness. You are free from all that.

10: Svaha!

Therefore, one should know
that Perfect Understanding is the highest mantra,
    the unequalled mantra,
the destroyer of ill-being, the incorruptible truth.
A mantra of Prajñaparamita should therefore be proclaimed:
Gate gate paragate parasamgate bodhi svaha.

A mantra is something that you utter when your body, your mind, and your breath are at one in deep concentration. When you dwell in that deep concentration, you look into things and see them as clearly as you see an orange that you hold in the palm of your hand. Looking deeply into the Five Skandhas, Avalokiteshvara saw the nature of interbeing and overcame all pain. He became completely liberated. It was in that state of deep concentration, of joy, of liberation, that he uttered something important. That is why his utterance is a mantra.

When two young people love each other, but one of them has not said so yet, the other person may be waiting for three very important words. If the first person is a very responsible person, he probably wants to be sure of his feeling, and he may wait a long time before saying it. Then one day, sitting together in a park, when no one else is nearby and everything is quiet, after the two of them have been silent for a long time, he utters these three words. When the second person hears this, she trembles, because it is such an important statement. When you say something like that with your whole being, not just with your mouth or your intellect, but with your whole being, it can transform the world. A statement that has such power of transformation is called a mantra.

Avalokiteshvara's mantra is "*Gate gate paragate parasamgate bodhi svaha.*" *Gate* means gone. Gone from suffering to the liberation from suffering. Gone from forgetfulness to mindfulness. Gone from duality into nonduality. *Gate gate* means gone, gone. *Paragate* means gone all the way to the other shore. So this mantra is said in a very strong way. Gone, gone, gone all the way over. In *parasamgate, sam* means everyone, the sangha, the entire community of beings. Everyone gone over to the other shore. *Bodhi* is the light inside, enlightenment, or awakening. You see it and the vision of reality liberates you. *Svaha* is a cry of joy or excitement, like "ah!" or "Wonderful!" or "Hallelujah!"

"Gone, gone, gone all the way over, everyone gone to the other shore, enlightenment, svaha!" That is what the bodhisattva uttered. When we listen to this mantra, we should bring ourselves into that state of attention and concentration, so that we can receive the strength emanated by Avalokiteshvara Bodhisattva. We do not recite the Heart Sutra like singing a song, or with our intellect alone. If you practice the meditation on emptiness, if you penetrate the nature of interbeing with all your heart, your body, and your mind, you will realize a state that is quite concentrated. If you say the mantra then, with all your being, the mantra will have power and you will be able to have real communication, real communion with Avalokiteshvara, and you will be able to transform yourself in the direction of enlightenment. This text is not just for chanting, or to be put on an altar for worship. It is given to us as a tool to work for our liberation, for the liberation of all beings. It is like a tool for farming, given to us so that we may farm. This is the gift of Avalokita.

There are three kinds of gifts. The first is the gift of material resources. The second is the gift of knowledge, the gift of the Dharma. The third, the highest kind of gift, is the gift of non-fear. Avalokiteshvara Bodhisattva is someone who can help us liberate ourselves from fear. This is the heart of the Prajñaparamita. Svaha!

11: A Tangerine Party

The Prajñaparamita gives us solid ground for making peace with ourselves, for transcending the fear of birth and death, the duality of this and that. In the light of emptiness, everything is everything else, we inter-are, everyone is responsible for everything that happens in life. When you produce peace and happiness in yourself, you begin to realize peace for the whole world. With the smile that you produce in yourself, with the conscious breathing you establish within yourself, you begin to work for peace in the world. To smile is not to smile only for yourself; the world will change because of your smile. When you practice sitting meditation, if you enjoy even one moment of your sitting, if you establish serenity and happiness inside yourself, you provide the world with a solid base of peace. If you do not give yourself peace, how can you share it with others? If you do not begin your peace work with yourself, where will you go to begin it? To sit, to smile, to look at things and really see them, these are the basis of peace work.

Sometimes at a retreat, we have a tangerine party. Everyone is offered a tangerine. We put the tangerines on the palms of our hands and look at them, breathing in a way that makes the tangerines become real. Most of the time when we eat a tangerine, we do not look at it. We think about many other things. To look at a tangerine is to see the blossom forming into the fruit, to see the sunshine, and the rain. The tangerine in the palm is the wonderful presence of life. We are able to really see that tangerine and smell its blossom and the warm, moist earth. As the tangerine becomes real, we become real. Life in that moment becomes real.

Mindfully we peel our tangerines and smell their fragrance. We carefully take each section of the tangerine and put it on our tongues, and we can feel that they are real tangerines. We eat each section of the tangerine in perfect mindfulness until we finish the entire fruit. Eating a tangerine in this way is very important, because both the tangerine and the eater of the tangerine become real. This, too, is the basic work for peace.

In Buddhist meditation we do not struggle for the kind of enlightenment that will happen five or ten years from now. We practice so that each moment of our lives becomes real life. And, therefore, when we meditate, we sit just for sitting; we don't sit for something else. If we sit for twenty minutes, these twenty minutes should bring us joy, life. If we practice walking meditation, we walk just for walking, not to arrive anywhere. We have to be alive with each step, and if we are, each step brings real life back to us.

The same kind of mindfulness can be practiced when we eat breakfast, or when we hold a child in our arms. Hugging is a Western custom, but we from the East would like to contribute the practice of conscious breathing to it. When you hold a child in your arms, or hug your mother, or your husband, or your friend, breathe in and out three times and your happiness will be multiplied at least tenfold. And when you look at someone, really look at them with mindfulness and practice conscious breathing.

At the beginning of each meal, I recommend that you look at your bowl and silently recite, "My bowl is empty now, but I know that it is going to be filled with delicious food in just a moment." While waiting to be served or to serve yourself, I suggest you breathe three times and look at your bowl even more deeply, "At this very moment many, many people around the world are also holding a bowl, but their bowl is going to be empty for a long time." Over forty thousand children die each day because of malnutrition. And that is only the children. We can be very happy to have such wonderful food, but we also suffer because we are capable of seeing. When we see in this way, it makes us sane, because the way in front of us—the way to live so that we can make peace with ourselves and with the world—is clear. When we see the good and the bad, the wondrous and the deep suffering, we have to live in a way that we can make peace between ourselves and the world. Understanding is the fruit of meditation. Understanding is the basis of everything.

Each breath we take, each step we make, each smile we realize, is a positive contribution to peace, a necessary step in the direction of peace for the world. In the light of interbeing, peace and happiness in your daily life means peace and happiness in the world.

Thank you for being so attentive. Thank you for listening to Avalokiteshvara. Because you are there, the Heart Sutra has become very easy.

The Sutra on the Middle Way

Kaccayanagotta Sutta

Contents

The Sutra on the Middle Way

I heard these words of the Buddha one time when the Lord was staying at the guesthouse in a forest of the district of Nala. At that time, the Venerable Kaccayana came to visit him and asked, "The Tathagata has spoken of Right View. How would the Tathagata describe Right View?"

The Buddha told the venerable monk, "People in the world tend to believe in one of two views: the view of being or the view of nonbeing. That is because they are bound to wrong perception. It is wrong perception that leads to the concepts of being and nonbeing. Kaccayana, most people are bound to the internal formations of discrimination and preference, grasping and attachment. Those who are not bound to the internal knots of grasping and attachment no longer imagine and cling to the idea of a self. They understand, for example, that suffering comes to be when conditions are favorable, and that it fades away when conditions are no longer favorable. They no longer have any doubts. Their understanding has not come to them through others; it is their own insight. This insight is called Right View, and this is the way the Tathagata would describe Right View.

"How is this so? When a person who has correct insight observes the coming to be of the world, the idea of nonbeing does not arise in her, and when she observes the fading away of the world, the idea of being does not arise in her mind. Kaccayana, viewing the world as being is an extreme; viewing it as nonbeing is another extreme. The Tathagata avoids these two extremes and teaches the Dharma dwelling in the Middle Way.

"The Middle Way says that this is, because that is; this is not, because that is not. Because there is ignorance, there are impulses; because there are impulses, there is consciousness; because there is consciousness, there is the psyche-soma; because there is the psyche-soma, there are the six senses; because there are the six senses, there is contact; because there is contact, there is feeling; because there is feeling, there is craving; because there is craving, there is grasping; because there is grasping, there is becoming; because there is becoming, there is birth; because there is birth, there are old age, death, grief, and sorrow. That is how this entire mass of suffering arises. But with the fading away of ignorance, impulses cease; with the fading away of impulses, consciousness ceases; . . . and finally birth, old age, death, grief, and sorrow will fade away. That is how this entire mass of suffering ceases."

After listening to the Buddha, the Venerable Kaccayana was enlightened and liberated from sorrow. He was able to untie all of his internal knots and attain arhatship.

Samyukta Agama No. 301

1: The Wisdom of the Middle Way[68]

The morning of the Buddha's enlightenment at the foot of the bodhi tree, he was so surprised. He had been meditating for the whole night. In the early morning, at the moment when he saw the morning star, he declared, "How strange! Everyone has the capacity to be awake, to understand, and to love. Yet they continue to drift and sink on the ocean of suffering, life after life."

Before he became the Buddha, "the awakened one," Prince Siddhartha had a strong will to succeed. He tried to use his mind to suppress his mind and body, putting himself through a period of practicing self-mortification and extreme austerity in which he almost died. Eventually, he accepted that forcing his body and mind in the practice wouldn't help him, so he adopted the Middle Way, a path between austerity and indulgence in sensual pleasure.

Soon after Siddhartha woke up and became the Buddha, he wanted to share what he had learned. His first Dharma talk was offered to the five co-practitioners who had practiced asceticism with him.

He said, "My brothers, there are two extremes that a person on the path should avoid. One is to indulge in sensual pleasures, and the other is to practice austerities that deprive the body of its needs. Both of these extremes lead to failure. The path I have discovered is the Middle Way, which avoids both extremes and has the capacity to lead one to understanding, liberation, and peace. It is the Noble Eightfold Path of Right View, Right Thought, Right Speech, Right Action, Right Livelihood, Right Effort, Right Mindfulness, and Right Concentration. I have followed this Noble Eightfold Path and have realized understanding, liberation, and peace. Brothers, why do I call this path the right path? I call it the right path because it does not avoid or deny suffering, but allows for a direct confrontation with suffering as the means to overcome it. The Noble Eightfold Path is the path of living in awareness."

From his very first Dharma talk, the Buddha spoke about the Middle Way, the Four Noble Truths, and the Noble Eightfold Path. He continued to teach on these subjects throughout his life.

When the Buddha appeared in the world, he was a great revolutionary. He taught that everything is impermanent and subject to change and that what we call "self" or "self-nature" doesn't exist. The Buddha's teaching of no-self was in direct contradiction to the philosophy and religion prevalent in India at the time, and it generated a strong reaction. Hinduism believes that each of us has a divine self (*atman*) that is eternal and is part of the great divine self (*brahman*).

When the Buddha was still alive, his teachings were clear and powerful. After the Buddha's death, the Buddha's disciples had to develop their own teachings to respond to the continued opposition from Hinduism. Sometimes they brought up new theories that were far from the original teachings of the Buddha. There was much back and forth as Hindu scholars and scholars from the various schools of Buddhism contradicted and challenged each other. In the second century, the Buddhist scholar Nagarjuna wrote the Madhyamaka Shastra, a commentary of the Buddha's teachings on the Middle Way, in an effort to return to and clarify the Buddha's original meaning.

The Sutra on the Middle Way contains the key Buddhist concepts of Right View: keeping an open mind and avoiding extreme perspectives and dualities, and Dependent Co-arising: the interdependent, mutually created nature of all things.

The sutra uses the term "Right View" to mean a view that transcends dualistic thinking and is not caught in worldly views. Worldly views, views based on the surface appearance of things, are fetters.

In the Diamond Sutra, the Buddha talks about four notions that affect all our views and perceptions. These four notions need to be thrown away.

The first notion we need to throw away is the notion of self. There is the idea that I am this body, this body is me or, this body is mine and it belongs to me. We say these things based on the notion that "I am." But a better statement would be, "I inter-am." It's closer to the truth in the light of interconnected-ness; we see there is no separate self that can exist by itself. You cannot exist without your parents, your ancestors, food, water, air, earth, and everything else in the cosmos.

By looking deeply into the nature of reality, we can throw away the notion "I am."

The second notion the Diamond Sutra advises us to throw away is the notion of person or human being. When we look into the human being, we see animal ancestors, we see plant and mineral ancestors. A human is made of non-human elements. If we take away the non-human elements, the human being would no longer be there. This is the oldest teaching on deep ecology. In order to protect the human being, you have to protect what is not human. Discriminating between human and nature is a wrong view.

The third wrong notion is that of living beings. We distinguish living beings from non-living beings. We distinguish humans and animals from plants and minerals. But looking deeply into living beings, we see elements that we call non-living beings: plants and minerals. You can see that plants and minerals are also alive. After meditation we see there's no real frontier separating living beings and so-called non-living beings.

The fourth notion to be thrown away is the notion of life span. We believe that we're born at one point in time, that we shall die at another point in time, and that in between is our life span. Most of us believe we'll spend seventy, eighty, ninety, one hundred years on this planet and then we'll be gone. But when we look deeply, we see this is a wrong perception. In our minds, to be born means that from nothing we become something; to die means that from something we become nothing; and from someone we become no one. But a cloud can't be born; it has come from the water in the rivers and oceans, and dust and the heat of the sun have helped create it. A cloud can never die; it can only become rain or snow. A piece of paper can't be born; it's made of trees, the sun, the cloud, the logger, and the worker in the paper factory. When we burn a piece of paper, the paper is transformed into heat, ash, and smoke; it cannot be reduced to nothingness. Birth and death are notions that cannot be applied to reality.

These four notions are at the foundation of our fear, discrimination, and suffering. When we are able to see them as wrong views, ignorance and suffering will no longer touch us. We'll no longer suffer because of our wrong views.

When we are caught in ideas of self, human being, living being, or life span, it's because we haven't been able to see Dependent Co-arising. When we are caught in the idea of a life span, we think, my life will only last a certain amount of time, and we start asking questions like, "Did I exist in the past?" "What was I in the past?" "When I die, will I still be there, and if I am, what will I be?" These questions only arise when we are caught in the ideas of self, human being, living being, and life span.

The Sanskrit phrase *pratitya samutpada* means "in dependence, things rise up." Pratitya samutpada is sometimes called the teaching of cause and effect. But that can be misleading, because we usually think of cause and effect as separate entities, with cause always preceding effect, and one cause leading to one effect. According to the teaching of Dependent Co-arising, cause and effect arise together (*samutpada*) and everything is a result of multiple causes and conditions.

For a table to exist, we need wood, a carpenter, time, skillfulness, and many other causes. And each of these causes needs other causes in order to be. The wood needs the forest, the sunshine, the rain, and so on. The carpenter needs his parents, breakfast, fresh air, and so on. And each of these things, in turn, has to be brought about by other conditions. If we continue to look in this way, we'll see that nothing has been left out; everything in the cosmos has come together to bring us this table. Looking deeply at the sunshine, the leaves of the tree, and the clouds, we can see the table. The one can be seen in the all, and the all can be seen in the one. One cause is never enough to bring about an effect. A cause must, at the same time, be an effect, and every effect must also be the cause of something else. Cause and effect inter-are; they give rise to each other. The idea of a first or a single cause, something that does not itself need a cause, cannot be applied.

Our difficulties arise when we forget this teaching and become attached to ideas and to things, believing that they are independent and permanent. When we embrace the interdependent nature of all things, forsaking all extremes, we will be on the path of a more peaceful and joy-filled existence.

2: Right View

In this sutra we study Right View in the light of the Middle Way. The Middle Way means not being caught in pairs of opposites like "exists" or "does not exist." The Middle Way could be wrongly interpreted as meaning that "exists" and "does not exist" are both possible, and that the Middle Way goes between them. But in fact it means that "exists" and "does not exist" are both ideas we need to go beyond. Our insight of Right View is based on our observation of conditioned existence.

> I heard these words of the Buddha one time when the Lord was staying at the guesthouse in a forest of the district of Nala.

The Chinese version of the sutra says Buddha delivered this discourse in Nala, in the kingdom of Magadha. The Pali version says it was delivered in Savatthi (Shravasti), in the kingdom of Koshala. Magadha and Koshala are ancient kingdoms of the Ganges River basin.

> At that time, the Venerable Kaccayana came to visit him and asked, "The Tathagata has spoken of Right View. How would the Tathagatha describe Right View?"

The Venerable Kaccayana was a high monk in the Buddha's Sangha. His question is about Right View, and the Buddha responds by speaking of the Middle Way. The Middle Way avoids extreme views and dualistic thinking. Because we have wrong views, we have wrong perceptions. Wrong perceptions are the ground of all afflictions: fear, anger, discrimination, despair. All these kinds of afflictions are born from wrong perceptions. Looking deeply into the wrong perceptions, ideas, and notions that are at the base of our suffering is the most important practice in Buddhist meditation.

Our happiness and the happiness of those around us depend on our degree of Right View. But Right View is not an ideology, a system, or even a path. It cannot be described; we can only point in the correct direction. Even a teacher cannot transmit Right View. A teacher can help us identify the seed of Right View that is already there in our garden, and help us gain confidence, and show us how to practice, to entrust that seed to the soil of our daily lives.

Store consciousness is the place where all our experiences can be found. It is like the hard disk in a computer. Everything we've heard and seen, every experience of our lives has been stored there. Mind consciousness—our conscious mind—plays the role of the gardener. We cultivate the soil with our daily practice of mindfulness, helping the seed of Right View to manifest and grow.

So mind consciousness is the gardener, cultivating the soil and nourishing the seed of Right View with our daily practice of mindfulness. Buddhist meditation is an attempt to integrate mind consciousness in every moment of our daily lives so we are aware of what is going on within us and around us, so that we can truly be ourselves. Otherwise we're on automatic pilot and we're not really living our lives.

The Middle Way is not caught in pairs of opposites, such as being and nonbeing; coming and going; birth and death; same and different; exists and does not exist. These are ideas we need to go beyond. Shakespeare said, "To be, or not to be: that is the question." But in Buddhism, we go beyond the idea of being and not being. Because we have wrong views, we have wrong perceptions, and because of those wrong perceptions we think that this world is real, or that this world is not real.

The phrase "wrong view" itself is not exactly accurate. Relatively speaking, there are right views and there are wrong views. But if we look more deeply, we see that all views are wrong views. No view can ever be the truth. It is just the view from one point; that is why it is called a "point of view." If we go to another point, we will see things differently and realize that our first view was not entirely right. Buddhism is not a collection of views. It is a practice that helps us eliminate wrong views. The quality of our views can always be improved. From the viewpoint of the ultimate reality, Right View is the absence of all views.

At the base of our views are our perceptions (*samjña*). In the Chinese character for perception, the upper part of the character means "mark," "sign," or "appearance," and the lower part means "mind" or "spirit." A perception always has a "mark," and in many cases that mark is illusory. The Buddha advised us not to be fooled by what we perceive.

In the Diamond Sutra, the Buddha told the monk Subhuti, "In a place where there is something that can be distinguished by signs, in that place there is deception."[69] The Buddha taught on many occasions that most of our perceptions are erroneous, and that most of our suffering comes from wrong perceptions. We have to ask ourselves again and again, "Am I sure?" Until we see clearly, our wrong perceptions will prevent us from having Right View.

To perceive always means to perceive something. We believe that the object of our perception is separate from the subject, but that is not correct. When we perceive a mountain, the mountain is the object of our perception. When we perceive the moon, the moon is the object of our perception. When we say, "I can see my consciousness in the flower," it means we can see the cloud, the sunshine, the earth, and the minerals in it. But how can we see our consciousness in a flower? The flower is our consciousness. Perception means the coming into existence of the perceiver and the perceived. The flower that we are looking at is part of our consciousness. The idea that our consciousness is outside of the flower is deluded. It is impossible to have a subject without an object. It is impossible to remove one and retain the other.

> The Buddha told the venerable monk, "People in the world tend to believe in one of two views: the view of being or the view of nonbeing. That is because they are bound to wrong perception. It is wrong perception that leads to the concepts of being and nonbeing."

These words of the sutra are very clear. We have wrong views, we have wrong perceptions, and because of those wrong perceptions we think that this world is real, or that this world is not real. We have to throw away these wrong perceptions. Throwing away is stronger than "letting go." It takes insight and courage to throw away an idea. If we've suffered, it may be because we've entertained an idea that we haven't been able to release.

There are those of us who believe in an immortal soul, that after the disintegration of this body, the immortal soul continues to live on and doesn't change. We know that everything is changing, that everything is impermanent. So the notion that there is an immortal soul that remains itself forever and ever is a wrong view called permanence. The other extreme is annihilation: the idea that something can disappear forever and that after we die, nothing is left. That is also a wrong view. We are used to seeing the world as a series of opposites.

When we invite a flame to manifest, we can ask the flame, "Dear little flame, where have you come from?" We have the notion of coming and going. But the flame has not come from anywhere. Her nature is the nature of no coming. When conditions come together, she manifests. So coming is a notion. Going is another notion. When the flame is extinguished we can ask, "Dear little flame, where have you gone?" And the flame will answer, "I have gone nowhere. When conditions are no longer sufficient, I cease my manifestation. My nature is no coming, no going." Even when the flame is manifesting, the flame of one second is not the flame of the next. There is input and output, birth and death, at every moment.

Several years ago during a retreat in northern Germany, the Sangha married a couple. The next morning the couple came before the Sangha of mindfulness to report to us on the teaching of impermanence and neither the same nor different. The young man looked at his bride and asked this question: "Darling, are you the same person I married yesterday or are you a different one?" Because things are impermanent, nothing can remain the same in two consecutive days or moments. When you love, you worry a little bit that the other person may no longer love you. You want to be assured all the time that she still loves you. The young woman looked at her new husband, smiling, and said: "Don't worry, my dear, although I am not exactly the same person you married yesterday, I am not a different person either." That is the truth. The notions of sameness and otherness should be thrown away. If we are successful in our contemplation of impermanence, permanence no longer makes sense.

> "Kaccayana, most people are bound to the internal formations of discrimination and preference, grasping and attachment. Those who are not bound to the internal knots of grasping and attachment no longer imagine and cling to the idea of a self."

Here, we have two words: "grasping," which means not letting go; and "attachment," which is like a crab catching hold of us and not letting us go. What catches us and will not let us go are our ideas, our wrong perceptions. We're caught in our ideas and perceptions, and therefore we're attached to them.

We each have a view of the universe. That view may be called relativity or uncertainty or probability or string theory; there are many kinds of views. It's okay to propose views, but if you want to make progress on the path of inquiry, you should be able to be ready to throw away your view. It's like climbing a ladder, coming to the fifth rung, and thinking you're on the highest rung. That idea prevents you from climbing to the sixth, and the seventh rung. You are caught. So in order to come to the sixth and the seventh, you have to release the fifth. That is the process of learning proposed by the Buddha. Buddhism fully practiced is free from dogmatism. If you worship something as a dogma, as absolute truth, you are not a good practitioner. You must be totally free, even from the teachings of the Buddha. The teachings of the Buddha are offered as instruments, not as absolute truth.

We have the habit of distinguishing between wrong views and right views. We say that permanence is a wrong view, and we use the Right View of impermanence to overcome the view of permanence. But you also have to be free from the view of impermanence.

The truly Right View, as the sutra tells us, is the absence of all views. According to the teachings of the Buddha, we have to throw away all views, including the so-called right views. Reality, things as they are, cannot be described in terms of notions and views. That is why so-called "right views" are only instruments to help us.

In the Ratnakuta Sutra, the Accumulation of Jewels, the Buddha said that if you are attached to the notion of existence, then the notion of emptiness might help to rescue you. But if you are caught by the notion of emptiness, no one can rescue you. You have to see the Dharma like that also. You should be free from the true teachings, let alone from the teachings that are not true. In the Diamond Sutra the Buddha says: "All teachings must be abandoned, not to mention non-teachings." The practice of throwing away your notions and views is so important. Liberation will not be possible without this practice of throwing away.

> "Those who are not bound to the internal knots of grasping and attachment no longer imagine and cling to the idea of a self."

The word "imagine" is the translation of the Chinese word that means to measure, to estimate, to conceive of. We have a conception about something. We say it's important or it's not important. We say it exists or it doesn't exist. Wrong perception means that we imagine things about the truth. We load this idea and that idea on to the truth. Actually the truth is not like that, but we think it's like that. Although we know that nothing is permanent, in our everyday lives we think of things as permanent. Even if we understand the idea that a separate "self" is a misperception, most of our thinking is based on seeing things as having a self. This kind of thinking is dangerous. These ideas tend to make us feel secure. But in fact they're based on wrong perception. The basis for all our grasping and imagining is our ideas.

At the center of our grasping and imagining, at the center of all our wrong perceptions is our idea about self. We think there's something called a "self," that there is a "me" and "mine." We have the idea that "I" exist, and that there are things that belong to "me," that are "mine." But who is this self?

When we look at a flower and ask, "Who is opening?" we don't need an "I" that is born, that grows old, and that will die. We think that if there's birth, there has to be an "I" that is born, if there is aging, there has to be an "I" that grows old, and if there is death, there has to be someone who will die.

In truth, birth is simply birth, old age is simply old age, death is death; there is no "I" in that. It is only when we are caught in the idea of self that we say there has to be an "I." Does the flower have a soul, a self, within it? Does it need a self in order to be born, to open, and to fade; does it need an "I" in order to exist? For there to be rain, there doesn't have to be an "I." Rain happens; you don't have to ask, "Who is falling?" In many languages, we have to say "it" is raining, implying there is a self that is raining. But if there is rain, is there a self in the rain? We get used to this way of speaking, that there has to be a subject, a self, and only then can there be an action. In English we say, "It rains." In Vietnamese we say, "The sky is raining" or "the weather is raining."

When we say, "I know the wind is blowing," we can divide this sentence into two phrases. One is "I know," the other, "the wind is blowing." This is truly a strange statement. How can there be wind that doesn't blow? As soon as you have wind, you have blowing; without blowing there is no wind, the blowing is part of the wind. Why not just say, "the wind"? It's the same when we say, "A cloud is floating in the sky" or "a flower is opening." If a cloud is not floating in the sky, then it's still the water in the river; if a flower is not open, it's not yet a flower, but a bud. There is also the phrase, "I know." Do we have to have an "I"? Just to say "know" would be enough, we don't need "I." "Know" is a verb, so it requires a subject, and therefore we have to have the word "I." If we wish to say the truth, just to say "rain" or "wind" or "cloud" is enough.

We've become accustomed to the habit of thinking and speaking in terms of a subject, a self. This has been happening for so many past generations. But, unfortunately, this idea that there must be a subject hides the truth from us.

3: Dependent Co-arising

They understand, for example, that suffering comes to be when conditions are favorable, and that it fades away when conditions are no longer favorable. They no longer have any doubts.

Here, the Buddha talks about suffering simply as a phenomenon, just like a picture or a table. The inclusion of the words "for example" makes this clear. Suffering is just being used as an example to represent all phenomena.

The Buddha is talking about causes and conditions. We find out about the Middle Way by observing and learning about conditioned existence. Cause and effect co-arise and everything is a result of multiple causes and conditions. The egg is in the chicken and the chicken is in the egg. Chicken and egg arise in mutual dependence. Nothing can arise independently.

"Causes and conditions," and "Dependent Co-arising" carry a similar meaning and are at the heart of the Buddha's teaching. "Causes" refers to the seed or principle condition. "Conditions" refers to the other necessary conditions that are not the principal ones. In the Chinese character for "cause," the word "great" is pictured inside four walls. If something is to become great, it must break through those boundaries. When you look at a mustard seed, it's small; the conditions aren't there for it to be large. But when the mustard seed is put into the earth and watered, it becomes a great plant. The conditions to bring the mustard seed to fruition are water, earth, fertilizer, warmth, and so on. Notice that the conditions are also causes. But the primary cause, of course, is the seed itself. The subsidiary causes are the conditions necessary to support the primary cause to develop.

In talking about causes and conditions, the Buddha used the term "Dependent Co-arising" (pratitya samutpada). "Dependent" means relying on each other. "Co" means together, simultaneously. Nothing can arise alone or stand on its own; everything is dependent upon everything else.

In the United States, although we celebrate Independence Day, we cannot really live without being dependent on other countries. Maybe we should celebrate "Interdependence Day," since one country has to depend on other countries in order to exist.

When we have a feeling of suffering and we look deeply into it, we can see that the suffering comes from various conditions that have caused it to arise. When we look deeply at a flower, we see that many conditions have come together to make the flower possible.

The same is true of a cloud or a table; when the conditions necessary for them to be are not there, then they will not be there. A person who observes in this way sees clearly and no longer has any doubts. We see that everything comes to be because of the coming together of favorable conditions, and when those conditions fall apart, that thing can no longer exist.

"Their understanding has not come to them through others; it is their own insight." This insight is called Right View, and this is the way the Tathagata would describe Right View.[70]

Everything comes to be because of various causes and conditions. Don't believe this just because the Buddha said it. Believe it because you've looked deeply and seen it for yourself. The Buddha always asks that we experience these things for ourselves and not accept them based on the words, teachings, or ideas of anyone else, including the Buddha. We don't want to repeat, like a parrot, the things that other people have said.

We have suffering; everyone has suffering. When we look deeply into the heart of that suffering, we see the causes and conditions near and far that have brought it about. We can see this on our own. No one else has to say this to us. It's with our own wisdom that we look into our suffering. Because we've been able to see this for ourselves, we have no doubts about our insight, we know that it is so. That insight comes from us, it's not something we receive from someone else.

Regardless of the number, when conditions that are related to each other come together, they bring about a phenomenon, and we have a perception of that phenomenon. Whether a Buddha is or is not present in the world to teach about it, Dependent Co-arising remains the basis of everything. This truth, or law, is always there in the field of all phenomena. This truth is always present in all dharma realms.

> "How is this so? When a person who has correct insight observes the coming to be of the world, the idea of non-being does not arise in her, and when she observes the fading away of the world, the idea of being does not arise in her mind."

"Being" or "becoming" occur in the *lokadhatu*. The lokadhatu refers to this world, the world of suffering, where things appear to be born and to die and to exist independently of each other; the grapefruit is independent of the lemon. But in the *dharmadhatu*, the realm of "things as they are," the lotus is not different from the meditation hall, a man is not different from his brother, all things are interconnected; in the one is the all and the all is in the one. All dharmas, all phenomena, dwell in the dharmadhatu. If we can touch them deeply, we can be in touch with their no-birth and no-death nature. This is the world of the dharmadhatu, *nirvana*. It is our way of living that determines whether we're living in the dharmadhatu or in the lokadhatu.

According to the teachings on Dependent Co-arising, all phenomena dwell in their Dharma nature, their nature of no-birth and no-death. We have our Dharma nature; the flower has its Dharma nature. If we can be in touch with that nature, we go beyond ideas of being born and dying. If we can be in touch with the Dharma nature of the flower, we won't see the flower as something that blooms and then dies, and that is separate from other things.

It is clear that the world is in the process of manifesting. It is clear that the flower is manifesting. So we cannot say it doesn't exist. We see that suffering is manifesting; we can't say that suffering isn't there. But when we can see and know something as it really is, we won't attach to it, and we won't weigh it down and burden it with ideas.

> "When a person who has correct insight observes the coming to be of the world, the idea of nonbeing does not arise in

her, and when she observes the fading away of the world, the idea of being does not arise in her mind. Kaccayana, viewing the world as being is an extreme; viewing it as nonbeing is another extreme. The Tathagata avoids these two extremes and teaches the Dharma dwelling in the Middle Way."

The notions that life span is this body or is not this body are two of the "extreme views" spoken of in the Sutra. The Middle Way goes beyond ideas of being and nonbeing, birth and death, one and many, coming and going, same and different.

The notions of existing and not existing come from our wrong perceptions. The Buddha says that we should go beyond the ideas of "exists" and "does not exist." When something manifests, we have the tendency to say it exists; and when it no longer manifests, to say it doesn't exist. This is a mistake that many of us make.

Plum Village, where I live, is situated amidst fields of sunflowers. When we do walking meditation in April, we don't see any sunflowers so we say, "There are no sunflowers," and we think of them as not existing. But a farmer driving along the road in April will see things differently. If we were to say to the farmer, "There are no sunflowers," he may say, "Yes, there are," because he has planted the seed. Then in May or June sunflowers will appear.

We're very quick to come to the conclusion that something doesn't exist. The farmer knows very well that in two months' time the field will be full of sunflowers. But we who don't know anything about farming will say, "There are no sunflowers," but our view is not in accord with reality.

The teachings of the Buddha are always the Middle Way, the way that goes beyond ideas of being and nonbeing, birth and death, one and many, coming and going, same and different, as well as ideas of not being born, not dying, not one, not many, and so on. The Tathagata avoids these extremes.

In eleventh century Vietnam, a monk asked his meditation master, "Where is the place beyond birth and death?" The master replied, "In the midst of birth and death." If you abandon birth and death in order to find nirvana, you will not find nirvana; nirvana is in birth and death. Looking deeply into the phenomenological world, we touch the true nature, the noumenal world.

"The Middle Way says that this is, because that is; this is not, because that is not."

These words are so simple but they're very deep. "This is, because that is." This is the meaning of interdependence. "This arises because that arises." The word "arises" is better than the word "born." This is the definition of Dependent Co-arising and it is repeated many times in the Original Buddhist sutras. "This is, therefore that is." "This is, because that is; this is not, because that is not." "This ceases to be, because that ceases to be." "This is like this, because that is like that." That is the best definition of Dependent Co-arising that we can give. If we smile, the mirror smiles back at us. If we are kind to others, they will be kind to us.

When people ask such questions as: "Is there a teaching in Buddhism about how the world came to exist?" "Who created the world?" "When did it begin and when will it end?" there is only one thing we can do, and that is to cite this phrase: "This is because that is; this is not because that is not." This is born because that is born. This ends because that ends. The flower is because the sunlight is because the seed is because the Earth is. This thing can be because other things are there. This is the teaching of Dependent Co-arising, and it is presented so simply. "This is because that is" is the highest reply we can give to questions about the existence of the world.

Just like all other things, time is a conditioned phenomenon. Time is conditioned by space, by earth, by water, by everything in the cosmos. This is true for a flower, it is true for our suffering, and it is true for all phenomena in the world. The question "What is the first cause?" comes from our ignorance. Questions such as: "Who created the world?" "Is there such a thing as time or not?" "When did time begin?" become very naive when we understand the teachings on the Middle Way. When we've understood these teachings we can go deeply into the teachings of Dependent Co-arising. Time is there because of space, space is there because of time; they are dependent on each other. This manifests because that manifests. This is latent because that is latent. We don't have to go to a teacher or a religion to answer these things. We only have to look deeply to be able to see for ourselves.

This is because that is. This arises because that arises. For there to be a father, there has to be a child; and if there is a child, there has to be a father. If there's an elder brother, there must be a younger brother;

and if there's a younger brother it's because there is an elder brother. There is night because there is day. These things rely on each other in order to exist.

"Because there is ignorance, there are impulses; because there are impulses, there is consciousness; because there is consciousness, there is the psyche-soma; because there is the psyche-soma, there are the six senses; because there are the six senses, there is contact; because there is contact, there is feeling; because there is feeling, there is craving; because there is craving, there is grasping; because there is grasping, there is becoming; because there is becoming, there is birth; because there is birth, there are old age, death, grief, and sorrow. That is how this entire mass of suffering arises. But with the fading away of ignorance, impulses cease; with the fading away of impulses, consciousness ceases; . . . and finally birth, old age, grief, death, and sorrow will fade away. That is how this entire mass of suffering ceases."

After listening to the Buddha, the Venerable Kaccayana was enlightened and liberated from sorrow. He was able to untie all of his internal knots and attain arhatship.

Here the Buddha speaks about the twelve links of Dependent Co-arising. The first link is ignorance (*avidya*), and it informs all the other links. *Vidya* means seeing, understanding, or light. Avidya means blindness, lack of understanding, or lack of light. The second link is volitional action (*samskara*), motivating energy, and the impulse to cling to being. The third link is consciousness (*vijñana*). Consciousness is filled with unwholesome and erroneous tendencies, which bring about suffering. The fourth link is the psyche-soma, mind and body. It is also called *namarupa*, name and form, referring to the mental element and physical element of our being. Both mind and body are objects of our consciousness. The fifth link is the six *ayatana*s, which are the six sense organs (eyes, ears, nose, tongue, body, and mind) accompanied by their objects (forms, sounds, smells, tastes, tactile objects, and objects of mind). These six ayatanas do not exist separately from mind/body (the fourth link), but are listed separately to help us see them more clearly.

The sixth link is the contact (*sparsha*) between sense organ and sense object; this brings about sense consciousness. When eyes and form, ears and sound, nose and smell, tongue and taste, body and touch, and mind and object of mind come into contact, sense consciousness is born. Contact is an important basis for feelings (*vedana*), the seventh link. Feelings can be pleasant, unpleasant, neutral, or mixed. We tend to become very attached to our feelings. The eighth link is craving (*trishna*), or desire. The ninth link is grasping, or attachment (*upadana*). It means we are caught, in thrall to the object. The tenth link is becoming (*bhava*), being, or coming to be. Because we desire something, it comes to be. We have to look deeply to know what we really want. The eleventh link is birth (*jati*). The twelfth link is old age, death, and decay (*jaramarana*).

The Buddha said that the teachings on the twelve links of causation are the essence of his teaching. The twelve links were never meant to be understood in a linear way, with each link leading only to the next. Each link could not exist without all the others; in this way we can say the links are "empty." Each link in the chain of Dependent Co-arising is both a cause and an effect of all the other links in the chain. In each there is ignorance, in each there is consciousness.

Studying the twelve links of Dependent Co-arising helps us diminish the element of ignorance and increase the element of clarity. When our ignorance is diminished, craving, hatred, pride, doubt, and views are also diminished, and love, compassion, joy, and equanimity are increased.

If you look into your body or your emotion in one moment of your daily life, you will see that all of the twelve links are present in that moment. These twelve causes and conditions lean on each other, are committed to each other, and bring about the great mass of suffering. Each one of the twelve links is in relationship with the other eleven. If you don't practice mindfully, you allow this cycle of suffering to continue.

When we practice mindfulness, we can see that the twelve links of Dependent Co-arising can be informed by wisdom instead of by ignorance. When wisdom is the first link, all the other links are influenced by it. For example, sometimes a feeling is accompanied not by ignorance, but by understanding, lucidity, or loving kindness, which can result in compassionate action. To say that feeling brings about craving is not precise enough. Feeling with attachment and ignorance brings about craving. In the cycle based on ignorance, living beings drift and sink because of their deluded minds. When feelings are conditioned by wisdom, Dependent Co-arising can also bring about mindfulness, liberation, and nirvana. The cycle based on clarity and awareness is the one in which the bodhisattvas realize awakening.

When you light up the lamp of awareness, you will see how the twelve links of Dependent Co-arising are working. You will say, "Let's not let the links work like that anymore, we've suffered enough already." When we bring mindfulness into the picture, our ignorance becomes less dark, and clarity arises. From mindfulness arises the clarity of consciousness. Within consciousness there is ignorance, but there is also the seed of awakening and mindfulness. If we light up the lamp of mindfulness it will make the darkness disappear.

Very often our suffering and despair help us to awaken; thus, clarity can come from ignorance. When the lamp is alight the ignorance in our attachment and despair will weaken and transform. Our clarity gives rise to *bodhicitta*, the great aspiration. If you have a great aspiration, it's because you've seen suffering, have awakened to the presence of suffering, and want to put an end to it. Clarity brings about bodhicitta, the aspiration to attain enlightenment for the benefit of all living beings. The great aspiration gives us the insight that we have to be there for all suffering beings.

In the cycle based on wisdom, we have something that's equivalent to psyche-soma. That is the *nirmanakaya*, the transformation body of the Buddha. We see our connection with all other living beings. Living beings contain hatred and darkness. Now our presence, like that of the flower, can bring freshness and happiness. The nirmanakaya is the form in which a bodhisattva is present. There are still the six senses, but now wisdom is their basis. For an ordinary person, the six senses are the cause of bondage because they have ignorance at their base. In the transformation body of the bodhisattva, the six senses are there, but they do not have ignorance in them; they have the great vow in them.

The transformation body of the bodhisattva is also in contact with the sense objects. There has to be contact between the sense organs and the object because the bodhisattva is in the world in order to be in touch. In that contact there is mindfulness. With mindfulness, there is clarity, great aspiration, and wisdom. Contact leads to feeling, but now feeling contains mindfulness.

When there is mindfulness, there will still be pleasant, unpleasant, and neutral feelings. But these feelings no longer contain ignorance; instead they contain great aspiration and wisdom. When there is a painful feeling the bodhisattva knows it is a painful feeling. When there is a pleasant feeling the bodhisattva knows it is a pleasant feeling. So there is no wrong perception within feelings; they are recognized for what they are. A bodhisattva can share the suffering of living beings. When she sees someone in great pain, she feels compassion, she suffers. But that kind of suffering increases her wisdom and nourishes her great aspiration. When there is mindfulness of feelings, they don't lead to craving, but to compassion and loving kindness. Seeing living beings suffer, the bodhisattva gives rise, not to anger, but to love and the mind of compassion. Living beings suffer, and because they suffer, they crave and are attached, and they spread their suffering around them. But the bodhisattva, although she feels this suffering, is still free, and has compassion and loving kindness. Loving kindness and compassion contain clarity; they are elements of true love; they don't lead to attachment, but to freedom. It's because the bodhisattva has compassion and love that she is always able to maintain her freedom. If clarity and great aspiration are lost, freedom is lost at the same time.

The substance of a bodhisattva is freedom. When the bodhisattva goes into life, she's not motivated by attachment or bondage, but by the great aspiration. The bodhisattva dwells in the dharmadhatu but is motivated by compassion and loving kindness to go into the world of birth and death. While he dwells in freedom in the dharmadhatu, he doesn't abandon the beings who are drifting and sinking in the world of suffering.

Dependent Co-arising is sometimes called great emptiness (*mahashunyata*). The word "emptiness" means free from all notions, ideas, and attachments. You can't say phenomena don't exist, you can't say they do exist, you can't say they're born or they die, you can't say phenomena are the same, you can't say they're different; all phenomena lie in their nature of emptiness and cannot be grasped.

This poem from Nagarjuna talks about emptiness and Dependent Co-arising:

All phenomena that arise interdependently,
I say that they are empty.
Words come to an end, because their message is false.
Words come to an end, because there is a Middle Way.

If we look carefully into the twelve links of Dependent Co-arising, we will see the teachings of emptiness. The Buddha said, whoever sees Dependent Co-arising sees the Buddha, and whoever has seen the Buddha has seen Dependent Co-arising. In our daily lives, we may ask, "Who am I? What am I doing here? Where did I come from? Where will I go?" These are philosophical questions. The Buddha said the reason we ask such questions is that we are caught in the idea of self, in the idea of me and mine. If we can see Dependent Co-arising, we will not ask these questions anymore.

The Buddha advises us not to study philosophy, but to give our time to looking deeply into reality, and to being able to see the true abiding of all dharmas, the suchness of all dharmas, the emptiness of all dharmas. When we see this, we will no longer be caught in the idea of "self," the idea of "is" and "is not," and in asking philosophical questions. When we see the nature of Dependent Co-arising, worldly views and worldly knowledge will no longer catch us, and we will go beyond the internal formations that are based on them.

When we can meditate on Dependent Co-arising we go beyond all these questions. The Buddha said, when we go beyond these ideas, we're like a palm tree that has had its top cut off. All our wrong perceptions will no longer arise. When we've been able to see the nature of interdependent arising, we'll overcome ideas of self, living being, and so on, and ignorance and suffering will no longer touch us. We'll no longer suffer because of our wrong views.

4: Walking the Middle Path

One day Buddha asked the monk Sona:

> "Is it true that before you became a monk you were a musician?" Sona replied that it was so. The Buddha asked, "What happens if the string of your instrument is too loose?" "When you pluck it, there will be no sound," Sona replied. "What happens when the string is too taut?" "It will break." "The practice of the Way is the same," the Buddha said.

The Sutra on the Middle Way has profound and wonderful meaning. But only when we discover how to apply the teachings in it to our daily lives can they be truly beneficial. Even when we are able to talk eloquently about the Middle Way, no-self, or Dependent Co-arising, we still need to ask: How can these teachings be put into practice every day?

The first way is to notice our attachment to the teachings themselves. Not only do views such as permanence and self need to be transcended, so do impermanence, nonself, and nirvana. The Buddha says the teachings are like a raft that helps us to the other shore. Once there, we leave the raft on the shore for others to use. The teachings, like the raft, need to be released. It's said that near the end of his life the Buddha said, "In forty-five years of teaching I have not said anything." In fact he said a lot things, but he didn't want his listeners to get caught in his words.

For ease of understanding, we speak of teachings such as impermanence, nonself, and interbeing as right views. But we know these are teachings to help us, they're not theories. For example, the notion of impermanence is to help us overcome the notion of permanence; it's not a truth to be worshipped. The teachings need to be handled skillfully so we don't get caught in them.

When presenting the twelve links of Dependent Co-arising, the Buddha says that "ignorance gives rise to impulses." "Ignorance" means that we don't understand what is happening, so we behave in a certain way. If we were able to see clearly, we would behave differently. Each one of us is caught, to a larger or a smaller extent, in our emotions, in our difficulties, and in our experiences of suffering in the past. Because we're caught, we repeat the same suffering over and over again. We have a habit energy of reacting to circumstances in a rote way. We tell ourselves that the next time that happens we won't react like this, we'll react differently. We're very determined; we make a promise to ourselves. But when that thing happens again, we still react in the old way—as we did two hundred years ago. So why do we keep repeating this? Every time we behave like this we make others suffer and we make ourselves suffer.

Our habit energy is what causes us to repeat the same behavior thousands of times. Habit energy pushes us to run, to always be doing something, to be lost in thoughts of the past or the future and to blame others for our suffering. And that energy does not allow us to be peaceful and happy in the present moment.

The practice of mindfulness helps us to recognize that habitual energy. Every time we can recognize the habit energy in us, we are able to stop and to enjoy the present moment. The energy of mindfulness is the best energy to help us embrace our habit energy and transform it.

The energy of mindfulness is the full awareness of the present moment. This energy is generated from the practice of mindful breathing, mindful walking, mindful drinking, mindful eating, and so on. The energy of mindfulness carries within itself the energy of concentration. When you are mindful of something, whether that something is a flower, a friend, or a cup of tea, you become concentrated on the object of your mindfulness. The more you are mindful, the more concentrated you become. The energy of concentration is born from the energy of mindfulness. And if you are concentrated enough, the energy of concentration contains the energy of insight. Mindfulness, concentration, and insight are the energies that make up the Buddha. These three kinds of energy can transform habit energy and lead to healing and nourishment.

A few days of practicing mindful breathing and mindful walking can make a big difference. And the practice should be pleasant, should not be hard labor. When you breathe in, you bring attention to your in-breath. "Breathing in, I know I am breathing in; breathing in, I feel alive." In that breath is your happiness.

Whenever habit energies arise, we can accept and recognize them and then they won't push us to behave in negative ways. We can say to our habit energy, "I will look after you, habit energy, I will discover what your root is."

Often, when I'm talking to a large group, giving a Dharma talk, I'll tell a story. Suppose I tell the story of a monk who doesn't practice, who just goes from festival to festival, memorial service to memorial service in different temples. He doesn't organize ceremonies in his own temple, but when he sees other temples celebrating, he goes to them. And he stays there all day. I may be telling this story just for fun, but some people may feel I'm reprimanding them specifically. I have no intention of directing what I'm saying to those particular people, but because they have that habit energy, they receive the story like an arrow, wounding them. When we suffer we make those around us suffer. We think we are the only person who is suffering, but in fact we are creating suffering for other people.

After one retreat I held, a student wrote to me and said: "I'd never felt so happy and secure as in this retreat, because nobody was allowed to talk. So I knew nobody would come and say things which would hurt me or say unkind things to me or about me." When I read that, I thought this person must have suffered a lot in the past. Probably people in his family had said things to him that hurt him very badly. I felt compassion for him. I knew how much he must have suffered. So we have to look back at our suffering and see how, without the energy of mindfulness, we suffer and we make others suffer. We may feel that it is because of someone's clumsiness or lack of mindfulness that we suffer, but we often do the same to others. Only when our light of mindfulness shines on all of us will we be able to take steps in lightness, ease, and freedom.

The suffering that we have borne in the past is immeasurable. Compared with our suffering of the past, our suffering of today is very small. So why do we continue to make each other suffer? In the great ocean the big fish are eating the little fish. A baby fish is swimming along and suddenly a huge fish comes up behind, opens up its mouth, and the little fish becomes the food of the big fish. There are bears that go down to the river when they are hungry and catch the fish in their paws and eat them. "Why aren't the other fish caught and eaten? Why am I caught and eaten today?" Ducklings are following their mother, and while the mother duck is eating worms, a large bird snatches up one of the baby ducklings. This is the kind of suffering we have been through in the past. We are that duckling; we are that fish. Sometimes the mother hen sees the danger and puts out her wings to protect her baby chicks, so that the large bird doesn't swoop down and take them away. Sometimes we've wanted to protect our children, but we haven't succeeded. And these sufferings take place in life all the time. We have suffered so much as birds, as fish, as trees, and all those sufferings have become a great mass of suffering within us.

Our Sangha, our practice community, plays an important role in helping us put an end to the habit energy of suffering. The Sutra on the Middle Way reminds us that the idea of a self is just a shell. Only when we can get out of the stiff shell of the self can we see that our suffering in the present is the suffering of our ancestors and of our descendants. We are the continuation of our mothers; we are our mothers. Our children, our students are already in us, suffering with us. So we should not waste a moment or a day of our practice.

Every day is an opportunity for us to practice liberation—liberating our ancestors and our descendants within us. With meditation, we can relive the moments of our lives that have been full of fear and suffering, and we can practice mindful breathing and breathe for all our ancestors and all our descendants. When I am breathing, I'm not breathing for one mother and one child, but for many mothers and many children. Breathing like that for ten minutes can bring liberation if we practice properly, and the insight we use in our practice is the insight of the Middle Way.

The teachings on Right View and Dependent Co-arising also offer us guidance on how to be with others. When we look deeply into others, we are looking deeply into ourselves at the same time. If we think the other person is someone other than us, that his or her success or failure has nothing to do with us, then we have not been successful in our looking deeply. The happiness of that person is linked to our own happiness. If we're not happy, the other person can't be happy, and our larger community will not be happy.

The monkey knows that the fruit with a lot of prickles is very sweet inside, so he uses a stone to break the skin of that prickly fruit. There may be people in our lives we feel are too difficult to talk to or be with. We see them as severe, not generous, not able to embrace and accept us. But that is only our first experience. There may be a great deal of love and compassion in that person, which is obscured by habit energies. If we look deeply and see what is obstructing that person, we can help them. If we can break the shell of habit energies we will enjoy the sweetness of the love that is inside. We can be like the monkey who is able to pierce the tough prickly skin and savor the fruit inside.

The aim of Buddhist practice is to go from the field of phenomena down into the level of substance, of true nature. We go from being caught in conventional designations—parent, child, I, you, flower, cloud, coming, going—down into the level of the Middle Way which goes beyond all conventional designation. Anger and hatred arise because we are caught in the conventional designation. If we look deeply and carefully, we will see ourselves in our parents and will see our parents in ourselves. When we can see that, we can be in touch with a very deep level of reality, and our suffering and sadness will evaporate.

If we continue to be imprisoned by the habit energies of the past, we will never liberate ourselves, nor can we liberate the thousands of generations of ancestors and descendants in us. But if in our daily lives, while we are washing up, cleaning the vegetables, driving the car, working in the garden, or watering the plants, we use that time to truly look at ourselves and each other to see our true nature and the true nature of others, we can gradually get out of the ropes that bind us. Our fear, our sorrow, our complexes are all born from our discriminating ideas of coming and going, self and the other. Looking deeply in our daily lives like this is the true work of the practice, the cream of Buddhist teaching.

When we first come to Buddhism, we can immediately experience mindful breathing and it make us feel better. There's a tendency to grasp hold of this and think, "If I can breathe, if I can smile, if I'm able to follow my breathing when I feel a bit angry, then that's enough already." This kind of thinking stops us from going deeply into the deep teaching of nondiscrimination that brings us to fearlessness, to the insight that helps us break through all our fetters. That is the greatest gift and the greatest fruit of the practice. If we're caught in ideas, caught in sorrow, caught in the way other people treat us, then that is a terrible waste of our lives.

The teachings on Right View and Dependent Co-arising offer us guidance on how to be with others. When we look deeply into others, we are looking deeply into ourselves at the same time. If we think the other person is someone other than us, that his or her success or failure has nothing to do with us, then we have not been successful in our looking deeply. The happiness of that person is linked to our own happiness. If we're not happy, the other person can't be happy, and our larger community will not be happy.

The insight generated from our understanding of the Sutra on the Middle Way can dissolve habit energy and generate the energies of great insight, love, and compassion. These energies can liberate us from suffering and help us to hand on to the future generations enough insight and love to release them from suffering like ours. We have to learn to live in happiness in the present moment. Every moment we walk in the present moment is a moment of liberation. Every step like this can liberate us and liberate countless generations of ancestors and descendants. With each step we walk with the Buddha.

THE SUTRA ON THE EIGHT REALIZATIONS OF THE GREAT BEINGS

FO SHUO BA DA REN JUE JING

Contents

The Sutra on the Eight Realizations of the Great Beings[71]

Wholeheartedly, day and night, a disciple of the Buddha should recite and meditate on the eight realizations discovered by the great beings.

The First Realization is the awareness that the world is impermanent. All political regimes are subject to fall; all things composed of the four elements are empty and contain the seeds of suffering.[72] Human beings are composed of Five Skandhas (aggregates) and are without a separate self.[73] They are always in the process of change—constantly being born and constantly dying. They are empty of self, without sovereignty. The mind is the source of all confusion, and the body is the forest of all impure actions. If we meditate on these facts, we can gradually be released from samsara, the round of birth and death.

The Second Realization is the awareness that more desire brings more suffering. All hardships in daily life arise from greed and desire. Those with little desire and ambition are able to relax, their bodies and minds free from entanglement.

The Third Realization is that the human mind is always searching for possessions and never feels fulfilled. This causes impure actions to ever increase. Bodhisattvas however, always remember the principle of having few desires.[74] They live a simple life in peace in order to practice the Way, and consider the realization of Perfect Understanding as their only career.

The Fourth Realization is the awareness of the extent to which laziness is an obstacle to practice. For this reason, we must practice diligently to destroy the unwholesome mental factors that bind us, and to conquer the four kinds of Mara, in order to free ourselves from the prisons of the Five Aggregates and the three worlds.[75]

The Fifth Realization is the awareness that ignorance is the cause of the endless round of birth and death. Therefore, bodhisattvas always remember to listen and learn in order to develop their understanding and eloquence. This enables them to educate living beings and bring them to the realm of great joy.

The Sixth Realization is the awareness that poverty creates hatred and anger, which creates a vicious cycle of negative thoughts and activity. When practicing generosity, bodhisattvas consider everyone, friends and enemies alike, as equal. They do not condemn anyone's past wrong-doings, nor do they hate those who are presently causing harm.

The Seventh Realization is that the five categories of desire lead to difficulties.[76] Although we are in the world, we should try not to be caught up in worldly matters. A monk, for example, has in his possession only three robes and one bowl. He lives simply in order to practice the Way. His precepts keep him free of attachment to worldly things, and he treats everyone equally and with compassion.

The Eighth Realization is the awareness that the fire of birth and death is raging, causing endless suffering everywhere. We should take the Great Vow to help everyone, to suffer with everyone, and to guide all beings to the realm of great joy.

These eight realizations are the discoveries of great beings, buddhas, and bodhisattvas who have diligently practiced the way of compassion and understanding. They have sailed the Dharmakaya boat to the shore of nirvana, but then they return to the ordinary world, having abandoned the five desires, with their minds and hearts directed toward the noble way, using these eight realizations to help all beings recognize the suffering in this world.[77] If the disciples of the Buddha recite these eight realizations and meditate on them, they will put an end to countless misunderstandings and difficulties and progress toward enlightenment, leaving behind the world of birth and death, dwelling forever in peace.

1: The Eight Realizations and the Eleven Guidelines for Daily Living

---

When I was seventeen and in my first year of novice studies at a Buddhist monastery in Vietnam, I had to memorize the Sutra on the Eight Realizations of the Great Beings. Over sixty years have passed, and I still find this text to be torches that help light my path.

In 1978, I became involved in a project to rescue Vietnamese boat people in the South China Sea. We printed the Sutra on the Eight Realizations of the Great Beings in a small booklet in Vietnamese to help the survivors as they found a new home somewhere in the world. Soon, we found this sutra to be very helpful for those in the West as well. All of us, whatever our past experiences, are struggling to realize full consciousness in our daily lives.

The most accessible way to approach the Sutra on the Eight Realizations of the Great Beings is to see each of the eight items discussed as a subject of meditation. In addition, there are eleven guidelines for daily living that can be found in the sutra. Although the form of the sutra is simple, its content is extremely profound and marvelous. This sutra is not an analytical treatise or a historical artifact; it's a realistic and effective approach to meditation and a guide for our interactions with others.

THE FIRST REALIZATION

The First Realization explains and clarifies the four basic subjects of Buddhist meditation: impermanence, suffering, no-self, and impurity. We must always remember and meditate on these four principles of reality. As mentioned in the sutra, if someone meditates on these facts, she will gradually be released from samsara, the round of birth and death.

Impermanence

This refers to the transient nature of all things. From moment to moment, all things in this world, including human life, mountains, rivers, political systems, are in constant transformation. This is called impermanence in each moment. Everything passes through a period of birth, maturity, transformation, and destruction. This destruction is called impermanence in each cycle. To see the impermanent nature of all things, we must examine this closely. Doing so will prevent us from being imprisoned by the things of this world.

Suffering

Suffering has to do with the emptiness of all things. The ancient people of India said that all things are composed of four elements: earth, air, water, and fire. Acknowledging this, buddhas and bodhisattvas understand that when there is a harmonious relationship among the four elements, there is peace. When the four elements are not in harmony, there is suffering.

Because all things are created by a combination of these elements, nothing can exist independently or permanently. All things are impermanent. Consequently, when we are caught up in the things of the world, we suffer from their impermanent nature. And since all things are empty, when we are caught by things, we also suffer from their emptiness. Awareness of the existence of suffering leads us to begin to practice the way of realization. This is the first of the Four Noble Truths.[78] When we lose awareness of and do not meditate on the existence of suffering in all things, we can easily be pushed around by passions and desires for worldly things, increasingly destroying our lives in the pursuit of these desires. Only by being aware of suffering can we find its cause, confront it directly, and eliminate it.

Selflessness (no-self)

Buddhism teaches that human beings are composed of Five Aggregates, called skandhas in Sanskrit. If the form created by the four elements is empty and without self, then human beings, created by the unification of the Five Skandhas, must also be empty and without self. Human beings are involved in a transformation process from second to second, minute to minute, continually experiencing impermanence in each moment. By looking very deeply into the Five Skandhas, we can experience the selfless nature of our bodies, our passage through birth and death, and emptiness, thereby destroying the illusion that our bodies are permanent. In Buddhism, no-self is the most important subject for meditation. By meditating on no-self, we can break through the barrier between self and other. When we no longer are separate from the universe, a completely harmonious existence with the universe is created. We see that all other human beings exist in us and that we exist in all other human beings. We see that the past and the future are contained in the present moment, and we can penetrate and be completely liberated from the cycle of birth and death.

Modern science has also discovered the truth of the selfless nature of all things. The approach of South African biologist and anthropologist Lyall Watson, for example, corresponds entirely with the principle of dependent origination and no-self.[79] Scientists who meditate continuously on the selfless nature of their own bodies and minds, as well as the selfless nature of all things, will one day easily attain enlightenment.

Impurity

In terms of the nature of our bodies and minds, impurity means the absence of an immaculate state of being, one that is neither holy nor beautiful. From the Buddhist psychological and physiological standpoint, all human beings are impure. This is not a negative judgment, but an objective perspective on human beings. If we examine the constituents of our bodies from the hair on our head to the blood, pus, phlegm, excrement, urine, the many bacteria dwelling in the intestines, and the many diseases present waiting for the opportunity to develop, it seems clear that our bodies are impure and subject to decay. Our bodies also create the motivation to pursue the satisfaction of our desires and passions. That is why the sutra regards the body as the place where misdeeds gather.

Similarly, the mind is the place where misunderstandings gather. Since we are unable to see the truth of impermanence, suffering, and the selfless nature of all things, our minds often become the victims of greed and hatred, and we act as if we are individual isolated beings who will live forever. So the sutra says, "The mind is the source of all confusion."

The Second Realization

"More desire brings more suffering" is the basis of the Second Realization. Most people define happiness as the satisfaction of all desires. There are five types of desire.[80] These desires are boundless but our ability to realize them is not, and unfulfilled desires always create suffering. When desires are only partially fulfilled, we continue to pursue their complete fulfillment, and we create more suffering. Even when a desire is fulfilled, we suffer when its fulfillment terminates. It is only after we become completely exhausted from this incessant pursuit that we begin to realize the extent to which we were caught in the insatiable net of desires and passions. Then we can realize that true happiness is really a peaceful state of body and mind, and this can only exist when our desires are few. Having few desires and not seeking fulfillment through the pursuit of the five desires are great steps toward liberation.

The Third Realization

Knowing how to feel satisfied with few possessions destroys desire and greed. This means being content with material conditions that allow us to be healthy and strong enough to practice the Way. This is an effective way to cut through the net of passions and desires, attain a peaceful state of body and mind, have more time to help others, and be free to realize the highest goal: the development of concentration and understanding to attain realization. Knowing how to feel satisfied with few possessions helps us avoid buying unnecessarily and becoming part of an economic system that exploits others, and it enables us to decrease our involvement in the pollution of our environment.

The Fourth Realization

Diligent practice destroys laziness. After we cease looking for joy in desires and passions and know how to feel satisfied with few possessions, we must not be lazy, letting days and months slip by neglectfully. Great patience and diligence are needed continually to develop our concentration and understanding in the endeavor of self-realization. We must use all of our time to meditate on the four truths of impermanence, suffering, selflessness, and impurity, the first four subjects of meditation. We must penetrate deeply into the profound meaning of The Four Establishments of Mindfulness, practicing, studying, and meditating on the postures and cycles (becoming, maturing, transformation, and destruction) of our bodies as well as our feelings,[81] sensations, mental formations, and consciousness. We should read sutras and other writings that explain meditation, correct sitting, and controlling the breath, such as the Satipatthana Sutta and The Mahaprajñaparamita Heart Sutra. We have to follow the teachings of these sutras and practice them in an intelligent way, choosing the methods that best apply to our own situation. As necessary, we can modify the methods suggested in order to accommodate our own needs. Our energy must also be regulated until all the basic desires and passions—greed, anger, narrow-mindedness, arrogance, doubt, and preconceived ideas—are uprooted. At this time we will know that our bodies and minds are liberated from the imprisonment of birth and death, the Five Skandhas, and the three worlds.

THE FIFTH REALIZATION

Concentration and understanding destroy narrow-mindedness. Among the basic desires and passions, narrow-mindedness has the deepest roots. When these roots are loosened, all other desires and passions—greed, anger, doubt, and preconceived ideas—are also uprooted. Knowing this, we can make a great effort to meditate on the truths of impermanence, no-self, and the dependent origination of all things. Once the roots of ignorance are severed, we can liberate ourselves and teach others to break through the chains of birth and death.

The first four subjects of meditation are to help us attain liberation. The next four subjects have the aim of helping others attain liberation, thus clearly and solidly uniting Theravada and Mahayana Buddhist thought.

THE SIXTH REALIZATION

Every person, no matter what their wealth, is equally capable of practicing generosity. Some people think that they can practice generosity only if they are wealthy. This isn't true. Some people who are very wealthy do practice generosity, but many only do charity with the aim of gaining merit, profiting, or pleasing others. People whose lives are grounded in compassion are seldom rich because they share whatever they have with others. They are not willing to enrich their lives financially at the cost of others' poverty. Many people misunderstand the Buddhist expression "practicing generosity" to mean casually giving five or ten cents to a beggar on the street if we happen to have it in our pockets.

The practice of generosity is more beautiful than that. It is both modest and grand. Practicing generosity means continually acting in a way that will help equalize the difference between the wealthy and the impoverished. Whatever we do to ease human suffering and create social justice can be considered practicing generosity. That is not to say that we must become active in any political system. To engage in partisan political action that leads to a power struggle among opposing parties and causes death and destruction is not what we mean by practicing generosity.

How can a person practicing "knowing how to feel satisfied with few possessions" also practice generosity? It is by living simply. Almost everyone who spends his or her life serving and helping others, sacrificing themselves for the sake of humanity, lives simply. If they live their lives worrying about making money and gaining merit, how can they practice generosity? Mahatma Gandhi lived a very simple life; nevertheless his merit helping humanity and saving human beings was immeasurable. There are thousands of people among us who live very simply, while being very helpful to many, many others. They do not have as great a reputation as Gandhi, but their merit is no less than his. It is enough for us just to be a little more attentive and aware of the presence of people like these. They do not practice generosity by giving money that they do not possess, but rather by giving their time, energy, love, and care their entire lives.

Practicing generosity in a Buddhist context means to consider everyone equal, not to discriminate against anyone. There are cruel persons and kind persons among the poor and destitute, just as there are among the wealthy, and we must not exclude the cruel ones from our practice.

As the sutra states, "Bodhisattvas consider everyone, friends and enemies alike, as equal. They do not condemn anyone's past wrongdoings, nor do they hate those who are presently doing harm." This expresses the spirit of Mahayana Buddhism. Poverty creates anger, hatred, and wrongdoing. If we teach Buddhist philosophy though lectures, but do not practice generosity to ease the suffering of others, we have not yet attained the essence of Buddhism. We should practice generosity with compassion and not disdain, without discriminating against people who, because of their poverty, have caused anger and hatred.

THE SEVENTH REALIZATION

While living in society, we should not be defiled by it. We must live in harmony with society in order to help others, without being caught by the five desires, living like the lotus flower that blooms in the mud and yet remains pure and unstained. Practicing the way of liberation does not mean avoiding society, but helping in it. Before our capacity to help becomes strong and solid, we may be defiled by living in society. For this reason, bodhisattvas meditate on the detrimental nature of the five desires and firmly decide to live simply in order to practice generosity without discrimination. Thus, living in society and not being stained by it is to practice the Six Paramitas. *Paramita* means to help others reach the other shore, the shore of liberation from sickness, poverty, hunger, ignorance, desires and passions, and birth and death. The Six Paramitas are giving, observing the precepts, using diligent effort, endurance, concentration, and understanding.

THE EIGHTH REALIZATION

We should create in ourselves the firm decision to help others. We must make a deep and solemn vow to overcome the difficulties, dangers, and suffering that may occur while helping others. Since the suffering in society is limitless, the willingness and devotion to practice the way of helping others must also be limitless. Thus, the Mahayana spirit is an endless source of energy that inspires us to practice generosity without discrimination. With the Mahayana spirit, we can withstand the many challenges and humiliations encountered in society and are able to continue to practice the Way. This will bring great happiness to others.

ELEVEN GUIDELINES FOR DAILY LIFE

The Mahayana Buddhist practice of the Six Paramitas is, in part, inspired by this sutra.

The Sutra on the Eight Realizations of the Great Beings is a great resource for meditation. But it is not intended for us to simply meditate on this sutra and then to continue living our lives as before. To fully benefit from this sutra, we must also practice and observe its teachings. Here are eleven guidelines for daily life, based on the insights found in the sutra:

I

While meditating on the body, do not hope or pray to be exempt from sickness. Without sickness, desires and passions can easily arise.

2

While acting in society, do not hope or pray not to have any difficulties. Without difficulties, arrogance can easily arise.

3

While meditating on the mind, do not hope or pray not to encounter hindrances. Without hindrances, present knowledge will not be challenged or broadened.

4

While working, do not hope or pray not to encounter obstacles. Without obstacles, the vow to help others will not deepen.

5

While developing a plan, do not hope or pray to achieve success easily. With easy success, arrogance can easily arise.

6

While interacting with others, do not hope or pray to gain personal profit. With the hope for personal gain, the spiritual nature of the encounter is diminished.

7

While speaking with others, do not hope or pray not to be disagreed with. Without disagreement, self-righteousness can flourish.

8

While helping others, do not hope or pray to be paid. With the hope of remuneration, the act of helping others will not be pure.

9

If you see personal profit in an action, do not participate in it. Even minimal participation will stir up desires and passions.

10

When wrongly accused, do not attempt to exonerate yourself. Attempting to defend yourself will create needless anger and animosity.

11

The Buddha spoke of sickness and suffering as effective medicines. Times of difficulties and accidents are also times of freedom and realization. Obstacles can be a form of liberation. The Buddha reminded us that the army of evil can be the guards of the Dharma. Difficulties are required for success. The person who mistreats one can be one's good friend. One's enemies are as an orchard or garden. The act of doing someone a favor can be as base as the act of casting away a pair of old shoes. The abandonment of material possessions can be wealth, and being wrongly accused can be the source of strength to work for justice.

The Sutra on Happiness

Mangala Sutta

Contents

The Sutra on Happiness

I heard these words of the Buddha one time when the Lord was living in the vicinity of Savatthi at the Anathapindika Monastery in the Jeta Grove. Late at night, a *deva* appeared whose light and beauty made the whole Jeta Grove shine radiantly. After paying respects to the Buddha, the deva asked him a question in the form of a verse:

"Many gods and men are eager to know
what are the greatest blessings
which bring about a peaceful and happy life.
Please, Tathagata, will you teach us?"

(This is the Buddha's answer):
"Not to be associated with the foolish ones,
To live in the company of wise people,
Honoring those who are worth honoring—
This is the greatest happiness.

"To live in a good environment,
To have planted good seeds
And to realize that you are on the right path—
This is the greatest happiness.

"To have a chance to learn and grow,
To be skillful in your profession or craft,
Practicing the precepts and loving speech—
This is the greatest happiness.

"To be able to serve and support your parents,
To cherish your own family,
To have a vocation that brings you joy—
This is the greatest happiness.

"To live honestly, generous in giving,
To offer support to relatives and friends,
Living a life of blameless conduct—
This is the greatest happiness.

"To avoid unwholesome actions,
Not caught by alcoholism or drugs,
And to be diligent in doing good things—
This is the greatest happiness.

"To be humble and polite in manner,
To be grateful and content with a simple life,
Not missing the occasion to learn the Dharma—
This is the greatest happiness.

"To persevere and be open to change,
To have regular contact with monks and nuns,
And to fully participate in Dharma discussions—
This is the greatest happiness.

"To live diligently and attentively,
To perceive the Noble Truths,
And to realize nirvana—
This is the greatest happiness.

"To live in the world
With your heart undisturbed by the world,
With all sorrows ended, dwelling in peace—
This is the greatest happiness.

"For the one who accomplishes this
Is unvanquished wherever she goes;
Always he is safe and happy—
Happiness lives within oneself."

1: The Greatest Happiness

The Pali version of this sutra is called the Mangala Sutta.[82] Mangala means a good omen, a forewarning of something to come, usually something positive that will bring happiness and prosperity. The word also connotes a blessing because in this sutra the Buddha teaches about the most important blessings, those things that bring happiness.

This sutra can be broken down, stanza by stanza, for meditation, as well as reflected on as a whole. It is broken down here, for closer study and reflection.

> "Not to be associated with the foolish ones,
> To live in the company of wise people,
> Honoring those who are worth honoring—
> This is the greatest happiness."

The greatest blessing is to have good, wise, kindhearted friends close by. We can't be happy unless we have a sane, healthy space within us and around us. We need a habitat that is beautiful and nourishing, and that gives us the safety and the freedom that we need.

It is a great blessing to be among friends who are practicing kindness and refraining from violence, stealing, and cruelty, and not caught up in addiction.

A community that practices love and understanding is the best antidote to addiction to drugs, alcohol, and casual and careless sex. When people suffer, they look for these distractions in order to forget their pain. But these things only distract us temporarily from our suffering, they don't heal us.

Our community can be a family that sustains us. We can't handpick everybody with whom we interact in our daily life, but we can choose to live among those who are kind and virtuous. When we can interact with those who are honorable and have great virtue, we are creating conditions that will bring us lasting happiness.

"To live in a good environment,
To have planted good seeds
And to realize that you are on the right path—
This is the greatest happiness."

"To live in a good environment" means to live in a place where the surroundings and all the activities have the purpose of nourishing us and building community. Without this base environment, we can't go very far. When we practice meditation together, eat together, or work together in a loving and aware way, we are nourishing our peace and harmony.

The physical environment and the presence of others is very important. Often, if we are home alone, even sitting for fifteen minutes of meditation seems impossible. We think we have so many other things to do, or perhaps we feel silly sitting alone like that. But if everyone around us is sitting, we find it much easier! That's why creating a nourishing environment is crucial. Only with this support, can we be a source of joy for ourselves and others.

Community—called Sangha in Buddhism—and time are the two ingredients of the universal medicine. If you can take that medicine every day for a number of years, then you have a chance. You become a plant, a tree, deeply rooted in the soil of the Sangha. Happiness and love become possible. And then you can go back and help your own blood family, your own spiritual community, and your society.

It's crucial that we all learn the art of Sangha building and figure out how to create a nourishing, harmonious environment in our lifetimes. If we do not have this base, then there is nothing to keep us on the right path and keep us from entering the hell realms or the realm of the hungry ghosts. We don't need to leave this Earth to look for hell. Hell realms are everywhere, even in the town in which we live. There are hell realms that we have visited, or that we have lived through, and we know that these hell realms are real. We may have been caught in situations of abuse, violence, cruelty, fear, or addiction. We may have been carried away by strong emotions, such as hatred, jealousy, or infatuation, and so committed unwholesome actions. And we know that all over the world countless living beings are suffering in situations of war, poverty, injustice, and environmental destruction.

Hungry ghosts are demons who are perpetually craving food but are unable to take in nourishment. Hungry ghosts are not a myth—they live among us as people who may have enough food and clothing but who are still hungry for knowledge, for love, for hope, and for something to believe in. We have to build community a little bit everywhere so these hungry ghosts can find refuge. It is the atmosphere of harmony and community that can help the hungry ghosts get rooted and undo their knots of suffering.

With our nourishing community around us, we can find the right path to stability, ease, and liberation. Having a path is wonderful. Seeing the path is already great happiness. There is no reason to be fearful or confused anymore. Once we have recognized the path, our sense of loss, confusion, and despair dissipate. Happiness becomes immediately possible.

> "To have a chance to learn and grow,
>   To be skillful in your profession or craft,
>   Practicing the precepts and loving speech—
>   This is the greatest happiness."

"To have a chance to learn and grow" means to have the opportunity to have a good education as well as to learn the Dharma. Learning is something that must happen every day, even for the Buddha! We want to have a vocation that does not cause harm to others or to the environment. When we can learn and practice our skills at the same time, we support ourselves and our families, this is already a great blessing. There are many lucrative vocations that keep us twisting and turning in bed at night because they are not ethical. Those vocations cause harm to others or to the environment, and they force us to lie and hide the truth. Even though these jobs may be lucrative, they cause us a lot of suffering, suffering that goes deep into our soul. When we are able to find a job that expresses our ideal of compassion, happiness arises, even if the job is not as lucrative. Having a vocation that does not cause harm to others, to the environment, and through which we can express our compassion is a cause for great happiness.

Twenty-five hundred years ago, the Buddha offered his lay students five precepts, or guidelines, to help them live peaceful, wholesome, and happy lives. We call them the Five Mindfulness Trainings. Mindfulness—the awareness of what is going on in our bodies, our feelings, our minds, and in the world—is the basis of each training. With mindfulness, we can avoid harming ourselves and others; we can protect ourselves, our families, and our society; and we can ensure safety and happiness, now and in the future.

Even if we are happy in our work and following the precepts, it still requires daily commitment to practice loving speech and refrain from speaking to others with harsh words. When we use loving speech, we avoid misunderstanding and much suffering. Even if other people use harsh language when talking to us, we will suffer less if we use only loving speech in return. When we have understanding and compassion, we have lightness and we can communicate well with other people, even those who are violent and cruel. We can accept them; we know they are unhappy and that they are victims of their own anger, violence, and discrimination. When compassion and understanding are in us, we are no longer motivated by the desire for punishment or revenge. Loving speech becomes available to us and communication becomes possible.

Without real communication, happiness can't exist. To be surrounded by family, friends, and a spiritual community that know how to use loving speech is a great daily blessing. Because happiness is possible here on Earth, the Buddha often spoke of practical blessings such as this.

"To be able to serve and support your parents,
To cherish your own family,
To have a vocation that brings you joy—
This is the greatest happiness."

Your parents are the ones who raised you and cared for you when you were little. Now that you are an adult, you can support your parents as they supported you. That is the highest blessing. There are many ways to support parents. We can offer financial support if we have that resource, but we can also offer spiritual and emotional support. Financial offerings are wonderful; however, more people suffer spiritually than financially. If we know how to practice and keep the mindfulness trainings, then we become a pillar of our family, able to support them in times of suffering and difficulty.

A long monastic history demonstrates this point. Although monastics don't hold jobs in the secular world and don't have money to send home to their parents, if they practice diligently, with equanimity and happiness, they are able to help many people and their family also benefits from this. In difficult times, they can be spiritual leaders, bringing reconciliation to their families.

A monk who practices successfully becomes the spiritual leader in his family, even though he may be very young. When a monastic opens her heart to intervene, her brothers, sisters, aunts, and uncles listen to her because she represents a source of spiritual love.

We do not need to become monastics to have this role in our families. If we use loving speech, let go of our attachment to outcomes, and base our acts on compassion and love instead of anger and jealousy, we can become pillars of support for our families.

As a practitioner, our aim is not to make a lot of money. Our aim is to transform the suffering in our hearts, to live in equanimity, peace, and happiness, and to offer happiness to our family and those around us. Our happiness multiplies exponentially when we see that we can bring happiness to those around us. This is reality, not superstition. In a retreat of five hundred people, there may be hundreds of them who come back to thank us after they have practiced. We can see the transformation in them. As each of us becomes more at ease and more aware of our capacity to love, we are more able to reconcile with our families and our loved ones if there has been conflict. Easing a long conflict with a loved one is a great source of happiness right in that very moment. We don't need to wait ten years to reap the happiness that is the fruit of our practice.

> "To live honestly, generous in giving,
> To offer support to relatives and friends,
> Living a life of blameless conduct—
> This is the greatest happiness."

"To live honestly" is to act virtuously, to be just, and to offer ourselves to life. To be generous is not simply to share our money, material resources, and technical knowledge; generosity does not require money. The offering of wealth, goods, or knowledge is only one of the many forms of generosity. There is a second form of generosity, offering the Dharma. We can always offer and model the way to practice to alleviate suffering. This offering is much more precious than the financial offering. Most precious is the third kind of offering, the gift of non-fear, *abhaya*. The greatest gift in life is to live without fear and to teach others to do so as well. The offering of material goods, of the Dharma, and of non-fear are gifts from Avalokiteshvara Bodhisattva.

Many people are victims of their fear. If we can alleviate someone's fear, that is the greatest gift that we can offer them. Our lives will be filled with happiness if we can help others around us. But if we spend our whole lives building up our names and our fortunes, then we cannot find happiness. We might have a lot of money, a big house, a luxurious car, but that's not real happiness. We can only taste real happiness when we can help others around us. And we have to start with those in our family and the dear friends around us. We have to help family, relatives, and friends first before we are capable of helping others outside our circle. If we're successful in helping our brothers and sisters in the Sangha, then we definitely will be able to help our loved ones. If, in our daily lives, we can't help our brothers and sisters, then how can we offer help to others? We have to be successful in helping the people around us alleviate their suffering. That is the highest blessing, and that blessing has a lasting effect.

To be able to act without regret is a source of great happiness. This means we have nothing to regret in our words or actions toward others. We should be able to ask ourselves, "Have I done anything to my teacher, my friend, my father, my mother, that has made me feel regret later?" Asking this question will help us avoid any hint of regret, and will ensure that our speech and actions will not cause harm to others.

When our speech and actions cause no harm, we face a future without remorse. If we are burdened with regret, happiness is impossible. If we have erred in the past, or said something that caused harm, we can transform that past action and regret through the process of Beginning Anew.[83] We can commit ourselves to acting and speaking peacefully in the future, and then lasting happiness will again be available to us. If we can transform our minds and be determined not to say things or act in ways that will cause regret, then our minds will be cleansed and become luminous, and all the mistakes and errors of the past will completely disappear.

This is practicing according to the teaching of the Buddha. The errors originated in our minds, and when we transform our minds, we have the determination to refrain from committing the same errors in the future. When we transform our minds, we are immediately cleansed. The guilt we feel is lifted and the dark past disappears. This is called the practice of Beneficial Regret and Beginning Anew. Only when we're determined to make a vow to ourselves and our Sangha, that we will not commit such acts or speak such words, can our errors and our guilt be lifted. But this requires a strong determination, and our determination won't be strong if we don't make this vow in front of both our Sangha and the Buddha.

Thus, kneeling down to prostrate, practicing Beginning Anew, and taking the Five Mindfulness Trainings with determination and resolve, will instantly make our guilt from the past disappear. When the mind is no longer loaded with guilt, then the guilt no longer exists. That's the principle of Beneficial Regret and Beginning Anew in Buddhism, being able to act without a hint of guilt. In English we can also call it "blameless conduct."

> "To avoid unwholesome actions,
>   Not caught by alcoholism or drugs,
>   And to be diligent in doing good things—
>   This is the greatest happiness."

Our society is organized in such a way that it creates lonely people by the tens of thousands every day. And when we carry such despair and loneliness within us, it creates a vacuum. We feel compelled to fill that vacuum and forget our suffering with drugs, alcohol, careless sex, and the kind of entertainment that destroys our bodies and minds. Guns, armies, and prisons can't solve the problem of drugs and alcohol. The only way to ease this sense of emptiness and loneliness is to create an environment where young people can live joyfully. And if we ourselves don't live joyfully, we can't help our children or provide them with a good environment either.

Any speech, act, or thought that we feel might cause harm to others or to ourselves, is unwholesome. Even a joke that causes others to suffer or hurts their feelings is unwholesome. Not only do the victims suffer, but the perpetrators also share the suffering. Though others can't read your mind, you still suffer from negative thoughts. You may suffer tremendously, even if you're the only one who knows it.

Anything that clouds our minds is considered an intoxicant, whether it's drugs, alcohol, or gossip. We consume these intoxicants thinking that they will make us happy, but only when our minds are clear does happiness truly become available to us.

We should also be diligent in doing good deeds. If there's any work that can bring happiness to ourselves or to others, we should do it without hesitation. Even when work benefits others, we too taste the fruit of happiness from it. These good deeds are blessings, and the happiness that comes from doing them will surely follow.

> "To be humble and polite in manner,
> To be grateful and content with a simple life,
> Not missing the occasion to learn the Dharma—
> This is the greatest happiness."

To be humble means that you don't put yourself above somebody else. We can learn to be humble and to have reverence for all others, even when they are younger than we are. A young child deserves to be treated with humility and respect.

Young children often invoke a true sense of contentment and gratitude, for they are content with very little. A stick can provide hours of joy and entertainment to a child. In order to be happy, we have to learn to live simply. When we live simply, we have much more time and we can be in touch with the many wonders of life. Living simply is the criterion for the new culture, the new civilization. With the development of technology, people lead more and more complicated lives. Shopping has replaced other activities as our mode for satisfying ourselves. The criterion for being happy is to live simply and to have harmony and peace in yourself and between yourself and the people around you, without aggressiveness, irritation, and anger. We must know the limit, we must know how much is enough. This is the antidote for wanting more and more and more. You know what is sufficient, what is enough for you.

There is a Vietnamese proverb, "Tri tuc, tien tuc, dai tuc, ha thoi tuc." That means, settling for "good enough" is enough. If we wait until all our needs and wants are met, we may wait forever. "Tri tuc" means "realizing that this is good enough." "Good enough" means being content with the minimum amount necessary. Your shirt and pair of shoes can last another year. It's all right for three or four people to share a desk for studying, there's no need for each to have her own desk. Settling for "good enough" in terms of simple living will bring us contentment, satisfaction, and happiness immediately. As long as we think our lives are not good enough, we will not have happiness. As soon as we realize our lives are good enough, happiness immediately appears. That is the practice of contentment.

In Vietnam there's a school of Buddhism called the Four Gratitudes. Just by practicing gratitude, we can find happiness. We must be grateful to our ancestors, our parents, our teachers, our friends, the Earth, the sky, the trees, the grass, the animals, the soil, the stones. Looking at the sunlight or at the forest, we feel gratitude. Looking at our breakfast, we feel gratitude. When we live in the spirit of gratitude, there will be much happiness in our lives. The one who is grateful is the one who has much happiness, while the one who is ungrateful will not be able to have happiness.

If someone offers you a teaching, a Dharma talk, take it. Seize any opportunity to learn the Dharma. A Dharma talk is not a lecture, but an opportunity to open ourselves up and allow the deepest levels of our consciousness to be penetrated and nourished by the Dharma. Listening to a Dharma talk can take the misunderstanding and ignorance out of us. It can take away our craving, anger, and hatred. The more toxins we remove, the more our hearts will feel light and free, and happiness will be possible. Happiness grows from inside out.

Those who conduct their life according to this principle will have lasting happiness.

"To persevere and be open to change,
To have regular contact with monks and nuns,
And to fully participate in Dharma discussions—
This is the greatest happiness."

When we can yield to reason and let someone correct us without becoming angry or resentful, then we will find that happiness remains with us. It is incredibly difficult, but when our brothers and our sisters point out our faults, the best thing we can do is put our palms together and bow in appreciation, with graciousness on our faces and in our hearts.

The benefit in being close to a monk or nun is the opportunity to learn the Dharma. That is why young men and women like to hang around monks and nuns at the temple. This is a very great blessing!

A Dharma discussion is an opportunity to express ourselves and to listen and learn from others. We can share our joys, difficulties, insights, experiences, and questions. Using loving speech and deep listening, we can also focus on important matters of concern, such as how to create a good environment for our children, our children's children, our larger community, and the Earth as a whole.

> "To live diligently and attentively,
> To perceive the Noble Truths,
> And to realize nirvana—
> This is the greatest happiness."

To live diligently and attentively means walking, standing, lying down, sitting, working, eating and doing everything in mindfulness.

The Four Noble Truths are at the heart of Buddhist practice.[84] Thanks to the Four Noble Truths, we will be able to practice and realize nirvana. Nirvana is something very concrete, the absence of afflictions and the presence of solidity, freedom, and well-being. To realize nirvana is to be completely liberated and cease all suffering while we are living in the world. All afflictions are dissolved, and only perfect equanimity remains. This is the full definition of happiness.

Because we've planted good seeds in the past, we now have the opportunity to live among the sages. In a good environment it's easy for us to plant good seeds—seeds of peace, joy, community, and happiness. Today we are blessed to be able to sit in the middle of a healthy Sangha that practices with diligence and with ease; we are reaping the benefit of the good seeds we have planted in the past. We need to continue our path and not abandon our good environment.

> "To live in the world
> With your heart undisturbed by the world,
> With all sorrows ended, dwelling in peace—
> This is the greatest happiness."

Although we are still living in this mundane world, our minds can be imperturbable. We don't need to be flustered by all that we see and hear. The practice of letting go is essential for our happiness. We distance ourselves from the influences that destroy our bodies and minds, so that we are able to release the many worries and concerns that consume us and prevent us from getting in touch with the wonders of life that we need for our nourishment. There are many things we cannot let go of, and so we miss the opportunity to get in touch with what is more important, and with what is refreshing and healing that is always available to us. We get caught in a kind of prison. Recognizing that these worries and concerns are not really important, we are able to release them, and suddenly happiness comes right away.

It's like when you leave the city behind to go to the countryside. It may take forty-five minutes or an hour to get out of the city, and when the hills begin to appear and the breeze begins to caress your face, you feel so happy because you've been able to leave the city behind you. All of us have had this kind of experience.

Have you ever met someone who seems to be skilled in the art of letting go? A friend or a teacher can remind us and help us let go of worry, craving, and concern, so we can be free to encounter the wonders of life that are in the here and the now. If we see someone living in this world who is not disturbed by the ebb and flow of life, not enmeshed in afflictions, that person has freedom, that person is solid. To see such a person is the highest blessing. When we master this quality, all of our worldly afflictions dissolve and we become indestructible, completely at peace. We can become that person by practicing happiness in the present moment.

> "For the one who accomplishes this
> Is unvanquished wherever she goes;
> Always he is safe and happy—
> Happiness lives within oneself."

The World-Honored One has said that we should not predict the future based on what happened in the past. We need to base the future on our own actions in the present. Our actions are our karma, and so are our thoughts, our speech, our intentions, and our attitude. If we live in the Dharma, we can generate our own blessings. Our happiness is a lasting one that can be carried on to the next life. We can find happiness no matter what situation we might be thrown into.

Wherever we may go, we will feel the secure protection of the Dharma. Wherever we may go, we will feel strong and solid. The solidity comes from the practice. The greatest blessing is not the one that falls down from the sky and is handed to us. The greatest blessing is the happiness that each of us can generate for ourselves.

A Short History of the Sutras

The first attempt to standardize or codify the Buddha's teachings came during his lifetime when one day in the Jetavana Monastery, two monks, Yamelu and Tekula, asked the Buddha if they could translate all his teachings into the classical meter of the Vedic language. They told the Buddha that they wanted to do so in order to protect the beauty and accuracy of the Dharma. But the Buddha didn't want his teachings to become a precious object reserved for a scholarly elite. He wanted everyone to be able to study and practice the Dharma in his or her own language.

About four months after the Buddha's passing, the Venerable Mahakasyapa convened a council on Mount Saptaparnaguha at Rajgir in order to orally collate all the Buddha's teachings. Five hundred elder bhikkhus were invited to attend this Collation Council, which was sponsored by King Ajatashatru of Magadha. The language of the collation would naturally have been Ardhamagadhi, the language of the Buddha. If the local districts later developed versions in their own languages, these would have been based on the collation of the Rajgir Council.

One hundred years later, a second council was convened in Vaishali to further collate the canon of the Buddha's teachings. On this occasion, seven hundred bhikkhus were invited to attend. After the Second Council, in 375 BCE, the community of bhikkhus divided itself into two schools: the Sthavira, which tended to be conservative, and the Mahasanghika, which tended to promote development and reform. The followers of the Mahasanghika were more numerous. In the three hundred years that followed, many other schools branched off from these two schools. According to the Samayabhedoparacanacakra by

Vasumitra, who belonged to the Sarvastivada school of the Northern tradition, there were eighteen schools in all.

A third council was organized in India at Pataliputra under the patronage of King Ashoka in 244 BCE, two hundred thirty-six years after the passing of the Buddha. At that time, perhaps because King Ashoka leaned more towards the Vibhajyavada sect, the Sarvastivadins moved to the north and established their base for development in Kashmir, where they flourished for more than one thousand years.

The number of schools proliferated because of the many different ways of understanding and commenting on the teachings of the Buddha. Each school has handed down its own versions of the *Tripitaka*, the whole of Buddhist scripture that includes the *Vinaya Pitaka* (the rules for monastic conduct), the *Sutra Pitaka* (Buddhist discourses and teachings), and the *Shastra Pitaka* (scholarly explanations and summaries of the sutras). All three pitakas of the Theravada school are intact thanks to the relatively stable ground for practice in Sri Lanka. The Tripitaka of this school is written in the Pali language, which originated in western India. The Theravada arose from the Vibhajyavada, which was a school opposing the Sarvastivada.

The sutras in this collection are of both Theravada (Pali and Chinese) and Mahayana (Sanskrit and Chinese) origin. However, because the word "sutra" is commonly used in the English language, we are using it here for the whole collection. We use the word "sutta" only when it is part of the proper name of a Pali sutta, such as Anapanasati Sutta or Satipatthana Sutta.

We translate the term "sati" differently in the words Anapanasati and Satipatthana. In the former, we use "full awareness," and in the latter "mindfulness." There are no diacritical marks used in these translations. All sutras are translated from the Pali and Chinese by Thich Nhat Hanh, with Annabel Laity and Anh-Huong Nguyen. Commentaries are in original English or translated from the Vietnamese by Annabel Laity and Anh-Huong Nguyen.

To keep the translations as close to their origins as possible, the text of the original sutras have been retained with the male pronouns, *he* and *his*, throughout, although the message is intended for practitioners of any gender.

Notes

1. For more on the life of the Buddha, see Thich Nhat Hanh, *Old Path White Clouds* (Berkeley, CA: Parallax Press, 1991).
2. Savatthi (Sanskrit: Shravasti): The capital of the Koshala kingdom, about seventy-five miles west of Kapilavatthu (Sanskrit: Kapilavastu), the birthplace of the Buddha.
3. *Bhikkhu* (monk) is the Pali equivalent of the Sanskrit word *bhikshu*.
4. The Pavarana Ceremony was held at the end of each rainy season retreat, the annual three-month retreat for Buddhist monks. During the ceremony, each monk present invited the assembly to point out the weaknesses he exhibited during the retreat, in order to improve his practice and his character.

   The full moon marked the end of the lunar month. Normally, Pavarana was held at the end of the month of Assayuja (around October), but during the year in which this sutra was delivered, the Buddha extended the retreat to four months, and the ceremony was held at the end of the month of Kattika (around November).
5. The full moon day of the retreat's fourth month (Kattika) was called Komudi, or White Lotus Day, so named because *komudi* is a species of white lotus which flowers in late autumn.
6. Field of merit: Supporting a good community, like planting seeds in fertile soil, is a good investment.
7. *Arahat* (Sanskrit: *arhat*): The highest realization according to the early Buddhist traditions. *Arahat* means worthy of respect, deserving. An *arahat* is one who has rooted out all the causes of affliction and is no longer subject to the cycle of death and birth.

   The root of affliction (Sanskrit: *klesha*, Pali: *kilesa*): The ropes that bind the mind, like greed, anger, ignorance, scorn, suspicion, and wrong views. It is the equivalent to asava (Pali): suffering, pain, the poisons of the mind, the causes that subject us to birth and death, like craving, wrong views, and ignorance.
8. The first Ten Internal Formations (Sanskrit: *samyojana*) are [1] caught in the wrong view of self, [2] hesitation, [3] caught in superstitious prohibitions and rituals, [4] craving, [5] hatred and anger, [6] desire for the worlds of form, [7] desire for the formless worlds, [8] pride, [9] agitation, and [10] ignorance. These are the knots that tie us and hold us prisoners in our worldly situation. In the Mahayana, the Ten Internal Formations are listed in the following order: desire, hatred, ignorance, pride, hesitation, belief in a real self, extreme views, wrong

views, perverted views, and views advocating unnecessary prohibitions. The first five are called "dull," and the second five are called "sharp."

The fruit of never returning (Pali: *anagami-phala*): The fruit, or attainment, second only to the fruit of *arahatship*. Those who realize the fruit of never returning do not return after this life to the cycle of birth and death.

9. The fruit of returning once more (Pali: *sakadagami-phala*): The fruit, or attainment, just below the fruit of never returning. Those who realize the fruit of returning once more will return to the cycle of birth and death just one more time.

10. The fruit of Stream-Enterer (Pali: *sotapatti-phala*): The fourth highest fruit, or attainment. Those who attain the fruit of Stream-Enterer are considered to have entered the stream of awakened mind, which always flows into the ocean of emancipation.

11. The Four Establishments of Mindfulness (Pali: *satipatthana*): [1] Awareness of the body in the body, [2] Awareness of the feelings in the feelings, [3] Awareness of the mind in the mind, [4] Awareness of the objects of the mind in the objects of the mind. For further explication, see the Sutra on the Four Establishments of Mindfulness.

12. The Four Right Efforts (Pali: *padhana*): [1] Not to allow any occasion for wrongdoing to arise, [2] Once it has arisen, to find a means to put an end to it, [3] To cause right action to arise when it has not already arisen, [4] To find ways to develop right action and make it lasting once it has arisen.

The Four Bases of Success (*iddhi-pada*): Four roads that lead to realizing a strong mind: diligence, energy, full awareness, and penetration.

13. The Five Faculties (*indriya*): Five capacities, or abilities: [1] faith, [2] energy, [3] mindfulness, [4] concentration, and [5] wisdom.

The Five Powers (Pali: *bala*): The same as the Five Faculties, but seen as strengths rather than abilities.

The Seven Factors of Awakening (*bojjhanga*): [1] full attention, [2] investigating dharmas, [3] energy, [4] joy (see note 21), [5] ease, [6] concentration, [7] letting go. These are discussed in Section Four of the sutra. The Noble Eightfold Path (*atthangika-magga*): The right way of practicing, containing eight elements: [1] Right View, [2] Right Intention, [3] Right Speech, [4] Right Action, [5] Right Livelihood, [6] Right Effort on the Path, [7] Right Mindfulness, [8] Right Meditative Concentration.

The above practices, from the Four Establishments of Mindfulness through the Noble Eightfold Path, total 37, and are called *bodhipakkhiya-dhamma*, the Components of Awakening.

14. Loving kindness, compassion, joy, and equanimity (Pali: *brahmavihara*): Four beautiful, precious states of mind that are not subject to any limitation, often called the Four Limitless Meditations. Loving kindness is to give joy. Compassion is to remove suffering. Joy is happiness that nourishes ourselves and others and does not lead to future suffering. Equanimity is relinquishing, with no calculation of gain or loss, no clinging to beliefs as the truth, and no anger or sorrow.

15. The Nine Contemplations: The practice of contemplation on the nine stages of disintegration of a corpse, from the time it swells up to the time it becomes dust.

16. Joy and happiness: The word *piti* is usually translated as "joy," and the word *sukha* is usually translated as "happiness." The following example is often used

to compare *piti* with *sukha*: Someone traveling in the desert who sees a stream of cool water experiences *piti* (joy), and on drinking the water experiences *sukha* (happiness).

17. *Dharmas*: things, phenomena.

18. Disappearance, or fading (Pali: *viraga*): A fading of the color and taste of each dharma, and its gradual dissolution, and at the same time a fading and gradual dissolution of the color and taste of desire. *Raga* means a color, or dye; here it is also used to mean desire. *Viraga* is thus the fading both of color and of craving. ·

19. Cessation, or emancipation, here means the ending of all notions, concepts, and wrong views as well as the suffering that is caused by these things.

20. Letting go, or relinquishing, here means giving up any idea or any thing that we see to be illusory and empty of substance.

21. "Joy" is the translation of *niramisa*. This is the great joy that is not to be found in the realm of sensual desire.

22. Discriminating and comparing: That is to say, discriminating subject from object, comparing what is dear to us with what we dislike, what is gained with what is lost.

23. Equanimity, or letting go (Pali: *upekkha*, Sanskrit: *upeksha*): The notion of giving up discriminating and comparing subject/object, like/dislike, gain/ loss is fundamental. The Buddhism of the Mahayana school has fully developed this concept.

24. See note 11.

25. See note 17.

26. The method of counting the breath has been widely accepted and has found its way into the sutras and commentaries. The Ekottara Agama (Zeng Yi A Han) (Sutra number 125 in the Taisho Revised Tripitaka, An Ban chapter, books 7 and 8) does not mention the technique of counting the breath, but it does mention the method of combining the breathing with the Four Meditative States. Chapter 23 of the Xiu Hang Dao Di (Sutra number 606 in the Taisho Revised Tripitaka, book 5), called "The Breath Counting Chapter," identifies the method of Full Awareness of Breathing with the method of counting the breaths. This sutra also refers to the Four Meditations.

27. Sutra 606 in the Taisho Revised Tripitaka, chapter 23.

28. Sutra 125 in the Taisho Revised Tripitaka.

29. Sutra 602 in the Taisho Revised Tripitaka.

30. Parthia: Ancient country in Southwest Asia (northeast modern Iran).

31. Sutra 125 in the Taisho Revised Tripitaka. Sutra 606 in the Taisho Revised Tripitaka. Tsa A Han, or The Samyukta Agama, is Sutra collection number 99 in the Taisho.

32. See note 11.

33. See the Sutra on Knowing the Better Way to Live Alone, this volume.

34. The Four Jhanas or Meditative States (Sanskrit: *rupa dhyana*, Pali: *rupa jhana*). The Four Formless Concentrations (Sanskrit: *arupadhyana*, Pali: *arupa jhana*).

35. Thich Nhat Hanh, *Present Moment, Wonderful Moment* (Berkeley, CA: Parallax Press, 1990).

36. Thich Nhat Hanh, *The Sun My Heart* (Berkeley, CA: Parallax Press, 1988).

37. See The Heart Sutra for a more complete explanation of this point.

38. Samyukta Agama 1071. The equivalent in the Pali Canon is the Theranamo

Sutta (Samyutta Nikaya, Sutta number 10). This version is translated from the Chinese by Thich Nhat Hanh.

39. The Bhaddekaratta Sutta (Majjhima Nikaya, Sutta number 131). This version is translated from the Pali by Thich Nhat Hanh.

40. See note 3.

41. Some *gathas* written by Ekavihariya can be found in the Theragatha (Poems of the Elder Monks), verses 537–546. In these poems he praises the tranquility of living alone.

42. This conversation, so similar to the one in Samyukta Agama 1071, is from the Theranamo Sutta, Samyutta Nikaya, Sutta number 10.

43. From the Samyutta Nikaya, Sutta numbers 63 and 64.

44. Madhyama Agama 166, which is the equivalent of the Lomasakangiya-Bhaddekaratta, number 134 in the Majjhima Nikaya.

45. Madhyama Agama 167, equivalent to the Ananda-Bhaddekaratta in the Pali Canon, Majjhima Nikaya 132.

46. In the Pali Canon, see the Nagita Sutta, Anguttara Nikaya chapters 5.30, 6.42, 8.86. In the Chinese Canon, see Samyukta Agama 1250 and 1251.

47. For the full text, see Thich Nhat Hanh, *Stepping Into Freedom* (Berkeley, CA: Parallax Press, 1997).

48. Master Dharmapala translated *bhaddekaratta* as *xian shan*. *Xian* means "virtuous" or "able," *shan* means "good," "good at," or "skillful." These two words translate *bhadda* and *ratta*. But the part *eka*, "alone," which lies between *bhadda* and *ratta*, has been overlooked, although it is fundamental to the meaning of the compound.

49. Arittha is referred to here as a "vulture trainer" to distinguish him from other monks with the same name.

50. The Pali version adds two other comparisons: an impaling stake and a slaughterhouse.

51. In the Pali version there are only nine divisions of the teachings. The Chinese version gives all twelve: [1.] Discourses (*sutra*), [2.] Teachings in verse (*geya*), [3.] Predictions (*vyakarana*), [4.] Summaries in verse (*gatha*), [5.] Interdependent origination (*nidana*), [6.] Instructions by simile (*upadesha*), [7.] Quotations (*itivrittaka*), [8.] Inspired sayings (*udana*), [9.] Stories of previous births (*jataka*), [10.] Extensive explanations (*vaipulya*), [11.] Wonderful teachings (*adbhuta dharma*), [12.] Giving definitions (*avadana*).

52. "Grounds for views" are the foundations that cause us to cling to views (Sanskrit: *drshti sthana*; Pali: *ditthi thana*).

53. The Chinese version is missing the fourth *skandha*, mental formations (Sanskrit: *samskara*; Pali: *sankhara*).

54. This sentence is not found in the Pali version. Instead, we find the following sentence: "When he understands that the self does not exist in this way, he is not upset."

55. The Pali version speaks of an external source first and an internal source second.

56. Internal formations are the psychological ropes that bind us, like knots of afflictions stored in the depths of our consciousness (Sanskrit and Pali: *samyojana*). Energy leaks are the afflictions that lengthen the time we suffer and tie us to the realm of birth and death. *Ashrava* is the Sanskrit word; the Pali is *asava*;

and the literal meaning is "to leak." The meaning can also be that of "affliction," synonymous with the Sanskrit *klesha* and Pali *kilesa*.

57. "Cannot be grasped" is translated from the Chinese (Sanskrit: *anupalabhya*, "not to be grasped").

58. See note 52.

59. "Becoming" (Sanskrit: *bhava*) refers to being born and dying in a cycle of birth and death. "Craving" (Sanskrit: *trishna*) and "becoming" are two of the twelve links of interdependent origination (Sanskrit: *dvadashanga pratitya sarnutpada*).

60. The first five internal formations are desire, hatred, ignorance, pride, and doubt. They are sometimes called "dull." The other five internal knots are personality views, extreme views, wrong views, perverted views, and views relating to rituals and prohibitions, and are sometimes called "sharp." The five dull internal formations have been uprooted and shattered and cannot arise anymore.

61. According to Indian mythology, Prajapati (Pali: Pajapati) is the progenitor or the creator of the world. This role is sometimes given to Indra, Savitri, Soma, Manu, and other deities. The Chinese version lacks the following sentence that appears in the Pali version: "I say that right here and now it is impossible to find any trace of the Tathagata." This sentence is also found in the Anuradha Sutta (Samyutta Nikaya, Vol. III, p. 118).

62. A *pacittaya* offense is one of the lighter transgressions of the monastic code. Confession to another bhikshu remedies the offense.

63. See The Diamond Sutra in this volume.

64. The Order of Interbeing is a lay and monastic order created by Thich Nhat Hanh in the mid-1960s to help victims of the war. Its members help others while basing all actions in their practice of mindfulness, concentration, insight, and compassion.

65. The eight "noes" are: no birth, no death, no permanence, no annihilation, no oneness, no otherness, no coming, and no going.

66. *Samjña* is the Sanskrit word for perception, notion, idea, or concept. The Chinese character of the word "notion" has two parts: the upper part means "appearance" or "mark" and the lower part means "mind." In our mind there's a mark and we catch that mark and we think it's the reality of the thing in itself. The Chinese characters for "mark" and "perception" are closely connected because "mark" is the object of perception, and "perception" in turn is the subject of "mark"; so we have a perception when our mind is grasping a mark. In Sanskrit object of mind is *lakshana*, and mind is *citta*. When those two are combined we have the word *samjña*, notion or perception.

67. Translation: Gone, gone, gone all the way over, everyone gone to the other shore, enlightenment, hallelujah!

68. The Sutra on the Middle Way translated here is number 301 in the Samyukta Agama; the Samyukta Agama is number 29 in the Chinese canon. The equivalent sutra in Pali is the Kaccayanagotta Sutta, Samyutta Nikaya 12.15.

69. See The Diamond Sutra in this volume.

70. The Buddha uses the term "Tathagata" when speaking of himself.

71. This sutra was translated from Pali to Chinese by the Parthian monk, An Shih Kao at the Lo Yang Center in China during the later Han dynasty (140–171 CE). The ancient form of this sutra is the culmination of several smaller works

combined. The sutra is entirely in accord with both the Mahayana and Theravada traditions of Buddhism.

72. The four elements are earth, air, water, and fire.

73. The Five Skandhas are forms, feelings, perceptions, mental formations, and consciousness.

74. A *bodhisattva*, "awakening being," is someone committed to enlightening oneself and others so that all may be liberated from suffering.

75. The four kinds of Mara are unwholesome mental factors, Five Skandhas, death, and distractions (e.g., fantasies or forgetfulness).

   The three worlds are desire and passion, form (without desire and passion), and formlessness (only mental functioning).

76. The five desires are being wealthy, being beautiful, being ambitious, finding pleasure in eating, and being lazy.

77. *Dharmakaya* means the body of the teaching of awakening. *Nirvana* is liberation from birth and death.

78. The Four Noble Truths are suffering, the cause of suffering, the end of suffering, and the Eightfold Path.

79. Dependent origination (Sanskrit, *pratitya samutpada*) means that any phenomenon arises and exists not on its own, but in a mutually interdependent web of cause and effect with all other phenomena.

80. See note 76.

81. The Four Foundations of Mindfulness are body, feeling, state of mind, and objects of mind.

82. The Mangala Sutta, sometimes called the Mahamangala Sutta, appears in the Sutta-Nipata and in the Khuddakapatha. It also appears in the Jataka (tales of the Buddha's earlier births, often in animal-fable form).

83. For the Beginning Anew Ceremony, see Thich Nhat Hanh, *Chanting from the Heart* (Berkeley, CA: Parallax Press, 2006).

84. See note 78.

Index

Parallax Press, a nonprofit organization, publishes books on engaged Buddhism and the practice of mindfulness by Thich Nhat Hanh and other authors. All of Thich Nhat Hanh's work is available at our online store and in our free catalog. For a copy of the catalog, please contact:

Parallax Press
P.O. Box 7355
Berkeley, CA 94707
Tel: (510) 525-0101
www.parallax.org

Monastics and laypeople practice the art of mindful living in the tradition of Thich Nhat Hanh at retreat communities worldwide. To reach any of these communities, or for information about individuals and families joining for a practice period, please contact:

Plum Village
13 Martineau
33580 Dieulivol, France
www.plumvillage.org

Blue Cliff Monastery
3 Mindfulness Road
Pine Bush, NY 12566
www.bluecliffmonastery.org

Magnolia Grove Monastery
123 Towles Rd.
Batesville, MS 38606
www.magnoliagrovemonastery.org

Deer Park Monastery
2499 Melru Lane
Escondido, CA 92026
www.deerparkmonastery.org

The Mindfulness Bell, a journal of the art of mindful living in the tradition of Thich Nhat Hanh, is published three times a year by Plum Village. To subscribe or to see the worldwide directory of Sanghas, visit
www.mindfulnessbell.org